MOTIVATION

as related to personality

McGRAW-HILL SERIES IN PSYCHOLOGY
HARRY F. HARLOW, *Consulting Editor*

John F. Dashiell was Consulting Editor of this series from its inception in 1931 until January 1, 1950. Clifford T. Morgan was Consulting Editor of this series from January 1, 1950 until January 1, 1959.

MOTIVATION
as related to
personality

DOROTHY RETHLINGSHAFER

DEPARTMENT OF PSYCHOLOGY
UNIVERSITY OF FLORIDA

McGRAW-HILL BOOK COMPANY, INC.
New York   San Francisco   Toronto   London

MOTIVATION as related to personality

PREFACE

My early interest in motivation was aroused by J. F. Dashiell's seminars at the University of North Carolina. At that time I first recognized the multiplicity of problems in this field. Later, while teaching both undergraduate and graduate courses in motivation, I was able to grasp what seemed to be the basic problems; these form the nucleus of this book and are outlined in Chapter 1 and explored in more detail in Chapter 3.

In writing this volume, I found that I could not produce a manageable book on both learning and motivation, so I abandoned learning to those psychologists concerned with "how we become what we are," i.e., those who write books on learning. I approached the problems generally subsumed under motivation, knowing that any attempted answers must necessarily be incomplete. I presumed to treat drives in performance without including the role of learning in need-related responses, and I presumed to consider goals without showing first how they were learned. Instead, I used as the focus of interest the evidence which suggested that transitory variables were shifting yet were constantly at work within man's activity stream. Behavior, or responses of the muscular system, is a part of the activity stream that can be more reliably recorded but may be less significant with regard to motivation than the other activities. I have emphasized the interaction of motivation and personality.

The illustrative material is primarily taken from experimental studies, although clinical and industrial observations are also included.

In this volume I have included a series of insets adapted from original sources. In the past I have used various books of readings in my teaching; however, the use of insets has a definite advantage, for they are concise, carefully selected, and can be presented adjacent to those topics in the text for which they have particular relevance. From the many sources available, I have chosen the specific insets for the following reasons: to elaborate technical points, to illustrate particular areas, to present views from original sources, and to introduce challenging questions for the student.

I am grateful to my friends, colleagues, and students for their comments concerning various sections of this book. In particular, I owe much to W. E. Caldwell for many stimulating discussions and to H. F. Harlow and W. B. Webb for their helpful criticism. My graduate assistants and departmental typists have been of invaluable aid.

Acknowledgment is made to the following sources for permission to reproduce materials: Williams & Wilkins Company, American Psychological Association, the *Journal Press*, *The American Journal of Psychology*, *The Journal of Personality*, *Endocrinology*, *American Journal of Orthopsychiatry*, *Life* magazine, and *Reader's Digest*. I appreciate the permission from Mr. Rube Goldberg, so generously given, to reproduce one of his cartoons. I wish to thank individual authors as well as publishers referred to at appropriate places throughout this text and included in references within the bibliography.

Dorothy Rethlingshafer

CONTENTS

CHAPTER 1

INTRODUCTION

Was the man framed? If so, who was to judge the appeal now lodged against his expulsion? The senior Fellows, who had been deceived during his first trial? The man, or men, who had contrived the evidence against him? With these problems the novelist C. P. Snow confronts his readers and subtly leads them into the labyrinth of human motivation. "Ambition, prudence, pride, probity, hatred—they interweave like the forces of a difficult chess problem; and, when the solution emerges, we see that a few small acts of negligence, misplaced loyalty, and subtle deceit have changed the lives of several score of men and women and have endangered the honor of a noble institution" (278).

To reveal the interwoven forces operative upon, within, and between men is the purpose of this volume, but we will be able to move only an inch or so in the long distance which separates psychology from understanding the motivation of men.

Guess we must, and often assume; check the hypotheses by appeal to experimental and clinical observations, and report what seem to be the most valid interpretations of the observations. Always we will be concerned with men, but in seeking some of the answers of shifting motivations in men, we will find that simpler organisms may be useful at times for experimentation.

Motivation and Personality

The personality of a man affects the degree to which motivational variables may be reflected in his behavior. And his motivation often leaves an impression upon the personality structure. This interaction is continuous. However, personality structure is to some degree consistent through time; personality structure, we will assume, is a fairly stable organization, though subject to slow changes. Motivational variables, on the other hand, are constantly shifting; they come and go. They

1

are transient influences upon performance and when not active are, as it were, nonexistent.

It is not possible to encompass in one volume what could justifiably be included in a treatment of motivation and personality. We are concerned primarily with motivation. When theories or studies of the personality seem particularly relevant, they are included.

Outline of This Volume

In one way or another, motivational changes are constantly occurring within the activity stream of man. A man may shift in his potentiality for action. If in some way his capacity for vigorous activity is raised or lowered, his motivational potentiality is changed. In Chapter 2 some of the significant variables in motivational potentiality are discussed.

In Chapter 3 a few well-established observations with fairly simple animals are used to illustrate activation, selection, and direction, as well as reinforcement. These areas will continue to be of interest in succeeding chapters.

In the fourth chapter are presented demonstrations of the significant investigative-curiosity tendency, some of which throw a new light on problems which arise in understanding arousal, selection, direction, and reinforcement of higher organisms.

Man fluctuates in the vigor of his movements. At one time he is extremely, perhaps even abnormally, excessive in activation; then he declines into less and less activity until we see the low level of deep sleep. In Chapter 5 the observed fluctuations in activation, not only in the immediate arousal but in the readiness for arousal, are developed.

Men can be placed in relation to each other along a continuum of their average level of activity. There are individual differences in personal pace. Some men are extremely active; others are of a generally low personal pace. The basis of individuality in personal pace is considered in Chapter 6.

Fluctuations in activation—in contrast to changes in personal pace—are temporary and short-term in length. Two constructs—nonspecific drive and drives (drive components)—are useful in interpreting activation fluctuations. Chapters 7 and 8 are concerned with these fluctuations.

Men are observed to move toward certain effects and away from others. The learned personal utility of the effects varies from man to man and from time to time within any one man's life stream. Once attained, some effects are to be reattained. Chapter 9 is concerned with goals, the to-be-reattained effects.

Phenomena in life of great interest to laymen as well as to psychologists are man's choices. To understand choices of men—or even to approach an understanding—more than motivational variables must be studied. An approach is made in Chapter 10. Sensitization—a basic process in selecting in all organisms—is first illustrated. To this are added descriptions of typical choice situations for men as they have been isolated in experimental studies. Choice by man involves the cognitive activities, i.e., focusing, perceiving, and remembering. That these are subject to changes from motivational variables is demonstrated in Chapter 11.

In Chapters 12 and 13 on tension and anxiety, some of the problems of concern in maladjustments are considered, and in the last chapter there are briefly reviewed studies relevant to the general question of the role of motivation in learning.

CHAPTER 2

ENERGETICS

**Men do not live by bread alone, but
if they have no bread they cannot live.**

There are two views with respect to the energetics of organisms. The older view, and one now considered incorrect, was that organisms are naturally inert. Man was viewed as "something static in his natural state; hence something upon which motion, life, and action had to be superimposed." He presumably came alive only through the application of special enlivening forces to which were attached such terms as "motives," "incentives," "needs," and "need drives." In contrast to this older view is a more recent one: Man is naturally active, and his arousal does not have to be explained, since by being alive he is to some degree aroused all the time. However, the continuous fluctuations in his degree of arousal, i.e., in the amount of his activity, can be traced to various determinants. Among these is his capacity for vigorous action, which includes the degree of energy, the "fuel," which he has available.

Significance of Plenty of Fuel. Man loses energy in every reaction. Even in the obtaining of foods from which he attaches energy, he loses energy. Under some conditions, such as in a dangerous situation, he may expend an extraordinary amount of energy. The feats of strength which have been recorded under extreme fear and anger are legendary. An energy reserve is obviously necessary to meet the emergencies of life, as well as to carry on the routine acts and daily physiological processes which permit the reduction of bodily needs. Nor can man long sustain creative work.

SOURCE OF ORGANISMIC ENERGY

When organisms are considered in relation to their environment, it is apparent that they derive energy from their surroundings. "In the case of animals, the primary source of energy is chemical; the food that they

4

take in is oxidized or burned and serves as fuel for the living engine.
Other types of energy which occasionally accrue to animals are unimportant" (267, p. 349). Organisms may derive a little heat from their
surroundings, a little mechanical energy from the push of the wind;
light energy may affect the eyes, but these are trivial sources of energy
in comparison with the chemical energy derived from foods. Though
the organism can build many of the materials that it needs, there are
certain essential food materials. The well-known dietary essentials—the
ten amino acids, three fatty acids, all the vitamins, and certain inorganic
elements—must be added to some of the so-called "nonessential" amino
acids and a good supply of carbohydrates. Without the so-called "non-
essentials," much of an animal's energy is spent in building up the
needed complex materials out of the essentials (440).

Simply to exist requires energy. To increase the drain upon the organism by an inadequate diet is to decrease the energy available for
motivational demands. Animal husbandry has long recognized the significance of diet to obtain maximum efficiency from domestic animals.
Industry has also tied energy expenditure to diet. Observation of laborers on a construction job in a south-of-the-border state is pertinent. A
change in the workers from "laziness and slovenliness" to "increase in
ability and inclination to do useful work" was traced to an excellent diet
introduced by the company. The social import of the use of men in this
fashion may be questioned; the significance of an adequate diet to the
energizing of men cannot be questioned.

WHAT IS MEANT BY ORGANISMIC "ENERGY"?

Different Views Concerning Organismic Energy

It is assumed herein that energy used by organisms is *physical* energy,
released into organismic activities of many kinds. The energy of a man
is said to be potential or kinetic. In general terms, the potential energy
of a man is that which his body possesses as an ability to do work by its
reactions. Forms of kinetic energy are seen when potential energy is released, a continuous process in living organisms. Attachment of energy
from the external world by organisms as potential energy implies that
energy has been transformed. Similarly, the expenditure of energy as
kinetic energy means that it has changed its form. Behavior implies energy transformation.

Not all psychological theorists accept the above interpretation of
physical organismic energy. Some assume that man has "mental energy,"
some kind of energy not identifiable with physical energy. In the

Freudian theory, as in a few others, there is the assumption of psychic or mental energy. The defenders of Freud state that there is nothing mystical, vitalistic, or supernatural about Freud's concept of psychic energy. Psychic energy can be assumed to arise from bodily energy, and in turn the psychic energy may be transformed back into bodily energy. Just how these supposed transformations take place is, however, unknown.

In most motivational positions, whether they include mental processes or not, the assumption is that organismic energy is physical energy attached from foods. Its release is seen in all kinds of organismic activities.

Energy Balance

Various factors affect the motivational potentiality of an individual, i.e., the degree of energy available for release into all activities. They include (1) the ease of obtaining sufficient and adequate foods; (2) the efficiency of the body (*a*) in conversion of the nutriments into energy, (*b*) in the storage of energy, and (*c*) in making it available for release. *Conversion of Nutriments into Energy, Storage, and Release.* It is the basic digestive-circulatory system that makes possible the attachment of energy after the food is ingested. Food energies are changed by the digestive system into a concentrated type of fuel. There are biochemical events (intermediary metabolism) by which foods are broken down into some simple compounds, then recombined in various ways to make the materials from which the different cells of the body get the energy for their activities. The significance of intermediary metabolism in the energetics of organisms is briefly outlined in Inset 1.

INSET 1. INTERMEDIARY METABOLISM*

A brief survey of intermediary metabolism is presented by Morgan and Stellar (440). Food materials are first obtained from the outside environment in such forms as carbohydrates, fats, and proteins. After being eaten, these materials are broken down in the alimentary tract to a form in which they can be absorbed into the blood stream from the walls of the intestines. After being distributed to different parts of the body—the liver, for example—the complex materials are further broken down to simpler compounds that can be used in chemical reactions by the cells of the body as a source of energy. At the same time, these simpler compounds may be used as building blocks to make various complex substances that the body requires. These processes of breaking down and rebuilding are the major aspects of intermediary metabolism and are basic in providing energy for the organism's activities of all kinds.

* Adapted from C. T. Morgan and E. Stellar, *Physiological Psychology*. New York: McGraw-Hill, 1950.

Intermediary metabolism of the major food materials takes place in a series of chemical reactions in which complex molecules such as glycogen and the fatty acids are dismantled section by section or assembled in discrete steps from their elementary compounds. Energy is, of course, given up in the process and "lost" as heat. Nevertheless, the body may manage to accumulate energy through the various steps of metabolism and "package" it so that it is ready in rather large units for instant and varied use. The secret of this success lies in a single but very unusual chemical grouping—the energy-rich phosphate bond. The bonds between elements or groups in a molecule always contain energy—*that is where the energy released in a chemical reaction comes from*—but the phosphate bond can hold unusually large amounts of energy. When it does, it is called the energy-rich phosphate bond. When ruptured, the calories released are significantly greater in amount than those released by ordinary energy-poor phosphate bonds.

The organism cannot be potentially ready for release of energy into any activities if there is failure at any stage of the obtaining of foods, their ingestion, or the conversion of nutriments into energy. There are various influences upon this total process, including age, health, size, sex, genes, periods of rest, functioning of the endocrine system: These and other factors may affect the conversion of energy from foodstuffs, its accumulation into certain specialized cells of the body, and its release into activities.

We now consider the most fundamental factor influencing the potentiality for being moved—the adequacy of the amount of foods ingested.

POTENTIALITY FOR AROUSAL

Motivational psychology is concerned, along with other problems, with the reactivity (activation) of individuals and with their capacity to be energized, to endure, and to persist in hard work. Privation from foods is shown to affect such motivational aspects. During famine or a semistarvation diet, the calorie deficit (energy expenditure less calorie intake) is paid at the expense of the energy stored in the cells of the body as fat, protein, and carbohydrates. The fat stored in the cells as adipose tissue plays no vital role in the life processes and consequently can, within limits, be drawn upon with impunity to supply the calories lacking in the semistarvation diet. But when this store of energy is exhausted, demands for energy are made upon the essential cellular constituents, and this last drain on the organism is soon reflected in a lowered energy reserve with a correlated loss in general vigor of behavior. Thus men subjected to long-continued semistarvation diets are reduced in potentiality for arousal.

Illustrations

A study of food privation was performed during World War II upon thirty-two young adult males who volunteered as subjects and were fed a semistarvation diet for twenty-four weeks (330). Their diet subjected the men to extreme food privation. The continuous loss of weight during the twenty-four weeks was approximately 25 per cent of their normal weight. The correlated changes in the physiological functioning of the men as well as in their work output were observed. A rehabilitation diet followed.

The effects of food privation on potentiality for arousal were apparent in four different kinds of records: (1) subjective reports of decline of interests, (2) physiological changes, (3) decline in general movements, and (4) lowered work output.

1. *Subjective reports.* Subjective reports from men under semistarvation diet indicated feelings of weakness, loss of ambition to study, narrowing of interests in external events, and loss of sexual desire. Emotionally the reported changes involved both depression and periods of irritability, including aggressive feelings.

It should be noted that privation from food represents an interference in a strong need with a consequent frustration; and frustration, we will later find, is a motivational condition correlated with a rise in drive tension. It might be expected that the frustrated, hungry men would attack the barriers between them and food. The subjects in this Minnesota study were, however, civilized men, volunteers for the study, who were on their honor to follow the rules in regard to decreased diet. They hoped to contribute to science and, in the long run, to the well-being of others. Even so, a few men broke rules and were discarded as subjects. The remaining subjects, being influenced by accepted social values, did not break the starvation diet. They could not, however, completely inhibit their feelings of frustration and consequent irritations. Their capacity to be moved decreased even while their frustrations increased.

2. *Physiological fitness.* The measured physiological fitness of the men declined during the weeks of food privation, another clue to the lowering of potentiality for activation. Among the many physiological changes observed in this study was a decline in the basal metabolic rate (BMR), a measure of the rate of oxygen consumption. As is indicated later, in Chapter 5, BMR is one of various indices to the arousal variations.

3. *General overt behavior.* There were clear indications of a lowering of the usual activation levels of the men. Movements were slow and restricted. Less variability appeared. Stairs were mounted one at a time, and the starved men sat or leaned against a wall when they had to wait for some appointment. In general, the men became apathetic and im-

mobile under the inadequate diet. Even if they had been aroused by fear or anxiety, their capacity to respond to these states was limited.

4. *Endurance on work tests.* A steady decline in endurance was measured, as indicated below, in both aerobic (steady moderate) work and anaerobic (short exhausting) work of such an intensity that it could be maintained for only a short time.

The aerobic work test consisted of a thirty-minute walk at 3.5 miles an hour on a motor-driven treadmill with a 10 per cent grade. Air, temperature and humidity were controlled. Various measures were used to obtain the physiological effect of the standard work periods upon the men as they went through twenty-four weeks of semistarvation and, later, as they improved during the recovery period. Among these measures, the record of the absolute heart rate during work of moderate intensity was relatively uninfluenced by semistarvation. However, the semistarvation diet brought a dramatic reduction in the *resting* pulse rate. Hence when the subjects worked, there was a greater increment in pulse, clearly demonstrating that the work was harder for the subjects in semistarvation than during the control period.

The anaerobic work test indicates the ability to work at high intensity. This test reflects capacity for movement. It is also considered a sign of endurance, a motivational problem related to willingness to "take" discomfort or pain. The subjects were asked to run a motor-driven treadmill with an 8.6 per cent grade at 7 miles per hour for five minutes or until exhaustion. The actual time of run decreased from 242 seconds on control tests preceding the starvation period to 50 seconds at the end of the experimental period.

Complete Deprivation from Foods

In the Minnesota study reported briefly above, the men were not completely deprived of all foods. They were on a privation diet. When a group of young adult males were deprived of *all* foods for 2.5 days and a second group for 4.5 days, the ability to perform exhausting work was definitely impaired after the first day of starvation and continued to decrease. There was no marked initial increase in the vigor of performance as a resultant of the deficit from all foods, though some studies with hungry men indicate that, at first, activity slightly increases (632). The hungry rat shows at first an activity rise, then later a fall if the food deficit continues.[1] The human infant, when deprived of food from 2 P.M. to 6 P.M., steadily increases in activity from the first to the last fifteen-minute period (307).

---

[1] Hull (299) writes of the negative or inanition component of the drive from food privation. This component represents a lowering of potentiality for motivational expression.

Relation of These Studies to Motivation

The above studies on deficits (whether partial or complete) from foods have significant implications for motivation. The first and the most obvious one is that if food deficits are too long continued, a bodily condition is reached after which the potentiality for arousal is impaired. Motivational potentiality for children is guarded by rearing them in conditions for normal health and growth. Society sets up school lunches for children who are on an inadequate diet, and they thus can be more active in school work.

A second conclusion from the Minnesota study is that a desire to work hard is not identical with the capacity to do so. As the capacity of the men to be active and to persist declined, their desire to do well on the tasks did *not* decrease. The observers of the starved men write that at all times the motivation (willingness to perform) of the men was high. Though the starved men had at the end of the weeks of food privation lost skill and capacity for work, and though they disliked the work tests, "their interest in their own abilities and the general desire" not to let the other fellow down and to provide valid data which might be useful far offset the dislike of the test situation. This is significant. It illustrates how a man's values may be pitted against unpleasantness and discomfort and force him to use the strength he has, even though it is limited. The food deficit reduced potentiality for movement but did not reduce the apparent desire to perform well, even in strenuous tasks. Some subjects believed that the score on the performance tests would be of social value in the study. Others were pitting their performance against their desire to be able to take the hard work.

Third, it should be remembered that no matter how hungry a man is or how oriented he is toward obtaining food—no matter, in other words, how strong are his demands—his energy reserve cannot be ignored. He is limited in his activation, endurance, and persistence by his fitness for activity. There is a constant interaction between psychological goals of whatever nature and the capacity to attain them. "Is it worth it?" "Can I do it?" These are questions inevitably raised when psychological demands are placed in opposition to the degree of energy required to satisfy these demands.

The motivational complexity of the Minnesota study is not yet completely revealed. These hungry men were not working for food. They were hungry, and food was all around them, but they did not steal or buy it. The study is in this sense not revealing of a natural state such as a condition of famine when the orientations of all are toward food.

Finally, we note that the extreme need for food affected the cognitive world, as do other organic changes in men. Under the long-term semistarvation diet, the psychological world of the subjects was focused on food even though they did not try to obtain it. The intense preoccupation with it made it difficult for the men to concentrate upon the tasks that they had intellectually decided to work on. If a man tried to study, he soon found himself daydreaming about food, foods he had eaten in the past, opportunities he had missed to eat a certain food when he was at this or that place. He would daydream by the hour about the next meal.

In general, any variable which affects adversely the amount of energy of a man affects his arousal and the continuance of any act once started. With a low degree of potential energy, a man may either use it up at a fast rate or expend the energy more slowly and less wastefully. In contrast, a man who has a high degree of potential energy can sustain activity for a long time, even at a high rate of energy expenditure, though the capacity to be active and a high level of arousal are not inevitably correlated. Any lowering of the amount of potential energy is a *limiting* factor upon the motivation of a man as indicated by the degree of energy expended. A lowered potentiality for arousal, however, does not necessarily affect the strength of the willingness to perform.

Motivational psychology, instead of concentrating upon deficits, should concentrate upon optimal conditions for vigorous activity of all kinds. An adequate diet is the basic factor for such optimal conditions. It is obviously not the only factor.

GENERAL DEMANDS UPON MEN FOR ENERGY

If we consider the balance of potential energy as something to be guarded just as Jack Benny guards his money reserves, then we can ask what are the demands upon man's reserves? First, what are the inescapable demands? One demand is the cost of staying alive, the primary maintenance cost.

Maintenance Costs

In order to remain as an intact system, man must obtain foods, water, and other necessary substances. He must protect the constant states of his internal environment. In these activities energy is lost. Energy is also demanded in overcoming resistance to movement, both external resistance, as from the wind, gravitational pull, and the contact of the feet with the ground, and internal resistance (the resistance of the body colloids, which prevents an animal from falling apart). Without the second —the internal resistance—a man would "tear his tendons, break his bones, 'pull' his muscles, strain his joints" (87).

And there is the maintenance cost of preserving the group, the demand for reproduction. Perhaps the serious-minded reader will be interested in the rate of loss of energy in lovemaking. The following description of the simple act of a man kissing a girl should perhaps lead to a congressional investigation of this waste of energy.

> When a young man kisses his girl, his liver supplies his adrenosympathetic system with glycogen for energy. In order to burn this extra sugar, his body releases insulin, vitamin B-1, and phosphorus. Meanwhile, an exchange of starch, phosphorus, and thiamine is going on between the thalamic and the cortical brain, that is, if the young man is doing any thinking, which is questionable. Then as his pulse and respiration rates rise, his consumption of thiamine and phosphorus increases because of the more rapid transfer of oxygen on the intracellular level. (Adapted from M. Torre, Kiss & Tell, Reader's Digest, May, 1958.)

Imagine the energy used by the adult in the reproductive act—a loss not too frequently deplored. Energy is used also in caring for the young and, in most civilized groups, for the weak and the aged.

Emergencies

A man who must escape from some choking rope must have a lot of potential energy or he cannot act on his need for air. A man under increasing temperature which is inducing a nonoptimal state in his body must not be too low in potential energy or he may not be able to move from the heat. A man suddenly faced with loss of life from destructive forces is not likely to survive if his basic energy level is low. However, the emergency reactions, including the concomitant fears, angers, and anxieties, are often "wasteful." Though emotional patterns in the non-civilized man had a use in preparing the organism for violent action, can we afford them now? And what of the feelings, the likes and dislikes, the hates and the longings, the states of euphoria and depression—are these wasteful in the energy expended? That stress is inevitable in life must be recognized. How civilized man may learn to respond to stress in a less energy-wasteful manner than appears in primitive expressions is slowly being revealed by studies of psychosomatic interactions. In Chapter 12 is reported Selye's significant theory (550) concerning alarm reactions.

Beyond Maintenance Costs

Though man must have bread to live, he does not live by bread alone. Motivational psychology is only beginning to touch lightly this metaphysical problem as one of concern to its students. Man for ages has gazed into the firmament and asked questions and found answers, but only recently has he seriously believed that he might move beyond his own planet. He now is learning to move into space. The cost is tremendous, and though he justifies the cost by pointing to the practical outcomes of the discoveries, he suspects that the cost is far beyond the value to maintenance of the group. Yet he continues. Nor is this a new trend in man; the distinctively human activities are creative—oriented, as is art or religion, to beyond-maintenance goals.

Civilizations and Energy Costs

Men are increasingly learning how cooperative action reduces maintenance costs and thus permits sufficient amounts of energy to be left over for release into nonmaintenance costs. Unfortunately, this progress has not reached, and perhaps cannot reach, the same degree in all geographic sections of the world. Men in the tropics and in the arctic region still use much energy in maintaining optimal body temperature. In other places, so much energy must be used in obtaining food that little is left over for creative activities.

Though most groups of men have passed beyond the daily routine, observed in nonsocial animals, of hunt, kill, eat, sleep—hunt, kill, eat, sleep, yet men live even today where maintenance costs are very high. Sherif and Sherif (558), in describing the primitive Siriono society reported by Holmberg (291), comment that although the food supply of the Siriono is sufficient "for survival, it is persistently inadequate." The tropical climate in which they live is highly unfavorable for preservation or storage of food. Arduous hunts for food must be made almost daily, and about a fourth of them are unsuccessful. The Siriono have only the most primitive weapons and few agricultural tools or skills. Domestication of animals is unknown. In short, the Siriono's waking hours are occupied with the exhausting and dangerous job of hunting and collecting enough food for survival (558, p. 438). A brief description is presented of some of the outstanding effects of this persistent food scarcity upon the Siriono culture and the individual's activity stream. Food and food getting are the basis of the Siriono's major anxieties. "When food is obtained, it is eaten without ritual, often furtively or at night so that it need not be shared." Food is the greatest single source of conflict in the group. Almost no food preferences are shown; "a hawk is devoured as voraciously as a partridge." The stealing observed is related to the taking of food on those few occasions when some is left unguarded. Food and successful hunting tend to dominate the dreams and fantasy of the Siriono. "Food is used as a lure for obtaining a partner in sexual activities. When food is scarce, there is little sexual activity. Sexual orgies follow a successful hunt."

The recurring problems of hunger influence the practices and social values of Siriono culture. "Since a man can seldom collect more food than is necessary for his family, the family is the functioning economic and social unit." The usefulness of the Siriono band is limited chiefly to serving as a source of sex and marital partners. The Siriono must often be on the move in search for hunting grounds; individual ownership of a garden plot, tree, and the like is therefore recognized only when such articles are used. Status and prestige are based largely on hunting prowess and food-getting ability, and "the almost constant preoccupation with food and the rigors of obtaining it have resulted in a sparse development of art forms, folk tales or mythology. Magic is related chiefly to food. The Siriono's concern merely to survive leaves little time for intellectual activity or for speculations on deities or an afterworld" (558, pp. 439–440). In other words, the high maintenance costs limit the number of channels of energy release and no doubt limit as well the endurance and persistence toward all goals save that of food; moreover, the scarcity of nutriments reduces even the capacity to obtain food. Of particular interest is the limitation upon the intellectual life.

Are not the societies of the Western world, such as the "practical" United States, also limited in the acceptable channels of energy release? Even in a food-surplus nation there is often a denial of the value of all acts save those that are "practical," those that can in some way be useful in maintenance. Such values may aid, of course, in the superior protection of the body, superior living conditions. Ease of living is not only tied to sufficient foods but to optimal temperature, to freedom from pain, to freedom from fear of enemies. Curiosity is encouraged in the "practical" world, but the outcome of the investigations is supposed to be in some way useful. Only by pointing out that applied research cannot proceed without basic research has the scientist in the practical United States been permitted to explore for the sake of exploration. Let us consider a simple example of the usual Western values. Observe the farmer of our Great Plains. Let us say that he is plowing a straight furrow in the spring. And we know that there are concomitant activities in which he could indulge himself. He might take pleasure in the act itself. Or he might think of his independence from the boss in the factory where he once worked; he could savor the completion of each furrow; he might stop and admire his work or think of the many others who have plowed before him, those who plowed even straighter or more crooked than he. He could feel the beginning of warmth from the spring breeze, look upon the swelling red buds, mistily reddening the black lines of the leafless trees, and pleasure in growth of life. But if he does he will most likely not meet the next payment on the mortgage.

This example is not merely the author's idiosyncratic criticism of the pressures in Western society to channel energy into the practical. Fromm

(207) suggests, as others have before him, that English and American culture accept as their dominant value that all energy should be directed toward work and the fulfillment of duty. The Horatio Alger myth is with us—the myth that we are born to strive onward and upward, that to go forward means to obtain material success, that all "upward motion must occur before death, in fact, several years before death, in order to allow some time for the enjoyment of whatever elevation one is capable of achieving" (459, p. 194). There is, says Murray, the marriage of greed and speed and an embrace of the machine as the surest and quickest way to paradise—a villa in Florida or California.

RELEASE OF ENERGY

Many variables affect the release of energy. Only a few are considered in this section. One general principle which affects the rate of release not only by men but also by nonhuman organisms is the "law of least effort."

The Law of Least Effort

Organisms are so structured that they naturally protect their motivational potentiality. Animals and man economize in their expenditure of effort. This tendency has been called the law of least effort. An organism expends the least amount of energy possible in order to reach a goal. Other things being equal, an organism learns to select the easier task rather than the hard, provided both end in the same result. A more formal statement of the law of less work is as follows: "If two or more behavior sequences each involving a different amount of energy consumption or work have been equally well reinforced an equal number of times, the organism will gradually learn to choose the less laborious behavior sequence leading to the attaining of the reinforcing state of affairs" (299, p. 294). (From the point of view of simple behaviorism it is assumed that the equal number of reinforcements make for equal habit strengths of the behavior sequences.)

Man does not always operate so simply. He might choose the task with the most work involved because he believes he needs a flagellant for some guilt which he carries. Or man may have acquired what Max Weber (646), the German sociologist, called the Protestant ethic: i.e., a man should want to work hard and earn money not simply to enjoy life but because hard work is admirable and likewise is acquisition of money. A man with this set of values considers that working hard and making money are per se "good." In this ethic hard work sometimes seems to be chosen over less difficult work though the ends attained might be even more enjoyable in the latter case. There are other reasons why a man or a simpler animal might not operate on the law of least effort. It is possible that there is no recognition of which is the easiest way to attain an end. The least-effort choice between more than one way to the same goal demands some understanding of the kind of work involved. Man, however, can learn to choose the less laborious task, that one which will attain the same reward as the more difficult one.

Even nonhuman subjects can learn to exert a sufficient amount of effort, and no more, as a means of obtaining a reward. See (626, 637, 136) and others (571). If given a choice among several ways, each differing in the work required but all ending in the same reward, they generally select the task which they have learned requires the least expenditure of energy.[2]

Quantitative Sets

Men learn to estimate how much effort is required to complete a task in a given time period. Knowing the quantity of work to be completed in a given time, they tend to adjust their rate of output accordingly. Their estimate of how fast they must work in order to get the job done may not be accurate, for it is affected by many factors. This inadequacy of a quantitative set is likely to be seen in daily life situations such as the industrial setting.

Studies of the quantitative sets adopted by men indicate that these sets vary according to whether the men have to work for a long time or a short time. In general, men set an initial higher pace for themselves in tasks which are not going to be continued than in tasks which are of greater length. The men do not start too fast in the longer work periods because they apparently have learned that they cannot keep up the fast pace. For example, the initial level of effort expended in simple addition was higher for subjects when told that they would have a small number of problems than for those who were told that a large number was to be done (347). Similar findings were reported by another investigator (37). Ross and Bricker (524) were interested in the effect of the size of a repetitive motor task (pulling a hand dynamometer) on the force exerted in the first pulls. This task permits a fairly direct measurement of energy expended. Assuming that the problem was not too easy for the subjects, the amount of the force exerted in the initial trials should be governed by the number of trials that the subject knows are to follow. Two studies were run. One used the directions: "Will you squeeze the dynamometer with all your force ten times." In a second study twenty pulls was the requested task. There was a significant drop in the initial

[2] The effort required, as learned from previous performances, may even prevent the initiation of a task. The response threshold may, however, be crossed if a highly inciting goal is anticipated.

level of force exerted as the magnitude of the total task was increased. The subjects, as it were, "saved" their energy for later work. It is interesting that a quantitative set may also be fixed by an illusion of a heavier work load than actually exists in a task (311).

SUMMARY

In this chapter the following problem was both directly and indirectly approached: What factors affect motivational potentiality? The first emphasis was upon the necessity of having sufficient energy. Motivational potentiality in terms of capacity for vigorous responses, endurance, and continuance is dependent upon an adequate energy reserve. Instead of emphasizing deficit motivation like a deficit from foods, which is often placed high on motivational lists, we suggested that a good diet is more important. Only psychologists seem to forget this.

The studies of semistarvation diet and of complete removal of all foods from young adult men illustrated how quickly capacity for work declined. That continuous scarcity of food will affect men who live in such conditions was demonstrated by the description of a primitive culture, the Siriono society, where food is not easily attained. The Sirionos' motivation, as compared with groups of people where food is more plentiful, was affected: e.g., great value was placed on food and on hunting. Other interests could not exist, since the men had little time and little energy for release into any activity save food getting. When food was absent, and it often was, there was little sexual activity. Creative activity was lessened.

Even the man in a well-established civilization where group cooperation permits a surplus of foods (though it is not always distributed) must spend some of his energy in maintenance of his body. But he has time for many other activities, some "practical," some not. We deplored, as others have, the emphasis in the Western world, in a food-surplus nation like the United States, on the practical.

Finally, rate of release of energy was briefly considered. There is a tendency for organisms to use the least effort possible to attain an end. The pace adopted in a task by a man is also influenced by the amount to be accomplished in a given time, but any quantitative set is not a simple matter. Many factors influence rate of energy release, as is later indicated.

CHAPTER 3

THE BIOLOGICAL APPROACH
TO MOTIVATION

What is described as the motivation of men differs according to the assumptions made about the nature of that organism classified as Homo sapiens. There are two general models of man which permit different motivational positions according to the model accepted. In the biological model, man is said to be similar to all other organisms, including the simplest animal on the phylogenetic scale. The biological model represents man as an animal. True, he is a complex one with a great capacity for learning, and he cannot be interpreted simply on the basis of findings from subhuman species.

Biologically oriented theorists in the field of motivation emphasize as man's primary urges those which all animals possess. These theorists acknowledge the determinants developed within the socialization of men, such as values, social ambitions, ethical goals, and guilt. However, the biological view of man considers such determinants to be outgrowths of learning based on man's "primitive" (animallike) nature. One of the main problems in this approach is, therefore, how the modification of motivation occurs in the life of an individual, i.e., how the child's simple needs are so modified that he later exhibits the many complex wishes and wants of adulthood.

A position in contrast to the above view is that men, by socialization, become qualitatively different from animals; men are said to be transformed by social evolution from animals into humans. No, or little, understanding of human beings can be obtained, it is assumed, by observations of nonhumans, even by studies of their social interactions.

In this chapter we approach motivation via the biological view of man, since it has posed many of the present-day problems of experimental and clinical interest. In later chapters, the motivation of man as transformed

18

by socialization will be considered, but it will be accepted that principles derived from simple organismic action are applicable to man.

The conventional biological view of man dominates the presentation of motivation in most elementary texts of psychology, which often list such tissue needs as those for foods and water as primary in arousal. Moreover, the assumption is openly or implicitly made that such tissue inadequacies, or their learned substitutes, are essential, or at least basic, in initiation of activity. This assumption is not in any fundamental conflict with the Freudian emphasis on the role of the instinctive urges of the id as energizing sources.[1] Freud was biologically oriented in his use of the id instincts like hunger and similar tissue-based urges and particularly in his recognition of the significance of the sexual urge, including its indirect as well as its direct manifestations.

The usefulness of the biological model in interpreting the complexity of man's motivations has generally been acknowledged. Variations of this conventional biological view appear in the different treatments of learning and of personality.[2] It has recently been subject to modification by an interest in the biological tendency observed in the higher animals to investigate the external world.

Contribution of Darwin

Following the general acceptance of the Darwinian theory of evolution, man was considered only one of the many organisms on this world and one whose nature would best be understood if this fact was not forgotten. The biological approach emphasized the high position of man in the hierarchy of organisms, but the difference between man and the lower animals was one of degree and not of kind. Darwin pointed to the resemblances in the sensory equipment among the vertebrates, to the similarities in their capacities to learn, remember, and reason. He assumed that man, as well as other mammals, possessed instinctive tendencies such as the tendencies to care for the young, to give mutual aid and sympathy, to seek at times others of his own kind. He thus sought to mark the similarities in the cognitive, affective, and motivational areas between man and other animals. Even man's values and the "promptings of right and wrong" were assumed to be rooted in social instincts, particularly in the ties that bound parents to their children. He sought in

[1] The assumption can be traced to McDougall's similar position on instincts (415); it was formalized in Dashiell's 1928 text of elementary psychology (138) in his emphasis on tissue needs as primary and was accepted by Tolman in his *Purposive Behavior in Animals and Men* in 1932 (614) and by Hull in his *Principles of Behavior* in 1943 (299).

[2] It has influenced the motivational views of Murray (457), Stagner (580, 581), Murphy (455), Klein (336), and to a lesser degree the theories of Maslow (404), Rogers (519), and Combs (125).

the lower animals some trace of what he found in complex and socialized man.

The students of the rapidly growing comparative psychology of animals moved to an even more restricted biological view—the view that man could only be understood by discoveries of laws concerning the functioning of the nonhuman animals. In other words, psychological principles were to be discovered on the lower level and could then be generalized to man. This assumption was forcibly stated by Dashiell (138) in 1928: "Man is an animal—a living organism. . . . Human psychology is rooted in living protoplasm and is to be *explained partly in terms of its antecedent history.* To understand the *fundamentals of human behavior* it is necessary *first* to observe animal behavior, for here, stripped of the complications produced by civilizations working upon more sensitive organisms, these fundamentals may more readily be noted" (138, p. 22, italics added).

Novikoff (467) in 1945, however, pointed to a limitation in this approach to man. Knowledge of the laws governing the lower level of animals, he stated, could be considered necessary for a full understanding of the higher level; yet the unique properties of the phenomena at the higher level (like man) could not be predicted a priori from the laws of the nonhuman animals. The higher animals were not merely an extension or elaboration of the lower or earlier in origin. Quantitative complications in biological evolution could become so great that there were qualitative differences with new, "emergent" properties. In other words, man could only be completely understood by studies of his own behavior. This modification of the biological view of man did not deny the value of comparative behavior studies; although the laws that hold on one phylogenetic level might not be adequate to explain all phenomena on the higher level, the former were never contradicted, reversed, or negated by the latter. Not even among the physical laws, any more than gravity itself, was there a principle known to be transgressed by the bodily mechanism. To put it another way, observations of the simplest organisms can reveal aspects of complicated man, but it must not be forgotten that man can never be thus completely evaluated, not even by observation of those primates which are next to him in the evolutionary scale. Species-to-species differences do not preclude the possibility of obtaining some consistent trends in organismic activities applicable to any living individual from the simplest to man, but the discovery of such trends still does not deny that man's capacities permit him to function on a higher biological level than that of the lower animals (465). We now outline the positive contributions of this modified biological approach to man as an aid in understanding his motivation.

Contributions of the Animal Model to Motivation

1. One of the contributions of viewing man as an animal is that it points up a characteristic (among others) which he possesses in common with all organisms, i.e., the inevitability of activity.

2. A second contribution of the biological approach to motivation is that the assumption of a completely rational man disappears under the impact of the animal model. The mind of man is no longer isolated from what is happening in his body.[3] It is accepted that man's sensing, perceiving, reasoning, remembering do not occur independently of his bodily tensions, and that often these tensions can influence behavior in an irrational manner, even without conscious awareness. Reasoning is no longer considered independent of the often nonrational emotions, feelings, and basic needs, particularly after biologically oriented Freud asked whether man was as logical as he often claimed. It is recognized that man's reasons for his actions are often given after the act. They are attempts to explain as he reasons why he (his self) would do so and so. Man is not necessarily incorrect, yet neither is he necessarily correct when by self-analysis he attempts to isolate what he calls his reasons for what he has done or will do. Freud popularized the concept of repressed sexual impulses which, he said, swayed man. He added that the logical reasons could actually be rationalizations or other self-defenses. So he stated, and this was finally accepted and incorporated into modern psychology.

The interrelationships between the mind and the changing bodily states are now frequently sought. Psychosomatic studies arose with the recognition that the mind and body could not be separately examined. Recently there has been an interest in the feedback upon the central processes from tensions in men generated in interpersonal relations. This interest moves even further from the pure biological approach.

3. The biological approach to motivation presents man as adaptive, as are all organisms, with a capacity for self-regulation. The identification and emphasis of this capacity is an important advance in studying man. He fortunately possesses, with all other animals, regulatory mechanisms. Most important for man is his capacity for adaptive learnings, which are useful in situations where his survival or the survival of the human species, is threatened. Social adjustments also occur when bodily survival is not immediately threatened, in fact, when the apparent reason for change in an individual's behavior is to get along with others. We

---

[3] The recognition of a relationship between mind and body did not originate *de novo* with the acceptance of the animal model. The speculations of Descartes, for example, foreshadowed a mind-body relationship.

even change (sometimes) because of the peculiarities of others, not in order to aid our own or their survival, but merely to agree, to conform, to be one of the group. The clinical interest in "adjusting man" is an outgrowth, in part, of an increasing interest during the present century in biological adaptiveness and in social adjustment.

4. A fourth outgrowth of the interest in the animal model are studies of simple behavior units. Among the first isolated for specific attention were reflexes, with stimuli marking the onset and a fairly invariable response as the end. Even before the interest in reflexes there had been an emphasis on a more complex behavior unit, the "instinct" as observed in subhumans. As is well known, much of behavior was at one time "explained" by calling forth the genies labeled instincts. They were, in fact, an improvement upon the earlier animistic concept of the soul as the mover of man. However, instincts were soon overused, i.e., were ever-ready explanations of why a man did so or so, and they gave way to regulatory activity phases initiated by tissue disturbances. These were accepted as motivational units superior to instincts or to the simpler reflexes. It was first postulated and to some degree supported by investigations that there were internal regulators which, when stimulated by tissue irritations, aroused central neural areas, and that regulatory behavior followed which ended with relief of tissue need. The identification of the mechanisms involved in the "registration" of a tissue need on the central neural system and in the release of need-directed behavior permitted controlled studies of the initiation and the continuation of variable responses which persisted until "relief" occurred (see Inset 2). Such a phase in the activity stream, from the onset of a need to the relief, is a regulatory act.

INSET 2. REGISTRATION OF TISSUE NEEDS*

Cannon early advanced his local stimulus theory of drives, i.e., the postulation of interoceptive receptors in the mouth, throat, or stomach as responsible for registration of tissue needs upon the neural centers. The implication was also present that these internal receptors were in some way responsible for learning need-related behavior. However, further evidence questions the internal receptors as the sole mechanisms in determining how such a tissue need as that for nutriment in the body cells influences the neural excitation centers.

There is reason to believe, writes Morgan (439), that any alterations in internal sensory stimulation may be indirectly the resultant of a change in blood chemistry. The role of humoral factors in initiation and in cessation of behavior under food and water deprivation has been demonstrated

* Adapted from C. T. Morgan, Physiological theory of drive. In S. Koch (ed.), *Psychology: A Study of a Science*, Vol. I. New York: McGraw-Hill, 1959.

in a great variety of recent experiments. Morgan points out that these experiments may be divided into two general groups: those in which the dependent variable is the rate of learning or extinction, and those in which simple preference between two materials, or the rate of ingesting such materials, is the dependent variable. Both types of experiment have made use of the stomach tube or fistula for getting food into the stomach without the animal's eating or drinking it, although in some cases the material has been introduced directly into the internal environment by hypodermic needle.

Those of the first type, using rate of learning as a measure of effect, have issued mostly from Miller's laboratories at Yale. Through a permanent fistula, fluid food has been delivered directly into the stomach whenever the rat performed a correct response. The general problem has been to determine how reinforcement administered in this way compares with normal reinforcement as his ingestion of food. Although there are many interesting results of these experiments, two facts stand out: Food administered directly into the stomach is reinforcing, though probably not so much so as food ingested in the normal way. When nonnutritive materials are introduced into the stomach, the result is not one of reinforcement. Moreover, the distension of the stomach by a balloon is negatively reinforcing. Although it is risky to interpret such results until we understand better the nature of reinforcement and its relation to learning, they indicate that mere stimulation of the stomach is not enough to change whatever must be changed to effect learning and that there are some specific humoral effects of food that are important in bringing about this change.

The second group of experiments with preloading of the stomach points even more clearly in this direction. With the single-stimulus method it is possible to measure relatively small changes in rate of ingestion, which presumably reflect drive level, within a very few minutes after loading the stomach with any desired material. Several different materials have been used prior to animals' drinking solutions of salt and sugar. Both the kind of preloaded material and its concentration make an important difference in rates of ingestion immediately following preloading. And the striking thing about the results is that they follow so quickly upon preloading, long before the material in the stomach has had a chance to be absorbed into the blood stream. Such results seem to mean that some humoral messenger is released into the blood or that in some cases water is withdrawn from the blood, thereby changing its chemical balance, and that this directly modifies activity in a "central motive state." Confirming this interpretation is the fact that substances injected directly into the blood stream cause about the same effects as the same substances placed in the stomach.

In spite of the recognition of the value of identification of tissue needs as origins of initiation and as continued supports for regulatory (adaptive) acts, a protest arose in regard to the overemphasis on such disturbances as being the basic motivational origins. Out of this protest has come an increasing interest in other biological (built-in) tendencies such as the tendency to be curious or to investigate, which the higher animals and man possess but which do not originate in, and are not necessarily aroused and maintained by, any tissue disturbance or any kind of irritation. The investigative act based on the built-in tendency to be curious is now of as much interest in motivational psychology as the regulatory need-relieving act; perhaps even more so.[4]

We now consider the contributions to motivation of studies of the regulatory act, which in its most natural form is observed in organisms under bodily irritations (disturbances). Some necessary definitions are first presented.

Definitions

"Adaptive," "regulatory," "homeostatic mechanisms," "adjustive behavior" are frequently used within the biological view of motivation. Biologically, the term "adaptive" refers to modifications in the body structure or in activities, modifications which tend to aid survival as changes occur in the internal or external field.

When is activity adaptive? This question is not easy to answer. Is only that activity adaptive which maintains the individual's own survival? Or the survival of his group? Tinbergen (609) in his studies of the instincts of the lower animals outlines some activities of direct advantage to the individual and others advantageous to the group. With respect to man, the meaning of the term adaptive becomes even more obscure. What is adaptive for man? That which protects the human species? That which protects his own particular nation? That which serves simply his economic group, or only his family? Or should the question of what is adaptive for man be answered by assuming that man is most truly humanlike in adjustment when he maintains his values (his standards of conduct) even against social values, even though his material possessions, his family, and his body are thereby broken? Questions of this sort, when answered by a "humanized" man, reveal his individual set of values.

Regulatory activity is "protective" (adaptive) in its final effects on the organism. The principle of regulation is appealed to frequently by physiological psychologists. It has also been applied to the behavior stream and to central events, i.e., when there are nonoptimal living conditions, animals are so structured that they exhibit changes in their activity stream which usually remove or reduce the nonoptimal conditions.

---

[4] In one sense the interest in curiosity and investigation is a return to an emphasis on instincts; however, by an increasing number of studies the mechanisms responsible for the origin and continuation of the investigative tendency are being isolated. In other words, the investigative act is not "interpreted" today by simply saying that it is an expression of the instinct of curiosity.

Other psychological terms may be employed to convey a meaning similar to the terms "adaptive" and "regulatory," e.g., "accommodative" (Klein); "purposive" (Tolman); "competence" (White); and "coping" (Maslow). Regulatory acts, to be considered below in more detail, may be based on inherent adaptive mechanisms, as is observed in the intake of oxygen and expiration of carbon dioxide. They may also refer to learned ways of adapting to variety of changes. Regulation is made possible by the capacity of animals, including men, to have physiological, cognitive, and behavioral corrective activities aroused whenever there is any threat to optimal conditions for living.

"Regulatory activities" has a broader meaning than "homeostatic mechanisms," that is, when "homeostasis" refers only to *optimal conditions in the internal environment* (see Inset 3). Homeostasis may be used quite broadly to refer to general optimal conditions like a pleasant sweet taste, freedom from anxiety, or having a high status.

INSET 3. HOMEOSTASIS OF THE INTERNAL ENVIRONMENT*

Viewed empirically, writes Dempsey (153), the physiological reactions of mammalian organisms present an array of contradictory and paradoxical phenomena. The heart rate and cardiac output may increase while the blood flow in a given region increases, decreases, or remains static. An accelerated respiratory rate may accompany muscular activity (exercise) or inactivity (panting). The glucose concentration of the blood may rise during depletion of the glycogen stores of the body, or, conversely, while the carbohydrate reserves are being augmented. Taken without reference to the total needs of the individual, these reactions can but bewilder the systematist. It is understandable, therefore, that a generalization rationalizing these and many other observations would be received gratefully by physiological investigators. Such a generalization was formulated by Claude Bernard (63) in 1859 and extensively documented by Walter B. Cannon (111) in 1932. Bernard was greatly impressed by the regulatory mechanisms that maintain the concentration of glucose in the blood at a nearly constant level. In a flash of intuitive insight he perceived this to be one example of a general law of constancy of the internal environment. Cannon, aware of many more examples in which a constant state is maintained and having investigated some of the regulatory mechanisms, applied a special name, homeostasis, to designate these steady states.

The internal environment is essentially the chemical medium supporting the neural system. Among these constant conditions therein which must be maintained, are, with mammals, the internal body temperature. It must remain fixed even though the temperature of the external environment is below zero or above 100 degrees. The acidity of the blood must remain

* Adapted from E. W. Dempsey, Homeostasis. In S. S. Stevens (ed.), *Handbook of Experimental Psychology.* New York: Wiley, 1951.

constant. A slight shift toward acidity would result in coma and death; a shift toward alkalinity would produce convulsions. There are other essential constant states of the internal environment, e.g., blood sugar level, salt and water balance, calcium and phosphorus balance, etc. These constant states represent optimal conditions (homeostasis) in the internal environment.

"Adjustive" is more frequently applied to the socially acceptable behavior which man exhibits as a member of a group. Of course, some activities physiologically regulatory, such as belching, are not socially adjustive, at least, not in the Western societies. Also, women who have suffered for the sake of the fashion of the day illustrate the conflict between physiologically healthy behavior and that culturally imposed in order to be socially acceptable. The concept of a truly adjusted man also implies an *integrated* personality, not simply a socially acceptable man.

REGULATION

The biological approach to man led to an interest in his regulatory (adaptive) acts. Man lives and moves in varying external fields. What he does is in part the resultant of changes in the *external* field. Some are disturbing to the organism. And man, like all organisms, also has an *internal* environment in which constant states must be maintained. And so, disturbances in the internal environment, as well as noxious external-in-origin stimulation, are important origins for regulatory behaviors. Disturbances in the central or cognitive activities, such as in remembering, in affective control, in inhibitory mechanisms, may likewise arise and be followed by adaptive behavior.

Some typical illustrations of simple regulatory acts are now presented, with the emphasis on behavioral adaptive changes.

Regulatory Acts of a Mammal under Painful Stimulation

An adult rat, as described by Hull (299), is placed into a box with two compartments. The floor is so arranged that electric shock can be a stimulus for the rat. When this painful stimulation is applied, the rat's behavior changes from the deliberate exploratory movements to an exaggeratedly—

> . . . mincing mode of locomotion about the compartment interspersed with occasional slight squeaks, biting of the bars which are shocking its feet, defecation, urination, and leaps up the walls. These reactions are repeated in various orders and in various parts of the compartment; sometimes the same act occurs several times in succession, sometimes not. After five or six minutes of this variable behavior one of the leaps carries the animal over the barrier upon the uncharged grid of the second compartment. Here after

an interval of quiescence and heavy breathing, the animal cautiously re-
sumes exploratory behavior, much as in the first compartment. Ten minutes
after the first leap of the barrier, the second grid is charged and the animal
goes through substantially the same type of variable behavior as before.
This finally results in a second leaping of the barrier and ten minutes more
of safety, after which this grid is again charged, and so on. In this way the
animal is given fifteen trials, each terminated by a leap over the barrier.
(299, p. 70. Reprinted by permission of Appleton-Century-Crofts.)

At the beginning there is increased variability in the rat's behavior;
with learning there is a decrease. This observation illustrates the acquisition of a change in the escape response pattern to a more adaptive
learned sequence of responses. Let us now assume that a buzzer has
sounded each time two seconds before the shock is turned on the grid
and has lasted until the animal leaped the barrier. The learning would
continue until the animal eliminated the original responses except that
of leaping the barrier. At some point the animal would begin occasionally to leap the barrier during the first two seconds of the sounding of
the buzzer before the onset of the shock. We may then say (1) that he
acquires an avoidance response, (2) or that he learns "something" about
the stimulus field, as is indicated by his isolation of the buzzer as a
warning signal and his jumping after its onset, (3) or that he has a
learned fear evoked by the buzzer. The animal placed again in the apparatus, and without shock being applied, would most probably show
by his behavior that the stimulus field (the buzzer or simply the walls
and floor of the apparatus) had changed in their motivational (energizing) influence. He would immediately attempt to leap over the barrier.
He would act as if he had learned to fear the stimulus field following
the associations with painful electric shock. Which of these three inferences are the animal's learnings cannot be precisely determined, but
probably he has changed in all three ways.

What has the experiment above told us about the motivation of a complex animal? We note first that characteristically this animal (like man)
shows greater activation, including initially emotional signs, when under
the disturbing painful stimulation, or, after learning, when under the
influence of the associated stimuli such as the buzzer in the above
demonstration.

Second, there is a variability, then a change in the responses, and then
a reduction in variation until finally the leaping of the barrier is evoked
immediately with the onset of the warning signal. This reduction in
response variation indicates learning. Motivationally, we are interested
in such learnings when the following questions are considered: (1) Did
the amount of irritating stimulation aid the learning? (Is amount of a
need drive a variable in learning rate and/or learning strength?) See pp.

320–326. (2) Did relief from pain strengthen learning? [If not, what was the reinforcing (strengthening) event?] These are problems both of learning and of motivation and are later considered under the topic of reinforcement on pp. 326–330.

Third, the organism usually orients differently to the total stimulus field after the onset of the pain. His selectings among potential stimulations are changed; e.g., he selectively orients to the barrier and to the warning buzzer. He also is selective in his responses (Chapter 10).

Fourth, the animal under painful stimulation is directed, moving toward escape from pain; even at the beginning of his escape attempts, we observe that what he does is in relation to the identified origin of the painful stimulation; later he seems directed to a learned, anticipated place "where there is no pain." There are behavioral signs of an anticipated goal (Chapter 9).

Finally, there are behavioral clues of an acquisition of a central learned fear. Additional questions: Is the animal being moved by a new motivational determinant—a central learned fear? Or has there been only an acquisition of an association (a conditioning) of a specific escape response to otherwise neutral stimuli, e.g., to the buzzer? A crucial experiment to answer these additional questions was performed by Miller (427). It is outlined below.

Learning under Acquired Fear

The apparatus used is illustrated in Figure 3-1. The two compartments were painted differentially, one white where the shock from the

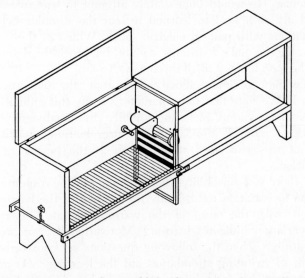

Figure 3-1. Apparatus used to establish a learned fear drive. Miller (430)

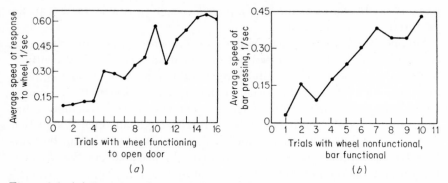

Figure 3-2. (*a*) Learning of a new habit (turning the wheel) during nonshock trials. Fear is the learned drive. Miller (430) (*b*) Learning a second habit (pressing the bar) during nonshock trials. Fear continues as the learned drive. Miller (430)

grid floor was given, the other black, the escape compartment. In the first ten trials the rats were given electric shock from the grid and allowed to escape through an open door into the black box. In five tests without shock the animals continued to escape by running through the open door.

A test of whether a central learned fear was energizing the animal was then made. The animal was placed in the white compartment where he had previously received shock. The escape door was closed but could be opened if the animal now turned a wheel. No shock was given, but the animal showed symptoms of fear such as urination, defecation, tenseness, and crouching. Moreover, he was energized; in general, his activity-level was raised. He performed a variety of new responses rather than simply the old responses, so that eventually he moved the wheel. The door then opened, and the animal escaped to the "safe" black box. Fear—learned fear—it was assumed, was the energizer for the variety of responses, including the wheel-turning performance.

A further test by Miller of whether animals so trained will show a general increase in energy release when in sensory contact with the spatial locus of former painful stimuli was made by so arranging the apparatus that the response to the wheel was no longer correct. However, a new problem was presented: The animal had to learn that by pressing a bar he could open the door and escape to the safe black box. At first, under the new problem, he continued to attack the wheel. Eventually these responses were extinguished, and other responses appeared. A new response (pressing the bar) that caused the door to drop and permitted escape was then learned. This is shown in Figures 3-2*a* and *b*. The most significant point of these experiments for motivational psychology is that new responses appear when the primary energizer, pain, is no longer present. The *inferred* energizer is a learned fear, an acquired drive component.[5]

Summarizing, we see that Miller's experiments (430) are of significance because he demonstrated not only that an animal would continue to perform in the same way under the conditioned stimulus (white box) as when stimulated by the original painful shock, but that the animal could learn new ways of escaping. In other words, Miller demonstrated that animals could learn not only to run through an open door when placed in a white box where shock had previously been given, but also to solve new problems. He inferred that (1) learned fear was the energizer and (2) its reduction was the reinforcer.

Presented above were a series of demonstrations posing motivational problems. These will be of interest in later chapters. One final demonstration of regulatory activity illustrates in more detail not only arousal changes but also shifts in selecting.

Self-regulation: Selecting by a Warm-blooded Animal in a Cold External Field

If the temperature outside a warm-blooded animal decreases, a number of activity changes occur which protect the temperature of the animal's body. The rate of heat production in the body will increase. There is also a "stepped-up" thyroid function, which improves the general metabolic rate through quickened heart rate and heightened muscular activity. In addition, the animal may increase its heat production by shivering. Other physiological and behavioral regulatory activities that reduce the rate of heat loss from the body will also take place.

> The superficial blood vessels will constrict; the hair of the body will erect, forming a good insulating coat in the case of certain furry animals; and the animal may roll into a ball, exposing only a minimum of body surface. At the same time the animal may behave in such a way as to reduce the heat loss and increase heat production. If possible, it will move to a warmer area of the environment. Given access to building materials and a variety of foods, it will build a nest, hoard large stores of food, increase its food intake, and select a diet of high caloric value. (440, p. 105)

Selecting is illustrated in the above regulatory unit. The warm-blooded animal in a cold external temperature is sensitized differently under the threat to his survival. He shows this change by selective orientation to objects which previously were ignored; e.g., he selects materials with which to build a nest and foods of high calorie value. Likewise out of his potential repertoire of responses, those appear which

---

[5] Drive and drive components (drives) are defined on pp. 115–117. Miller held that the fear was a covert response which set up "strong" stimuli arousing the rat as did the painful stimuli. Our inference in regard to fear would locate it more centrally.

aid his survival in this nonoptimal condition. He shivers, rolls into a ball, or moves away from the cold region.

We next turn to another capacity of higher animals—capacity to be directed.

Direction in Regulatory Acts

Within a regulatory act and, we shall see later, also in behaviors which cannot be so classified, it is possible to identify ends and, after learning, goals which mark the completion of phases in the continuous activity stream. In the first illustration above, the rat receiving painful stimulation reached an end on each trial when he jumped over the wall to the nonirritating box; he presumably had relief from pain. This relief closed a short regulatory phase in his activity stream. Later when the associated buzzer sounded, presumably he atttained relief from learned fear by jumping before the shock came.

In the observations of the adaptive responses of animals in a cold environment it was assumed that the end was a reduction of heat loss. These ends to regulatory phases in the activity stream are arbitrarily identified and described by an outside observer. It is not claimed that with the onset of a regulatory act any increase in activation and shifts in choices are in order to reach an end. Rather, all that is said is that goals are observed and that there is often agreement among observers in regard to identification of them, though with man it is not easy to determine the goals toward which he moves.

CONCLUDING STATEMENTS

The motivation of organisms may be viewed in different ways. In this chapter we have considered the contributions to motivation of a few systematic observations of regulatory activities. These studies posed significant problems. To answer these problems has been accepted, in part at least, as the duty of motivational psychology: e.g., (1) to account for activation variations, (2) to interpret the changing selections of individuals, (3) to account for directional tendencies, and (4) to determine the interaction of motivation and learning.

How Should Answers to These Problems Be Sought? Can answers to these problems be found by studies of a regulatory act? Its stages were described above. They are familiar to psychologists: First, there is the initiation of the regulatory attempts after the onset of some kind of disturbance or after a learned warning sign; then follow the initial increases in activation; there may occur signs of changes in selective orientation to the external field with shifts in response patterning; variability in behavior can be observed if the disturbance is not removed; and finally, there may be behavioral signs of relief in the ending of that regulatory phase in the activity stream. Such a description—even if it were more detailed—is unfortunately not of much value in understanding the behavior. It is as absurd as attempting to understand the movements of atoms by watching an atomic explosion. Instead, one problem must be approached at a time. For example, it is known that anticipated goals affect both arousal and selections and also determine directional control to an important degree, but it is difficult to study simultaneously all three changes. Hence, in the following chapters each of the different functions of goals, as well as of other motivational determinants, will be considered separately. By such isolation it is hoped that the complexity of events subsumed under the vague term "motivation" may be illuminated.

Biological but Nondeficit Tendencies

The contributions of the biological approach have not arisen solely from studies of pain, hunger, cold, or similar tissue disturbances. There are biological tendencies which are not based on deficits of necessary substances or conditions but which may influence the progress of a regulatory act and, more important, may operate between such homeostatic episodes. One tendency to be considered in the next chapter is that of investigating the external world (and the inner "world" of experiences) —a tendency which is quite significant in the activity streams of the higher animals, particularly of man. At least, man, having greater intelligence, has been more successful in his investigations of relationships among natural phenomena, and he is apparently the only animal who can examine his own experiences. There is no "existentialism"[6] for the apes. The development in the psychology of motivation of the biological tendency to sense, to investigate, to explore, to understand, is canceling the overemphasis on need-based motivation. The curious man often attempts to discover that which he knows will not reduce in any way any of his primary or social needs.

Before concluding this chapter we call the reader's attention to a motivational "formula" useful in interpreting observations of bodily need-based acts. The formula, however, has been applied to many activity phases the need-reducing utility of which is minimal or absent, and hence the formula is subject to criticism.

A Motivational Formula and Its Criticisms

One motivational formula is as follows: "Equilibrium—disturbance to equilibrium—attempts to return to equilibrium." The assumption is that

---

[6] The term "existence" comes from the Latin root *ex sistere*, meaning literally "to stand out," "to emerge." The existentialists seek to understand man as a being who is always in the process of emerging, becoming. They are concerned with experiences as such.

the organism is not aroused unless there is some antecedent for the on-set of a state of disequilibrium. In other words, the activities of organ-isms are said to increase under disturbance to equilibrium and are in-fluenced by the particular nature of the disturbance. The organism may not effect immediate removal of the disturbance, but if regulation is completed, there is restoration of optimal conditions. Satisfaction, re-laxation, pleasure, and/or relief are supposedly present at completion. (To avoid any implication that the formula is static, the assumption is made that new sources of disequilibrium are frequently appearing.)

Many of the theories of motivation today have in common the basic assumption that *all* activity tends toward the elimination of exciting states, toward equilibrium, or as one technical phrase has it, toward drive reduction. These theories hold that all excitability, all striving, have their original or immediate source in the disturbance of organic equilibrium. The more severe the disturbance, the greater is the urgency to reduce tension. Man, it is assumed, learns ways of detensioning. Here the Freudian and behavioristic models are alike; similar to many other theories, they hold quiescence, complacency, drive relief to be the goal of action. In contrast to this view is the warning: "Attempts to reduce drive" should not be the automatic description whenever signs of strug-gle are observed in a man's activity stream. A disturbed man, a restless man, might even be attempting to increase drive by seeking one goal after another. Or he might be attempting to move away from a condition of boredom, from a static state into an active one.

A reverse motivational formula may be at times equally sensible. Rise in activity can be considered the result of too little activity, too much equilibrium, rather than the reverse. Cannon (111), to whom is often attributed the first emphasis upon homeostasis though it was a principle already observed by others, placed a limitation upon its application. He assumed that the physiological homeostatic mechanisms were useful to protect the internal environment but also to free man "for adventure and amusement." With homeostatic devices that keep "constant" essen-tial *bodily* processes, Cannon assumed that man was thus freed from the slavery of the details of bare existence—"free to enter into agreeable relations with others, free to enjoy beautiful things, to explore and to understand the wonders of the world, to develop new ideas and interests, and to work and play, untrammeled by anxieties concerning bodily affairs." With essential needs met, the priceless unessentials could be freely sought (111, p. 323).

Next considered is a biological tendency which cannot be classified as regulatory or nonregulatory. The investigatory-exploratory tendency may operate with, or at times independently of, regulation, or even in conflict with it.

CHAPTER 4

THE INVESTIGATIVE-

EXPLORATIVE ORIENTATION

Why did Columbus sail westward in spite of the dire warnings against the unknown? Why does man today plan to go to the moon? Why does any man want to visit the moon and why "in heaven's name" would Bill Smith volunteer to ride the rocket ship? Because the moon is there? Because it is a challenge? Perhaps Bill's hopes are the same as men's in general. He has a desire to achieve, or a hope that conquering space will aid his country. There are both practical and nonpractical outcomes of the investigative-exploratory tendency. The purpose of this chapter is to consider a few of its various manifestations.

The investigative-curiosity tendency, not dependent on any need state, is a significant determinant in the motivation of higher animals, particularly man. The recognition of this nondeficit biological tendency is an important advance in motivational theory, for it questions any simple need-based biological position. As Morgan (439) points out, though perhaps too hopefully, "If it is characteristic of people that they are motivated to explore, manipulate, and experience their environment, then personality theory need not indulge in any great gyrations to explain the seemingly complex motives found in people" (439, p. 667). Moreover, to the degree that it can be demonstrated that the investigative-curiosity tendency will support persistent performance and permit learning, then questions are raised whether drive relief, or the reward symbol of relief, is essential for reinforcing (strengthening) performance.

Recognition of Significance

Exploration, or the investigative-curiosity tendency, is not a recent arrival in the taxonomy of motivational tendencies. McDougall (415)

34

in 1926 recognized its importance in man and suggested there were individual differences in the innate strength of curiosity. These differences
were apt to be increased, he believed, during the course of a man's life,
curiosity growing weaker for lack of use in those in whom it was innately weak and stronger through exercise in those in whom it was innately strong. In men of the latter type it might become the main source
of intellectual energy and effort; to its impulse could be traced most of
the purely disinterested labors of the highest type of intellect. Mc-
Dougall wrote: "It must be regarded as one of the principal roots of
both science and religion" (415, p. 61).

Not only in man but likewise in his phylogenetically close neighbors,
there is a tendency toward persistent, thoroughgoing, and systematic examination and trial of objects and situations, or so write two early scientific observers in *The Great Apes*. In the monkeys this tendency is con-
spicuous, and in the apes it is obviously more serviceable than in any
animal except man. "Clearly, in all of the primates the assemblage of
activities, suggested by the term curiosity, constitutes a highly important
partial basis for progress. . . . It would be difficult to exaggerate the
psychobiological value of curiosity in primates. Its complete description
will ultimately throw a flood of light on many puzzling aspects of behavioral adaptation" (663, p. 573).

Turning to a keen observer, Freud, we find that he too paid his respect to curiosity by attributing knowledge and investigation to sub-
limated forms of acquisition, while the energy with which it worked
supposedly came from the "looking impulse" (*Schaulust*). The impulse
to acquire, according to Freud, was derived from the desire to incorporate external objects, which characterizes the oral stage of the psycho-
sexual development. The looking impulse was one of the partial impulses
contained in the libido. It also was said to underlie certain perversions
of voyeurism. It may appear to the reader that Freud's *Schaulust* which
can lead to voyeurism is a far cry from the tendency to be in active relationship with the world, but Freud's emphasis on the sexual origin and
expression of curiosity is nevertheless another indication of the widespread consideration of this organismic tendency.

Other psychologists have not neglected this general tendency. Bartlett
(40), writing in *Remembering*, used the concept of "effort after meaning." Lewin (365) postulated a need to structure the field. Woodworth
(659) early emphasized the role of perception in learning, i.e., the thesis
that perception was always driven by a direct inherent motive which
might be called the will to perceive. "Whatever ulterior motives may
be present from time to time, this direct perceptual motive is always
present in any use of the senses. It is impossible to look without trying
to see or to listen without trying to hear. To see, to hear—to see clearly,

to hear distinctly—to make out what it is one is seeing or hearing—moment by moment, such concrete immediate motives dominate the life of relation with the environment" (659, p. 123). In his 1958 *Dynamics of Behavior*, Woodworth again speculated that the "direction of receptive and motor activity toward the environment is the fundamental tendency of animal and human behavior. . . . It is the all-pervasive primary motivation of behavior" (660, pp. 124–125). He added, "We are not pretending that the organic needs are derived from the tendency to deal with the environment. The organic needs are autonomous" (660, p. 128). However, investigation, whether it appears or not in the reduction of needs, has its own immediate satisfactions: e.g., "a child on a visit, if given the run of the house, will locate not only the pantry and bathroom but also a surprising number of things that are interesting because he can do something with them. You cannot expect him to keep busy most of the time attending to his organic need" (660, p. 131).

Goldstein (223, 225) advanced a similar hypothesis when he wrote that the basic drive, the only drive by which the life of the organism is determined, is the "tendency to actualize its nature, to actualize itself."

One of the manifestations of the investigatory tendency is an orientation toward the external origin of any change in the sensory input, such as a change in a sound or in brightness. Pavlov names this orientation the investigatory reflex, the "what is it?" reflex (see Inset 4).

> It is this reflex which may bring about the immediate response in man and animals to the slightest changes in the world around them, so that they immediately orient their appropriate receptor organ in accordance with the perceptible quality in the agent bringing about the change, making full investigation of it. The biological significance of this reflex is obvious. If the animal were not provided with such a reflex, its life would hang at every moment by a thread. (481)

INSET 4. THE "WHAT IS IT?" REFLEX*

Berlyne (62) has outlined the results of investigations of physiological processes which are a part of the orientation reflex.

Orienting behavior has been recognized by Russian experimenters as a worthwhile topic for research ever since Pavlov paid his respects to it. But advances in neurophysiological knowledge and recording techniques have caused the Pavlovian concept of an orientation reflex or orientation reaction to be modified, extended, and given a new impetus to investigation in Soviet laboratories.

The major conclusion yielded is that outwardly visible orienting behavior —the postural changes and receptor adjustments that are classed as orient-

* Adapted from D. E. Berlyne, *Conflict, Arousal, and Curiosity.* New York: McGraw-Hill, 1960, pp. 81–83.

ing responses—forms part of a whole constellation of physiological processes permeating the entire organism that can be elicited by the onset, termination, intensification, weakening, or modification in any other way of any kind of stimulation. The components of this many-sided orientation reaction, as revealed by the experiments of Sokolov and others (567, 568, 569) including American investigators, e.g., Davis et al. (148), and Dykman et al. (168), are as follows:

1. Changes in Sense Organs:
   a. The pupil of the eye dilates.
   b. Photochemical changes lowering the absolute threshold for intensity of light occur in the retina.
2. Changes in the Skeletal Muscles That Direct Sense Organs:
   a. The eyes open wide and turn toward a source of visual stimulation; this action is often accompanied by movements of the head, the trunk, and even the whole body.
   b. The head turns toward a source of sound.
   c. Animals prick up their ears.
   d. Sniffing occurs, especially in animals that use their olfactory sense much more than man.
3. Changes in General Skeletal Musculature:
   a. Ongoing actions are temporarily arrested.
   b. General muscle tonus rises, increasing readiness for activity in the skeletal muscles. Kvasov (350) has called this phenomenon the "What's to be done?" (*chto delat'?*) reflex by analogy with Pavlov's "What is it?" reflex.
   c. There may be diffuse bodily movements and vocalization.
   d. There is an increase in muscular electrical activity detectable with the electromyograph (148).
4. Changes in the Central Nervous System:
   a. Alpha waves, when present, disappear and give place to faster, more irregular EEG (electroencephalogram) activity.
   b. When slower EEG waves representative of drowsy and somnolent states are present, they are replaced by alpha waves.
   c. If, however, fast waves in the beta (14 to 30 cycles per second) or gamma (over 30 cycles per second) range are already present, the orientation reaction will not produce an EEG change.
5. Vegetative Changes:
   a. The blood vessels in the limbs contract, while those in the head expand.
   b. The GSR (galvanic skin reflex; an increase in the electrical conductance of the palm and the sole) occurs.
   c. There are cardiac and respiratory changes whose exact nature varies.

Pavlov adds that, strictly speaking, no stimulus within the animal's range of perception exists to which it would be absolutely indifferent. In a normal animal the slightest alteration in the environment—even the very slightest sound, faintest odor, or smallest change in intensity of illumination—immediately evokes the reflex, the "what is it?" manifestation. However, if these stimuli keep recurring, they spontaneously and rapidly weaken in their effect. And there is thus selection among them for further examination.[1] Some of such brief orientations are often followed by a further investigation of the stimulating source or sources. In other words, the investigatory tendency may manifest itself in a variety of ways, all of which usually increase the number of sensory contacts.

Observations of Curiosity in Children

The young child tends to use all of his extereoceptive receptors to increase sensory contacts. The child also frequently uses his hands and lips as a means of increasing the sources of stimulations. He may "explore" an object with lips and mouth, to the delight of the child and to the horror of the parents.

Piaget (487) in his observations of early development notes that a child not only is influenced by the stimulating environment but in turn exerts an influence on it. Even the very young child's behavior often suggests that he is trying out the effect of different responses upon some stimulating source. With an object never observed before, he seems to be asking what will happen if he pushes it, drops it, eats it, tastes it, kicks it, smashes it, gets it wet, or throws it. And when he perceives the effects of his actions, he may try out again the same responses, observing whether he obtains the same effect. He is a beginner in the field of science, but he *is* beginning. A higher stage in the development of the investigative tendency is observed when relationships are sought. For example, the child may test the relationship between the felt weight of an object and the perceived quickness of its fall after he releases it. One child almost a year old indicates such active experimentation. White (653) reports Piaget's observations:

> At 10 months and 10 days Laurent [the child], who is unfamiliar with bread as a nutritive substance, is given a piece for examination. He manipulates it, drops it many times, breaks off fragments and lets them fall. He has done this kind of thing before, but previously his attention has seemed to be centered on the act of letting go. Now "he watches with great interest the body in motion; in particular, he looks at it for a long time when it has fallen, and picks it up when he can." On the following day he resumes his "research." (653, p. 319)

He grasps in succession a celluloid swan, a box, and several other small objects, in each case stretching out his arm and letting them fall. Sometimes

---

[1] That this investigatory tendency in man is not solely the resultant of his socialization is indicated by its appearance in nonhumans. It is a biological (inherent) tendency.

he stretches out his arm vertically, sometimes he holds it obliquely in front of or behind his eyes. When the object falls in a new position (for example on his pillow) he lets it fall two or three times more on the same place, as though to study the spatial relation; then he modifies the situation. At a certain moment the swan falls near his mouth; now he does not suck it (even though this object habitually serves this purpose), but drops it three times more while merely making the gesture of opening his mouth. (487, p. 269)

And when the older child can move through space—crawl, walk, run —then he can even more quickly contact new sensory fields and complete an examination. He is not yet capable of an effective investigatory act, but what he discovers may be quite exciting to him. In general, children placed where there are many potential discoveries do not seem to be annoyed nor to dislike the opportunities to investigate. In fact, if we can speculate in regard to their feelings, it can be said that they enjoy investigations. It is observed that a change in the external field is more "fun" than monotony. For example, the hypothesis that novelty is pleasing was supported when children showed signs of frustration if interrupted in their play with new toys, even though they had their old toys returned (36).

What is unusual is a child who has adequate sense organs and uses them only in a limited fashion, who can perceive the external world but is lost within it, who can manipulate but is indifferent, who can walk but does not attempt it, and who, though he can babble and make a variety of sounds, is mostly silent; a child who makes little or no use of his investigative capacities is an abnormal child. In other words, curiosity in a child does not have to be explained.

The above speculations would not have been of much concern to motivation if there had not been experimental demonstrations that new sensory contact and/or enlargement (enrichment) of the external field can act as a reward, and that learning of difficult problems can occur when the support for the necessary continued performance seems dependent upon this type of rewarding effect. We now turn to some experimental studies of the investigatory tendency.

Experimental Demonstrations and Some Questions

In an experiment, Nissen (464) used the open alley type of maze devised by Dashiell (137) as a reward place for rats. They were tested in an obstruction box for the strength of their exploratory tendency. It was assumed that the experimental animals would cross an obstruction more often to obtain the rewarding opportunity to explore than control animals that ran into a bare chamber. This was confirmed. Harlow and others have demonstrated that permitting increased use of exterocep-

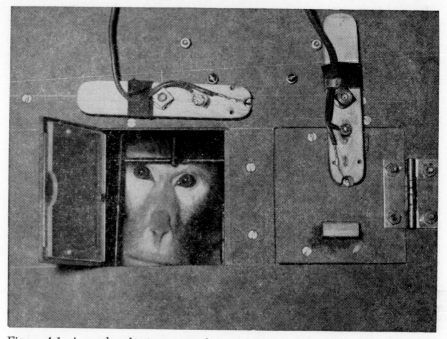

Figure 4-1. A monkey having a visual reward after a correct response to a color-discrimination problem. Butler (100)

tive sense organs supported the continuance of learning tasks. The role of an increased visual field in rewarding animals (monkeys) in discrimination learning is illustrated in a report below by Harlow (247) of a study by Butler (100). The front of the essential apparatus is shown in Figure 4-1. It consists of a wire cage covered by an opaque box.

At one end of the box are two windows so designed that they may be covered by differentially colored cards. The windows are hinged and open outward to light pressure unless locked by a locking device. In front of the windows inside the lightproof box is an opaque screen which can be raised or lowered by the experimenter. The monkey enters the cage, which is covered by the box and which is at all times dimly illuminated. The opaque screen is then raised and the monkey is given 30 seconds in which to respond to the colored cards. If the monkey makes an incorrect response, the locking device is activated, and this automatically turns on a small light outside the apparatus, the opaque screen is lowered by the experimenter, and a 30-second interval is interposed before the next trial. If the animal makes a correct response, it is rewarded by being allowed to look through the window for a 30-second period. At the end of this time, the opaque screen is lowered, and thirty seconds later another trial is started. (247, p. 37)

Twenty trials a day are given for twenty days, and as indicated in Figure 4-2, fairly rapid and efficient discrimination learning for the visual exploratory reward takes place. Repetition of the study (104) yielded similar results.

The above experiments pose significant problems for motivational research. Among them are:

1. What is responsible for the *arousal* (the activity) of the monkeys? Why did they not simply go to sleep or, at least, lapse into inactivity? There was no irritant, no need to be active.

2. A second series of problems concern the specific orientations of the animals, i.e., their first selective focusing on one particular part of the external field (the colored cards). And why is the specific motor channel of release—the touching of the correct card—continued? Why do the monkeys not engage in the many other activities—grooming, jumping, watching, listening—of which they are capable?

The animal could have consistently so moved the latch that the door did *not* open. But he did not. Why not? The selective evocation of a particular response over others is a motivational problem, but it is also, we will see later, a learning problem and a problem in understanding the cognitive activities.

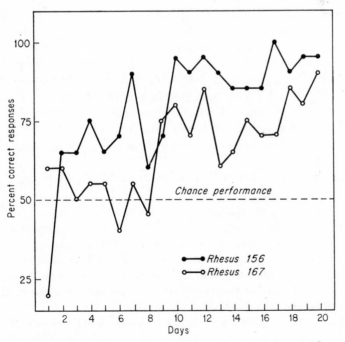

Figure 4-2. Discrimination learning by monkeys motivated by visual exploration. Butler (100)

3. The correct response is learned. What is the *strengthening* mechanism? Apparently the "reward" is "looking out the window." Why is this rewarding? Is there any need relief?

4. A final problem is posed by the above study in any attempt to identify the *direction* toward which the animal is moving in his many responses. Is there, for example, a goal?[2] And what is it?

Suggested Answers. Let us consider the question why the monkey was aroused, i.e., active, during the observations.

Actually it is not essential to account for activity in organisms, but there always remains the problem of accounting for a shift in degree of arousal *and* for the channels of release of energy. Why did the animal engage in the response of "opening the door"? We know this response is followed immediately by the sight of a more varied external field. Is this enriched visual field the important variable? Butler in another study (101) investigated the effect on the opening-the-door performance when several objectively different external fields were used. The purpose of the second study was to determine the length of time that changes in the visual field would support the opening of the door. Animals were tested ten continuous hours a day for six consecutive days. The number of openings and length of time the door was held open were recorded automatically.

The results indicate that (1) the effect of an enriched visual field sustained performance, and (2) the influence of the visual fields varied according to the specific objects presented. Most responses of opening were made when another monkey could be seen; next was the sight of a toy electric train in motion, which elicited more activity than the sight of food (Figure 4-3). As is indicated in Figure 4-4, when a homogeneous visual field was present following the opening of the door, there was little performance as contrasted to the effect when a monkey could be seen. In general, it is a *stimulus change* which is significant in maintaining the performance.[3]

In the above situation with monkeys as subjects, there are signs that the continued use of a specific motor channel—the opening of a door—was influenced by an anticipation of an enriched visual field. The behavior of the animals suggested that the change in the stimulus field was anticipated and that it was a to-be-attained effect (a goal), not something to be avoided. Learning occurred. Other studies have supported these findings with the laboratory rat as subjects (151, 60). A change in the visual or the auditory stimulation favors the continuance of performance of a motor task.

Children will perform on a simple task for visual rewards. The main-

[2] A goal is a learned anticipation of a to-be-attained effect.
[3] Manipulation per se was to a lesser degree also involved (103, p. 169).

Figure 4-3. A view of an electric train serves as a reward for pushing open the door of an enclosed box. Butler (101)

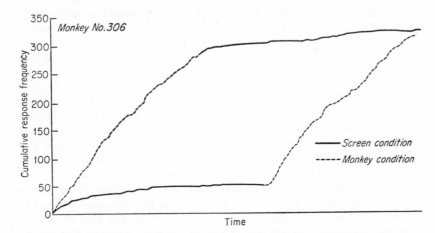

Figure 4-4. Different visual incentives affect response rate. Responses during two tests of sixty minutes each were recorded. On one-half the tests the visual reward was the view of another monkey, and on the other half, a visual homogeneous field. Butler (103)

tenance of play behavior by nursery school children has been studied by Hayes (256) when the reward was a stimulus change. Children were invited to play simple games, such as dropping marbles through a slot and retrieving them in a tray or pressing a lever that produced noise. The subjects would become satiated with any one game, but changing games served to reinstate play behavior to its original level—a finding similar to that reported for chimpanzees.

Why does the organism "like" a stimulus change? Why is it rewarding? Apparently there is an inherent (built-in) tendency to stay in contact with changing stimulation (at least under certain circumstances). This has sometimes been phrased as a liking for variety or novelty. One of the early studies of stimulus deprivation employed students at 20 dollars a day to remain in an isolated cubicle with all extraneous sources of stimulation greatly reduced. Among the other findings was a report of a growing strong aversion in the subjects to the monotonous environment. In spite of the high rate of pay, they could stand only a few days of the isolation from change (66). Inset 5 reports clever methods of overcoming the monotony of solitary prison confinement.

INSET 5. A PRISONER IN SOLITARY*

The ingenious prisoner may overcome to some degree the horror of solitary imprisonment. The following is a report by a woman, a British subject, isolated in a Hungarian prison for a large part of seven years.

A habit of mind stood me in good stead during my seven solitary years. I cannot remember ever having just waited anywhere—not even for a train or in a dentist's office—without some physical or mental activity. And in my dark cell I was now emancipated from the pressure of time; there was no more clock watching, no more hurrying to keep appointments. So I had the first opportunity in many years to think over and digest all that I had learned during these years.

I began by reciting poetry and later translated poems from one language to another. I discovered that rhymes came easily to me, and from there to composing doggerel was but a step. Being deprived of physical activity, because of horror of treading on the muck on the floor, I was just beginning to tire of a mental diet consisting entirely of poetry when, nine days later, I was transferred to another cell. Here I was to remain in complete isolation until I was removed to a prison outside Budapest in May 1954.

This new cell, though still in total darkness, was a Ritz Hotel by comparison. It was on the ground floor instead of in the cellar and the bed had a straw mattress. Although the cell was only about five feet by ten feet, there was a narrow concrete furrow deeply worn by countless feet that had walked endlessly to and fro. In time, I did the same.

* Adapted from *Reader's Digest*, July, 1959. From *7 Years Solitary*, (c) 1957, by Edith Bone. Reprinted by permission of Harcourt, Brace & World, Inc.

In imagination I walked the streets of all the great cities of Europe where I had lived; I recalled their rivers, their buildings, their monuments. Quite naturally I began to call on my friends and acquaintances in those cities, and as I am talkative by nature these visits were very real. Thus there was no lack of human companionship, even if it was only in my imagination.

I first used my fingers to count the kilometers, but I lost count every time I was interrupted by the guards. So I made 30 pellets out of bread, ten of them small, ten medium and ten large. Each time I passed the table at the foot of my bed, I put down a small pellet; when I had put down all the small pellets I picked them up and put down a medium-sized one and started all over again. When I had put down ten medium-sized ones I put down a large one. Even in the dark I was able to keep count of the distances covered.

One day after more than five months of darkness, the electric light which formerly had been turned on only at meals was left on after breakfast.

Now that I had light, I could evolve better methods of keeping count. The obvious thing was to substitute an abacus, or counting frame, for the pellets. The only material I had was the black convict bread which I got but could not eat. Being unkneaded, unleavened and almost unbaked, the sticky mess, after proper treatment, hardened into something very like plastic.

It took me months to work out the problem of how to use this so that the "beads" would slip easily on the "wires" of my abacus—thick sorghum straws from my broom.

Before I thought of making the abacus I had tried to take an inventory of my vocabulary in the six languages which I speak, but I failed because I always lost count. With the abacus this problem was solved; in the end I could enumerate 27,369 English words and a total in all languages of close on 100,000. There were, of course, many more inventories that one could make. How many birds could I name? How many trees? How many flowers? How many makes of cars? How many wines? How many characters in Dickens?

The guards were keen to prevent me from knowing what was going on outside my cell. Naturally, even though I was only mildly interested, I decided to pierce my door for a spyhole through which I could look out, just as the guards could look in through their spyhole, which is a feature of every prison door.

January 27, 1952, was a memorable day for me, I got my spectacles back and was given writing materials and the use of the prison library. That day marked the end of my singlehanded struggle with solitude. From then on I had books and ever since I first learned to read, books have always been my closest friends and allies.

NOVELTY OF THE STIMULUS FIELD

The energizing effect of a "novel" field was hypothesized in 1926 by McDougall (415) when he wrote that the native excitant of the instinct curiosity "would seem to be any object similar to, yet perceptibly different from, familiar objects habitually noticed" (p. 60). Montgomery (432) much later stated on the basis of experimentation that a novel stimulus situation evokes an exploratory tendency, that exposure to the new situation reduces the strength of the tendency. He added a significant observation: During a period of nonexposure to a stimulus, the tendency recovers in strength. Campbell and Sheffield (110) found that without a "gross change in the auditory and visual environment" there was little increase in the movement of rats in activity cages, even when the rats were deprived of food.

Novelty of a stimulus object depends upon the particular individual involved in the interaction with the object. There is no way of predicting with certainty what will be novel to any one individual. There are, however, some criteria of value in identifying what in general are novel stimuli. We start with unfamiliarity: e.g., an object is novel if it is known that the object's specific sensory pattern has never been encountered before by the individual. Also, the least recent stimulation has the most novelty. Studies of the effect of new stimulations upon the exploratory behavior of rats include Nissen's observations (464) on number of crossings of an electrified floor grid of an obstruction box in order to contact new objects, like wooden blocks or corks, not present in the home cage. The rats made an average of six crossings in order to contact and examine objects which were new to them. (Three crossings was the number expected when the incentive compartment was empty.)

A novel stimulus may be characterized not only by unfamiliarity. Novelty may also result from odd or unusual patterns not necessarily arising from infrequent sensory contact. The stimulus elements may be familiar, but their combination is unusual. A rooster on top of a boy's head is novel; the combination is incongruous though both a boy and a rooster are fairly familiar stimulus objects. Berlyne (58) was interested in the exploration by rats of any one *odd* or *different* object introduced in a group of three objects, regardless of the degree of familiarity. His procedure was first to sate the animals with eating and drinking and second, after habituating them to the testing box, to place them with a group of objects and observe them for five minutes. The objects used were three unpainted wooden cubes or three hollow rings presented in groups of three or in mixtures. In one part of the study, three similar objects were placed together, such as three cubes; then after five minutes of contact with these, the rats were taken out and put in their home cages for ten minutes; then followed a five-minute test again with the same three similar objects, which Berlyne now called familiar objects. (At least the rats had had a previous five-minute survey of them.) After a ten-minute rest period, another test was made by introducing the rats to two of the familiar and similar objects and one *odd* object. Two blocks, for example, would be placed with a nonmatching (odd) ring. The time spent in exploring (contacting) each stimulus was recorded.

A slightly different procedure was followed with another group of rats, who were placed this time with two similar and one odd stimulus object, *all unfamiliar to them.* Five minutes of testing for exploration was followed by ten minutes in home cages, and again five minutes with the objects again, which had some familiarity now for the rats. The general conclusions: There was greater contact (1) with the unfamiliar and (2) with the odd stimulus.

Observations with human subjects indicate that the unfamiliar, the varying, the odd, and/or the complex visual patterns attract. Varying one part of a visual field and keeping the rest constant resulted in longer fixation times for the *varying* part (61). Figure 4-5 indicates an increasing time in surveying the changed stimulus element of the visual field in successive exposures of a few seconds each. In another study (59) the incongruous and the surprising visual forms produced more responses when the subjects were free to give themselves as many quick exposures to visual patterns as they wished to do. Likewise, the complexity of a visual configuration is a positive variable in increasing the length of time of eye fixations (61). As is seen in Figure 4-6, complexity of a visual configuration is increased by irregularity of arrangement, amount of material, heterogeneity of elements, irregularity of shape, incongruity, and incongruous juxtaposition. Novelty is not a simple dimension. In summary, novelty of a stimulation may be traced to lack of previous organismic contact or to infrequent (or at least not recent) contact. In

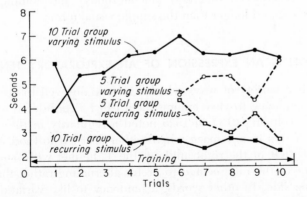

Figure 4-5. Fixation time increases on a new stimulus element in successive visual fields. The divergence is greater for the ten-trial group. The same stimulus element (animal) recurred on one side of the presentation screen while a new figure (new animal) appeared every time on the other side. Berlyne (61)

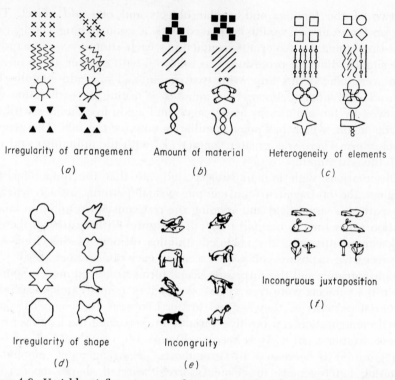

Irregularity of arrangement

(a)

Amount of material

(b)

Heterogeneity of elements

(c)

Irregularity of shape

(d)

Incongruity

(e)

Incongruous juxtaposition

(f)

Figure 4-6. Variables influencing complexity of a visual field. (a) Irregularity of arrangement, (b) amount of material, (c) heterogeneity of elements, (d) irregularity of shape, (e) incongruity, (f) incongruous juxtaposition. Berlyne (61)

addition it is observed that odd (incongruous) and complex stimulus patterns are focused longer than the simple visual forms.

ALTERNATION IS AN EXPRESSION OF AN EXPLORATORY TENDENCY

If there is a variety of ways which lead equally well to the same end effect, any tendency to vary among them can be considered evidence of exploration. Tolman (613) in 1925 noted a regularity in the alternating of choices of rats in a T-maze where either arm led to food. Whether a rat chose the left or the right angle of the T, he met with "success," but at least some of the rats seemed to prefer alternating rather than settling down to one side. In other words, a tendency to like variation was observed.

The evidence for alternation in successive trials on a single-unit choice is well established. Several interpretations have been advanced: (1) a reactive inhibition[4] or fatigue-like product which brings a cessation of a response; (2) a stimulus satiation or avoidance of the place just contacted; and (3) a similar view that alternation is one manifestation of the exploratory tendency, i.e., approaching least familiar places.

Montgomery (432) set up a definitive test to determine whether rats were avoiding the response just evoked or avoiding the stimulus just contacted. By using a double T-maze, that is, a cross-maze with goal boxes at either end, the rats could be started so that (1) they could go to the same goal place twice in succession and thus show different turning responses, or (2) they could go to different goals and thus repeat the same turning responses (see Figure 4-7). If the subjects chose the second possibility, the interpretation was that alternation behavior resulted from place avoidance rather than response avoidance. The major source of alternation was found to be in the avoidance of recontacting the same place rather than the avoidance of the same turning response. This finding confirmed earlier observations of Dennis and Sollenberger (154) and Montgomery (432). Glanzer (221) further confirmed this tendency for rats to alternate contact with alleys (stimuli) rather than to alternate turns (responses) in a maze.

The interpretation that exploration is controlled in some measure by a tendency to respond to relatively new stimulation was again found in a study of Montgomery (434). Rats explored one empty maze for five minutes and were immediately transferred to another maze identical in size, shape, and color. The exploration in the second identical maze was

[4] There are a variety of psychological meanings for the term "inhibition." Reactive inhibition, a concept advanced by Hull (299), refers to a response-produced decrement in repeating that response.

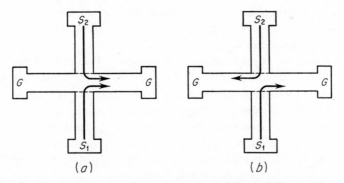

(a) (b)

Figure 4-7. Double T-maze, or cross maze, with goal boxes (G) at either end. Animals are started at S_1 on odd-numbered trials and at S_2 on even-numbered trials. (a) The left side of the diagram shows the behavior of a hypothetical animal who is influenced by a tendency to alternate right and left responses. (b) indicates behavior of the animal who alternates stimulus contacts. The latter behavior is more frequently observed.

compared to that exhibited when other groups were transferred to another maze slightly different in some respect, as in luminance. The results: The less the difference, the less the exploration in the second maze. These results contradict the reactive-inhibition hypothesis and support the tendency to explore the unfamiliar and also the least satiated stimulus, even if not unfamiliar, as the basis for alternative choices.

Are the above behavioral changes signs of curiosity or are they an expression of a general activity drive? If exploration is merely a release of "excess energy," a manifestation of a general activity drive, then there should be no order or system in the exploration. An analysis, however, reveals that the animals tend systematically to traverse that part of a maze occupied least recently. The general activity drive would not easily account for the rapid decrease in amount of exploratory behavior over a short period of time. Only one-fourth to one-third as much activity occurs during the fifth minute of maze exposure as during the first minute. Nor does a need for activity provide a basis, writes Montgomery (434), for predicting the differential amounts of recovery of exploratory behavior produced by varying the luminance of the maze.

MANIPULATION

Manipulation of objects has long been observed in the higher animals, even when no particular end other than the manipulation itself seems to be served. Dogs and cats cannot manipulate, since they have no hands; but they can paw, nudge, smell. The chimpanzee manipulates objects available to him and often also uses lips to examine objects. The curious animal, the child, and the investigating man may smash or tear apart, thus isolating some of the parts of the whole object. It is not merely increased sensory contacts but solutions to puzzling events which are served by manipulations.

Observations of Manipulation in Subhuman Primates. A tendency to manipulate the external world is sufficiently strong in monkeys that learning to solve mechanical problems is apparently supported by it. In a systematic study of manipulation, Harlow, Harlow, and Meyer (251) used rhesus monkeys as subjects and compared two matched groups in the solving of a mechanical puzzle when the manipulation of the puzzle did not lead to any special end such as food or water. The experimental group of four rhesus monkeys was given twelve days of experience in manipulating the puzzle. Another matched group, the control subjects, had the puzzle placed in their home cages for the same period of time, but the puzzle was unassembled. Hence the control monkeys could become familiar with the parts of the puzzle but not learn the solution. The purpose was to determine whether the experimental animals would learn the solution of the mechanical puzzle even though they were given no extrinsic reward for it. On two test days following twelve days of opportunity for learning, observations of both groups of animals were made. The experimental animals showed a total of thirty-one solutions and the controls four solutions in forty tests used. On the basis of these results the human experimenters postulated a manipulation drive, "strong and extremely persistent," to account for learning and maintenance of the performance. It was further hypothesized that drives of this class represent forms of motivation which may be as primary and as important as the homeostatic drives (hunger, thirst, etc.).

Since *no* extrinsic reward was given to the experimental monkeys for "monkeying" with the puzzle and learning it, their superiority on test days supports the assumption that there is a primary tendency for manipulation. A similar study using a more complicated puzzle (246) supported the above findings of a manipulative tendency, a tendency not easily subjected to satiation. For example, after the animals had learned the puzzle, the experimenter reset the puzzle every six minutes through the course of a ten-hour test session. The monkeys continued to work on the problem for the entire period, although there was a decrease in the number of devices manipulated. Moreover, the manipulative tendency appears in infant monkeys even before they have reached the age to handle solid foods (250, 405). Apparently this is a biological

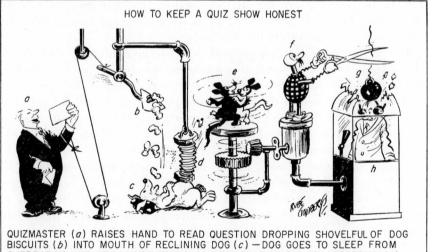

HOW TO KEEP A QUIZ SHOW HONEST

QUIZMASTER (*a*) RAISES HAND TO READ QUESTION DROPPING SHOVELFUL OF DOG BISCUITS (*b*) INTO MOUTH OF RECLINING DOG (*c*) — DOG GOES TO SLEEP FROM OVEREATING AND HEAVY BREATHING PLAYS DANCE MUSIC ON ACCORDION (*d*) — WALTZING MICE (*e*) REVOLVE VIOLENTLY, CAUSING MECHANICAL BARBER (*f*) TO CUT STRING, DROPPING IRON BALL (*g*) ON CONTESTANT (*h*) RENDERING HIM UNABLE TO ANSWER QUESTION, THUS KEEPING PROGRAM FREE FROM CORRUPTION

Figure 4-8. "Manipulation." Cartoon by Rube Goldberg. (*Newsweek*, November 16, 1959)

tendency of sufficient strength to support long-continued activity centered on one aspect of the external field, permitting learning and/or problem solving.

Man's gadgets, even those not useful but intrinsically pleasing in their clever "Rube Goldbergisms," are illustrative of the attraction that manipulation has for the human species. Figure 4-8 represents how absurdly this strong tendency may be expressed.

The above experiments would suggest that manipulation springs from a primary dispositional tendency rewarding in itself, though no doubt it could be strengthened by extrinsic rewards or nullified by associated painful stimulation.

BODILY NEEDS AND INVESTIGATIVE-CURIOSITY TENDENCY

Are bodily states the basis for investigative tendency? The answer is a definite no. Neither curiosity nor manipulation is a deficit drive, nor must either be supported by nonhomeostatic needs for its appearance. They are too all-pervasive, too likely to be aroused under many and diverse conditions, to be dependent on any specific need state either present now or historically an influence. Though they have a biological utility, they are not needs; they are innate tendencies. Action is often traced to stimuli from the external environment; internal stimuli may also be objects of curiosity, and manipulation of parts of the body is observed. In general, however, the exploratory, manipulatory, and/or investigatory behaviors are evoked by new or changing stimulations, the sources of which are external to the body.

Just as the monkeys manipulated puzzles apparently for the sake of the manipulation and were also interested in changes in the external field sufficiently that new unneeded learnings occurred, so man is excited and maintained in directed lines of performances without any support from his bodily need. In other words, he will investigate for the sake of the investigation. Perhaps the most suggestive systematic observations which would support the significance of the investigative-curiosity motivation in adult man is in the variety of interests which he reports on standardized questionnaires. Though there is no evidence, pro or con, that the interests of men are developed on the basis of curiosity alone, the wide individual differences suggest that more than the common bodily needs are supporting the growth of those interests.

Bodily Needs Are Related to Exploration. There is a complex interrelationship between bodily needs and the investigative-exploratory tendency. Particularly in complex mazes, exploratory behavior is increased by hunger (62). Fehrer (183) tested the hypothesis that the greater amount of exploration on the part of hungry subjects was due to a greater tendency to leave a familiar place. Rats were familiarized with a box, being left within it for approximately 24 hours, and they were then permitted to explore a new box. Hungry animals entered the new box sooner and more often and stayed there for a longer period of time than food-sated subjects. Montgomery (433), on the other hand, demonstrated that deprivations of food (24, 48, and 72 hours) significantly reduced the amount of exploratory behavior, the maximal decrement occurring at 24 hours of food deprivation, with no further reduction up to 72 hours of deprivation. These last results contradict the common assumption that exploratory behavior increases in amount when a primary drive arises. There are two possible explanations: (1) Food or water deprivation strengthens certain behaviors that are incompatible with the kind of exploratory behavior measured, or (2) the presence of a strong primary drive component like hunger may decrease exploratory drive. Too strong a bodily need may prevent the perceiving of objects and their spatial loci which might be *later* useful to the organism. This point, though not easily proved with subhuman subjects, was advanced by Tolman (618) as a possible reason why very thirsty rats might not notice food locations. In some latent-learning studies, it was found that the perception by rats was restricted frequently to only the aspects of the external field to which they were immediately sensitized by their immediate bodily need.[5] Even if they ran over food pellets on their way to water, thirsty rats did not seem to have perceived the food. At least, later when hungry, they showed no behavioral signs that the food pellets and their location had been noted. Human subjects also report a narrowing of their external field when under strong bodily needs. The general interests of the human males under a semistarvation diet declined; their orientations were narrowed upon foods and pictures of foods (330). The decreased range of cues used by human subjects in solving problems as drives increase in strength is illustrated on pp. 257–258.

In contrast, other observations suggest that investigations of "puzzling" aspects of the external field are likely to occur to the degree that solutions will serve an immediate practical need. Organisms are often confronted with problems of how to reduce their bodily needs, and their continuance in attempts to solve the problems are in part based on the need drives. The following observation—admittedly anthropomorphic in the description—was of a food-deprived rat confronted with a puzzling event in his external field when he was attempting to reduce his hunger. He became oriented toward his external world in which the puzzle arose. Having been trained to pull a lever which opened a door to the goal box, he could then run into the box, where he always found a food pellet

---

[5] Latent learning is acquisition of learning presumably without any need-drive reduction, and without being immediately overtly apparent.

upon a small piece of white paper. One day the author, who was the experimenter, did not place the food pellet in its regular position on the small bit of paper. The rat, having performed correctly by pulling the lever in the right direction and entering the usual food box, found no pellet. He sniffed around, then ran out of the goal box back to the lever, pulled it correctly again, and hurried to the place where the food pellet had always appeared. Again, no pellet of food. The rat picked up the piece of paper in his teeth and ran out to the lever, placed it near the lever, pulled correctly, and turned to the piece of paper. The experimentor is sorry to say that the attempt to solve the puzzle was not successful with this hungry rat, for again there was no food pellet; and the rat ceased lever-pulling for that day and probably lost interest in solving problems that were presented by the huge gods who kept him in cages.

Deterrents to the Development of Curiosity

The arousal of pain or fear is a deterrent to further investigation in animals and in men. Montgomery and Monkman (435) introduced shock into a novel maze, and the exploratory behavior decreased. Shock given prior to the animals' being placed in the maze was not a deterrent. Fear is a deterrent of expression of curiosity. Butler (102) found that a barking dog in the external field brought cessation in monkeys of "opening-a-door and looking-out." Animals are probably frightened by the sound or the sight of a strange animal. The curiosity of a child and a man is often stopped in its expression along a certain line when pain arises, but if the damage done is not too extreme, the child or man may change the form of his behavior yet not discontinue investigation of the object or situation associated with the pain. In fact, he may become more curious about what brought on the painful effect.

Habituation is the chief antagonist to novelty. Yet unchanging school materials—the maps, the books, the arithmetic problems—can be kept stimulating for the learners. The good teacher presents and re-presents in such a fashion that novelty does not disappear. A map continues to be novel under many re-presentations when it is studied each time in a new way. The value of teaching machines may lie in their novelty to the school children.

CONCLUDING STATEMENTS

The discussion has centered upon studies which illustrate how a biological tendency—the investigative-curiosity tendency—affects performance and permits learning to occur. We have seen that learning can be established when what follows the correct response is stimulus change.

Manipulation for the sake of manipulation has also been observed in the primates and learning occurred.

One antecedent condition which is known to arouse behavioral signs of approach and exploration is novel stimulations. Even places in the external field recently contacted for a few minutes have less "attraction," as indicated in choices of paths in a maze, than the not-so-recently contacted routes. Novelty of stimulation is the resultant of the organism's having had no previous or recent sensory contact. In addition, novelty is related to varying, to odd or incongruous, and to complex stimuli—all of which may owe their novelty to unfamiliarity. Also, puzzling stimulus changes arouse investigation.

Exploration of new sensory fields permits knowledge of the environment in which the organisms must move. Exploration may aid in the reduction of needs. These investigative activity patterns are observed in various phylogenic levels of organisms; they have reached their highest development in man. His greater capacity for symbolization—used in abstracting, concept forming, reasoning, creating, imagining—permit exploration, manipulation, and general investigation at a level which the subhuman animal is incapable of reaching.

In spite of the difficulty of obtaining evidence, it appears that simply finding out things is in itself pleasurable. There is truth in Asch's statements when he writes of social conditions under which some live which can impair and distort the individual's tendency to make sense of the world and to stand in a meaningful relation to the surroundings.

> The need for sensible action, for knowledge, for positive goals can be weakened, satisfied too easily, and stifled by conditions, in the social field and by forces within the person. Social oppression can produce a fear of knowledge and an attitude of not wanting to think. It can result in resignation, readiness to abdicate to authorities the prerogative of passing upon what is true or false, and hatred of those who lack this attitude. Personal oppression can strike at the roots of confidence and impair the objective orientation, producing instead a preoccupation with one's safety or cynicism. (24, p. 302. (c) 1952. Prentice-Hall, Inc.)

And, we add, induces depressing boredom.

CHAPTER 5

ACTIVATION

Activity is characteristic of organisms from the simplest animal to man. Any organism is in constant motion, internal or external, though the degree of movement fluctuates. Almost at the instant when the sperm penetrates the egg membrane (as observed in marine eggs), a violent churning and streaming begins to agitate the protoplasm; new membranes are elevated from the egg's surface, and embryonic development begins. Such marked intracellular changes are accompanied by sharp changes in respiratory activity. Observe also simple marine animals and you are immediately struck by the degree of energy expended in "spontaneous" movements—in movements which appear unorganized and undirected but continual. Such activity, seemingly internally aroused, appears in the pink sea anemones with their curling, twisting tentacles; in the pulsating jellyfish; in octopuses with their restless suction tubes moving over the surfaces of the water tank in which they have been placed.

Activity is not solely a property of living systems. The stars move in their courses; the water moves in a rushing current to the sea; the tides come and go, attacking the sea walls; the wind comes unseen through the open window, and the papers fly from the table. The missiles pursue their moving targets; the houses crumble under the blasts of the explosions; the ground trembles; the rocks grind upon each other, and the earth quakes. And man too is moved by these unleashed forces. He is pulled by gravity and falls when in unbalance; he is pushed or even lifted skyward by the winds in the tornado; he rides the current of the river and thus moves more swiftly down the stream. He is crushed by the explosive forces of the "released" atoms.

Motivational psychology of man is concerned with the drama of man's movements within and against these physical forces. He holds himself in a state of strain so that gravity is overcome. He can resist the force of the wind and is not blown willy-nilly where he does not want to go, and he often turns against the current of the river and moves upward toward

56

the headwaters. As long as man is alive he can move with or against the external forces. He will not simply be moved. We can say with emphasis that motivational psychology does *not* have to account for arousal—for man is always to some degree aroused—but it must face the problems posed by the continuous variations in arousal of organisms.

To illustrate what is meant by activation, with rises and falls therein, let us observe a man throughout the twenty-four hours of a day and night. Starting in the evening we see his activation decrease as his usual time for sleeping recurs. As drowsiness gives way to deep sleep, the records of electrical activity (EEG) from his cerebral cortex change in pattern. The gross musculatures are relaxed and their contractions (when they occur) are infrequent, sending few return impulses to the central nervous system. The sympathetic or emergency division of the autonomic nervous system is minimal in activity. The man does not respond to ordinary stimuli; he is asleep. Yet, even within deep sleep—a condition close to zero activation—there are still slight variations in his degree of excitation. Though his sensory thresholds are high, loud sounds, painful stimuli or any intense sensory input will break through. And when the alarm clock rings, it usually results in a stimulation strong enough to break the threshold, and the man awakens. Then begin the multiple activities of the day. Being awake, he is more responsive to stimulation. More muscular responses are involved, which in turn send back afferent impulses to the central nervous system (CNS).

Whether it is a very busy day or a fairly humdrum one, there are constant fluctuations in energy expenditure. Then as evening comes, the activity level gradually falls. (With some men their peak of arousal is reached in the evening and early hours of the night, particularly young men "on the prowl.") Sleep and its period of inactivity descends at last. The cycle of the rise and fall within the twenty-four hours has been completed, only to start again with dawn.

There are also short-term cyclical changes which can be observed rather frequently during the waking period. Even in the day the man becomes briefly drowsy and then more alert, a state only to be followed by a lowered excitation level which again may be followed by a rise. Such short-term variations imposed upon the twenty-four-hour cycle of sleep-waking are frequent: Rises and falls occur not only in alertness but in exciting emotions, in depressing affective states, in sensory acuity, in rapidity of movement, in degree of tensed concentration.

Some General Statements

In the assuming of activity as an inherent attribute of a living system, there is no evocation of an entelechy, of a supreme mind which moves the creatures on this earth. Rather the assumption of organismic activity as inevitable in its simplest meaning merely recognizes the obvious fact that being alive demands the attachment of energy and the release of energy. Nor in the descriptive phrase "spontaneous activity" which is later used is there any implication that activity is freely "willed" into being. It is determined. It may seem at times that internal changes are solely its determinants, but no individual is ever entirely free from interaction with the external world. By means of complex receptors, organisms are in constant contact with external events. And many internal and external determinants are responsible for the rate of energy expenditure at any moment in time and for the particular channels into which it is released.

A man's average activity-level may be at a low or high over hours, even days. In a manic person, for example, the overall level is not a normal waking level. Characteristic high and low levels are considered in a later discussion of personal pace, where the emphasis is placed upon the factors which determine the individual differences in the overall (average) level of activity. At this point we are interested in the determinants of fluctuations in activation no matter what is the man's usual pace. Even the hyperactive man is not continuously "driven" to the same high degree. During certain periods he appears inactive, almost inert. And similarly the hypoactive individual, though generally performing feebly with little vigor or intensity in his activities, is capable of an even lower, or sometimes a higher, drive than he usually exhibits.[1]

The individual pattern of the fluctuations may be described as frequent or as infrequent in rises and falls. The swing also may be from extreme activity to great sluggishness. Or a lesser range in variations may be observed in an individual.

All cycles are under the influence of nonmotivational determinants. If the health of the individual is poor, if little food had been ingested for some time, or if for some other reason there has been an exhaustion of the potential energy available for release into activity, the cyclical pattern is affected. For example, the man would be inactive longer than he would be active, and the peaks of his increased activation would not be so high.

ACTIVATION CONTINUUM

To define the two poles, or extremes, of the continuum of activation, we seek examples of the lowest activation possible and, at the other end, of the most extreme excitation. Death represents zero activation, but for a living organism there is no zero activity. However, there is at times minimal arousal such as in deep sleep, in a trance, or in a "frozen" con-

[1] Drive is defined on p. 116.

dition before a cardiac operation. The hibernating animal is on an even lower level of activation than man can obtain. The other pole of the continuum is represented by an extreme amount of activity, such as the frenzied excitement of the hypermanic. But it is difficult to mark the intervening stages, the steps which indicate an increase from the minimal arousal through an average amount up to an abnormally high excitement. In other words, there are no well-established units of activation as there are inches on a yardstick. How much change takes place in energy expenditure between the lowest level of activation recorded and a discriminal rise? Such a question cannot at present be answered. This limitation does not preclude measures of degree of activity, i.e., amplitude, number, pressure exerted, speed of running.

Activation is a valuable construct even as intelligence is a useful dimension, though it too has no zero point and there are no equal units. And even as the continuum of intelligent functioning can be described by subcontinuums, so can the activation continuum. There are several related subdimensions of activation to be considered later, such as depressing-exciting emotions, low vigilance–high vigilance, relaxation-tension, and no continuance–high persistence.

ACTIVITY STREAM

Activity is a broad term. Organismic activity may refer to the metabolism of a single cell, to such internal physiological activity as digestion of food as well as other necessary life-sustaining activities of the internal environment of an organism, and to central neural activities. In experiential language there also are sensing, perceiving, remembering, thinking, and planning; i.e., "cognizing." And the activity streams of organisms encompass the variations in emotions and concomitant changes such as the internal secretions by endocrine glands of hormones into the blood stream, with the resulting marked changes in total organismic functioning. They also encompass the action of the muscular systems, which are capable of slight tensions or of vigorous contractions with resulting overt movements of the parts of the body. The total activity stream of a man involves all these energy transformations and others not here listed.

The total activity stream may be said to have a hierarchical arrangement, with interaction among the "layers" as well as with changes over time in the order of arrangement of various energy transformations, i.e., in their "position" of dominance. Some activities are merely necessary for supporting the organism as an intact structure. Other activities are directly involved in the immediate main, or dominant, direction of the organism; others may appear to be in conflict with the dominant direction. They vary in the degree of awareness which an individual has of each; they vary in the number of parts of the body structure involved and in the degree of influence that they have on the structuring within the hierarchy of activities. Such a hierarchal arrangement is illustrated below in the description of a child running a race.

A Hypothetical Illustration of a Short Phase in an Activity Stream of a Child. The following illustrates the complexity of energy transformations which may be observed in a short time period during the life of a child. It points up the dynamics of the activity stream.

Let us say that a child is running a race with the other children. Note that we have said in this illustration that the child is "running a race," though at times a child may seem to be merely running. Observations of the total activity stream reveal physiological events, some of which have a minimum of involvement in running a race. Other physiological activities are, however, greatly altered to conform with the main act. There are increased heart rate, change in respiration rate, and other emergency reactions. There is inner excitement, perhaps of some degree of specificity. The child also varies in his central activities in other ways as he moves behind or ahead of his competitors. There is perhaps a remembering of what his father told him about winning races; let us assume a father who has said that winning is not so important as trying. Or possibly the social value of "beating the other fellow" may have been taught this child, and thus there is the anticipation of the goal with an increased expenditure of energy. Or there may be perceptions, images, and ideas not related to the main goal of the moment, e.g., a color of the dress of a spectator may briefly register, a sudden recall of an unfinished task at home may occur, or a disagreeable feeling of the dryness of his throat may have a fleeting dominance even while speed is increasing as the end of "running the race" is approached.

Nor does the above description, which is confined to the overtly observable or the fairly easily reportable activities, illuminate those below the level of awareness. To use an analogy from Freud, the description does not include that part of the iceberg which lies below the surface, out of sight, hidden from the individual as well as from the observer. For example, hostility against his father, not acknowledged by the child or observable in any way, may be supporting an unknown desire to lose the race.

As is apparent from the above, the concept of arousal (activation) incorporates a variety of energy exchanges in the life stream. Some of these facets of total activation are closely related to each other; some are not.

Our next concern is with the recurrences in intensity, i.e., with the degree of the energy released irrespective of its form, irrespective of whether a man is walking, eating, or fighting. These changes in intensity of activation may be periodic or aperiodic. Their origins are both internal and external to the organism. The first illustrations presented below of changes in the activity stream represent fairly regular periodic rise and fall in amount of energy expenditure.

ILLUSTRATIONS OF CYCLES IN THE ACTIVITY STREAM

Diurnal Cycles of Activity

A diurnal rhythm designates the twenty-four-hour cycle of changes which recur with day and night. Nocturnal, auroral, vesperal designate general rhythms when the marked variations in activation center around the night, morning, and evening hours. Changes in the amount of light may not be the only external antecedent condition to which the diurnal activity variations may be geared. Changes in temperature may, for instance, be an equally important extrinsic determinant.

Man's Diurnal Rhythms. Man's diurnal rhythms are subject to modification by the immediate influence of external stimulations as well as by continuous conditioning of the internal mechanisms to the varying work and play schedules of man. Some of the recurrent changes of general activities of men which may be included under twenty-four-hour cycles are sleep-wakefulness and activity associated with eating at regular intervals.[2] Both, of course, are influenced by internal and external environmental factors and by learning.

Oscillations in Efficiency

The search for periodicity in performance has a long history. As early as 1905 Seashore and Kent (549) reported periodic waves in continuous mental work. Philpott (486), concerned with the problem for twenty years or more, has sought to demonstrate geometric periodicity, but his conclusions have been contradicted by Richardson (508), who by statistical tests supported randomness rather than periodicity.

It appears that there is no typical *diurnal work curve* for all types of jobs, though there may be *within a specific factory* a regularly recurring acquired work curve or curves correlated with the nature of the work and the external conditions. Freeman and Hovland (202) summarized various school and industrial studies of types of diurnal curves of output. In spite of great variation, the balance of evidence suggests an afternoon

[2] The temperature of the body also has a slight daily variation. And there is "the daily variation in the frequency of cell division in the epithelial and muscular tissues. The numbers of dividing cells in the skin and in muscle are greatest in the middle of the night, and few can be found in the afternoon. The hypothalamus is rhythmically changing and shifts with the day and night, as is seen when one travels quickly by air to the Orient, but the seasonal control is absent" (270, p. 115).

superiority for sensory and motor performance but little agreement as to the time when complicated mental work can be done most efficiently. Indices of diurnal variation by means of cycles of activity may include rise and fall in sensory acuity, attention, changes in mood, and affectivity. Irritability may follow a periodic alternation that reappears each twenty-four hours.

Long-term Cycles in Work Output. Hersey (274) hypothesized that men undergo long-term rhythmic cycles in industry. He found by intensive and frequent interviews and other observations that male workers undergo cycles of productivity and morale. "Cycles for some individuals are as short as 14 days while for others they are as long as 52 days, with an average of about 35 days. At the high points of the curve, a man shows increased productivity and zest for work. Somewhere between these periods, he shows a disinclination for mental effort, planning, and concentration. But it is said that the low periods for some men seem to be the 'breeding ground' for later exhibitions of creative production" (233, p. 340). Another investigator has found supporting evidence for such cycles (647). "A rhythmic cycle of about 48 days was found in handgrip measures in one subject. A fluctuation pattern that is as dramatic as this one is reported to be," suggests Guilford, "would seem to merit serious attention" (233, p. 340).

Sleep Rhythm

In whatever manner sleep is described and to whatever antecedent conditions it is traced, there is no doubt that it represents a recurring depression in the activation-level of the organism. Whether the changes are reported as a shift in the EEG pattern,[3] in cognitive changes, in physiological variation, or in the decline of overt action and in the decrease of general alertness, the sleep pattern may be said to come and go. The sleep rhythms change with maturation and are subject to conditioning. Sleep has been called a need, though all the necessary antecedent conditions to bring the low level of activation observed in sleep are not definitely known. Deprivation from sleep is inevitably followed by a return to it.

Both intrinsic and extrinsic factors are involved. Kleitman (337) writes of wakefulness of necessity when extrinsic sources arouse the organism: There is "heavy" sensory inflow. However, he points out that wakefulness of choice may be maintained, a phenomenon which suggests intrinsic control.

Sleep-wakefulness is an example of a rhythm in activation that will vary greatly with conditions but cannot be abolished. Even forced wakefulness as in torture ends in collapse. Kleitman (337) illustrates the in-

[3] See Table 1.

Table 1. Psychological States and Their EEG, Conscious and
Behavioral Correlates

Behavioral continuum	Electro-encephalogram	State of awareness	Behavioral efficiency
Strong, excited emotion (fear, rage, anxiety)	Desynchronized: low to moderate amplitude; fast mixed frequencies	Restricted awareness: divided attention; diffuse, hazy; "confusion"	Poor: (lack of control, freezing up, disorganized)
Alert attentiveness...	Partially synchronized: mainly fast, low-amplitude waves	Selective attention, but may vary or shift; "concentration," anticipation, "set"	Good: (efficient, selective, quick reactions) organized for serial responses
Relaxed wakefulness.	Synchronized: optimal alpha rhythm	Attention wanders —not forced; favors free association	Good: (routine reactions and creative thought)
Drowsiness..........	Reduced alpha and occasional low-amplitude slow waves	Borderline, partial awareness, imagery and reverie; "dreamlike states"	Poor: (uncoordinated, sporadic, lacking sequential timing)
Light sleep..........	Spindle bursts and slow waves (larger); loss of alphas	Markedly reduced consciousness (loss of consciousness); dream state	Absent
Deep sleep..........	Large and very slow waves (synchrony, but on slow time base); random, irregular pattern	Complete loss of awareness (no memory for stimulation or for dreams)	Absent
Coma..............	Isoelectric to irregular	Complete loss of consciousness; little or no response to stimulation; amnesia	Absent
Death..............	Isoelectric: gradual and permanent disappearance of all electrical activity	Complete loss of awareness as death ensues	Absent

Source: Lindsley (373).

teraction of external and internal influences upon this inherent cyclical
activity. From the day of birth, the baby is subject to training from the
social environment. External stimuli impinge on an individual during
the day. Muscular activity and, in turn, the activity of the nervous system
increases, the latter then augmenting muscular activity. As the mus-

cles get tired, not only from overwork but from postural or tonic activity inherent in being awake, there is a reversal aided by the onset of darkness, the lowering of the air temperature, and the cessation of noises, characteristic of evening in the social routine of living. When the reversed trend of activity has reached a certain low ("drowsiness level"), it becomes harder to remain awake. Sleep occasions a further drop in activity until the diurnal minimum is reached; then proprioceptive impulses from the muscles, cramped by prolonged maintenance of certain positions, increase from more frequently "turning over" as the night goes on. When, in addition, visceral impulses (from stomach, urinary bladder, etc.) and external environmental influences increase with the advent of morning, it becomes more and more difficult to remain asleep.

Seasonal Cycles of Activity

Cyclical behavior fluctuations may be closely tied to seasonal changes; the hibernation period of such animals as the bear or squirrel represents a seasonal depression. Internal and external sources are responsible for seasonal variations in activation. Recurring external influences, terrestial and cosmic, may be synchronized with the cyclical activity of the internal tissues; and there follow behavioral changes. One of the many observations is a change in the spring in the diurnal activity pattern of white-crowned sparrows (182). This change was attributed to a gradually improving metabolic state correlated with increase in activity of the anterior pituitary. An overall increase in activity was observed as well as a greater nocturnal activity. Man, however, is only mildly seasonal. See Chapter 13 in Bartley and Chute (43).

Origins of Activity Cycles

The above cycles in energy output are under the influence of more than one factor. Three general origins of these variations are: (1) intrinsic (inherent) rhythms; (2) extrinsic (external) recurring events; (3) recurring tissue needs and periodic or aperiodic secretions of the endocrine glands. (These three are not independent.) In addition, there is the inevitable role of learning.

Intrinsic Rhythms. Some of the most simple rhythms can be illustrated in the periodicities of plants, as in the opening and closing of flowers, in pollen production, in the movement of leaves, in the electrical excitability of the mimosa (648). Intrinsic periodicity in the activity of the tactile receptor of a simple animal was early suggested by Coghill and Watkins (124). They noted that there appeared in the *Amblystoma punctatum* an intrinsic cycle of irritability. When various specimens were tested at fifteen-minute intervals during their development, they showed a pronounced synchrony in the fluctuation of their sensitivity to tactile stimulation. Hunger was excluded as a possible explanation, since every cell in the body of the larva had its own food in the form of yolk. They concluded that the fluctuations in irritability must have their origin in an intrinsic periodicity of organismic processes which may be the primary factor in the waking and sleeping of animals generally. Fatigue as it is ordinarily understood was said not to be involved. The phenomenon which they describe may represent "a general, primitive type of periodicity which may underlie many more complex forms of behavior, such as the running cycles of the rat" (44, p. 224).

In Tracy's work with fish embryos (622), it was observed that after hatching they typically lie quiescent at the bottom of the tank, yet also show at different times sudden and apparently spontaneous movements. Tracy attributes these movements to cumulative changes in the blood of the organism, the consequent reactions being either a result of direct stimulation of the nerve centers or of stimulation of specialized receptors in the blood vessel system. Possibly these responses involved a modification of existing thresholds of excitation in the CNS so that this threshold change rendered effective what were previously ineffective peripheral stimuli (112, p. 294).

Tracy drew some interesting conclusions from his studies. As reported by Carmichael (112), if external conditions were held constant, the activity of organisms might be largely determined by their own life processes. The whole organism would then "beat" in its own environment, much as the primitive heart cells beat in the environment of the fluids in which they are developing. In other words, "were it not for changes in the external environment, behavior would be rhythmic, as it is in an excised muscle maintained under certain conditions in a balanced salt solution" (112, p. 294). Tracy concluded by saying: "From the beginning and more or less continuously during its whole existence, the animal is driven through its environment as a result of stimuli which arise periodically in connection with its metabolic processes" (622, p. 345).

There is an apparent *intrinsic rhythmic* character of behavior in a newborn infant. When a newborn babe is placed in a stabilmeter-type crib, there are observed oscillations in his gross movements. Kleitman (338) reports a periodic rise and fall of activity-levels of infants. These fluctuations with a periodicity of fifty to sixty minutes are discernible whether the infant is asleep or awake. Kleitman suggests three possible origins of this primitive rhythm in activity of the infant: It may be (1) correlated with metabolic variation, (2) a pacemaker discharge, or (3) a fatigue-recovery phenomenon. Like the cardiac and respiratory cycles in activity, it tends to lengthen with age.

Intrinsic Rhythms and External Events. Internal and apparently inherent mechanisms are synchronized with recurring external stimulation changes with resulting changes in activity. Though there is increasing evidence of accurate biological clocks among various species (181), the physiological cycles are controlled, or at least monitored in phase and periodicity, by environmental changes. One such change which can act as a "timer" is the proportional amount of light to dark together with a change in temperature. "Because of its fixed annual periodicity the change in daily photoperiod frequently is more advantageous than other environmental factors as a timer or Zeitgeber in an environment with regular seasons" (181, p. 71). The degree of independence of an intrinsic mechanism from external control varies; the intrinsic control may be dominant, or it may not. In one study insects naturally more active during the night were reared from the larval stage in continued darkness, yet gave essentially the same performance as recently collected adults. Harker (245), however, reports some evidence of early *extrinsic influence*. She found that rhythm of activity correlated with light-dark changes in the Mayfly nymphs is dependent on the eggs' being exposed to a normal light-dark cycle. The rhythm is absent from nymphs bred from eggs kept in continuous light. A single exposure to the light-dark cycle is enough to establish the rhythm; and once established, it continues regardless of external conditions.

Often an inherent cycle is so affected by external events that it does not appear without these events. Diurnal cycles can be reversed, though not always immediately, by artificial light so that day becomes night. In other words, when the rise and fall in activity-level is synchronized with the rise and setting of the sun, this rhythm may be changed by artificial light. The change in the rhythm is not immediate in all animals with the external light-dark shift; *any lag is considered evidence of intrinsic control.*

Learning and Cyclical Tissue Changes

Already established rhythms may be broken if the external field is changed. Disruptions of learned eating and sleeping cycles in human subjects occur when some of the normally available cues are withheld for a period of a few days. It is reported (67) that after a few days in an isolation experimental chamber, the human subjects may ask for the usual breakfast foods in the evening and for dinner in the morning. Apparently certain extraneous cues are normally responsible for the maintenance of behavioral cycles, and with the disruption of these cues the cycles may correspond only roughly to the physiological changes on the basis of which the cycles were initially established.

There are limitations upon the modifications of rhythms of activity when they are based on recurring humoral, gastric, or other bodily changes, but modifications occur. Infants get hungry at fairly short intervals and certain extraneous cues unrelated to the underlying physiological changes can be systematically associated with the recurring hunger. These extraneous cues—like the appearance of mother or of the bottle—are correlated first with the usual behaviors aroused under the need for food. Sucking movements, for example, start with the sight of the bottle. Thus, the anticipatory feeding responses come to be elicited by the conditioned cues, and *if* these cues appear at regular intervals, the feeding behavior reappears at those intervals. Also we can observe that in the adult the sounds of dinner being prepared are associated with preparation for eating.

Is the hunger state (the physiological change) conditioned, or is merely the feeding behavior conditioned? Or both? General observation would suggest that hunger is not conditioned. If there is not too much of a time gap between the association of anticipatory cues for eating and the onset of the actual physiological condition for hunger, anticipatory responses are conditioned. It is not possible, however, to arouse by conditioned stimuli the hunger state (or related food approach and eating) *when the animal is food-sated.* In other words, the behavioral cycles do not become completely independent of the underlying processes.

Learning New Cycles in Energy Release. Cycles in activation may be modified, but can new ones be established? Finger et al. (192) reported that spontaneous activity increased if reinforced when animals were moved from the activity wheel directly to food. Activity in a free-response field might also be thus reinforced and reappear at intervals, i.e., if systematic association of activity-then-reward continued at regular intervals. Such a learned cycle might be so well established that reinforcement would no longer be necessary. Conditioning to time intervals has been reported.

A physiological recurrence with appropriate behavior was established by Spragg (579) in chimpanzees by giving daily injections of morphine. Thus a new cycle was acquired—both the recurring physiological condition and the correlated begging for the morphine injection reappeared at intervals.

Frequently in the lives of men, acquired cycles appear in the realm of behavior but not necessarily with accompanying physiological cycles. There are the stereotyped reappearing behaviors associated with the work day, with the weekend, even with vacations. Each day has its usual reappearing behaviors—the clang of the alarm clock is followed by the rising, eating breakfast, the going-to-work, the coffee break, and on and on. The daily maintenance determinants in a particular society keep certain behaviors recurring. Such cultural schedules may be stronger than the desires of individual men upon whom cycles are imposed by the group.

Abnormalities in Recurrences

The normal repetitions observed in the activity stream of men are usually adaptive, either serving physiological needs or in some way adjustive to social demands. There are, however, recurrences in the activity flux which indicate that the normality of the controlling and releasing mechanisms is out of order. The rhythmic motor habits of disturbed children—such as head rolling, head banging, bed rocking—are abnormal recurring overt responses. There are, of course, many other abnormal repetitions observed among children and adults, sometimes within the activity streams of individuals called normal and sometimes within those of the more seriously disturbed.

Since the time of Freud, it has been generally accepted that many such repetitive phenomena as dreams, emotional outbursts, unpremeditated acts, slips of the tongue, laughter irrelevant to the situation, and gestures represent in more or less disguised form unconscious and repressed needs, wishes, wants of the individual. Such also may be expressed in children's play or in their drawings and paintings. (A host of projective techniques has made use of this assumption as a means of understanding the "hidden" aspects of personality.) Maslow (403), citing Fenichel (185, 186), suggested that some of the repetitive phenomena are attempts to cope with problems even if the problems are not at the level of awareness. [Again the perseverations are possibly only expressive, i.e., not functional (not beneficial) to the patient.] The repetitive behaviors which seem to be attempts to cope with insoluble problems are similar to those of the fighter hopelessly outclassed but desperate, who gets up off the floor again and again, only to be knocked down again and again. Maslow adds: "Apparently the insecure human organism cannot accept defeat gracefully. He must keep on trying again and again, useless though this may be" (403, p. 370). Among the repetitive activities, possible attempts to cope with failure are recurring feelings of insult or humiliation, unconscious jealousy and envy, persistent compensation for inferiority feelings, the compulsive and persistent promiscuity of latent homosexuals, and other vain efforts to remove a threat. And there are the tics, rituals, and other symbolic acts and the neurotic "acting out"—all examples of repetitive response patterns sometimes functional in indirect fashion.

Abnormalities in cycles of *arousal* are equally disturbing or even more so. The mood changes, correlated with restriction of movement, may be followed by extensive, even violent, activation.

CLUES TO ACTIVATION CHANGES

When a man shifts in his immediate position on the activation continuum, moving toward greater arousal or toward less, there is a change in the demand for energy expenditure. All the energy transformations cannot be simultaneously recorded. Even the attempts to record behavioral changes—the overt movements—are never complete. There are, however, a large number of devices for recording variations in the activity flux. Some of these are critically examined below. (Any attempt to determine if a change in activation has occurred should employ as many records as are experimentally justified.) Both physiological and behavioral changes are used as indices to activation changes. In addition, evidence of changes in central affective excitement can be obtained from verbal reports of men as well as by more indirect methods of determining feelings and emotions as experiences.

Physiological Indices

The measures of physiological changes considered as clues to activation changes include scores on variations in BMR, pulse rate, respiration rate, GSR, muscular tension records, and EEG records. See Inset 6 for a brief development of these physiological measures of activation changes.

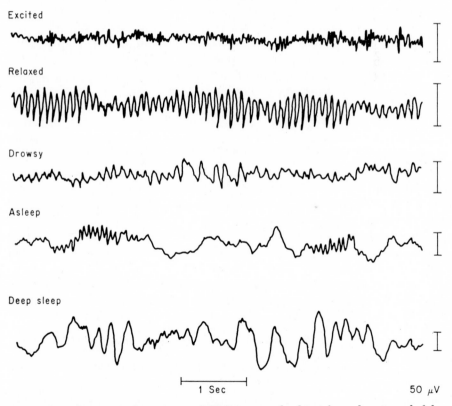

Figure 5-1. Changes in the patterns of EEG in normal subject from sleep to wakefulness to excitement. Jasper (313) (Courtesy of Charles C Thomas, Publisher, Springfield, Illinois)

EEG Records. The assumption that there is an activation continuum was early suggested by patterns of electrical activity of the brain, as shown in EEG records. The patterns of firing of nerve cells within the brain vary as man passes from a state of deep sleep into light sleep, waking, and greater activity. On the EEG records in deep sleep there are large low-frequency waves. In light sleep and drowsy states the frequencies are not as low as in deep sleep, but there are more low-frequency waves than in the wakeful states. In relaxed condition but awake, most individuals have a predominance of waves in the alpha range of 8 to 12 cycles per second. As alerting and exciting conditions predominate, there is a change in the records from a regular synchronized appearance to an irregular desynchronized tracing, usually of reduced amplitude.

Table 1 and Figure 5-1 illustrate the correspondence between the EEG patterns and the arousal continuum. Malmo (394) has reported a slow decline in EEG rate, palmar conductance, heart rate, and respiration during sleep, commencing with drowsiness and continuing through the onset and later stages of sleep. Studies also reported by Malmo of the reverse condition—when there is sleep deprivation—indicate a progressive rise in palmar conductance and respiration and a progressive decrease in the amount of alpha activity.

The EEG records of individuals when alerted and later when relaxed are presented in Figure 5-2. As indicated, blocking of alpha is corre-

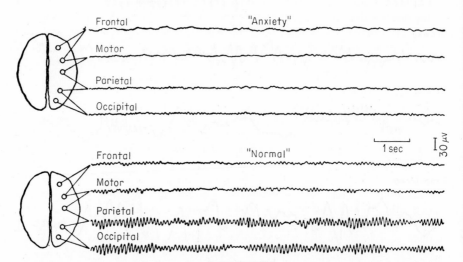

Figure 5-2. Electroencephalograms illustrating absence of alpha waves in the records of a patient in an "anxiety" state and the well-regulated alpha rhythms of a "normal" subject. The first record should not be considered pathognomic of anxiety. Records of normal and anxious individuals cannot always be so readily differentiated. Lindsley (372)

lated with rising tension. The top record of Figure 5-2 shows the block-ing of the alpha rhythm during apprehension. An apprehension pattern of the EEG is also reported for clinical patients in an anxiety state.

INSET 6. PHYSIOLOGICAL INDICES TO AROUSAL VARIATIONS

Frequently used measures of physiological reactivity include records of changes in the electrical activity in the brain, i.e., EEG records, skin conductance, muscle action potentials (electromyographic records), basal metabolic rate, and others.

1. EEG records represent changes in the electrical activity of large masses of nerve cells. Distinctive wave patterns—as indicated in Figure 5-1—are observed as the individual changes from deep sleep to highly alerted states (313).

In relaxed wakefulness there is a predominance in the alpha range. Alpha rhythms appear as fairly rhythmic (approximately ten per second) potential oscillation during a relaxed state and in the absence of special stimulation. Almost any brief stimulation is followed by blocking of the alpha rhythm. The blocking of the alpha rhythm disappears in normal subjects following cessation of the stimulation which brought it on *unless* there remains a startle from the stimulation resulting in surprise. This alpha blocking is a flattening and a desynchronization in the rhythm. The resultant is a pattern in which there is a high frequency (20 to 40 cycles per second) and a low amplitude. The flattening effect can be seen in the EEG at the top of Figure 5-1. It is also similar to that indicated in Figure 5-2 from subjects who were generally apprehensive or anxious. It has been called the "activation pattern" (372).

2. Another of the widely used indices to level of activation is the elec-trical conductance (or its reciprocal, resistance) of the skin, usually of the palms of the hand. The conductance of the skin varies constantly. The absolute level at any given time has superimposed upon it more rapid variations that result from stimulation. The latter is called the galvanic skin reflex (GSR). McCleary (408) in his review of the GSR points out that it was discovered sixty years ago but that the physiologists do not yet know exactly what it is. And the psychologists do not yet know ex-actly what it indicates in regard to the functioning of the individual. The present status of the GSR is not, however, as uncertain as the above would indicate. It is known that the GSR reflects the skin resistance to an electric current either exogenous or endogenous in origin. Resistance is in some way tied into sweat gland activity, which in turn is under the influence of the autonomic nervous system. Psychologically, the GSR has most frequently been said to be an index to short-term changes in excitement or reactivity of the individual to stimulation. However, the slow downward changes in skin conductance in subjects as they become gradually habituated to a situation (144) or the progressive upward changes in conductance during a vigil (393) are of as much or more interest in understanding activation changes as is the GSR.

3. Objective clues to arousal changes are also obtained by recording electrical potentials from muscles. These electromyographic records may be obtained from any muscle group. A significant point in regard to interpretation of muscular tension records is that there is a continuous sustained contraction, or tonus, of skeletal muscles. The muscles of our arms, legs, trunk, and neck receive a continual barrage of nerve impulses which keep them in a state of partial contraction. There are also shifts of tension in specific muscle groups (394).

4. BMR, a measure of readiness for activity, is the minimal heat produced when measured from fourteen to eighteen hours after the individual has eaten and is at rest but not asleep. It represents the energy expended to maintain respiration, circulation, peristalsis, muscle tonus, body temperature, glandular activity, and the other vegetative functions.

5. In addition to the above physiological indices to arousal variations, there are others such as respiration rate, blood pressure, heart beat, skin temperature, oral temperature, pupillary response, salivary secretion, gastrointestinal activity, tremor and steadiness, eye blink, and blood chemistry (661).

Further evidence that the alpha blockade (see Inset 6) represents arousal was added by a report from Lansing, Schwartz, and Lindsley (355). These investigators recorded both the reaction time and alpha blocking. First, an alert condition was established by using a preparatory warning signal preceding a visual stimulus to which the subjects were to react. When the warning signal produced alpha blocking prior to the visual stimulus, reaction time was markedly reduced. Also when the foreperiod was lengthened, the reduction in reaction time as a function of the length of the foreperiod followed the same time course as did the degree of alpha blocking as a function of the foreperiod interval. The EEG blockade as a sign of alertness is thus again substantiated.

Studies of the arousal changes as indicated by physiological clues from measures of skin conductance and muscle-action potentials are later developed on pp. 79–83. We now turn to the overt signs of arousal variations. (The relation of activation level to the cortical bombardment by the ascending reticular activating system, ARAS, is discussed on pp. 124–125 in Chapter 7 on general drive.)

Behavioral Changes as Indicating Shifts in Arousal

Assume a man moves from sleep into observable reactions; there appears at first a straightening out of one limb from some uncomfortable contraction into a position of greater ease. Then as the waking is completed, the man probably moves his total body into a new posture; sometimes he immediately rises and starts the many overt reactions characteristic of the human species.

Behavioral indices to level of activity may be obtained from measures of both "spontaneous" and "forced" responses. There is no hard and fast line between spontaneous and forced movements. Spontaneous responses are interpreted in various ways. By the use of the term "spontaneous" it is not meant that the responses are uncaused. Spontaneous behavior is illustrated by diffuse restlessness when there is no orientation toward a goal and when there are no immediately pressing conditions for movement.

Forced responses are predictable: e.g., when a nonaquatic animal is placed in water, he must move in an appropriate swimming pattern or sink to the bottom and die. A man placed on a treadmill is *forced* to move.

Records of Spontaneous Responses. The spontaneous behavior of an organism is often recorded in fields where he may move but is not forced to move, i.e., not forced by any experimentally introduced activator. For example, the young mammal—rat or child—placed in a stabilmeter may or may not move.[4] However, if recordings are made over a sufficient period, there will finally be some overt responses. A revolving drum apparatus may record general locomotor activity in rodents, or pedometers may be used on sheep, pigs, and men. The individuals may then be allowed to move as they wish in their usual geographic fields (498). Monkeys were fastened by a 9-inch chain to a 2.5-inch rod so that the movement of the monkey caused the rod to activate a counter (517). A monkey-size pneumatically mounted activity cage was devised to record general movement (203).

Other methods of measuring spontaneous behavior include recording the total area covered in an open field or in an open-alley maze (Figure 5-3). Dashiell in 1925 (137) determined the number of units entered in

[4] The living cage or crib is so mounted on tambours or microswitches that slight or gross movements may be recorded. See (498) and (453) for discussion of instrumentation for recording spontaneous activity.

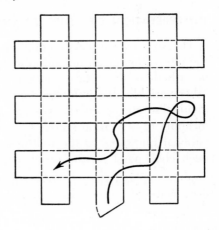

Figure 5-3. Dashiell's open alley maze used in recording exploratory behavior. Dashiell (137)

a standard time period by hungry and nonhungry animals. He found that food-deprived rats ran into 43 units as contrasted to 27 units for rats which had just been fed. (There was no exit in the maze.)

General Clues to Activation Changes as Observed in Either Spontaneous or Forced Responses. Wittenborn (655) set up rating scales of behavior of men in respect to the following nine aspects of what he described as "overt potentiated drive." These aspects, which are signs of degree of arousal in any organism, include: (1) *threshold,* i.e., the force or intensity of the stimulating situation required to elicit a response; (2) the *latency* of the response, a similar objective recording of readiness for arousal; (3) *amplitude* of the response, which is, of course, often considered a sign of degree of arousal; (4) *speed,* which though a complex measure, gives some indication of the level of activity; (5) *duration* of a response, often used in attempts to determine how aroused an individual is by some motivational antecedent; (6) number of *repeated elicitations* of the response, which, Wittenborn hypothesizes, show how ready an individual is for action; (7) *variety of stimuli* which will elicit a response; (8) *number* of *similar* responses (the greater the number, the higher the assumed facilitating drive); (9) *superfluity* of *behavior,* which is the final index to the degree of readiness for activation (e.g., one man may blink his eyes, jump, yell, and wave his arms at an exciting stimulus; another less "superfluous" in his behavior may only blink his eyes).

That these nine signs of the vigor of a man's activity can be used with some degree of reliability in rating scales was demonstrated with a sample of young psychiatric patients observed by two raters in terms of "resistive reactions to superiors" and also of "attention-seeking reactions to superiors" (655). (It was assumed that habit strength was high and approximately uniform among the individuals in respect to the responses rated.)[5]

INTERPRETATION OF CLUES TO GENERAL ACTIVATION LEVEL

The significance placed upon any activation measure in understanding the motivation of an individual must take into account what can only be described as the total situation. Obviously this includes among many other variables the immediate antecedent conditions acting upon the individual's rate of energy release. There are no simple answers to the meaning of activation scores, but they throw some light upon such motivational questions as the following: Is the man really aroused? Has he been challenged by the problem? Is he emotionally aroused and likely

[5] Less subjective methods of recording than rating scales have been devised for these indices.

to "explode," an emotional response which will leave him even lower in depression? These questions also demand knowledge of the total personality structure of the individual being observed. A few motivational studies directly approach the interaction of personality and the immediate activating conditions: e.g., are individuals whose personality is characterized by high anxiety likely to respond to painful or noxious events in a different fashion from individuals of low anxiety? And what would be the difference in their activation changes? These and similar questions have been raised in a few studies, and answers have been given by the use of some of the many indices to activation changes.

The use of any activation records should take into account the specific observational method employed, including its reliability as well as its relation to the other methods used to determine arousal or some aspect of arousal. The interpretation of any activation score is also dependent upon knowledge of the following: age, or maturational level; sex; weight; health; structural defects, if any, and other stable characteristics of the individual observed, including his personal pace.

The *overt behavior pattern* may be misleading in regard to the immediate degree of total arousal of lower animals and particularly of men, subject as the latter are to modifications of their behavioral expressions. The inherent response patterns of subhumans may be misleading with respect to the degree of arousal brought on by some antecedent condition. For example, the inherent response pattern forced under painful stimulation would not always and immediately suggest any arousal change; perhaps even a decrease would be implied, though other clues would suggest that the animal had risen in his inner activation. For example, Kimble (332) recorded responses of rats to unavoidable electric shock, ranging from 0.0 to 0.9 milliampere in 0.1-milliampere steps. Both ascending and descending order of presentation of shock was used. Three categories of behavior in response to shock were reported: (1) no overt response, (2) jump, and (3) flinch, considered similar to what other observers have called "crouch" or "freeze." One significant point of the study for motivational psychology is that with an increasing amount of electric shock there were more and more of the overt avoidance responses. See Figure 5-4. Under increasing noxiousness of the stimulus, the subjects were forced into more overt responses, a clue to increased inner excitement. But, no doubt, the animals were increased in activation even from the beginning of the application of the painful stimulation. A test would consist of the measurement of their physiological reactivity from the beginning of painful stimulations. The variations in activation, in other words, cannot be determined by any simple interpretation of a few clues. The total activity stream must be considered.

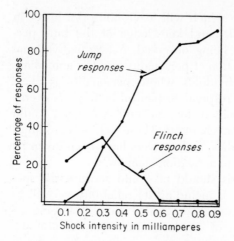

Figure 5-4. As shock increases in intensity, a greater degree of overt movement is observed. Kimble (332)

Most significant in understanding rises and falls in activation are the corresponding changes in effectiveness of performance. The general relationship is illustrated by an inverted U-shaped curve. As general activation rises from low to high, it reaches an optimal level; then as it further increases, it is nonoptimal for some or all performances. When a man is not active, when he is drowsy and inert, he is not in an optimal state for most tasks. And when he is too highly activated, his performance is likely to be less effective. In Chapter 7 concerning general drive the question of optimal excitation for effective performances is reopened.

SUBDIMENSIONS OF THE ACTIVATION CONTINUUM

There are at least four interdependent subdimensions of the general activation continuum: (1) affective excitement, (2) alertness (vigilance), (3) muscular tension-relaxation, and (4) persistence. Each of these is now discussed as it is related to general activation, but the reader must keep in mind that each possesses a degree of autonomy. For example, arousal level and degree of persistence are positively correlated, yet there are observations which suggest that high persistence can occur in some situations when the usual level of arousal of the individual is quite low.

Emotional Changes and Activation

The question has been raised whether there are different emotions or whether there is merely a continuum of low to high excitation. The assumption herein is that different phases in the total activity stream may be dominated by specific affective activity patterns which can at times be differentiated as emotions and at other times cannot be easily distinguished from each other. It is established that these affective variations are correlated to some degree with other activation changes.

Emergency Emotions. Those particular changes in the total energy transformation called exciting emotions (fear and rage) represent emergency or preparatory patterns of responses. The correlation between arousal and strong emotions was recognized by studies which demonstrated the essential identity between the physiological patterns of strong emotional states and those arising from the stimulation of the sympathetic nervous system (372). The physiological effects for which the sympathetic branch of the autonomic nervous system is responsible are of such a nature that they can support overt flight or combat. They are emergency reactions; they represent mobilization of energy, as stated by Duffy (164, 165).

Emergency reactions may be too violent when threatening conditions arise in the *social* field. There are many inhibitions against violent animallike action in civilized man. The preparation, the physiological processes changing so that quick and vigorous responses are possible, is not followed by the outer behavior for which the inner preparation was made. Even violent words, much less violent attack, are socially frowned upon. Thus the inner stirred-up state has no direct outlet, but the tension remains to harm the normal physiological functioning or is displaced into abnormal behaviors. When a man mobilizes for action, he often cannot release the responses which would best serve him in restoring his normal functioning. He remains for a while under tension even if by socially acceptable cunning he removes the threat for which he "overmobilized" himself. Stress is then present: i.e., if the organism cannot take care of the tension overload, the homeostatic mechanisms start to break down.

The Less Exciting Conditions. It has been observed that "after a stimulus to the sympathetic function has been removed, the parasympathetic system may overcompensate slightly before it, itself, returns to its prestimulation level of activity." (650, p. 348.) This is possibly a part of the physiological pattern of relief, or satisfaction. The sympathetic, and possibly both branches of the autonomic nervous system, may be in a hyporeactive state. There is also reduced metabolism; changes in heart rate and blood pressure are minimized during depression. These physiological reductions, if substantiated in conditions identified by other signs as nonexciting conditions, would suggest that certain affective states mark a low level of the activation continuum.

Vigilance—Low-to-High, or the Alertness Continuum

"To activate" means not only to make active but also to render a person ready for activation. Motivational psychology is concerned with the conditions which make for alertness, readiness for response. Often direct and immediate release into action is not possible. Rather, the organism must be ready. The wild animal, i.e., the hunting, tensed animal, may be required to withhold responses until the appropriate moment to strike with teeth or talons. Similarly a man must often be in restraint of action.

During alertness there may be restraint imposed in waiting for signals before responses can be made. During this waiting period the degree of vigilance must not decrease. Interest in "vigilance" has arisen because of the increasing necessity for men on guard to detect warning signals on radar screens. (See Inset 7.) The word "vigilance" has replaced "attention" and "set" in this field largely due to the influence of Mackworth (387), who borrowed the term from Head. Studies of many variables affecting detection of signals (monitoring, or as the British say, watchkeeping) indicate that the amount of sensory input is an important one (77, 149, 150). A continued sensory input, whether from signals being given or from extraneous stimuli, aids in maintaining percentage of correctness of reports. Figure 5-5 shows an increase in detection of signals on a simulated radar-viewing test as the number increased. Support for the importance of varied sensory input in voluntary control of vigilance is added by the observation that difference limens for luminance are impaired in continued measurement, but if one allows the observer to stand up and stretch, the DLs recover. Any restriction of sensory input from proprioceptive and tactual sources contributes to a decline in vigilance (417).

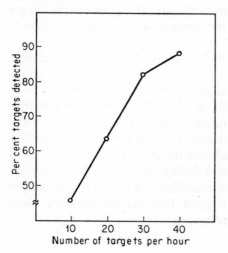

Figure 5-5. Per cent of signals (targets) detected increases as there is an increase in the average rate at which the targets appear on a screen. The points are averages for four subjects, each on four 3-hour periods of search. Deese (149)

INSET 7. VIGILANCE IN PROLONGED AND REPEATED SESSIONS*

Although there has been considerable recent work on the problem of vigilance, the laboratory work has typically been over somewhat limited periods of time (one to four hours), and when more extended periods have been considered, they have typically been *in situ* and have suffered from the lack of control. This is a report of an exploratory laboratory experiment using relatively prolonged periods (nine hours), during which it was possible to exercise considerable control over the stimulus variables and obtain somewhat refined measurements of responses (645).

The primary question asked is: "In a situation of prolonged continuous monitoring, when the stimulus definitely stimulates the signal-receiving sense organ and response is a simple on-off, essentially fatigue-free response, do men show characteristic individual or group patterns of response change within and/or between repeated sessions?"

In this study, three sailors responded to tone signals by pressing one of two keys. One key was pressed for an increasing tone and the other key for a decreasing tone. They did this for nine hours a day without interruption for five successive days. One hundred eighty-four signals were given each day with a varied pattern of intervals between signals. Within a given day there was an increase in general latency of response to the signals. In two of the subjects there was also an increase in variability of response latencies, but the third decreased in variability. Over the five days of testing there was a tendency in one subject to increase in latency and in another to decrease, but the third showed no consistent trend. These findings emphasize the individual difference factors in vigilance. Errors (pressing the wrong key or missed signals) were surprisingly few.

"One final point should be noted about certain applied implications of these data. Monitoring of simple relatively frequent signals over long periods of time can be done quite effectively." One man missed only six of the over nine hundred signals presented over the five days, another eight, and the third nineteen. Since these misses did not bunch in any given period for the three men, the use of two men monitoring such signals would result in extremely low probability of a signal being missed by both. Further, the response latencies are quite short, averaging 1.05 seconds for the three men.

General Level of Readiness in Relation to Short-term Changes in Readiness. A fundamental problem in understanding variations in activation of men is the relation of the overall level of readiness to immediate short-term excitability. It is observed that any individual man is at times ready for stimulation and at times less so and that some men on an average are generally more sensitized by stimulation than other men. Studies investigating short-term excitability have used the GSR. In addition,

---

* Adapted from Wilse B. Webb and Robert J. Wherry, Jr., Vigilance in prolonged and repeated sessions. *Percept. Mot. Skills*, 1960, 10, 111–114.

there are records of the individual skin resistance levels *before* specific stimulations. The GSR indicates a short-term "burst" of inner excitement, but this is superimposed upon the general level of the individual's immediate overall excitation level, or readiness. Let us say a man is showing *on an average* a certain amount of resistance to an electric current; then he is stimulated by a noise, a word which "taps" some emotional experience, a painful stimulation, a task to perform (like adding two place numbers), or a request to solve a reasoning problem. Under such stimulations he generally shows a temporary decrease in the skin resistance (actually an increase in arousal) and then a return to the original level. Many studies have been concerned with such transitory fluctuations rather than with the average conductance level of an individual. The latter is slower in change but is more representative of the overall readiness level. These two are, however, related: In general, the lower the average conductance level, the smaller the GSR.

Readiness for a Specific Stimulus. Various conditions force differential selectivity among potential stimuli. A man often becomes hypersensitive to some stimuli, obtuse to others. Whatever is the sensitizing factor, it intensifies responsiveness to some stimuli, reduces or inhibits responsiveness to others. Man both focuses and filters the potential stimuli provided by the environment. When a man "feels the urge" of ambition, he may show a higher level of overt activity than previously exhibited; he is more reactive to all stimulation; his general alertness seems stepped up, but there is also increasing selective attention to those sources of stimulation perceived as furthering the ambition.

In studies of food selection under qualitative needs there is evidence that children are more sensitive to (more likely to choose) foods which will reduce their specific needs (664, 669). On the other hand, under the influence of a loud noise the individual may be somewhat more alert to any stimulation, but he is not likely to be more sensitive to a particular source of stimulation unless he is afraid or curious. Then stimuli within the general locus of the source of the noise are observed. This selecting capacity of organisms is discussed in Chapters 10 and 11. Any organism is constantly exhibiting selectivity, or otherwise it would simply fly to pieces in its attempt to respond simultaneously to every irritation.

Achievement and Degree of Specificity of Readiness. A variety of interests may reflect a diffuseness of general readiness and handicap an individual in any continued development of some specific capacity. Diffusion in readiness for any stimulation may prevent persistence in scholarly work. In a study by Parrish and Rethlingshafer (478) highly intelligent but failing college students were found to have a greater number of interests outside of the scholastic field than a similar group of also highly intelligent and successful students. The implication is obvious: The failing students were alert to many sources of "interesting" stimuli with a resulting superfluity of activities, those which were necessary for passing courses of study being only some of many. The failing though intellectual students were ready for bridge and also for the physics book, for the rare books as well as the sturdy classics, for the vigorous rock and roll as well as for the sounds of the chemistry laboratory. They were ready for too much.

Variations in Muscular Tension, Another Subdimension of Activation

Variations of arousal can be scored by measures of muscle action potentials in different parts of the body. The amount of motivation affects the degree of arousal as indicated by increased muscular tension. When human subjects performing in a tracking task were offered bonuses of several dollars as well as threatened with painful stimulation, the muscular tension significantly rose (585). In another study (396) using both normal subjects and two kinds of clinical patients, muscular tension was recorded when the subjects were told that a pain stimulus would be applied to their forehead and was then recorded after a *warning* signal, during the pain stimulation, and *afterwards*. As indicated in Figure 5-6, there was a gradual rise in muscle potential up to the onset of the pain stimulation and a slight fall thereafter. (There were some slight differences according to whether the EMG was obtained from the forearm or neck.) Even more important was that the three groups of subjects varied in the amount of reactivity as well as (to a lesser degree) in the pattern of reactivity. The clinical patients with a history of headache complaints showed greater tension and a different body locus than the other patients. Normal subjects were less reactive in this situation. Malmo (394) also reports that patients with well-developed localized muscle-tension symptoms have greater tension in the "symptom area" under the stimuli of distracting noises or with the return of memories of traumatic experiences. One woman, for example, whose symptom area was in the left thigh had an increase in this muscle group when placed under a mild stress situation.

Preparatory Muscular Tension. Muscular tension has long been recognized as involved in a state of vigilance. Don't relax if the "enemy" is around. And in the modern small classroom, it is axiomatic: "Don't even look sleepy, or the professor will call on you." Of course, the "smart" student learns to "beat" this. "Look sleepy," is his advice, "when you know the answers, and look wide awake, all attention, when you don't know the answer." The degree to which muscular tension actually increases readiness is not easily solved. The armed forces have long considered that a soldier's alertness is improved by muscular tension. The soldier is placed in postural tension under the word "Attention," and *then* the order is given. To what degree such a postural change reflecting muscular tension is useful in attending is not established, though it is generally agreed that an individual alertly awaiting an event is in an increased state of tension.

The adaptive value of muscular tension is also observed when prepara-

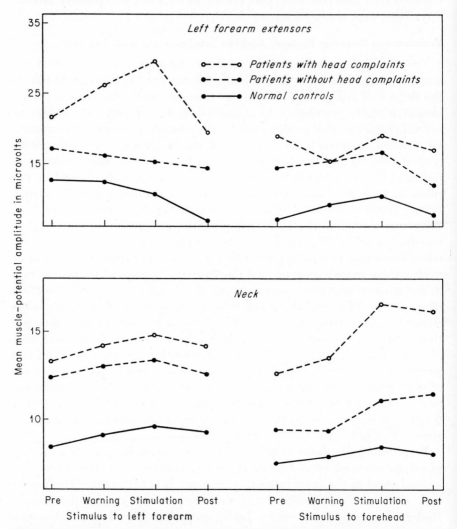

Figure 5-6. Muscle potential under anticipation and actual aversive stimulation of patients and control subjects. *Pre:* rest period of five minutes, following instructions. *Warning:* at end of rest period, brief warning was given that stimulations would begin. *Stimulation:* ten stimuli (on arm or forehead) spaced one minute apart. *Post:* rest period of three minutes. Malmo, Wallerstein, and Shagass (396)

tory adjustments for an oncoming noxious painful stimulus prevent the excitation aroused by the shock from "overflowing" into irrelevant discharge channels. When in a conditioning experiment a shock is given to a certain limb and a signal precedes the shock, tension develops in that part of the body about to receive the shock. If a person is prepared, that is, *if* he is in an optimal tension, he is more likely to react to a noxious stimulation in a compensatory manner than if he has no preparatory tension. When a shock falls upon an individual who has no particular set for it, the consequent overt activity is much more extensive and intensive than when some antecedent tension is more centered in those muscles specifically utilized in the withdrawal act. This same adaptive value of preparatory tension is illustrated in daily life when the communication of bad news is first preceded by a preparatory warning. The stress is not as damaging when the individual is to some degree prepared.

Muscular Tension as an Aid in Overcoming Distractions. Understanding of motivational and of personality individual differences has been increased by experimental attempts to untangle the relationships between tension (of various manifestations) and performance (of diverse kinds). Without attempting to unravel all the complexities involved in a long series of studies, we will simply illustrate how muscular tension (an optimal amount) has a facilitative effect in adaptation to distractions. Its value for adaptation to distracting stimuli was reported by Freeman (201) when two adults were subjected to distracting noise while writing (with the right arm). As seen in Figure 5-7, the results indicate that there was no difference during the quiet periods in muscular tension among the records on left and right arm and left leg. When noise was introduced, the effect of the distracting stimulus was to increase the tension in all parts of the body, but with repetition of the distraction the irradiation effect become less prominent. The concentration of the muscular tension was then in the limb being used (the right arm).[6]

All variations in muscular contractions affect general drive. Muscular contractions via proprioceptive afferent input increase central excitation. Muscular tension as a general origin of arousal is adaptive unless extreme. In contrast, the tension factor described as "nervous tension" by Guilford (233) is nonfacilitative of adaptive performance. Tension as nonadaptive is considered in later chapters.

Persistence, Low to High Degree

When it is said that a man is highly persistent, this term usually encompasses more than one attribute of the man. It implies that he is likely to *continue* any task, once started; that he will *endure* difficulties, fa-

---

[6] The intercorrelations reported among measures of muscular tension in different parts of the body are in general low (123).

tigue, pain, boredom, even fear and rising anxieties; that he, as a persistent man, will *not* be easily *distracted;* that he has the *sufficient energy reserve* not to be soon exhausted; that he might possibly be *inflexible,* perseverative, with more physiological inertia than most men. Nor would the above list of the attributes of a persistent man be complete without reference to the possibility of *negativeness* (perhaps expressed as stubbornness), inability to "let go," because any activity is likely to ego-involve a persistent man and any cessation be considered as ego-threatening. Factor analyses (500, 604) have isolated continuance, strength, endurance, control, perseveration as factors of what is called persistence.

Obstruction Techniques as Measures of Persistence. A rather gross measure of persistence is to place a barrier before a subject when he is under some motivational condition and record the attempts to overcome the barrier. (His score is then compared with others of his own age, sex, species.) The motivational conditions that have been often used with the obstruction method are the primary need drives, and the purpose of the studies is to determine which one brought out the most continuance in a group of animals such as the laboratory rat. Other motivational conditions studied with human subjects use interruption as the barrier in order to reveal some aspect of their persistence.

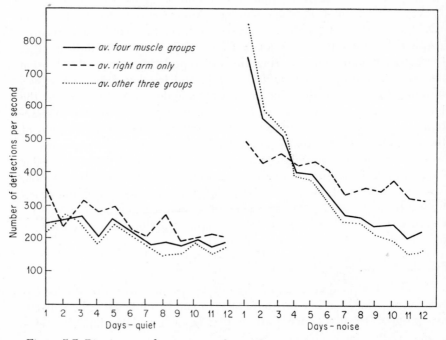

Figure 5-7. Rise in muscular tension with introduction of noise. Freeman (201)

Moss (443) reported in 1924 the results of food-deprived rats (groups of four rats without food for 12, 24, 48, 72, 96, and 144 hours) who were faced with an electrically charged grid between them and food.[7] (All animals first had an opportunity to cross to food without receiving any electric shock.) If an animal did not cross the grid within one hour after the test began, it was subjected to further starvation. No rat deprived of food for only 12 hours had sufficient drive to "take" the electric grid, but by 144 hours of food starvation all rats had crossed.

The results in these obstruction methods using laboratory rats have not been easily interpreted. When the number of crossings of a standard electrified grid to a standard food reward in a standard interval (twenty minutes) is recorded for a hungry animal, there is no way of determining how much each of the following contributed to this continuance or persistence score: the hunger state, the anticipation of the food, the frustration of the barrier, and the amount of pain actually received. Learning is also an unknown contributing variable.

In order to make comparisons from one motivational condition to another, it is necessary to ask whether the goals (incentives) are unequal or equal: e.g., is one bite of food equal to one sip of water or one short contact with a female, if the animal is a male? What we need, said Tolman in one of his many writings, are *standard* goal objects. But what is a standard goal object? One difficulty in identifying it is illustrated when we ask what is a standard female for a sexually aroused male. Her identification would be interesting.

Barrier Technique with Human Subjects. Human subjects have been given a goal task—such as fitting a puzzle together—and then interrupted. In several studies the observed behavior of various kinds of subjects indicated a range from low to high tendency to continue the interrupted puzzle tasks. Figure 5-8 gives the distribution of scores on the tendency to continue for normal children, for retarded children (IQ between 50 and 70), and for college adults. There is no great difference in the distribution of scores on this aspect of persistence in the three groups of quite diverse humans—all, however, having been trained in the American culture. This tendency to keep on going is well ingrained in individuals of the practical United States.

[7] Warden and his collaborators at Columbia University improved upon Moss's general technique described above. An elaborate electrical unit devised by Jenkins, Warner, and Warden (315) minimized individual differences in susceptibility to shock. Also see Muenzinger and Waltz (450). Other improvements on the Columbia Obstruction Method over Moss's technique are reported by Munn (453). Measures of tendency to continue in the rat also include the Pittsburgh Obstruction Unit, sand-tube obstruction apparatus and a paper window obstruction device, strength of pull exerted by rats, and speed of running (587).

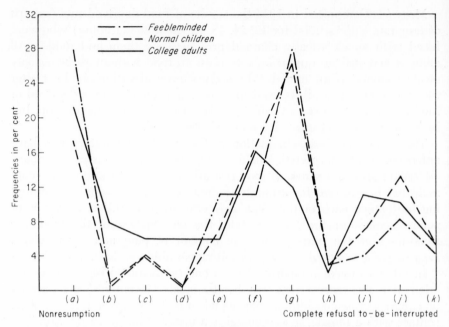

Figure 5-8. Frequencies in per cent of different behaviors following interruption of tasks. Three groups were used: feebleminded children, normal children, and college adults. Types of behavior following interruption: (*a*) no resumption; (*b*) tendency to resume; (*c*) part-refusal to be interrupted and no resumption; (*d*) part-refusal to be interrupted and tendency to resume; (*e*) no refusal to be interrupted and delayed resumption of two to five minutes; (*f*) no refusal to be interrupted and delayed resumption of one minute; (*g*) no refusal to be interrupted and immediate resumption; (*h*) part-refusal to be interrupted and delayed resumption to two to five minutes; (*i*) part-refusal to be interrupted and delayed resumption of one minute; (*j*) part-refusal to be interrupted and immediate resumption; (*k*) complete refusal to be interrupted. Rethlingshafer (499)

QUESTIONS REGARDING ACTIVATION AND SOME SPECULATIONS

The assumption of an activation continuum presents new questions of interest to motivational psychology. Would the reduction of sensory input both from the internal and external sources (at least as far as it is possible) affect the activity-level in any way? Would the absence of stimulation lead to a comatose state? Or to no change in activity? Or to a reduction of muscular action but to no decrease, perhaps even an increase, in dreaming, thinking, remembering, planning?

The above problems can be rephrased: (1) Does man like some degree of stimulation? (2) Does he work better when supported by the usual incidental sensory inputs? (3) Is there an autonomy of activity so that the absence of stimulation does not eliminate self-arousal?

Hebb (258) postulated a theory (later to be revised) of autonomous activity or a self-motivating central nervous system. He wrote that this assumption was based on the belief that living things simply by being alive were active. With the demonstrations of spontaneous activity in CNS it seemed "that the conception of a drive system or systems was supererogation" (261, p. 246). In other words, states of hunger or pain, or similar biological need states or their surrogates, were assumed to be significant in channeling the release of energy but *not* in initiating activity, i.e., not in arousal. However, in 1955 Hebb (261) questioned his earlier assumption of an autonomous activity of the CNS, citing among others the study of Bexton, Heron, and Scott (66), who found that males of the human species, well fed and physically comfortable, who were paid handsomely to do nothing, see nothing, and hear or touch very little for twenty-four hours a day were disturbed by the *lack* of external and internal stimulating events. The primary needs were met very well, and the secondary rewards were high. Nevertheless, these subjects after four to eight hours developed a need for stimulation of almost any kind. These young, normal, healthy men had their organic needs reduced to a minimum, and their external environment also was an unchanging field. Yet these subjects reported a dislike for this situation. In addition, there was disorganization in their cognitive activities.

Why did the thought processes break down in such an external field, and why should the organization of behavior not be promptly restored with restoration of a normal external environment? To answer his own questions, Hebb turned to stimulation as necessary for toning up or keeping active the neural arousal systems of CNS. Recognizing also that the amount of stimulation may become disruptive, he assumed that an optimal point of stimulation might be reached and that thereafter disorganization might occur to the vigilance of organisms. Though no one particular stimulus is always needed to initiate an animal's movement, behavioral activity, he pointed out, requires a background of sensory stimulation.

Possible answers to the above questions on the relation of stimulation to activity seem to be as follows: (1) Man likes some degree of stimulation; (2) he seems to work better with some degree of drive support from external stimulation; (3) activity is not entirely dependent upon stimulation, though it seems helpful in keeping the individual aroused. It is known that extreme reduction of stimuli from the external world is punishing.

Restriction from Movements—Does It Lead to Increase in Activation?

Restriction from movements may be followed by an increase over the normal amount. Who has not seen children rushing from school confinement? Systematic studies of the rat also support the assumption that restriction from overt movements, if not too long continued, leads to increased activity. Shirley (560) forced inactivity upon rats by requiring them to live in small cages for periods of one, two, three, and five days. The cages were so narrow that the rats could with difficulty turn around. When locomotor movements under normal living conditions was compared to those after restriction, it was found that one to two days of deprivation increased movements about 25 per cent while longer periods of restriction lead to a decrease in subsequent activity. Of interest is the additional observation that naturally inactive rats tended to become more inactive after rest while the most active rats tended after deprivation of motion to become more active, thus suggesting that the stable individual differences in the usual pace are significant in temporary variations in activation. Hill (282) tested male rats following 5, 24, and $46\frac{1}{2}$ hours of confinement. The rats could lie at full length but not stand on their hind legs or walk except by circling. Food and water were present. (External stimulation was not controlled.) Figure 5-9 indicates that after release the mean running rose according to period of deprivation from activity. The younger animals were more active after restriction was removed than the older animals. In another study, longer

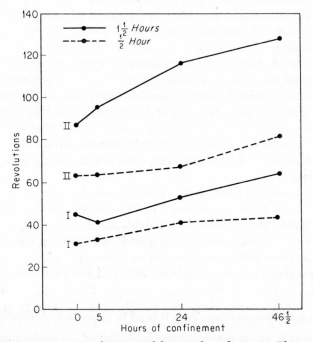

Figure 5-9. Activity rise as a function of hours of confinement. The mean running activity is presented for the entire $1\frac{1}{2}$-hour test session and for the initial $\frac{1}{2}$-hour test session. Group II consists of slightly younger rats than Group I. Hill (282)

periods of restriction from movement were correlated with a decrease in running (283).[8]

Some organisms seem to like locomotor activity sufficiently well so that it itself may act as a reward to sustain the performance of bar pressing. Kagan and Berkun (326) used the rewarding effect of permitting the animals to run after they had pressed a bar a certain number of times. Such animals were superior to control subjects in their performance in bar pressing. (When put on a fixed-interval, intermittent-reinforcement schedule, the mean superiority of the experimental animals increased.)

Does Man Ever Resist Activity?

Man may not like certain forms of energy release, i.e., what he calls work, though at one moment he may report that an activity is work and later it is not. One of the practical problems of motivational psychology is to determine what keeps a man achieving. In teaching adult classes in North Carolina, the writer found that there was a division among the men in regard to whether learning was work or not. Though all were volunteers for adult classes, for some the school was definitely work, but for others it was not. Some were extrinsically motivated, they wanted to learn, particularly arithmetic dealing with fractions, in order to get a superior job in one of the many furniture factories. Others simply wanted to learn.

They varied in their capacities for improvement, but this was not the differentiating factor in determining their liking for school. Some with very low capacity enjoyed any school activities. One man who could not write was given a sheet of paper, and as it was unlined, the teacher suggested that his work would first be to draw some lines upon it before he practiced his letters. Diligently he started to cover all paper available with well-drawn lines and stated that he would *like* to do this all day. That which will bore one man is what another wants to do; quite a fortunate state of affairs if the men find what they like to do.

In a more systematic study reported by Hebb (257) a large number of school children aged six to fifteen years were told that they need do no school work unless they wanted to and that the punishment for being noisy and interrupting others was to be sent to the playground. The reward for being "good" was to be allowed to do more work. Under these conditions the children discovered within a day or two that they preferred work to no work. They also learned more arithmetic and so forth than in previous years. To what degree parents' attitudes would be pressure sources in such a situation would be of interest. Children when

[8] The recording instrument is also a variable in determining whether there is an increase or a decrease in movements (284).

left alone certainly enter into many performances which permit learnings of many kinds. Practical motivational psychology, however, has the problem of getting children to release energy into those activities that permit the learnings which the social situation demands. Children who learn easily might be able to learn more if given greater freedom than is usual in the schoolrooms, but if not guided, there are many, even the highly intelligent, who would never learn necessary social skills.

GENERAL CONCLUSIONS

The activity stream of a child or a man is not simple; there are many energy transformations taking place concomitantly. Not all can be simultaneously recorded, but some methods have been devised for estimating the immediate degree of arousal of a subject. Simply by observing a child or man we see the rise in arousal from sleep to waking and the increased activity through the day until finally that cycle is completed with the return of sleep, only to start again at dawn.

Cycles of activation characterize all organisms. Man exhibits the simple intrinsic cycles, and he is subject also to the recurring changes in the external field correlated with the daily and seasonal events. His intrinsic cycles in activity may also be modified to some degree, and he acquires new cycles in activation, synchronized with his schedule of living in a particular social field.

Abnormalities are observed in cyclical behavior changes. The rhythmic motor habits of disturbed children or of adults include head-rolling, head-banging, torso-swaying. There are also repetitive tics, rituals, and other symbolic acts. Manic-depressive cycles, from very high to abnormal depression, represent the extremes of fluctuations in arousal.

The clues to activation changes may be found in any aspect of the total activity stream. All the energy changes cannot be recorded simultaneously, but any attempt to determine the activity-level variations should employ as many recording devices as is experimentally feasible.

Objective records can be obtained of physiological and behavioral changes as clues to increase or decrease of reactivity. Among the physiological indices are scores on variations in basal metabolic level, pulse rate, respiration rate, and other similar physiological activities. The assumption of an activation continuum was early suggested by the changes in brain waves as man passes from sleep to waking to greater and greater alertness.

Behavioral changes in variations of level of activity can be recorded of spontaneous and of forced movements. The records of spontaneous responses are made when there are no experimentally introduced origins of arousal. There are forced movements when an animal must move or die. Animals may also be systematically stimulated in order to determine their arousal level and changes therein.

Other general clues useful in determining the activation level were listed by Wittenborn (655): (1) threshold, (2) latency of response, (3) amplitude, (4) speed, (5) duration, (6) repetition of responses, (7) variety of stimuli eliciting a response, (8) number of similar responses, and (9) the excessive amount or the superfluity of behavior.

Activation continuum is not a simple dimension. Certain aspects of activation have been isolated for specific observations.

1. Often high activation is correlated with a rise in emotionality, particularly of the emergency emotions, the fears and angers. At one time biologically adaptive, they may be, if extreme, socially nonadaptive. Since overt expression of them is frowned upon, the resulting unrelieved tension may create a stressful condition. There are also the extremely depressed emotional conditions.

2. The construct of activation includes not only overt arousal but also readiness for arousal. Interest in the conditions which raise and maintain vigilance (alertness) has increased due to the present fear of the onset of a push-button war with little warning. Vigilance is highly necessary for the men who watch the borders of a country.

3. A high degree of arousal affects the persistence in activity. Persistence is revealed in a variety of ways: in continuance, endurance, control over distractibility, strength, perseveration, negativeness. According to the degree to which a man is characterized by these personality traits, his "scores" on "persistence" are affected. Certain antecedent conditions might bring out continuance, for example, or endurance might be exhibited.

4. The number of energizing conditions is reflected in muscular tension records. Preparatory muscular tension supports focused responses rather than diffuse and widespread reactivity. In general, muscular tension rather than relaxation aids readiness to respond. Stimulation, including that arising from contracted muscles, is helpful in alertness. Specificity in the locus of muscular tension is of increasing interest in identifying symptom tension areas.

Any consideration of general activation and the subcontinuums raises two problems which are entangled: the problem of the determinants of transient variations in arousal and the problem of the stable interindividual differences in activation. In Chapter 6 the second problem is considered under the topic of personal pace. And in Chapters 7 and 8 the concepts of drive and drive components are introduced with a return to the question of determinants of transient variations in activation.

CHAPTER 6

PERSONAL PACE

Men are often compared with each other in respect to their usual pace. The man with a low personal pace is indifferent to many of the excitations in his external world. Not exactly comatose, but often in the arms of Morpheus, he is slow in movements even when he is aroused to action. He shows less intensity and less extensity of reactions and may be more easily "stopped" in contrast to men who are energetic in manner, easily aroused, and rapid in movements, or who give other signs of high pressure toward activity. And there are many men neither extremely high nor low in their personal pace. The individual differences in energetic level are recognized in the practical judgments of men: the Italian speaks of the lazzarone, or the afternoon farmer, the French of the fainéant, or the do-little, the Australian of the sundowner, the American of the Weary Willie. And in contrast are the men of force, of vigor, of an unusually high activity-level.

Let us consider a lazy man, the man of low personal pace. The following is a stereotyped picture of a lazy man in the Western culture, where he is not usually admired. Little disturbs him as he lies in the shade day after day, neither the gnats nor the bugs that crawl upon him. His eyes are often closed against the sun, though he may not be asleep. He hears not the call of his wife to fetch and carry nor does the sight of any unfinished task disturb him. Even his ragged children do not move him from his rest. When the sun is down, he may rise, finding the easiest way to some source of food. Primary needs activate him, but he spends as little energy as possible to reduce them, nor does he often anticipate these needs. Like the grasshopper of the fable, he makes no preparation for the winter; he accumulates no store of goods. His critics find nothing admirable in his dependence upon others to provide.

Many variables determine a low personal pace. The lazy man may be suffering from malnutrition because he has little to eat or because his diet is lacking in some essential food material. In spite of a full stomach,

he may be starving. Or for other reasons he may be deteriorating physiologically so that his capacity to attach, store, and release energy is inadequate. His energy-releasing mechanisms may be inherently inadequate, or they may be impaired by disease. Also involved in a personal
pace are the early failures in reaching goals as well as the present opportunities to realize some gain by activity. And significant are the values
accepted in a man's self-development. Note, for instance, that in the
hypothetical lazy man described above, no tension was aroused by his
unfinished tasks. The social signs of his failures did not mock him. His
self-image, even his self-ideal, was apparently a "lazy man." Activity for
the sake of activity did not characterize him. He would appear to be an
exception to the previously advanced assumption that man is naturally
active, investigatory of his surroundings because he is curious. However,
in that assumption, that it is natural to be active, there is no implication
that organisms do not differ in their degree of activity.

Concept of Personal Pace. Each individual is characterized by a particular activation-level fixed to some degree by a variety of interacting
factors operating in his life stream. Figure 6-1 represents two hypothetical men, Abel and Benjamin, of whom Abel's usual level is somewhat
higher than that of Benjamin. The latter is nearer the lazy personal pace.
Of course, there are short-term fluctuations around the average pace. In
other words, there is an *average pace for each individual* from which

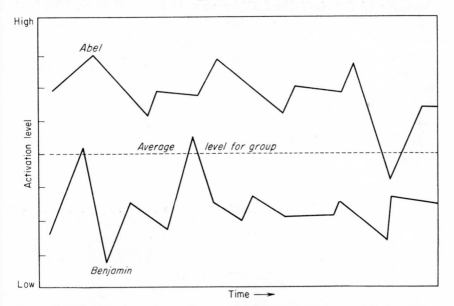

Figure 6-1. Fluctuations in personal pace of two hypothetical men (Abel and Benjamin) compared with the usual activation level of the group to which they may be
compared.

transitory changes in the amount of his activity can be observed. When a man is awake, the transitory fluctuations may be extreme; or again, there may be little shift up or down from his usual pace. These fluctuations were considered in the previous chapter and will be returned to in Chapters 7 and 8. The *determinants* of personal pace are of concern in this chapter.

Each man has his own pace which is characteristic for him though the forms of his behaviors will vary greatly. With aging or poor health, or simply because the man moves into a less exciting environment, there may be some modification of the general level. However, there is a lag in any change in personal pace. The pace of the young man may continue in the man of forty, even of fifty or sixty, but either he then collapses or there is finally a forced though gradual slowing down.

A man's personal pace, which we will see is in part gene-determined, is also subject to climatic and cultural influences. In the tropical climates men so respond that their usual pace will not exhaust them. Cultural differences are significant: It is said that the North American pace leads, among some social classes at least, to high tension and sometimes bodily exhaustion. Status striving and a higher pace are said to be most present in the upper middle class. The determinants of each man's personal pace are, however, complex, and there is constant interaction among the determinants.

Stability of Interindividual Differences in Personal Pace. The best evidence of the reliability of individual differences in general activity-level comes from studies of subhuman subjects. Among litter mates of rats, there are stable individual differences, with some animals running in a revolving drum 200 revolutions per day and others 20,000 (498). Other species exhibit individual differences in degree of movements. One highly active monkey and an inactive one maintained their relative positions in respect to each other on four test days at a temperature of 0°C (156). See Figure 6-2.

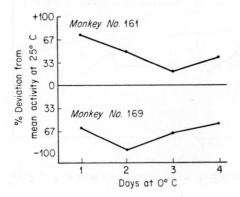

Figure 6-2. Consistency in individual differences in level of activity of two monkeys at 0°C. Active monkey (#161) is contrasted to inactive one (#169). DeVito and Smith (156)

The significant point is that the individual differences in activity-level are fairly stable. The subjects on retests do not greatly change their relative positions on the activation continuum. Even when some short-term energizing condition—such as hunger—is induced in *all* subjects, all will then step up their general activity rate; but they will remain in approximately the same relative positions with respect to each other as observed when their needs were minimal. If an active rat—one who scores high on locomotor behavior—is made hungry, he continues to have a score superior to that of a less active rat who is equally deprived of food. The size of the correlations obtained by Anderson (16) between activity scores on animals when their biological needs, such as for food, were minimal and when they were strong indicates stability in individual differences in running activity.[1] Scores were obtained both when food and water were available and when the same animals were food deprived. The correlation between these two sets of scores was .86. A correlation between activity scores of rats when and when not water deprived was .88, and when and when not sexually aroused was .70.

Gene-determined individual Differences in Overall Activity-levels

Heredity is in part responsible for consistent individual differences in activity-level. This is supported by studies on breeding active and inactive animals, as well as by examination of the various manifestations of excitability, reactivity, etc., in already established breeds of animals. Observations of human infants also support stable individual differences in reactivity before the external environment can greatly affect the constitutional makeup of the individuals (218).

Breeding Active and Inactive Animals. By breeding active animals with each other and inactive with inactive, there can be isolated two strains of animals that differ significantly in the group means. Rundquist (526) demonstrated that an active and an inactive strain of rats could be bred. (The criterion for "active" was the performance of the animals in a revolving drum for the last fifteen days of a total of twenty-one consecutive days in the drum. The rats were allowed to become adapted to the apparatus before records were obtained. They were kept in darkness during testing. As shown in Figure 6-3, a large difference in running between the active and inactive strains becomes apparent.) Since the environmental conditions remained *approximately* constant for the two groups, it was concluded that heredity influenced the levels of activity. The inactive strain had more sterile matings and took longer to reproduce. Litters were smaller among the inactive group than the active.

---

[1] Correlations between activity scores when animals were under different drives were low.

Females were more active than males. This was true for both strains of rats, active and inactive. After the first inactive animals died out, another inactive strain was bred (85, 86). Again, the inactive females were superior in level to the males—even more so than in the first study. As they grew older—to an age of 55 to 76 days—females continued to be more active than males. Apparently, it was easier to breed a lazy male than a female.

Rundquist and Bellis (527) compared the respiratory metabolism of the F 15 generation of active and inactive strains of rats. The difference between the average number of calories per gram of body weight per hour for the two strains by sex was significant.

Active and inactive strains have been found in other subhuman species. Mice of two strains (browns and albinos) differ in activity-level

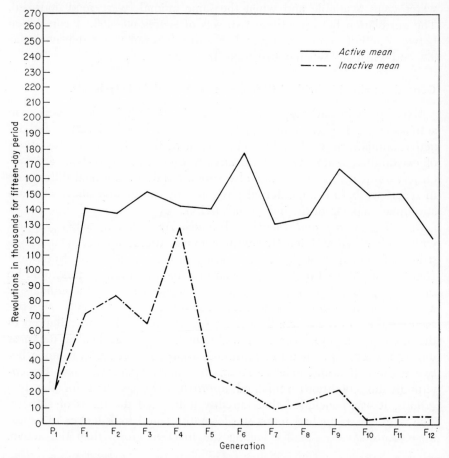

Figure 6-3. Activity means of active and inactive male rats by generation. Adapted from Rundquist (526)

(209). The browns are more exploratory than the albinos in an open-ended maze when allowed to explore for six 100-second periods. Browns entered an average of over 400 sections; an albino averaged less than 10. When interbred, the resulting hybrids were closer in activity to the active browns; apparently there is an overall dominance of the "activity" genes (in these subjects at least, as defined by the activity test used).[2] James (308) bred two types of dogs sufficiently different in average activity-level to be described as "active" and "lethargic." Purebred basset hounds were lethargic, while German shepherds were the active type. The first-generation hybrids showed intermediate characteristics. Within each type of dog, there were variations among individuals, but the range was more limited in the purebred group.

General Reactivity of Already Established Breeds. Any lover of dogs knows that they differ in temperamental characteristics; some are impassive and indifferent, others nervous and excitable. Fuller in a systematic approach to the temperament of dogs of different breeds subjected each animal to a variety of stimulating conditions, such as the presence of another dog, the ringing of a bell, handling by another person. Records were made not only of the observed changes in behavior but also of physiological reactions such as respiration and heart beat. He found four activity types: (1) the impassive, showing little internal or external reactivity; (2) the repressed, which had an increased heart rate and irregular respiration under the standard stimulations; (3) the nervous, with marked internal responses and visible trembling, even becoming convulsive in extreme cases; and (4) a milder excitable animal, with rapid breathing but only moderate heart increase. As is often true in any attempt to type animals or humans, there were mixed types and also a variety of reactions in the same individual, so that he might not seem to belong to any type. A follow-up study (208) by Fuller, using a rating scale extending from hypoactive (submissive) to hyperactive (struggling and aggressive), again indicated that dogs varied consistently in overall reactivity. (Heart rate was not, however, correlated with the ratings on the overt manifestations of individual excitability.)

One final point on the reactivity differences among dogs. Terriers, known as highly active and excitable animals, lived with beagles, passive and "inhibited" animals. After living together, each animal was given an opportunity to indicate his preference for companionship among those with whom he had lived. Each animal made a choice among every possible pair. In all cases both types of animals chose beagles (309). Thus apparently even the nervous terriers did not enjoy the companionship of their own kind; the hyperactive preferred the impassive for companions, and the lethargic beagles also wanted none of those excitable terriers.

[2] See Fuller and Thompson (211) for a review of similar studies, pp. 246–251.

Heredity as a Possible Factor in Personal Pace of the Very Young Primates. The earlier the activity differences among individuals appear, the more support there is for the assumption that heredity is influential.[3] And the newborn of the primates differ greatly in their activity and their passivity, in their readiness to respond or in their willingness to be inactive. Kinder (334) observed young chimpanzees over a period of $3\frac{1}{2}$ years at the Yerkes Laboratory; there was a degree of stability in the rate or tempo of activity of each animal. The relative standing of the individuals remained fairly constant in repeated behavior samplings. (The environment was highly uniform for these young chimpanzees.)

Infants of the human species differ reliably in the temperamental differences of activity. This is one of the obvious phenomena in infant growth studies. Fries (206), using two tests, was able to classify infants as quiet, moderately active, or active. Infants were classified, for example, as quiet if their startle response lasted less than ten seconds, active if it lasted twenty-five seconds or more. Those in between were typed as moderately active. Fries further reported that after five years the infants in general conform to their previous activity patterns. Gesell (218) reports consistency in rankings received by children at ages one and five in such behavior patterns as energy output, motor demeanor, emotional expressiveness, reaction to restriction, and other attributes. Such individuality may be the resultant of constitutional differences which appear at an early age and affect the readiness for reacting. That environmental factors may be significant in consistent differences among children in their energetic levels is not denied. For example, the emotional climate of a family, as a possible factor in personal pace, is considered on p. 106.

Summary. Heredity affects to some degree the usual pace of an individual. Breeding of animals has resulted in active and inactive groups. That heredity is in part responsible for individual differences in the personal pace of the young of subhuman primates, as well as of the children of men, was suggested by the early appearance of these activity differences in young chimpanzees and in infants of the human species.

Genes, Enzymes, and Personal Pace. We have seen that heredity is an influential factor in individual differences in personal pace. How? One possible answer is that such differences are based on the relationship between genes and enzymes. Enzymes control the breakdown of foodstuffs to simpler metabolic products and make available energy for the synthesis of cell constituents, for the liberation of heat, for the mechanical work of muscle and excretory cells, and for the electrical events constitut-

---

[3] All forms of behavior, including those which appear under selective breeding, are subject to prenatal and postnatal environmental influences. There is no denial herein of this obvious fact.

ing nerve action currents. Though the exact relationship is not known, "genes can make for the presence or absence of enzymes or determine the particular structure they have. Then, in turn, the loss of enzymes through gene mutation may block a step in metabolism. Or if their structure is seriously deficient, they may become relatively inactive and slow down metabolic reaction by becoming very slow pacemakers" (440, p. 89). And since metabolism proceeds stepwise, "the over-all rate of metabolism can be no faster than the slowest reaction in the metabolic pathway." One enzyme in a chain of reactions may become so inhibited that it slows the entire metabolic cycle. "In cases of such metabolic blocks in animals or man, the resulting loss of energy and essential compounds can stunt the individual's growth and even impair mental functions" (440, p. 88). Here is suggested a *possible* factor in limiting an individual's usual energy level.

Somatotypes and Personal Pace

Attempts to classify individuals into body types, each with their own temperamental traits including activity-level, have appeared at intervals in the history of man, from the observations of Greek philosophers to Sheldon's elaborate measurements of differences in body structure and corresponding temperamental components. Hippocrates, the Greek founder of medicine, for example, distinguished between two physical types: the *phthistic habitus* (long, thin) and the *appolecticus* (short, thick). Huter around 1880 initiated modern thought on the subject by formulating three types: the cerebral, the muscular, and the digestive. Other so-called basic types were advanced by Kretschmer (345) in 1925: the leptosome, the athletic, the pyknik, and a fourth, the dysplastic. Sheldon (555) in 1940 presented a method of classification of human males according to physical measurements of their body structures. Individuals were said to differ in the degree to which they possessed the following three physique components: mesomorphic, endomorphic and ectomorphic. More than one body measurement was used to determine the presence of these components. Careful anthropometric measurements were necessary to determine the various physique components, such as recognition of a high mesomorphic by "uprightness and sturdiness of structure," and of an individual high in the ectomorphic component by "linearity and fragility." The individual high in endomorphic component was characterized as being "soft and spherical." See Table 2. Some individuals had more of one component (as measured on a seven-point scale) than of the other body components; most often, however, the somatotype was mixed, i.e., the individual would have some of the body characteristics of the dominant mesomorphic and also about the same amount of the other two components.

Does Each Body Type Have a Different Personal Pace? It was early suggested that there was a physiological basis for temperamental differences: the Hippocratic temperaments, advanced in the time of the early Greek culture, were the choleric, melancholic, sanguine, and phlegmatic. As the terms suggest, these early typings of men implied that they differ emotionally. Child (121) supported, though to a lesser degree, the relations reported by Sheldon (555, 556) between temperamental characteristics and body types. (We are here interested only in aspects of energetics.) The somatotype high in the mesomorphic component was found to be more active than other body types lacking this component. The dominant mesomorph was said to have very forceful responses, a high drive for physical activity, and relative insensitivity to pain. The man high in ectomorphy was said to be fast but not forceful in his responses. Social influences upon the final personality which might emerge in a dominant mesomorphic individual were not forgotten by Child, who writes that ruthlessness might be correlated with mesomorphy in a society with weak sanctions against physical aggression. Ruthlessness would be encouraged in such a society but not in another. Similar hypotheses may be made in regard to the other body types.

There is limited evidence that a dominant mesomorphic individual prefers a nonsedentary occupation. In a study of delinquent, as contrasted to nondelinquent, boys, the former were predominantly mesomorphic (222). The mesomorphic male is also more likely to be found in a group of men beginning service as military fliers, i.e., as compared with a sample of college males of similar age. The significant point is *not* that there is a relationship between the dominance of mesomorphy and the "careers" of delinquency or of aviation. Rather, a predominant

Table 2. Components of Physique and Assumed Temperamental Characteristics

Physique	*Temperament*
1. Endomorphy—predominance of soft roundness; relative overdevelopment of digestive viscera	1. Viscerotonia—tendency toward relaxation, love of physical comfort, pleasure in eating, sociability
2. Mesomorphy—predominance of bone, muscle, and connective tissue; heavy, hard, rectangular physique	2. Somatotonia—tendency toward assertiveness, energetic activity, love of power and risk, physical courage
3. Ectomorphy—predominance of linearity and fragility; relative to his mass, the ectomorph has greatest sensory exposure and largest brain and nervous system	3. Cerebrotonia—tendency toward restraint, introversion, love of privacy and solitude, inhibition

Source: Anne Anastasi, *Differential Psychology.* New York: Macmillan, 1958, p. 172.

mesomorphic individual is more likely to seek an active occupation. Timidity, with a withdrawn and quiet manner, is not characteristic of those who are primarily mesomorphic, nor is timidity likely to be characteristic of a delinquent or of a man who is selected to fly a plane or to enter any similar vocation.

Note that in one study following 1,646 accepted candidates for military flying, there was no clear evidence of the superiority of any one of the three Sheldon somatotypes in achievement in military flying (175). Rather, there were present factors leading to greater selection of the individual high in the mesomorphic component. The conclusion was that mesomorphy was related in some manner to the total complex of factors which led the subjects studied to become eligible for, apply for, and be accepted for service as military fliers.[4]

Body Movements and Temperamental Traits. The interrelations among different personality measures and expressive movements (as well as other aspects of an individual response) have been studied. A general trait based on "tempo" (ranging from low to high), so that one individual can be contrasted to another in this characteristic, is suggested by observations of movements when the subjects are not aware of being observed. The tempo of an individual is revealed in walking, writing, talking, and gesturing, and in intensity of voice (592).

Ratings were obtained in one study (563) of the general activity of apathetic schizophrenic women (ages nineteen to fifty-six) on a seven-point scale of general activity. The correlations on reratings were as high as .95. When lively music was introduced, the activity was temporarily raised, but a high correlation (.88) was found between the base activity level and the ratings of the patients during the period of music.

The concept of a personal pace would be better supported if a general speed factor were found in a variety of measures, whether of motor or mental activities. Though there is some evidence of a general motor-speed factor, Guilford (233) writes that specific factors rather than one general factor provide the truer description.

Physiological Factors as Related to Personal Pace

A characteristically "tuned-up" or excited physiological state *should* be found among individuals of generally high personal pace. And the reverse should also be true: a person of characteristically less excited physiological condition should be low in activation-level.

Sympathetic versus Parasympathetic Dominance. In approaching the problem of the characteristic physiological levels of arousal of men, it

[4] A final evaluation is not attempted here of the identification of assumed physique components and any possible relationships with temperamental characteristics, including differences in personal pace (see 302, 157).

has been asked if some individuals are dominated by the sympathetic and others by the parasympathetic division of the autonomic nervous system. This is a question concerning the relation of the autonomic nervous system to personal pace. In other words, does each person have a characteristic state of balance between the sympathetic and parasympathetic branches of the autonomic nervous system? Wenger (649) reports a positive answer to the question. In samples of young children and of adult males, Wenger found an autonomic-balance factor. The concept of autonomic balance assumes that individuals characterized as having a chronic tendency to dominance of the sympathetic are more excitable and more predisposed to anxiety, and the reverse holds for parasympathetic dominance. Of course, people are not classifiable into sharply contrasting groups. The autonomic balance is a characteristic which is normally distributed, with relatively few individuals showing marked dominance of either the sympathetic or parasympathetic division. In one study of school-age children, measures of autonomic functioning were obtained in a resting state. About the same number of children showed sympathetic dominance as parasympathetic dominance. The extreme children on the sympathetic end of the distribution were more easily aroused to "emotional behavior," while the children with scores at the other end of the autonomic balance scores were more calm (650). Moreover, the scores of children on the autonomic index have a significant correlation on retests a year apart (323). There is also some evidence of a possible hereditary basis for individual differences on the dimension of autonomic balance. Studies of similarity in pairs of twins, ordinary siblings, and randomly chosen children indicate that the closer the heredity, the higher the correlations. The correlations were .45 for twins, and .30 for paired siblings. For not-related children the correlation was .05.

The cause-and-effect relationships between emotionality, defined behaviorally, and sympathetic dominance are unclear.[5] Wenger (649) found that Army Air Force personnel returning from combat areas with operational fatigue deviated from normal individuals in the direction of sympathetic dominance, and psychoneurotic personnel deviated further in the same direction. Guilford (233) comments: "This result might be taken to mean that those with combat fatigue were suffering from a mild psychoneurosis and both groups were reacting with residual fear to the combat situation."

A small group of ulcer patients had essentially normal scores. A small group of asthma patients showed an average tendency toward sympathetic dominance. "Patients of these different types who show sympathetic dominance may be in mental trouble because of their autonomic

[5] See pp. 149–155 for methods of identification of emotionality.

condition, or they may be reacting in a somewhat panicky manner to their mental troubles" (233, p. 338).

Personal Pace and Thyroid Functioning. Persons suffering from hypothyroidism are characterized by sluggishness, inertia, and dullness. There is a low pulse and respiratory rate. Hyperthyroid individuals have symptoms of increased nervous tension, excitement, and anxiety. The reactivity of the autonomic nervous system is exaggerated. The patient is characteristically jumpy, overactive, and restless.

Wenger (649) by factor analysis has demonstrated individual differences in thyroid functioning in children and in Air Force personnel. Two variables carried the load of demonstrating an underlying common variable: volar conductance and oxygen consumption. The oxygen-consumption variable identified the factor. As with all variables affecting personal pace, endocrine glands and their secretions must be carefully evaluated as determinants of an individual's overall level of activity. Striking relationships are sometimes observed at the pathological extremes of glandular functioning, but correlations within the normal ranges of functioning are more difficult to demonstrate. The trait of general activity-level is probably attributable to more than one gland, among other determiners. In one individual it can be attributed more to one and in another person, more to some other. "Systematic and comprehensive correlational studies between glandular disposition and behavior traits will require years of patient study before we have the facts" (233, p. 128).

Individuality in Patterns of Physiological Reactivity. Before leaving this brief review of individual differences in various physiological functions which possibly affect the usual pace of a man, some attention should be given to the individuality of the overall *pattern* of physiological scores on general reactivity. It is not one measure which is important but the interrelations of all the measures; moreover, one physiological reaction may be low and another high for a particular man at any one time, but the important point is that the total pattern or profile of scores is fairly stable from situation to situation. Figure 6-4 illustrates such profiles of two men performing in different tasks under high and low motivational conditions. Note how heart rate, as well as other physiological indices to reactivity, is the same whether the subjects are working on arithmetic or on a tracking task. There is some variability as the situation changes, but the overall pattern remains the same. The general level of reactivity is thus fixed in spite of the variety of conditions through which a man must move in his daily existence. Lacey and his associates (351, 352, 353, 354) called attention to individuality in physiological reactions under stressful conditions. Women subjects who were pregnant and hence under some degree of stress were further put under a mildly stressful situation by a test that emphasized speed of verbal responses. Each showed a characteristic pattern of autonomic reactions in repetitions of the situation. Some reacted relatively more strongly in terms of one measure such as the GSR, others in terms of systolic blood pressure, and others in other ways.

Summarizing the above, we can ask what has been revealed in regard to the lazy man, and others like him, whom we previously described. This hypothetical lazy man had a very low personal pace. No complete answer can be obtained to the questions why he would have such a generally low activity-level and why highly energetic individuals are present in any group of men. And the men who are in-between in personal pace are not easily interpreted.

A few of the possible determinants of a stable personal pace were reviewed above. It has been suggested that heredity may play a role. Ac-

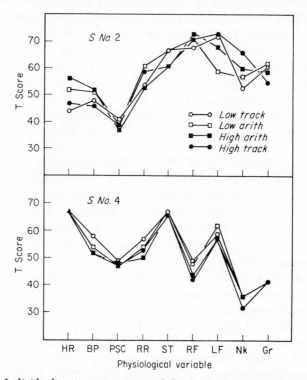

Figure 6-4. Individuality in patterning and level of physiological activity. Scores from two subjects in physiological responses during performance of arithmetic and tracking tasks, each under high and low "motivation." The measures used were: HR—heart rate; BP—systolic blood pressure; PSC—skin conductance; RR—respiration rate; ST—skin temperature; RF—muscle tension in right forearm; LF—muscle tension in left forearm; Nk—muscle tension in neck; and Gr—grip pressure. Schnore (541)

tive and inactive animals can be bred, and active and passive strains of animals can be identified. With men, the physique—the somatotype of Sheldon—is to a degree correlated with the usual energy release. A man of a high mesomorphic component is likely to be active, aggressive, and, if society permits, perhaps ruthless. But such statements are quite tentative. Too many variables affect the personal pace to be certain that a particular level of activity can be expected of a somatotype with dominance of a particular physique component. It is interesting to note that delinquents (boys) and military pilots were slightly dominant in the mesomorphic component. However, a mesomorphic component (uprightness and sturdiness of structure) did not mean that success in an active career inevitably followed.

Physiological differences among individuals of high to low overt reactivity have been found, but relationships have not yet been too accurately isolated. We can speculate that the lazy man might be dominated by the parasympathetic division of his autonomic nervous system, and that possibly he was so dominated from his first appearance in the demanding world. His lack of emotionality could thus be understood. However, a direct cause-and-effect relationship between emotionality and the autonomic nervous system is not established. Early experiences can so mold a child that he is generally overexcitable or depressed. Traumatic experiences and the general excitability of individuals are correlated, though again the exact relationships remain unknown.

The influence of the thyroid in reactivity is known to exist, and dramatic examples occur. Abnormalities in personal pace are likely to be related to the thyroid functioning.

Finally, we noted above that individuality in patterns of scores of physiological reactivity has been established. The profile remains the same from one situation to another. Exactly how stable such profiles would be under *extreme* stress is another question. We can guess that the lazy man previously described would have a different profile in physiological reactivity than his neighbor who is running himself to death to meet his taxes.

Environmental contributions to personal pace were not ignored above. The punishments and rewards of society for certain kinds of activity inevitably affect personal pace. There now follows a brief development of the influence on personal pace of the geographic and social medium in which men live.

Environmental Contributions

The pressures of the group with which an individual identifies, whether at the level of awareness or not, exert some influence. The overall activity-level of an individual is affected by his social field. The influences of geographic factors such as temperature and humidity may, if stable themselves, also lower or raise the usual levels of all individuals in the physical field. However, individual differences, constitutionally determined, would probably remain. There are such possible factors as diet, occupation, the number of primary or social needs, the number of frustrations in early life. There are the usually unknown effects of the associations of a child with parents and siblings. One observation reported by Fries (206) is that active children of maladjusted parents tended to become even more hyperactive while the naturally quiet children became more quiet. In other words, the children with such parents tended to deviate further from the median point on the scale and move toward the extreme positions on the activity-passivity scale. If the children in these homes developed neuroses at an early age, it was reported that startling reversals might appear. The basically active child might thus present the false appearance of being passive, and the naturally quiet child might become hyperactive. In contrast, children of adjusted parents were more likely to retain their original activity position or move toward the general median.

Self-concept and Personal Pace

Our lazy man, as we said above, might value inactivity. No tension was aroused in him by his unfinished tasks. The pressures of society did not create goals for him. How would he describe himself? Unfortunately we cannot ask him, but college students who differ in the values attached to activity have been asked questions like the following: "Do you often feel bubbling over with excess energy?" "Are you happiest when you get involved in some project that calls for rapid action?" "Are you the kind of person that is on the go all the time he is awake?" "Do you usually eat more rapidly than the average person?" If our lazy man answered "No," which he most probably would to these, he would score low on *general activity*. In the Guilford-Zimmerman Temperament Survey a *general activity* score is said to represent drive, energy, and activity. "If coupled with the right kinds of other qualities, this is good. If coupled with the wrong kinds, it may be bad. High activity has the general effect of exaggerating the appearance of other qualities. In many ways, it may be regarded as a kind of catalyzer. If an individual is inclined to be domineering, his high status on G will make his domineering more obvious and overt, etc." (238, p. 8; see also 239).[6]

[6] Factor analyses by Lovell (380) and Thurstone (606) of factors isolated by Guilford and Guilford (235, 236, 237) reduced thirteen to six "super-factors." "General activity" reappeared among the super-factors (second-order factors).

Items testing for "general pressure toward activity" were included in the Guilford-Martin personality inventory. These correlated .51 with "ascendancy" (another factor in the inventory) and −.27 with "lack of nervous tension and irritability." [A reliability of .79 (estimated) was reported for G.]

PERSONAL PACE AND ACHIEVEMENT

It is necessary to distinguish between the accomplishments of men and their energetics, for the former are affected by variables (such as opportunities and education) which have slight influence, if any, on personal pace. In fact, a high level of activity may not permit a man to make many contributions to society. The highly active individual may be too quick, not cautious enough, and thus lacking in the necessary skills for accomplishment. Moreover, the active man, particularly in a competitive society, may be subject to more interferences and thus develop a quicker emotional responsiveness. And though intense emotion is beneficial in situations demanding above all things a great output of muscular energy, skill and shrewdness are better served by lower degrees of general activation. The cognitive activities—reasoning, planning, judging—are not always served by high personal pace. Impulsiveness is supported, unfortunately, by a high level of excitation. Cognitive control over choice thus is weakened. Action is evoked before "thinking" can occur. Hyperactivity can be as destructive of the continuance of goal acts as is hypoactivity. The extremely active child, especially if he has passed well beyond the normal range, is likely to vary in multiple directions, changing from one goal to another. In a sense he never has goals, since he is bound to the immediate stimulus of the moment. See Inset 8.

INSET 8. ABNORMAL PERSONAL PACE OF A CHILD*

Loss of Controlled Direction in the Extremely Hyperactive Child. An illustration is now presented of a child with abnormal hyperactivity, the aftereffect of a moderately severe case of encephalitis. Goodenough (226) reports that the following represents notes taken by a psychologist at a behavior clinic. Wishing to get a picture of the boy's usual behavior, the psychologist decided to leave the child entirely alone for a period of fifteen minutes.

A small waiting room for children, equipped with a sandbox, toys, and picture books, was vacant at the time. The psychologist took him there, directing him to sit down and wait and stating that he would soon be sent for. B. W. agreed very cheerfully, and the psychologist left but remained within visual range.

The boy's eyes fell on the sand table. Instantly he sprang up, seized a small shovel, and began to dig, scattering the sand in all directions. He then noticed an unframed picture thumbtacked to the wall above the table. He jumped onto the table, gazed at the picture for a few seconds, then tore it down, crumpling it into a ball which he tossed away. He then jumped to the floor again and for a moment continued to dig in the sand until

* Adapted from Florence L. Goodenough, *Exceptional Children*. New York: Appleton-Century-Crofts, 1956, pp. 372–373.

his attention was diverted by the sight of a drinking fountain in the hall. He spent a moment or two in turning the water on as far as he could and making it squirt all about by putting his thumb over the stream. He then ran back to the sand table, returning with a handful of sand which he proceeded to pack into the fountain. At this point, the psychologist stepped forward to intervene, but B. W. did not wait for her expostulations. He ran full speed down the hall to a door through which he escaped, followed by the psychologist. Outside was a playground with swings, in one of which a small girl was slowly swinging back and fourth. With no apparent ill will but treating her exactly as he might have treated any other obstacle, B. W. pushed her out of the swing and jumped into it himself, pumping vigorously for a moment and then trying to climb up the rope. He paid not the slightest attention to the crying child on the ground who, more frightened than hurt, picked herself up and ran off. However, he may have anticipated punishment, for when he caught sight of the psychologist, he ran back at once into the building. An open door attracted him, and in he went. A clerk was sitting at a desk, behind her on the wall was a calendar. Onto the desk he leaped, scratching its polished surface with his heavy shoes. He shoved the clerk aside, snatched the calendar, and tore off the leaves one after another.

Although only eight minutes of the observation period had expired, the psychologist decided to terminate the experiment at this point. It is noteworthy that like many such children, this lad would yield cheerfully and at once to verbal commands or requests. These constituted a new stimulus, to which he responded as readily as he did to those suggested by other sounds or sights. But his obedience lasted only until something else claimed his attention, when he would be off like a flash.

A *hyperactive* child is harmed by too quick reactions, but this is an incomplete picture. If such a child can make quick and accurate judgments and continue one line of action, then the high level of readiness for performance will take him into many tasks and possibly lead to many accomplishments. It does not follow, of course, that what goals he reaches are either biologically adaptive or socially admirable.

The *hypoactive* child is handicapped by his slowness; he enters into few activities, explores little and misses much of the exciting world in which we all live. He is, however, aided in one way by his low personal pace. The reduction of his variability, which usually accompanies his hypoactivity, at times permits quicker learning. It is interesting, at least, that a brain operation which reduced the general level of activity of rats led to superior learning in a maze compared with control subjects. (Variability may be harmful, but as is true of so many characteristics of organisms, not necessarily so.) *Intelligence* may overcome any handicap of a low reactivity. The hypoactive child continues slowly along a narrowly directed line of action, not expending much energy; but if intelligent, he is able to perceive how to obtain goals with a minimum of activity. And the hyperactive person, if intelligent, is able to gather quickly much knowledge of his world. These speculations we now leave for a slightly better-documented finding. Intelligence is positively related to physiological fitness, though the correlation is not high. Terman's studies (598, 599, 600) of high-IQ individuals indicate that the highly intelligent person is likely to be superior in physical fitness.

The breeding by Tryon (625) of maze-bright and maze-dull animals permits an examination of the question: are the bright animals generally more energetic than the dull? Heron and Yugend (273) found for one group that bright rats had higher basal metabolic rates than the dull animals. The experimenters suggest that, as the high metabolic rate means a greater need for fuel, the bright animals were more motivated to get food in a maze. Kruse (348) also found that male maze-bright rats of the F 17 generation of Minnesota's breeding experiment were slightly but not significantly superior in feeding; they ate more than dull animals. The experimenters also noted that the bright animals were more emotionally upset by the changing of the feeding schedule and by the routine of obtaining records.

Learning and Personal Pace. Learning is related in a complex manner to the level of activity.[7] Too much activity leads to nondiscriminative responses. Animals (dogs) classified as of the active type by James (308) were more difficult to train in a conditioned feeding and a conditioned avoidance response than were those who were less active. They were likely to respond impulsively to the wrong stimulus. Similarly, overactive fox terriors were hindered in delayed response problems compared with the more placid cocker spaniels (210). Chimpanzees also do not solve problems well when too emotional. The highly anxious man or woman does not learn complex tasks as easily as less anxious individuals do.

The Work Pace

Productivity in the industrial situation is closely related to the normal work pace which is adopted by the workers or forced upon them in some manner. Note that what is the normal work pace represents what all the working force or subgroups therein accept as the normal rate for a particular work situation. The group standard may be too high for some workers and too low for others, considering what pace they are actually capable of holding to during the work day. Their personal pace affects

---

[7] We assume that the "law of least energy" operates in all living organisms, but this does not deny that men differ potentially and actually in their levels of energy expenditure. By learning, men save energy, but learning is not necessarily followed by reduction in energy release. It permits release of energy into new directions.

to some degree how closely they follow what is considered by the group as the acceptable work pace, but more significant is the criticism of their fellow workers. This criticism is chiefly directed against the man with a high work pace (the rate-buster). Many consider him a threat. By his fast production he implies that everyone could do better, and then management might possibly step up the expected production or attempt to lower the money rewards.

There are individual differences with respect to the conformity by the men to the standard which the group considers an honest day's work. When a bonus is offered or there is opportunity for a raise, some men are rate-busters; they go beyond the group norm. Other men are indifferent; and between the two extremes are the great majority of workers. They follow a fairly well-defined group standard in their rate of work, going neither too fast nor too slow.

Identification with Different Groups Affects the Work Pace. The men who follow a group norm in regard to their work pace believe that to produce at too fast a rate will inevitably affect everyone. These men identify with their fellow workers. On the other hand, some men identify with management or with social groups *outside* of the work situation. Their work pace is correspondingly affected. For example, a man in a blue-collar job may identify himself with an upper social class. He may want to take his family into that class, to which he believes he belongs or which he simply hopes to join. His work pace will thus be affected, since productivity frequently leads directly to more money or involves movement upward to jobs of higher prestige or more authority. Attempts to move into an upper class are, however, said to be minimal among industrial workers (81).

Identification with the union also presents some interesting effects on the work pace. "In some plants," write Brayfield and Crockett, "high productivity is not a deterrent to active union participation" (81, p. 419). The goal of high production is not, however, likely to lead to the attainment of goals connected with union activities.

Workers may also identify with civic groups outside the industrial situation, and there are many goals in these groups which require only minimal financial and occupational rewards from productivity. Active participation in veterans' organizations, in churches, in civic organizations may be carried out by individuals at all levels of the industrial hierarchy. Social rewards not related to productivity, from such activities may lower the work pace but obviously not the personal pace. Men whose chief identification is with such civic groups may have a high personal pace, but it will be reflected only slightly in their *work* pace. Since work pace is so strongly affected by the group norm of how hard a man should work, it may not reflect his personal pace to any degree.

CONTRASTING ATTITUDES

Whyte (654) has described the attitudes of three kinds of industrial workers in situations when a bonus was offered for production over a standard amount. The overall personal pace in each of these three typical workers is indirectly revealed by his descriptions of (1) the man with a low work pace; (2) the extremely productive worker who goes far beyond what is accepted by the workers as an "honest day's work," i.e., beyond what is considered by the group as a correct pace; and (3) the man in the middle, representing the work pace of the majority. The following description is from Whyte (654).

The Man below the Accepted Work Pace

For purposes of contrast, let us examine the two extremes in productivity. Take the case of a worker whose mean performance over a period of two years is only 52 per cent. He admits he was once interested in making bonus. But no more. You've got to keep your nose to the wheel. You can't stop for a visit, or you'll lose everything you've made. And even if you're willing to work like hell, you can't be sure of making anything. If I come out here and be a mule for eight hours, I want something to show for it. Suppose you plan on making so much bonus every pay—so you can buy a car or something. You'd have to ball the jack the whole turn and every turn. Inside of a week you wouldn't have a friend in the shop. And even if things was fixed so you could make your regular bonus by working like hell—I still wouldn't want it if I had to make somebody sore to get it or have the whole shop down on me. Don't misunderstand me. I'd like a little bonus. But they don't give it away, and I won't pay the price they want—be a —.

The Rate-buster

Contrast this with the statement of one of the top performers: I'm out here to make money. If any of these damn loafers think they can stop me, let them try it. I keep my bills paid an' don't owe anybody a damn cent. I mind my own business and look after my job. I'm always on time. I never lay off an' I don't sneak out early. The company can count on me, so why the hell should I care what a bunch of damn snoopy bums think of me?

Such striking differences do not come about by accident. They can be accounted for in a perfectly objective manner by comparing social backgrounds and present social activities of the two groups. We also find that the response to economic symbols is not an isolated phenomenon but rather fits in with a pattern of responses by the individual to his social and economic environment. (654, p. 41)

The Man in the Middle

Between the two extremes we find the majority of the workers. As might be expected, most of them combine in themselves characteristics of both extreme types. That is, one may be a country-born Republican who saves his money but belongs to several clubs outside of work and participates in the informal plant society, while another may be a city-born Democrat whose range of social contacts outside and inside the plant is small but who does not go against the group.

The middle performers are pulled both ways, as is indicated by this quotation from an elderly machinist who averaged 125 per cent over a two-year period:

I worked under the same damn system forty-five years ago and thought when I left that I was done with it. Nobody gets any good from an incentive system. It makes bad feelings among the workers, between the workers and the checkers (personnel who apply the incentive) and between workers and the bosses.

Now you take that son-of-a-bitch over there (nodding toward a rate buster), the incentive system made him what he is. He's got a bad principle and the system brought it out. He'd cut the workingman's throat for a nickel. I've told him to stay away from my machine and not to speak to me because I'd feel insulted. I value my fellow worker's opinion above the dollar.

This incentive business gets hold of you before you know it. My health is as good as it ever was, yet last summer I got so damned nervous because of the aggravation that I spent seven weeks in the hospital. That ate up all the bonus I ever made.

The thing that's so damn aggravating is that one job pays twice as much as it should and the next only one-fourth what it should. What you make you lose. And when you get one that pays high, the boss comes around and rides your ass to get it out right away—and you have to kill it. When it runs low, I raise hell with the checker and he takes it to the engineers. They promise to do something about it. Then they say their hands are tied and they can't change it. (654, pp. 46–47)

For the top and bottom producers the incentive system presents no conflict. The rate-busters have renounced the group; the bottom producers have renounced the incentive. It is the men who set a high value on both money and group ties that are pulled in opposite directions. Work rate is not only affected by personal pace but also by the attitudes of the workers.

CONCLUDING STATEMENTS

Personal pace is not a simple construct. There are many manifestations of its influence in the lives of men and many determinants of it. It is apparently influenced by heredity in each individual but is subject to many environmental variables. Contributing to the usual pace of a man are differences in physiological functioning, possibly related to differences in the components of physique such as those isolated by Sheldon. The personal pace is certainly not independent of the social and physical (geographic) fields in which the man moves. It can be affected by mal-adjustments of parents, which in turn affect the children of such parents. Physical diseases may create abnormalities in personal pace. The over- or under-reactivity of the thyroid creates dramatic differences in personal pace.

As is illustrated in studies of work pace, the group with which an individual identifies may affect his rate of energy release, at least in work situations. Attempts to achieve a prestige status affect the work pace, but the majority of workers in industrial situations set up their specific standard for rate of production and attempt to force it upon all others. This group norm is considered a protective device against management. Men of high personal pace may have difficulty adapting to the group norm.

Other traits are related to personal pace. Impulsiveness is supported by a high personal pace. Aggressiveness may be a personality attribute of an individual who functions rapidly. Murphy, speculating in regard to the development of children, writes that energy level or general activity-level is probably of considerable importance in the development of patterns of aggression, ascendance, cooperation, sympathy, and the readiness to develop coping techniques when threatened or frustrated (456, p. 627).

CHAPTER 7

FLUCTUATIONS IN ACTIVATION:
NONSPECIFIC DRIVE

The previous chapter indicated that each man is characterized by his particular and stable level of activity, i.e., his usual or personal pace. We are now concerned with the rise and fall in the arousal of individuals. Even the characteristically hyperactive man is not manic all the time. There are fluctuations in his rate of energy expenditure. At times he slows down, is inactive; moreover, he sleeps, though no doubt he is more restless in his sleep than is the hypoactive individual. And the man of a slow personal pace may in some situations be greatly activated.

Some Questions

What energizes man? And what deenergizes him? What presses down the accelerator? And what determines the slowing down? What increases energy expenditure? And what decreases the rate of the use of organic fuel, i.e., the energy attached from foods? There is a variety of antecedents for changes in arousal. Sometimes the arousal-level variations are observed even though the antecedent conditions of the assumed drive changes are not known. Depressions in activation, for example, appear: A man becomes slow, lethargic, indifferent to stimulation, not even moved by what in the past easily excited him. Behavioral and physiological indices indicate a fall in overall activation, but the antecedents of this depressed phase, which may last a few minutes, an hour, a day, or longer, are not always identified. The man cannot report them to his friends or even to his therapist (if he has one). At another time this same man may show all outer signs of high level of arousal, of high degree of activity. But again he cannot identify the antecedents of his high level of activity. He says he "feels fine, has a lot of drive." Why? He doesn't know. In other words, the antecedents of the arousal changes may not be immediately apparent.

If a clinician is asked by a client *why* he has certain unaccountable ups and downs, perhaps even abnormal and frequent fluctuations such as

114

from an extreme manic phase to a low depression, the approach will inevitably involve the personality of the client. However, to seek the *immediate* events which are energizing or depressing to a man is a different approach from analyzing personality as it is involved in the nature or quality of his variations in drive. The approach to activation fluctuations as they are determined by personality manifestations should be distinguished from any motivational analyses attempting to isolate the short-term fluctuating variables influencing a man's activity-level. A complete interpretation of fluctuations in the degree of energy expended would obviously depend upon both motivational and personality variables and, as indicated in Chapter 2, upon his potentiality for release of energy.

The clinical interview and the experiment are alike in that they both use hypotheses concerning the origins of excitation or depression. They both test their hypotheses, though by different methods. Basic in both approaches is the attempted isolation of the conditions (or at least some of them) which lead to the activation changes. The clinician may seek the normally depressing (or exciting) events, though he is usually more concerned with pathological disturbances of activation. The clinician, with the aid of the client, tests his hypothesis, and if it is confirmed, there may follow further analyses preceding the restructuring of the personality so that events may not again extremely depress, excite, or panic the client. The clinician's conclusions are most often in terms of the individual. In an experiment it is more usual to test general antecedent conditions for arousal changes and thus provide some general knowledge of activating determinants.

In the development of motivation and personality variables as they pertain to activation, two related concepts are used: (1) drive and (2) components of drive (drives). We now consider these constructs: first, their definitions; second, their development in different psychological theories; and finally, the evidence for inferring a varying drive with specific components therein.

GENERAL DRIVE AND DRIVE COMPONENTS

Two constructs frequently used in interpretations of arousal changes are nonspecific drive and specific drive (drive components). They are inferred intervening variables.[1]

---

[1] The intervening variable was introduced into psychology by Tolman (615), who was interested in central events (see pp. 733–749 in 341). Essentially, intervening variables are inferred central events between the onset of observed antecedent conditions and correlated activity changes.

Drive is the inferred central neutral excitation. Changes in antecedents (as in stimulating sources) with observed correlated variations in activation permit the inference of changing drive level.

Nonspecific Drive

It is said that a man's general (nonspecific) drive has changed when he is observed to be highly excited; when his high degree of arousal is decreasing, his inferred general drive is said to be decreasing. Nonspecific, or general, drive is central neural excitation. There is a constant flux in this central drive, as is manifested by frequent increases and decreases in the arousal level as well as in the readiness for arousal. When a man moves slowly, with little energy expenditure in any activity, and is indifferent to all potentially exciting sources, it is inferred that his general drive is low. And when he is ready for *any* action, when his alertness is high, then he can be described as having a high general drive level. The number of measures of activation outlined in Chapter 5 indicate the variety of available indices to the rise and fall of drive. General drive is differentiated into specific drives both by maturation and by learning.[2]

Drive Components (Specific Drives)

Origins of the specific drives are traced to antecedent conditions as these are correlated with activity patterns. These patterns are interrelated experiential, physiological, and behavioral changes. For example, there are known correlations between continued painful stimuli and changes to an activity pattern which is reported as fear, observed as a negative orientation to sources of pain, measurable as increased physiological reactivity, and recorded as withdrawal behaviors. In one study (160) the stimulating electric shock was reported for one group as 0.4 milliampere and for another group as 0.2 milliampere. The high-current group made more extra avoidance responses between shocks and responded more promptly. Thus there can be inferred for the high-shock group a stronger specific drive component of pain-fear. There are many other specific drives: e.g., hunger, thirst, and other need drives, and the arousing and depressing emotions such as anxiety, complex hate, frustration, disappointment. There are drives which originate in social interactions, as in status striving; drives based on exteroceptive stimulations. We have previously reviewed the curiosity-investigative tendency evoked by novelty of stimulation. Specific drives are further described in the next chapter.

The presence and the strength of many drive components cannot be objectively determined. For example, the amount of drive increase from an insult cannot be determined. There are many ways of insulting a person and many degrees of effect on the individual involved. The degree to

[2] General drive, in contrast to personal pace, changes according to situational variables. A man of low personal pace may show a temporary rise in energy output when there are threatening signals of danger in the situation. His drive rise may be briefly quite marked, but he remains a man of *usual* slow personal pace.

which an individual is drive-involved after an insult can, however, be rated by an observer and verbally reported by the individual insulted. Also, physiological scores can be obtained, as well as records of the vigor of action. His direct or indirect attacks, for example, may be recorded by measures of speed, strength applied, persistence of responses.

Two Categories of Drive Components

Drive components are based on (1) transient conditions and (2) latent organizations. The latter, when active, function like the transient drives. Transient drives are like the grin of the cat in *Alice in Wonderland*. It was there in splendor; then it completely disappeared from the horizon. Such drives exist temporarily; then they are gone. Where is hunger, once the stomach is full? And does fear, unlearned or learned, exist once it has subsided? Or curiosity after it is sated? Or love caress once it has been killed? Or noise exist after it ceases? Or pain, when the irritation is removed? These and other drives are transient states, their strength not subject to learning. They do not grow stronger under repetition. What *is* learned may be a correlated behavioral expression or possibly a modification of the physiological pattern, as well as new initiating antecedents for some, at least, of the specific drives.

In contrast to the transient specific drives are those based on learned dynamic traits (dispositional variables). The latter often lie fallow in the form of latent neural organizations, but once moved from passivity they function in ways similar to the transitory drives. Their active phase is transitory, but their basic organizations are a part of the learned systems in the neural areas. The role of those dynamic dispositional variables that are drive-related is slowly being determined. McClelland et al. (413) and Atkinson (28) have established, for example, the significance of need-achievement and have considered how it may be changed from a passive or latent organization into one of the functioning motives (drives) (see Inset 9).

INSET 9. INSTIGATORS*

In order to change a latent dispositional variable from a passive to an active role, instigators are designed to arouse human drives in experimental settings in as lifelike a way as possible.

Historically the most important of these attempts were those initiated by Sears (546) and others to induce ego involvement, success, and failure by the use of various types of instructions appealing to the achievement need and/or by manipulation of reported performance scores relative to levels of aspiration or to norms reported for other competing individuals. In the

* Adapted from D. C. McClelland, Methods of measuring human motivation. In J. W. Atkinson (ed.), *Motives in Fantasy, Action, and Society*. Princeton, N.J.: Van Nostrand, 1958.

same tradition were many of the studies of the Yale group in *Frustration and Aggression:* Attempts were made to induce frustration experimentally by such techniques as taking a bottle from a baby, preventing Boy Scouts from seeing a movie they expected to see, keeping college students up all night, producing direct conflict between two overt motor responses, and the like.

McClelland (410) and Atkinson (28) report different antecedent conditions used to induce the need-to-achieve. Every attempt was made to provide a setting which, in males, at least, would genuinely arouse *achievement strivings.* References were made to "intelligence" or "leadership capacity," and in some cases it was arranged that the subjects do well or poorly at actual tasks. Furthermore, it was not assumed that the relationship of the administrator to the subjects could be disregarded, that mechanical recitation of obviously "phony" instructions by anyone—even a pretty coed or a confused graduate student—about any task—even canceling X's and O's—would succeed in producing achievement striving.

Human motives more or less successfully aroused in addition to the achievement motive include the following. The *affiliation motive* is aroused by exposing subjects to public sociometric judgment and by rejection from fraternities which students wanted to join. The *sexual motive* is aroused in males by nude female slides and by proximity to an attractive female "lure" and in females by musical stimulation. The *power motive* was presumably aroused among candidates for an election during the suspense of waiting for the ballots to be counted.

SOME CONVERGING POINTS OF VIEW IN REGARD TO DIFFUSE DRIVE AND SPECIFIC DRIVES

Drive as a central fluctuating and diffuse state of neural excitation, with specific components therein, is not a new concept. It is, however, a controversial one. There are various theories of general drive.

Drive as Noxious Excitation

One view, though a questionable one, of general drive is that it is based on the degree of irritation to which the organism is subjected and from which it is presumably continuously attempting to escape. This view arose within that biological approach to motivation which assumed that the organism had to be irritated before it changed from a state of inertness to arousal. Hunger was, therefore, equated with pain, maternal motivation with discomfort from distended mammary glands, sex drive with the male's distended seminal vesicles. Moreover, it was found that an associated neutral stimulus could acquire the irritating or noxious property of such conditions. This view thus assumes that *any* increase in arousal necessarily is based on the onset of an irritating event. And it is further assumed that any increase of any of the specific drives is irritating and is inevitably followed by attempts to reduce irritation. Mowrer thus suggests that there is "an element of fear common to all primary drives, when they reach moderate to great intensity" (446, p. 163). This theory of mass irritation as basic in arousal is implicit though not significant in such diverse theories as outlined by Freud and Hull. Hebb, Allport, and Harlow have protested against this view. This theory that drive rests on irritations is not adequate, for it ignores the observations of changes in arousal which are *not* correlated with irritations. This view is also based on the assumption that organisms must be irritated to be activated. We assume that man's general drive rises and falls, but we do not assume that the basic antecedents to these shifts in excitation are necessarily disturbing.

Freud's approach, different in most respects to the above view of general drive, is now considered.

Freudian Theory: General Drive and Drive Components

Freudian theory is based on the assumption of a general drive. In much of Freudian writings there is the suggestion of the diffuseness of organismic energy. Freud postulates a *general* instinctive energy, the origin of which is the id. The id is said to be the source of psychic energy which is released by all the instincts.

Two general categories of specific drives called the life and death instincts are also postulated. That particular part of the psychic energy released into the life instincts is the libido. And since Freud ignored to a large extent his category of death instincts, general drive in his theory is often assumed to be the libidinal energy.

The psychic energy (general drive), being frequently barred from direct release, is often displaced, according to Freud, from its original and more natural objects and "invested" in such diverse activities as gardening, social work, athletic contests, daydreaming. This is a significant aspect of the Freudian concept of general drive, i.e., the "freedom" assumed for its attachment to a variety of objects. Psychic energy is assumed to be easily displaced. Cathexis, the attachment of this general energy to new outlets, is according to Freudian theory continuously taking place. The energy of the id is assumed to be in a fluid state, easily shunted from one action or image to another action or image. The displaceable quality of drive is said to be due to the id's inability to form fine discriminations between objects. "Objects that are different are treated as though they are the same. The hungry baby, for instance, will take up almost anything that it can hold and put to its lips" (241, p. 41). It is implied that there is "a certain indifference about the path along which the discharge (of energy) takes place, so long as it takes place somehow" (205).

This displaceable attribute of the psychic energy continues even after the ego has "trapped" energy from the id. Ego energy can be displaced to form new object-cathexes and can thus permit a whole network of derived interests, attitudes, and preferences to be formed. "These ego-cathexes may not directly satisfy the basic needs of the organism but they are connected by associative links with objects that do." The energy of the hunger drive, for example, may include such cathexes as an interest in collecting recipes, visiting unusual restaurants, and selling chinaware. This spreading into channels "only remotely connected with the original object of an instinct, is made possible by the greater efficiency of the ego in performing its fundamental job of gratifying the instincts" (241, p. 42).

The Freudian theory of motivation has undergone many slight and major revisions. Gill (220) in Inset 10 summarizes some of the trends in the changing psychoanalytic motivational theory. He points out that there is increasing recognition of derivative or acquired motivational variables.

INSET 10. TRENDS IN MOTIVATION WITHIN PSYCHOANALYTIC THEORY*

Psychoanalysis, writes Gill, always has been and continues to be a theory that centers on motivation in human behavior. Uniquely characteristic of psychoanalysis is the kind of motivation it postulates: drives rooted in the biology of the organism. These drives are sexual—in the broader sense in which the word is employed in psychoanalysis—and aggressive. They are characterized by their urgency, by their intimate connection with various kinds of bodily behavior—both in terms of one's own body and the bodies of other people—and by the rather bizarre quality of their mode of function when viewed in the light of ordinary conscious motivation.

Psychoanalysis has not given up this conception of primitive drives, but it has somewhat changed its view of their place in personality functioning and has added to its theory to account for other kinds of motivation as well. Whereas the psychoanalytic theory of motivation was formerly restricted almost entirely to primitive drive, it now includes a complex hierarchy of motivations that implies a progressive taming of drives with advancing development and progressive infusion of the drive representations with cognitive elements reflecting external reality. Its view of the dynamic relationships of the various levels of the motivational hierarchy has so changed as to increase the emphasis on derivative motivations—to which it has always paid some attention—though by no means diminishing the emphasis on more primitive motives.

Behavioristic (S-R) Constructs of General Drive and Drives

In S-R behaviorism Hull (299) accepts a general drive, the immediate nonspecific state or general condition of the nervous system to which all

* Adapted from M. Gill, The present state of psychoanalytic theory. *J. abnorm. soc. Psychol.*, 1959, 58, 1–8.

the specific drives contribute. The specific drives are inferred excitation patterns, i.e., drive stimuli based on primary need conditions for food, water, air, and elimination, as well as secondary (learned) drive stimuli.[3] Discrimination among these drive patterns is assumed to be acquired by the growing child.

Hull does not seem to grant as much "fluidity" to general drive as is implied in the Freudian model, though he implies that any one of the specific drives *may* motivate into action a habit acquired under another one of the drives.[4] Hull even flirts with the concept of sublimation when he writes of the action of the endocrine substances in lowering the reaction threshold of *all* effectors. His suggestion is that there is a generalized tendency to "facilitate action of *all* effectors," i.e., a general drive analogous to the Freudian libido. A sex hormone, Hull points out, might arouse action based on any habit "however remote the action from that involved in actual copulation" (299, p. 252).

A basic assumption in Hullian theory is that drive and habit interact in a multiplicative fashion to determine response strength. Drive is nondirective—is "aroused by a variety of antecedent conditions and becomes manifest in behavior through its capacity to multiply existing associative tendencies (habits)" (90, p. 135). See Brown (90), pp. 99–107 and 135–136. When general drive increases, all habits are facilitated, i.e., have more "excitatory potential." Both facilitative as well as irrelevant (interfering) habits for a particular performance are sensitized by rising drive.

General Drive Correlated with Emotionality

Within the framework of the Hullian theory, Spence (576, p. 132) presents a hypothesis that "the drive level (D), in the case of aversive situations at least, is a function of the magnitude or strength of a hypothetical response mechanism, designated as r_e (an emotional response), that is aroused by any form of aversive stimulation." The theory that general drive is a function of the strength of emotional response was extended by Spence and Taylor (577) to the measuring of individual differences in emotionality by a test called the Taylor Manifest Scale (MAS). This test is one operational definition of the emotional-responsiveness variable. In various studies, the MAS was used as a measure of characteristic differences in emotionality among men and women. Predictions were made on the basis of the Hullian theory. One such predic-

---

[3] *Drive stimuli* were originally postulated to account for the "registration" of the primary drive condition (need) on the central excitation flux or drive (D). Otherwise-neutral stimuli acquired drive property by association. Thus within Hullian-influenced theory learned drives were accounted for by the secondary drive stimuli.

[4] Experimentation has given this assumption some support. For example, on p. 135 are reported studies demonstrating that a motor habit learned under hunger may be evoked under thirst. Other studies of combined drives are there presented.

tion was that individuals with higher drive level (greater emotionality) would find the learning of complex associations most difficult because the higher the drive, the greater the response probability of evocation of interfering associations.

Purposive Behaviorism and Concepts of Drive and Drives

Tolman (620), a purposive behaviorist, leans toward the concept of nonspecific drive with specific components therein. He assumes a "big need" described as "a libido or a source of general energy." This is conceived to be in contact more or less directly with all the specific needs (specific drives).

The increasing specific drives thus, according to Tolman, originate from the more general drives. When a drive is blocked at any level of development, it is "converted" into a *specific* behavior propensity. Such new behavior propensities tend to be abandoned when they do not prove to contribute to the original goals. The docility (modifications) is assumed to be less limited in those conversions which occur as a result of learning than in those which occur as a result of Freudian "dynamisms" such as fixation. See pp. 168–170.

Murphy's Use of General Drive and of Drives

In the personality theory by Murphy (455), the basic motivational hypothesis is that all activity is traceable to tension, that tension is "need" for acting, and that tension, need, and motive are one and the same. Supposedly there are tensions of many sorts: e.g., mechanical tensions, as in muscles; chemical tensions; the surface tensions of individual cells. "The living body is a complex system of interrelated tensions, partially discharging, partly blocked from discharge, but in some sort of intercommunication" (455, p. 89). Murphy adds that there is nothing in the life of the organism to suggest that the vital organs are either more or less important than are the other tissues with reference to this uninterrupted activity. Tissue tension thus is, in his theory, the basic origin of activation (the source of general drive). He assumes specific drives and attempts to show how *canalization* may be the mechanism responsible for specificity in general drive. See pp. 170–171.

Neurophysiological Models for Drive and Drives

A neurophysiological model based upon earlier views of Morgan (437) and Lashley is developed by Stellar (583). Excitatory and inhibitory centers in the hypothalamus, or related neural areas, are assumed to determine the "amount of motivated behavior," i.e., level of general drive. These centers are assumed to be under the influence of a large number of excitation sources, i.e., all the afferent impulses arriving at the hypothalamus (or related areas). In Figure 7-1, Stellar indicates the possible origins of excitation input to the central arousal area. There are the incoming excitations from external stimuli; from internal chemical and physical factors such as hormones and blood temperature; and from cortical and thalamic centers which exert both inhibitory and excitatory influence. In addition, Stellar writes of the drive of the hypothalamus that determines the level of excitability and, therefore, the amount of motivation (583, p. 19).

A neurophysiological approach to the concepts of general drive and of specific drives is presented by Morgan (437, 438, 439), who writes of a "central motive state" (CMS). It is assumed that different drives (like hunger and thirst) involve different neural systems, *but there may be considerable overlap of these systems* (suggesting the existence of nonspecific drive). Without denying the importance of stimuli (internal or external in origin), Morgan stresses the humoral factors as influential in an onset or disappearance of central motive states. A CMS has the following properties: (1) Once the central state is set up, it persists without outside support from further excitation (although that it can "coast and perseverate" does not mean that it continues indefinitely); (2) general activity accompanies it; (3) it is responsible for the emission of patterns of behavior characteristic of the state, without specific receptor stimulation; (4) it sensitizes the organism to respond selectively to some stimuli and not to others and to select certain response patterns over

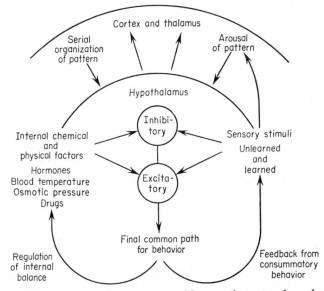

Figure 7-1. Stellar's diagram illustrating possible contributors to hypothetical excitatory and inhibitory neural centers. Stellar (583)

others. Morgan assumes that a CMS is responsible, in part, for the emission of very specific behavior patterns, such as sexual behavior, eating, or elimination. Thus Morgan postulates a cue as well as a general energizing function for a CMS.[5]

Neurological and other findings support the concept of specific drive components. There are, for example, discoveries by the neurophysiologists of neural "centers" in the hypothalamic region for hunger, thirst, sleep, and possibly others (438, 583).

A Neural General Arousal Center. Neurological theories in regard to general drive, and to the possible specificity therein, *are based in part on studies of the functions of the reticular area* and its interconnections with sensory tracts and with cortical areas described below in Insets 11 and 12.

INSET 11. THE RETICULAR FORMATION*

Structurally the reticular formation has been known for many years, but its functional role was poorly understood and has been largely overlooked, apparently in deference to the ascending sensory and descending motor pathways, the cranial nerve, and other nuclei surrounding it. The reticular formation consists of a rather dense network of neurons which forms a kind of central core extending from the medulla of the lower brain stem to the thalamus in the diencephalon. It extends through the region of the pons and the midbrain tegmentum upward through the caudal portions of the hypothalamus and subthalamus.

INSET 12. ASCENDING RETICULAR ACTIVATING SYSTEM (ARAS) †

In addition to the well-known classical or specific sensory pathways which carry messages to the brain via direct routes with few synaptic relays, there is a second sensory system, or an *unspecific sensory system.* This system, writes Lindsley, is rooted in the *reticular formation* of the lower brain stem, which forms a central core extending from the medulla to the thalamus. It is composed of multineuronal, multisynaptic paths which slow conduction through it. Branches from classical afferent pathways lead into it. The reticular formation and its upward extensions project upon widespread areas of the cortex in contrast to the specific sensory system, and when activated it causes desynchronization or differentiation of electrocortical activity. This unspecific or diffuse influence of the ARAS upon the cortex has as its primary role the maintenance of a waking state. This is its *general arousal function,* which causes the electrical activity of the cortex to shift from a sleep picture (with synchronized slow waves) to waking (with

---

[5] The sensitizing function of drives is discussed in Chapter 10, Selecting.

* Adapted from D. B. Lindsley, Psychophysiology and motivation. In *Nebraska Symposium on Motivation.* Lincoln, Nebr.: University of Nebraska Press, 1957, p. 57.

† *Ibid.,* pp. 95–96.

alpha waves). There is also believed to be a *general alerting function,* which causes a shift from synchronized alpha waves of the relaxed waking state to low-amplitude fast waves of a desynchronized pattern, thus creating a general attentive state. Differential excitation in the reticular formation and/or some combination of interaction between thalamus and cortex may give rise to a *specific alerting function,* in which attention may be focused on a single sense modality or on a specific stimulus within a modality. The alerting functions, both general and specific, appear to play a role in perception, including the elaboration and integration of incoming messages. The ARAS and its activating functions are supported by impulses feeding into the reticular pool from collaterals of all sensory paths and also from corticoreticular fibers. Thus cortical events, as well as sensory events, enter into the energizing of the ARAS, with resulting changes in consciousness, attention, perception, and perhaps learning.

Figure 7-2, a simplified view of the arousal neural area and some of its interconnections, indicates how these could lead to an indiscriminate spread of afferent excitation to cortical areas. This spread of excitation is described as a "toning up" or "alerting" function of this general arousal area. In a normal external environment with the usual amount of stimulation, afferent currents are transmitted, in part via the reticular area, to *wide* cortical areas, and serve to "tone up the cortex." This could be the basic origin of nonspecific drive. The afferent inputs via direct sensory tracts to specific cortical areas, however, are it is assumed, more likely to arouse action "related" to these specific inputs.

A *general* drive is assumed by Hebb (262), who considers the possibility of *specific* patterns in that drive. Though the assumed arousal system may be a generalized drive mechanism, it is said to be excited by different conditions, including primary drives like sex or pain drives. Differentiation within the hunger drives, such as a drive for particular vitamins or protein, is also accepted. The general drive and the specific

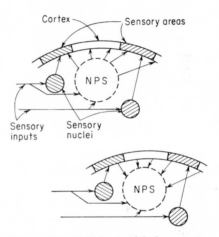

Figure 7-2. Hebb's simplified presentation of a nonspecific projection system (NPS). Two specific sensory paths are shown, the hatched circles representing two thalamic sensory nuclei, each connected with its own special cortical area. Each sensory input also sends branches into the NPS, which mixes up excitations from these different sources and transmits them indiscriminately to the cortex (upper diagram). The cortex also sends excitations to the NPS (below). In other words, cortical processes can contribute to the level of arousal. The NPS usually refers to the reticular formation. By permission from Hebb (262)

patterns may involve different segments of the arousal system—"presumably with parts of it in common, but also with other parts specialized for the separate drives" (262, p. 158). Hebb's drive theory is illustrated by his discussion of anger and fear. He suggests that anger and fear have a common core of undirected, and undirecting, emotional excitation (arousal) and that the differences which exist between two such emotions could lie in the cue functions of afferent input, not in the kind of arousal. "In anger, for example, the stimulus excites the arousal system, and also excites S-R connections and mediational processes that result in attacking behavior. In fear, the stimulus excites the *same* drive state (as in anger) but different cue functions, which determine flight." Hebb adds: "In some circumstances fear readily turns to anger, suggesting that they are closely related. The victim of a practical joke who is first frightened, then becomes angry when he perceives the situation, is an example; a comparable case is that of a chimpanzee who, not hearing the experimenter approach, showed startle and fear on being touched, and then when she saw what had happened became angry" (262, p. 159). The arousal itself does not differ; the distinction between anger and fear in these cases seems to lie in different cue functions, i.e., in capacity to release different action patterns.

The views of Lindsley (374) in regard to general drive also include the role of ARAS in regulating arousal. He writes that motivation requires an activator and that it is the reticular formation which has been shown to have such a function. It is sensitive not only to all types of internal and external sensory stimulation but also to events originating in the cortex. Its excitation leads to changes in the electrical activity of the cortex, and such changes are often accompanied by changed posture and behavior.

Summary. The constructs of general drive and of specific drive components have been incorporated in various theories concerning man's activity. Though the theorists differ in the significance attached to these constructs, there is agreement on the necessity to account for the general arousal of man, as well as for the specificity of channels of energy release in the activity stream.

Within the Freudian model of man, general drive is assumed to be psychic energy ready for release into a variety of forms, either into the unlearned id impulses or into contact with cathected (learned) objects. Hull accepts general drive, but he does not deny specific drives, primary and learned. Drive stimuli in Hull's theory furnish specific cues in the evoking of different adaptive behaviors. Otherwise-neutral stimuli also may acquire general drive properties or be associated with specific drives. Tolman's purposive behaviorism has stressed specific drives derived from more general need drives. Drives within his theoretical system have at times changed their labels; the essential construct remains, however.

Murphy hypothesizes a general tissue tension and some specificity in drive.

The neurophysiologists have been concerned with isolating the areas in the neural regions which are possibly responsible (1) for specific drives and (2) for general arousal. The reticular activating system as a possible neural area involved in the variation in general arousal, including vigilance, was briefly considered in the text and treated in more detail in Insets 11 and 12.

Though the above theories are different in many ways, they all are attempts to account for (1) variations in the general energetic levels of organisms; and (2) variations in the appearance and vigor of specific activity patterns, as are illustrated by eating, investigating, withdrawal. The appearance of specifically channeled rather than diffuse release of energy is a problem of concern in various areas of psychology. We will consider in the next chapter the identification of specific drives, and later in Chapter 10, Selecting, will return to the problem of selective release of drive-correlated activities. We now consider some systematic observations which substantiate the inference of a varying general drive.

OBSERVATIONS SUPPORTING THE CONSTRUCT OF GENERAL DRIVE

Evidence supporting the concept of general drive has been obtained in various studies, some of which grew from and/or were supportive of the above drive theories.

Neurological Support for General Drive Construct

Neurophysiological studies substantiating the existence of a neural arousal center lend support to the construct of general drive. It has been found that excitation by collaterals from direct afferent neurons may spread into the reticular area or arousal area. The afferent excitation then is diffusely relayed into cortical areas, tuning up (alerting) the cortex in general. Fuster (213) found that direct neural stimulations of the reticular formation of monkeys while performing visual discrimination resulted in increased speed of reacting, improved discriminatory accuracy, and lowered thresholds of recognition. The inference is made that these alerting functions are set in motion by an increase in afferent input via the reticular formation, irrespective of the specific external source of excitation.

Displacement

General drive is supported by clinical and experimental observations emphasizing displacement phenomena, i.e., the tendency of organisms when blocked to release excitation into other than the original act. The displaceable attribute of general drive is illustrated in the activity stream of higher organisms who are blocked by physical or social barriers. Frustration, the emotional state which arises following continued interference, adds to the general drive level, as is indicated by the rise in general amount of activity following interference. There is observed, after blocking, an indiscriminate rise in the vigor of responses, an intensification of any ongoing act. The drive release may be in channels quite unrelated to the original source of the interference. Such *displacement* of drive observed with frustration has different manifestations. One manifestation is when a new stimulus is reacted to as if it were the absent one. A mother after losing her child may displace her love to other children.

Displacement may also be of any responses, including aggressive ones, to new stimuli. Miller (428) demonstrated that an animal frustrated in fighting by the absence of its fighting partner, will turn its aggressive responses upon other sources of stimuli. These new stimuli which evoke fighting may be similar to what the animal was originally fighting: e.g., rats who were frustrated in fighting other white rats attacked a small white doll which was present. There is thus indirect release of the blocked drive.

The significant role of similarity between the original stimulus and the one to which a response is displaced has been assumed by Miller. The difficulty, however, of determining what are "similar stimuli" challenges any simple interpretation of the diffuseness of drive as the resultant of stimulus generalization. Displacement, we suggest, is not solely generalization along a stimulus continuum. The new stimulus is not *necessarily* similar in some way to the old one. In fact, lack of "appropriateness" of the new stimulus is a good indication of diffusely released drive. For example, that which is called "scapegoating" in social interaction is the release of drive tension to an inappropriate stimulus. A minority group such as the Negroes is reacted to aggressively by a lower-economic white group. This is called displaced aggression, i.e., aggression by the "poor white" whose drive is displaced to the colored group from its original stimulus target, the wealthy strata of society. The poor white presumably stays keyed up under his economic frustrations from the landowners and may respond with a burst of energy release, often inappropriately, to any stimulation even including the colored race. His drive may be displaced upon an innocent source in an aggressive and destructive form. In other words, a scapegoat receives the force of the built-up and lingering excitations, since a direct expression against the original and "real" source of his frustrations is inhibited, the real sources presumably being the wealthier white group. Freudian theory and clinical and social observations both suggest that energy aroused in a *blocked* impulse may be displaced. Illustrative of the above is the significant increase in verbally expressed prejudice toward the Negro reported by adults after a relatively mild, experimentally induced frustration (failure on puzzles) (129).

Displacement of Blocked Drive to New Responses. Displacement may also refer to the evocation of a new response to the original stimulus when the organism is blocked in responding in his usual manner. Even subhuman subjects show this displacement phenomenon: When cranes are interrupted in fighting, or ducks in copulation, the birds begin to preen, a response not at all similar to the old one. Lorenz interprets these response changes by assuming that neural "energy" aroused in the original blocked act is displaced to another act.

There are limitations on *overt* displacement. Fear, for example, when blocked in direct expressions, is most probably released in a withdrawal response, not in approach. Inhibition and rising inner drive may appear rather than any overt response displacement of the general drive. The blocked drive then is better described as increasing tension (see Chapter 12).

Hormones and Nonspecific Drive

Certain secretions in the body have effects upon other tissues or organs in the body. The secretions from those specialized cells called the endocrine (ductless) glands are chemical substances called hormones. They pass into the blood stream and are carried to all parts of the body. Hormones from these endocrine glands are known to be supportive of general arousal. An indirect proof of this statement is that activity in general is dramatically reduced by the removal of one of the following: pituitary, adrenal, possibly thyroid and parathyroids, and gonadal glands. See Figure 7-3.

Increased Stimulation, External in Origin, May Change the Level of General Drive

The construct of general drive is confirmed by the evidence that external stimuli may add to overall excitation. Stimulus dynamism, as suggested by Hull (300), refers to the contribution to central drive excitation by external-in-origin stimuli. An increase in number as well as in intensity (objective) of the sources of afferent excitation increases arousal.

Brown (88) found that hungry rats pulled harder against an attached weight when they were going to food associated with a brightly illuminated screen. Cattell (116) found quicker reaction time to light as it was increased in intensity. Kessen (329) studied stimulus dynamism with rats trained to avoid an electric shock by turning a wheel to a light signal preceding shock. This light was varied in intensity by using six light bulbs (from 6 to 300 watt) as conditioned stimuli. The intensity of the conditioned stimulus was significantly related to the number of avoid-

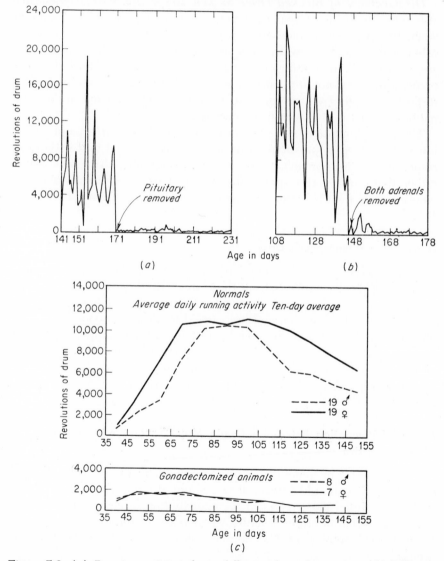

Figure 7-3. (a) Running activity of rats following hypophysectomy; (b) following adrenalectomy; (c) Top: Activity of nineteen normal males and nineteen normal female rats; Bottom: Ten-day averages for eight castrated males and seven spayed females. Richter (509, 510)

ance responses, speed of responses, and wheel turns per unit time. Dramatic evidence of the diffuseness of excitation is also present when external stimuli do not distract from but rather increase the vigor of any already ongoing action. For example, the excitation after the stimulating pattern called a loud noise[6] may be followed by a rise in energy released into any act. Morgan (441) early established that the *force* of a finger movement in a task somewhat similar to typewriting increased under bells, buzzers, and phonograph records. The general drive level, as inferred from increased energy expenditure in the pressure of fingers, was uniformly *raised* by these noises. When noise continued, however, adaptation occurred to the external stimuli and the drive excitation decreased. Further evidence that there is, at first, increased drive level under external stimuli is the finding of greater oxygen consumption under noise (661).

Muscular tension rises under noise and then subsides with the apparent adaptation to the stimulus. Davis (145) found that muscle action potentials increased in the presence of noise. On the fifth day of testing, however, the tension of the muscles was virtually unaffected when noise was presented. Davis also reported a rise in emotionality as indicated by a decrease in skin resistance at the onset of a five-minute noise period (143). Before the end of the period the overall drive level gradually returned to normal—to approximately the value of a control group sitting quietly for ten minutes. Further studies have substantiated these findings (146, 147).

Subhuman subjects may be raised in their performance level of a learned act by noise. Morey (436) studied the swimming and running speed of rats when subjected to a loud sound—an auto horn placed 5 feet above the starting box. Among his results were: (1) A sound which is simultaneous with swimming facilitated a rat's behavior; (2) both speed and error elimination were facilitated; (3) the response did not change *if* the noise was not concomitant with movement, i.e., a sound stimulation preceding swimming did not seem to have any facilitative effect on subsequent movement. An interesting observation was that if the water was maintained at body temperature, the swimming rat might prick up his ears and even turn his head when the sound started. Pavlov's "investigatory reflex"?

Physiological Costs of Noise. Further evidence, reviewed by Plutchnik (489), that noise is a general energizer comes from studies of increased physiological activity as the auditory intensity increases. There is a rise

---

[6] What is noise? The acoustical engineer, according to Berrien (64), defines noise as an unwanted sound. Paradoxically, psychologists seem to lean toward a definition couched in more physical terms. High frequencies, intermittency (irregularity), and high decibel level are characteristic of auditory stimuli called noise.

in blood pressure following a loud, unexpected sound (381) and a decrease in peristaltic contractions and flow of gastric juices following two 10-minute periods of noise (565). Also, subjects exposed to intermittent noise at 105 decibels while taking an intelligence test show a significant increase in pulse rate during the noise condition (127). And when auditory stimuli near the pain threshold in intensity are presented at one-minute intervals, a complex pattern of responses occurs, which includes increases in palmar-sweating, EMG, and respiration amplitude, decreases in pulse and finger volume and respiration rate, and an increase and then a decrease in pulse rate (148). Men exposed to ten-minute periods of jet engine noise at 120 to 150 decibels and to a 1,300 cycle per second siren reported heating of the skin, vibration in parts of the body, muscular weakness, and excessive fatigue, all of which disappeared within a week after the cessation of tests (477). In another study using even more intense auditory input, it was found that flies, mosquitoes, roaches, and caterpillars were killed within minutes, while human subjects developed skin burns, slight dizziness, and unusual fatigue (6). In contrast to these two reports, there was no measurable effect of jet engine noise at about 120 decibels on a wide variety of physiological measures of one-hour periods of exposure for ten days and two-hour periods for five days (193). "The difference in results between this last study and the preceding two may be due to the lower intensity noise and to the difference in the distribution of energy in the different frequency ranges" (489, p. 143). The extreme effects of strong auditory stimuli indicate nonoptimal drive or tension (see Chapter 12).

Industrial Production and Noise. If noise adds to general drive, then men working under it should be more productive, though perhaps at a physiological cost. Berrien (64) in an early review points up the contradictory results of noise on industrial production. Presumably, if noise is "helpful" in its contribution to general drive, it should step up production. This is not always found. Excess drive (tension), however, may be present. Many factors affect industrial production, and in most cases they cannot be controlled sufficiently in the real industrial situation to determine clearly what noise does to the work output of men.

There seems to be no doubt that noise affects the vital processes even though there are reports of quick adaptation (414). Adaptation, however, may be accompanied by a lowering of the basic energy-level of the individuals "suffering" from the noise, i.e., workers may be "worn out" more quickly under intermittent noise even though the adaptation appears to be complete. Long-term studies need to be performed. The nature of the noise, the age of the men, the length of time they have worked, and other variables would probably be significant in determining the diffuseness of rising drive from noise and the consequent physiological cost. Time periods already studied are in days or weeks; hence, the fact that continuing systematic physiological effects have not consistently been found should not necessarily be accepted as proof that there are no changes. "Maybe," writes McCormick, "we just have not been bright enough to figure out how to measure some physiological costs. In everyday experiences people sometimes say that they 'feel' more tired when working under noisy conditions than under quiet conditions. Whether such 'feelings' have any foundation in physiological changes is not yet detected or whether such feelings are completely subjective and without any physiological basis is something that yet needs to be found out" (414, p. 199).

General Drive Level as Changed by Stimulation within a Social Field. The complex social field of man has its own contribution to central drive. Though it is unknown to what degree an interpersonal relation engenders stimulation peculiar to itself, it is noted that social interaction increases the general arousal of the individuals in interaction. The specific nature of the interpersonal interaction is a variable in this drive increase.

Social stimuli as sources of activation have also been observed among the lower animals. Fish swim more rapidly when together than when alone (5). Various observations indicate that there is a facilitative effect on the eating rate when others of the same species are present. James (310) points to social facilitation on the amount eaten by dog puppies. He adds that the position of dominance in the group affects this social facilitative effect. The more dominant the animal is, the *less* affected he is in eating rate by the presence of other puppies, provided competition is not involved.

Many of the unlearned or learned behaviors are not evoked except under the stimulating effect of the presence of other individuals. Obviously, in mating reactions the presence of the partner represents a facilitating stimulus. In the interpersonal relations among men, the complex social field has its particular drive contribution which varies as that field varies. Sociological observers have stressed the excitement engendered by the restless movements of a crowd before it turns to mob action. Heider (266) in *Psychology of Interpersonal Relations* writes of stimulations as "request from others," "command from others," "reaction to the lot of others." These suggest interrelationships in a variety of social fields between social stimuli and personality. For example, a man might show most clearly the dynamic trait of aggression when in actual contact with stimulation from others of his own personality structure.

Combined Specific Drives

General drive construct is supported by the observations that the energetic level of performance is affected by varying combinations of specific drives. Hull in 1943 cited studies which indicate that satiation with food did not entirely eliminate a learned performance acquired under a need drive for food, thus suggesting the presence of "irrelevant" drive sources supporting the performance. Other studies followed, demonstrating (1) that performance level under one of the specific drives may be changed when another of the specific drives is added; or (2) that if the original drive source is removed, an irrelevant drive component may itself evoke the habit learned under the absent original drive source. Some of these studies are presented below.

1. Combined specific drives may increase the level of performance. Hull (242) found a significant increase in spontaneous activity with the addition of greater environmental stimulation and a further increase in activity with the addition of a food-deprived state. The subjects (male rats) in revolving drums were first under the influence of a minimum of external stimulation, i.e., in darkness, with a uniform temperature and with little auditory stimulation save the sound of the moving wheels. Moreover, the animals were neither hungry nor thirsty. In Figure 7-4, the line marked "normal stimulation" represents the activity-level under these motivational conditions. The activity-level rose when the external stimulation was increased (flashing lights and "considerable increase in auditory stimulation"). Following these changes in the external field, the animals were also deprived of food, and there was a further additive effect on the drive level.

Summational effects of combined drives on general movement were also found in a test of hunger with the exploratory tendency. Dashiell (137) in 1925 placed hungry rats in the open-alley maze and found the

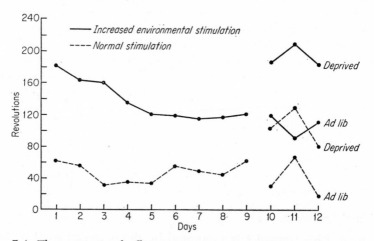

Figure 7-4. The summational effect on rise in running activity following, first, increased external stimulation and, second, food deprivation. Hall (242)

amount of their activity greater than that of food-sated animals. Some studies have supported the finding that the combination of novelty of stimulation and bodily need drives increases the degree of activity (183). Extreme hunger also enhanced the degree of the startle response to an auditory stimulus (422). Not all evidence is positive (433, and 243, pp. 84–87).

2. Habits learned under one specific drive may be evoked under other drives after removal of the original drive component. Webb (642), Brandauer (80), and later Webb and Goodman (643) demonstrated the contribution of irrelevant drives to the preventing of experimental extinction of a habit. In one study (642) the animals under food deprivation were trained for four days and then were satiated with food but deprived of water for either zero, three, twelve, or twenty-two hours. There was increased resistance to extinction according to the amount of the extra or irrelevant drive from water deprivation. Brandauer (80) confirmed these findings. Because there is difficulty in eliminating a food need drive when the animals' thirst is increased, the above studies were questioned as evidence that a habit learned under one of the drives may appear in the absence of this original drive source. In other words, the increasing performance of the habit when the irrelevant specific drive from thirst was added was said to be supported by the still-present hunger. Webb and Goodman's study (643), however, reaffirmed the observations that a habit learned under one specific drive may later be evoked by irrelevant drives in the absence of the original one. They trained hungry rats to push one of two bars in order to obtain food. After training trials, the animals were food satiated and returned to the box for a five-minute test session in which there was recorded the frequency of pushing the bar originally followed by food. Then the apparatus was flooded with half an inch of water. Under this irrelevant drive antecedent, the frequency of performance of the habit learned under a food need was significantly increased. Support for the generality of drive was thus affirmed. Siegal (562) reports confirmation of Webb and Goodman's results.

SOME PROBLEMS

The Plus-and-minus Effects of Combined Drives

There is not always a simple additive effect upon arousal by combining specific drives. The onset of fear modifies behavioral expression of pain in complex ways. Hunger and thirst, if simultaneously present, are known to interact, though this interaction is not yet precisely charted. In Webb and Goodman's study reported above, preliminary observations indicated that irrelevant drives from electric shock or noise brought forth crouching responses or highly disturbed behavior but not the habit learned under food need. The particular channel of motor expression observed in combinations of drives is a function of the degree of dominance of one drive component, as well as of the strength of the correlated motor patterns.

Anxiety counteracted the performance learned under hunger. Estes and Skinner (178) found that a tone, after being associated with painful shock, depressed an established rate of pressing a bar under food need. It can be inferred that a learned anxiety drive is evoked by the tone after association with painful shock and that this anxiety depresses overt responses to obtain food.

Anxiety may be more diffuse in its effects than other specific drives, at times increasing the vigor of any ongoing performance and again, as in the study above, depressing a specific habit. Ullman (628) reports that the emotionality (anxiety) generated under continuous irritations (electric shock) raised the general activity-level, and in this study the rise was expressed in greater consummatory activity (eating). Ullman suggested that eating thus became a general anxiety-reducing mechanism. Woodworth (660), however, questions whether anxiety can ever support a positive functioning of the organism, such as an approach to food.

The interaction among drive components and their correlated reaction tendencies may result in an alternation of the dominance of drives. One may be dominant over another, only to be shelved by the first. The particular level of central excitation, the immediate amount of nonspecific drive, may be increased; other drives, when combined, subtract from the general excitation level, nullifying the energizing effects of one or several other drives.[7]

This is an incomplete development of the concept of general drive. Drive rise, for example, may be excessive and result in general disruptions of organismic functioning. If noise while you work makes you angry, then the drive rise is detrimental, though a continuation of the distraction may finally bring complete adaptation to some, or to all, subjects.

The discussion above also has stressed those drive sources which raise general drive. Less consideration was given to variables correlated with a lowering of arousal. In Inset 13 there are listed the general signs of a decrease in reactivity when an individual is depressed.

---

[7] More than one drive component may be influential in determining the degree of arousal, but only one is in control (at any moment in time) of the selecting (editing) mechanisms, *unless* there is a breakdown in the usual integration normally characteristic of the activity stream.

INSET 13. DEPRESSION*

An extensive list of behavior indices presumed to be associated with depression follows. The prevalence of these indices in representative samples of depressed persons will define depression empirically. Factor-analytic methods may reveal subgroups within depression. It would be a fallacy to select items purely on the basis of frequency of occurrence, since some items may be compelling and crucial despite their infrequent occurrence and may be pathognomonic or point to atypical forms of depression. Some of the behavior indices related to depression have been studied by various investigators; others are merely mentioned in the clinical literature. Conclusive evidence does not exist for any behavior item, since at best, it is only represented by isolated studies (675).

1. General Physiologic Functions
   a. Food intake: decreased
   b. Fluid intake: decreased
   c. Gastrointestinal tonus and motility: low
   d. Gastric acidity: low
   e. Elimination: constipated
   f. Absorption of food: decreased
   g. Total body weight: loss
   h. Appetite: loss
   i. Sleep pattern: disturbed
   j. Gonadal functions: diminished or suspended
   k. Epinephrine secretion: increased
2. Neuromuscular Factors
   a. Skeletal muscle motility: slow and inhibited
   b. Muscle tonus: high
   c. Reflexes: hyperactive
3. Perceptual-Motor Functions
   a. Reaction time: slowed
   b. Decision time: slowed
   c. Input-output: limited reactivity
   d. Stimulus reproduction: slow and accurate
   e. Pain threshold: high
   f. Tolerance for pain: high
   g. Tolerance for fatigue: high
   h. Perceptual acuity: precise
4. Environmental Contact
   a. Interaction with others: minimal
   b. Range of interests: narrow
   c. Expectation from others: rejection, devaluation, punishment
   d. Reaction to overtures from others: withdrawal

* Adapted from Herbert Zimmer and James Foy, Depression: Definition and determinants. In D. Willner (ed.), *Decisions, Values, and Groups.* New York: Pergamon Press, 1960, pp. 305–307.

    e. Expression of feelings: minimal
    f. Evaluation of reality: accurate
    g. Involvement with environment: detached
    h. Sexual interest: diminished
    i. Suggestibility: low
5. Value Orientation
    a. *Weltanschauung:* pessimistic
    b. Self-evaluation: depreciating
    c. Perceived status: low
    d. Self-preservation: neglect or self-destruction
    e. Responsibility: frightened by
6. Subjective Feelings
    a. Range: boredom to despair

The "Ground" on Which a Stimulus Occurs

Increase in stimulation raises general drive, but it must be remembered that the degree of contrast between stimulus and background is a variable in stimulus dynamism. The contextual interpretation of stimulus dynamism is supported by the following study. Animals responding to a white card on a black background in a jumping apparatus exhibited significantly shorter latencies than a similar group responding to a black card on the black background. When a white background was employed, the subjects responded significantly more rapidly to a black stimulus card (79). The ground on which a stimulation arises may be more complex than is implied in the above. The meaning of a stimulus determines in part its general drive contribution. A whisper in time of danger may arouse a tremendous outburst of energy compared with a situation when the background is different—in other words, when there is little or no danger.

There are outbursts of energy release, violent actions which have no relation to any measure that observers can obtain of the amount of immediate sensory excitation. The reverse is also observed: a large amount of receptor excitation, as indicated by the area of receptor stimulated *or* by the physical characteristics of the stimulating source, is not necessarily related to the activity-level change which follows. There is, as Dashiell (138) and later Brown (89) pointed out, a *marked disproportionality between the energy content of a stimulus and the energy expended in the response.* The faint shadow in a graveyard may lead to exceedingly vigorous action in a superstitious person. Such behavioral relations have many physical analogies: e.g., "the disproportionality between the minute energy required to press the trigger of a gun and the tremendous energy released thereby from the cartridge" (89, p. 3). And as stated, the reverse can be found: A tremendous amount of energy may be released by the objective stimulating agent and little energy released by the organism. The unexpected explosion usually releases a large amount of energy by the organism, but if expected, the loud sound may have little or no activating effect.

The lack of any simple relationship between input and output is also illustrated if there is a removal of the original stimulating source but the removal is *not* followed by a cessation of the correlated response. If the energy output has been stepped up by the application of a large amount of electric shock, the removal of the shock does not necessarily lower the rate of organismic energy expenditure—not immediately, at least. It can be even observed that the rate of output may be stepped up. Why? Is there continuation of the high drive level? Possibly. At least the individual seems to stay keyed up and may then suddenly respond, perhaps inappropriately, with a burst of energy release to the slightest stimulation.

Another illustration of the lack of relationship between input and output: Assume that some otherwise neutral and slight stimulus precedes shock or is concomitant with it. This slight objective stimulus may later evoke the vigorous reactions that are usually correlated with painful stimuli. The neutral stimulus, it is said, has acquired drive properties. It is more arousing than before the associative learning. This learning was demonstrated on pp. 28–30 of a report by Miller (427).

Pathological Conditions in Relation to Loss of Stimulus Contact

Sensory deprivation is used in prisons (solitary) as punishment. And experimental studies of the effects of removing stimulation have shown a loss in vigilance, abnormalities like hallucinations, and in general a dislike of the situation. Men prefer neither too much nor too little external stimuli. What constitutes an optimal amount varies according to unknown conditions. The hermit avoids stimuli, at least those of a social origin. The extrovert seeks the stimuli of the social field.

Another of the pathological conditions to which man is subject is the individual's loss of sensory contact. In such an abnormal condition, the usual transformation of potential stimuli to actual excitations does not occur. The patient is no longer in contact. The loss of contact may be a persistent narrowing upon only one small part of the potential field. Such would be the pathological condition of centering upon organic sensations. It should be noted, however, that a narrow sensory field may simply represent an attempt to solve a problem. The concentration of the scientist on one narrow aspect of potential stimuli is not pathological.

General Drive and Muscular Contractions[8]

Muscular contractions have a two-way relation to central drive. As general drives go up, muscular excitation increases, and in turn there is a feedback via the proprioceptive tracts to the arousal neural centers, including the reticular area. There is thus an increase in the general drive level. Support for this generalization is accumulating. It is observed, for example, that emotionality and excitation in skeletal muscles are related. "In general, with increased emotion we are more tense muscularly, but, also, with increased muscular tension we are more emotional" (650, p. 372).

Vigilance and Stimulation

A man on watch is aided in his vigilance by the amount of sensory input. (See Chapters 5 and 11.) Stimulation contributes to general vigilance, but with repetition any one pattern of stimulation rapidly declines in arousal value. A change in stimulation, however, realerts the observer. Evidence that novel stimuli are arousal sources is indicated by the observation that there is greater GSR with the first presentations of a stimulus. Also, long intervals between stimulus presentations sustain this arousal characteristic of a stimulus, presumably because of the little-understood process of adaptation, which cannot reduce novelty as quickly as when stimuli are presented close together in time. In the sleeping cat a series of unfamiliar sounds (A-B-C) produces arousal, i.e., wakes up the cat. With an increasing number of repetitions the arousal decreases; now the cat neither wakes nor shows any effect of slight arousal on the EEG. (The effect of stimulation on the EEG records is illustrated in Figure 5-1.) If the stimulus pattern is changed (C-B-A), "the cat again wakes up, and the EEG shows the full arousal picture. When an animal, therefore, looks at a fully familiar object or scene, the arousal effects must be small, and if no need-associated stimuli are present, the probability of response is low. But if a strange object is introduced, or if familiar objects act in an unfamiliar way, producing arousal at the moment when the animal perceives the new element in the situation, the probability of response is high" (262, p. 174). Selective vigilance is also illustrated by the observation that the elephant may ignore all the stimuli from his herd but immediately is alerted by the presence of a human. Apparently the readiness for even a familiar stimulus may

[8] There is no single satisfactory technique for the measurement of drive. The objective method of recording action potentials from muscles is often inadequate because no one muscle group reflects general drive. Combined activation measures— ratings, pressure exerted on stylus, as well as GSR and records of action potentials— should be used if experimentally possible.

not be "lost" if its onset is associated with fear. Hediger (265) implies that the captive sleeping elephants are immediately aroused by slight stimuli from humans because of a degree of fear. At least, they sleep through many other changes in the external field, such as those arising from movements of their own species.

CONCLUDING STATEMENTS

What has the above added to our understanding of motivation? We have been concerned in greater detail than in Chapter 5 with the arousal variations of individuals. The constructs of general drive and of specific drives were advanced. The first aids in interpreting the *diffuseness* of activation of the organism which sometimes can be observed, the second in understanding any *continued control in the specificity of the channels of energy release.*

Several theoretical positions, reviewed above in regard to the arousal variations of organisms, incorporate these constructs within their own models of man. The theorists hold different positions in regard to how nonspecific drive with specific components functions. Nor do they agree in regard to the origin of specific drives, though some imply that the first condition of the neonate—at the higher organismic level—is nondifferentiated drive. Some theorists also imply that the general drive is based on bodily irritations from need conditions. This assumption was questioned.

The construct of general drive is supported by various lines of evidence. Neurophysiological findings have tentatively isolated a general arousal center, the reticular area.

The displacement phenomenon is also support for the diffuseness of general drive excitation. If blocked in the release of drive into some usual channel of expression, an individual may show displacement to some new stimulus. Another child may receive the love of a mother who has lost her own child. Or an individual prevented from responding in an aggressive manner may displace his aggression upon an innocent source. This stimulus (a scapegoat) may receive the full force of the blocked drive. Since interference is often followed by frustration, not only the original drive but the drive increase from this frustration may be released in attacks upon a scapegoat. The diffuseness of general drive is also shown by substitute responses. When blocked in an approach to a goal, an individual may exhibit substitute responses which do not attain the goal but apparently serve as a drive release.

Further support for the construct of general drive is provided by evidence of stimulus dynamism. It is observed that a general drive contribution to any ongoing act may arise from external-in-origin stimuli.

We noted above, for example, that noise may "feed" its excitation into already ongoing acts. Social stimuli, as well as other specific origins of excitation, add to or in some cases subtract from the overall excitation level. The ground on which a stimulus arises is also a significant variable in determining its drive contribution.

Combined specific drives may increase the vigor of performance. They may increase diffuse activity. Also, a habit learned under one drive component may later be evoked by another of the specific drives in the absence of the original one. However, there is not observed a simple additive effect upon general drive level when the number of specific drive components is increased.

One of the problems in interpreting nonspecific drive is the plus-and-minus energizing effects observed from various combined drive components. Other problems which need answers include the disproportionality between the stimulus input and the energy expended in responses. There are, moreover, pathological conditions which arise when stimulations are reduced in amount or when the individual loses contact with the external field. There are in addition problems in understanding variations in vigilance, which rises with increased general drive.

When general drive increases beyond an optimal degree, the resulting tension condition is nonfacilitative. (This point is developed in Chapter 12.) Studies in the next chapter support the energizing and deenergizing functions of the inferred specific drives.

CHAPTER 8

FLUCTUATIONS IN ACTIVATION:

SPECIFIC COMPONENTS IN DRIVE

A man is usually centrally influenced by a variety of excitation sources. He may be concomitantly thirsty, sexually primed, and irritated by a cut thumb or by sore muscles exercised too strenuously the preceding day. He may be anxious about the outcome of some particular plan that he has in mind, perhaps depressed by the anticipation of a decrease in prestige or by a threat of money loss. And there are possibly worries about his children and anxiety about his mother mixed with a recurring elation whenever he remembers the promising smile of his blonde stenographer. And there may be within his external environment many energizing sources of stimulations: noises and flashing lights to which he may find difficulty in adapting. And there may be deenergizing extrinsic agents acting upon him. The temperature of the room may have risen so that he cannot proceed at his usual pace. Fatigue may be increasing; the day dies, and a need for sleep arises.

Yet there may also be challenging problems on his desk. New questions are posed by callers in his office, and he wants to solve the problems, to work until he finds the answers. He is curious. Let us also assume he has a learned tendency to achieve, which an unsolved problem sets into action.

And there are possibly recurring memories, some bringing an affective arousal. He remembers a quarrel with his wife, and there is an expectation of a renewal when he goes home; if more fortunate, he remembers only the fun of the weekend with his family and plans another trip.

In the previous chapter the evidence reviewed supported the use of the construct of general drive. This evidence did not negate specific drives.

143

In fact, it suggested that at intervals there are differential central excitation patterns, i.e., drive components within the general drive flux. General drive, as previously indicated, is in a constant state of change, in part the resultant of variations over time of specific and overlapping drives. In other words, specific changes in arousal can be traced to antecedents for fears, pains, status striving, loves, hungers, ego protection, and other drives. But these do not equally affect the drive level. Nor are they equal in the frequency of their appearance. Most investigations, in fact, have centered on those antecedent conditions the onset of which are known to be correlated with increased excitation. Among these, the primary need drives based on deficits and on painful stimuli have had most intensive study. This chapter will be concerned with these and other antecedents with respect to their correlations with specific activation changes.

Functions of Specific Drives

1. Specific components in general drive affect the overall energetic level of the organism. This was considered in the preceding chapter.

2. Drives are also correlated with an increase or decrease of energy released into specific activity patterns. Drives are thus specific energizers or deenergizers.

3. Drives have "cue" functions. In the review of drive theories in the previous chapter one function of drives was noted—the cue or sensitization function. This function is accounted for in different ways according to the particular theorist. Drive stimuli in the Hullian theory are said to cue off associated responses. Morgan writes of "selective valves." Hebb emphasizes the cue function of drives as well as their general drive effect. Drives, we shall see, are variables at choice points. They structure the perceptual field and affect other cognitive mediating activities.

4. Drives are one of the variables which sustain goal directions (Chapter 9).

The second of the above-noted functions of specific drives will be emphasized in this chapter.

On What Basis Are Specific Drives Inferred?

What criteria justifies the inference of specific drives, i.e., of specificity within the general-drive flux? For example, when can we say of others, or of ourselves, that there is anger rather than fear? Or curiosity rather than boredom or anxiety? One sign of the onset of one of the drives is the rise and/or fall in the vigor of a specific performance. Hunger may be inferred by an appearance of increased eating or a decline in hunger by a decrease in food-related responses. Similarly, thirst is identified by the specific behavior of drinking. These behavioral changes can be used as clues to such need drives whether the eating is by knife and fork or by chopsticks, whether drinking is lapping from an open stream or sipping from a silver goblet. Note that a degree of specificity of response patterning is not a sufficient criterion. Rather, there must be signs of a change in *vigor* of specific performances in order to infer the onset of one of the drives.

The above criterion is difficult to apply. There is no rigidity in the behavioral forms of expression of any of the drives, except perhaps in compulsive acts. Variability must be expected: e.g., a child may not eat when, according to hours of food deficit, he should be dominated by a hunger need drive. Even the absence of any behavioral sign of hunger is no safe criterion that there is no hunger. Similarly, the absence of running away does not indicate the lack of fear either in the child or man. Withdrawal is not a certain sign that fear is a dominant component of drive. *Men may withdraw, without fear,* from a place or person *judged* dangerous. Some specificity is, however, observed in correlations between "usual" antecedents for drives and identifiable behaviors.[1] But the question remains open of distinguishing the contribution to these correlations of unlearned and learned organizations from the contribution of the specific drives.

More than behavioral clues aid in the identification of specific drives. Specific physiological activities may be correlated with behavioral clues, e.g., to a limited degree, emotions can be identified by the nature of the physiological changes for which the autonomic nervous system is in part responsible. An example is that antecedent conditions such as noxious stimulations or learned signals of oncoming danger are correlated with fear signs. The activity changes identifying fear include fairly specific behaviors of escape and withdrawal and the physiological changes described on pp. 155–156.

Finally, there are the reported changes in experiences associated with the onset of components of drives. When a man reports he is afraid, is this not a valid criterion of the onset of the fear drive component? Self-reports are suspect but are assumed to be valid as clues to how the man himself observes his energizers and deenergizers. Drives sometimes can also be identified by projective tests, as is illustrated on pp. 151–152.

DRIVES BASED ON EXTEROCEPTIVE STIMULATIONS

Some stimulations external in origin are more imperious than others. Not only do they affect general drive, but they may have dominance over the activity stream. The stimulations which are dominant may be star-

---

[1] The usual antecedents for specific drives are identified in part in the following pages.

tling, unusual, or novel; they may be visually vivid; they may be irritating, noxious, or painful. The excitation pattern forces its way into central dominance. Then it may be the basis for increased release of energy into fairly specific activities.

Novel Stimulation as an Origin of Specific Drives

Novel stimuli arouse an organism, and there follow changes in the specificity of channels of energy released. Evidence is presented in Chapter 4 that after the introduction of novelty into the external field, there is an increase in arousal, with the specific behavior being approach and investigation. The novelty of stimulations may maintain performance at a sufficient level to permit learning (see pp. 39–42).

Noxious Stimulation

Significant as arousal sources are noxious stimulation and painful irritation. They are both general and specific energizers.

As antecedents in raising general drive, noxious stimuli are correlated with diffuse release of energy. As specific antecedents for a component in drive, they are correlated with withdrawal. As stated above, it is possible to withdraw in many ways. Man, for example, may withdraw in social interaction by not communicating, by simply moving away, or by more subtle ways of escape from an irritating person or persons. That there are many ways of withdrawal does not deny that withdrawal exists.

Other stimuli, though they do not arouse pain receptors, may produce bodily irritation, described as extreme cold, extreme heat, cold-wetness, or extreme brightness. These and other noxious stimulations are followed by a rise in general drive and at times act as antecedents for specific drives.

Noise is an antecedent for one of the specific drives. Noise also affects general drive. As it increases in irritation, it may be an antecedent for one of the specific drives with sustained correlated withdrawal from the origin of the noise. It is both a general energizer and a specific origin for withdrawal.

Aversion to Bright Lights or to Continued Darkness as Evidence of a Drive Component. When the antecedent condition of a bright light arouses signs of negative orientation and sustained withdrawal movements, a drive component may be inferred. That such may be strong enough to sustain performance until learning occurs was demonstrated with rats in a multiple-choice situation. The organism was activated by a brightly lighted place and ceased movement in darkness (195). Light, however, is not inevitably avoided. That an increase in luminosity will increase the rate of responses (bar pressing) was established by Barnes and Kish (38). Mice had access to two bars, one of which, when pressed, provided an increase in illumination. The subjects pressed this bar more frequently than the other. They thus increased contact with light rather than avoiding it.

The apparent contradiction that both "light-on" and "light-off" are responded to positively may be the result of differences in the intensity of the light. If an extremely bright light is presented, aversion would arise and sustain any performance which leads to its removal. If an animal is in darkness, however, the onset of a mild light might be rewarding, since nonnoxious changes in a homogeneous stimulus field are usually acceptable. Both the species of the subjects as well as the ground on which a change in luminance occurs would be significant variables in determining the onset of behavioral avoidance following a change in luminance.

Contact Stimulation in the Tactile Domain

The tendency of the young of mammals to cling to soft surfaces, as studied by Harlow with monkeys, is another identified origin of positive orientation, movement toward, and continued contact with stimulation of a specific domain. In a study of monkeys clinging to "mother substitute objects" (252), "cloth mothers" were found to be superior to "wire mothers" in evoking continued contact. (See Figure 8-1.) Dog pups also prefer cloth mothers to wire mother substitutes (304). The feeding place, *if* associated with the substitute mother, is an added supportive factor in the release of continued contact with soft surfaces.

Some early reports by Watson and Morgan (638) suggest another stimulus domain which is allied to increased physical contact between children and parents and later between sexual partners. The excitation of the erotogenic zones such as the sex organs is followed in the human male infant by stretching, spreading of fingers and toes, cooing, extension of the arms, and perhaps erection of the penis, and in general, with older children and adults, by movements which increase or continue the stimulation. Harlow (249) more recently has shown how early contacts of real mothers and infant monkeys are essential for normal development of later sexual behavior as well as later maternal, and possibly paternal, responses. These affectional responses are delayed or completely absent in the adult monkeys whose early years are in social isolation.

EMOTIONS AS SPECIFIC ENERGIZERS AND DEENERGIZERS[2]

Emotionality ranges from high arousal to deep depression. General drive is thus affected. Distinctive emotional patterns, however, also occur within the general drive flux. We are at this point concerned with such

---

[2] Emotions when extreme are disorganizing of other ongoing activities. However, even when extreme they continue as drive components, in other words as motivational determinants, since they affect activation level. See (361, 641, 665) for a discussion of emotions, disorganizing or directing.

Figure 8-1. Illustration of influence of contact stimulation in the tactile domain. Young monkeys prefer substitute cloth mothers. The feeding place is also a factor in any preferred contact. Harlow (249)

specificity in emotionality. Within general drive, emotionality seems to be a concomitant stream of excitation or at least a "tributary," but it is at times marked by emerging specific patterns of affective excitation. The identification of emotional patterns has, however, been a troublesome problem for psychologists.

Identification

The problem of identifying specific patterns of affective variations of men and women is one of the earliest problems which a child must solve.[3] "Is Mom really angry or can I get away with it?" And as the child

[3] A similar problem exists for the parents in regard to the child's affective variations. Maturation, it is suggested by Bridges (82), permits differentiation of specific emotions from general excitement. Learning adds its influence in setting up specific action patterns.

develops, he must determine in his relations with his own peers what are their "real" emotions. He learns, though sometimes with difficulty, to identify sorrow in others and to speak kindly to them; to identify hatred and to adjust accordingly; to distinguish between fear and anger; to know when he is boring in a social field and when he is pleasing; and to discriminate the false from the real signs of pleasure in his company. The Greeks bearing gifts were suspect in the ancient days. The reality of their feelings had to be determined by careful watch. And today the problem remains of identification of the emotions and feelings of others as well as of ourselves.

Philosophers and psychologists have speculated concerning the attributes of what can be reported as fears, elations, joys, sorrows, and delights. And the poets have drawn on their own experiences and sought to share them with others. Can such affective central events be identified? An attempt is made below to illustrate the problems of description of the elusive central changes reported as feelings and emotions.

Dimensions of Emotions. If various dimensions (attributes) of *any* affective condition could be isolated, then it should be possible to place any specific affect at some point within a manifold. Let us assume that an emotion of elation is being scored in one of the dimensions—in intensity, for example. If high in intensity, would elation also be high in physiological involvement? Assume introspection indicates that the elation should be placed toward the pleasant end of a pleasant-unpleasant continuum. What relation would this score have on a depression-excitement dimension? A possible additional dimension would be libidinal excitement, ranging from slight reactivity, as under mild tactual stimulation, to an increase in excitement similar to that observed in stimulation of the erogenous zones. Where would an elation most probably be placed on the libidinal continuum, if such a continuum exists? Perhaps slightly above the neutral point.

Then there is a possible continuum of the attribute of anxiety, though not, perhaps, independent of pleasant-unpleasant attribute. Could all affective variations be said to have a degree of anxiety? Could it be reasonably said that when in love, an elated man is slightly anxious, or has a degree of anxiety? When a man is angry, is there also some anxiety, though probably less than in a fear state? Is it possible to find anxiety in disappointment? In depression? In joy? Or would it be more reasonable to assume that anxiety is an independent emotion? How would one describe anxiety?

That any one emotion may be a complex of interacting affects is better supported by the following study than by the above speculations. Schlosberg (539) had college students rate pictures of facial expression of emotions, using two dimensions: (1) pleasant-unpleasant and (2) acceptance-rejection. Probably the use of other dimensions would have improved the results, but even with these two he was able to obtain from the combined ratings for each facial expression scores which closely predicted the pictured emotions as independently judged. Correlations as high as .96 were obtained between scores, *using the combined two dimensions* and *direct judgments* of the emotions expressed. Schlosberg (540) in addition has presented a first approximation to a three-dimensional model. There is the activation continuum on the ordinate, and the other two dimensions are pleasantness-unpleasantness and acceptance-rejection.

Clues

What are the clues by which we mold our behavior according to the affects (feelings and emotions) of our friends and our enemies? And what are the clues by which a man identifies his own emotions? And what clues of emotional involvement can be, or have been, used by the clinician in attempting to aid the men and women who have sought for direction in their emotional difficulties.[4]

Verbal Clues. The validity of feelings a man *verbally* reports has long been questioned. Even before Freud and his emphasis on ambivalent attitudes (often below awareness) there was a recognition that whether it was love or hate a man felt could not be easily identified, even by the man himself. For example, the courts of law have been interested in whether a man killed when he was insane with rage *or* when he coldly planned the murder *or* when he was fearful at the moment of the killing. Yet the man's verbal report is not greatly trusted. It is his actions previous to the crime—whether they showed systematic planning (even if crudely attempted)—that permit more valid inferences regarding his "guilt," with cold anger being considered more reprehensible than fear.

Priests have also asked questions concerning the emotions which were present when a man moved into some immoral act and have assumed that they could obtain a valid report, since, as with clinicians, fear of *hostile* judgments was removed. The reported feelings after the sin—the repentance and the sorrows—were, however, of more interest, since in them lay the aid to saving the man's soul.

Physiological Involvement in Emotions. Emotions are defined in one physiological text as "activity and reactivity of the tissues and organs in-

---

[4] No attempt will be made herein to review all which is at present known concerning the sources of identification of emotions and feelings. The studies of projection of affect can be found in (28, 134). The physiological involvements are reviewed in various sources (22, 505, 650). Behavioral changes, including facial expressions and gestures, are described in (317, 318, 661); results of introspective accounts of affects are treated by Titchener (49, 611) and in clinical cases by others (17, 519, 520).

nervated by the autonomic nervous system" (650, p. 343). The writers of this definition state that an emotion may, though not necessarily, involve skeletal muscular response and mental activity. Within the framework of this physiological definition, verbal reports of such states as anger or pleasure cannot alone be proof of the affective states. Without the presence of altered visceral action, to say we are "happy," or we "hated" to lose the football game, or we "love" our dog, is merely to express attitudes and is not by the above definition of an emotion considered acceptable. Wenger et al. write:

> That we all are aware of and experience emotion is unquestioned. That we perceive external stimuli as potential satisfiers or annoyers and react to them emotionally is obvious. That we perceive certain visceral events (such as a stomach cramp or a fast-beating heart) and report them as "feelings" is also clear. That we vaguely perceive certain other visceral changes and report them as feelings of happiness, anger, disgust, embarrassment, or depression is our contention. But when one uses such words to report a change in "feeling" *in the absence* of real change in visceral functions, then we should have to say that no change in emotion is represented, no perception or feeling of change, and, therefore, that the reaction is ideational in nature. (650, p. 354)

Whatever the reaction of the reader to such a stringent physiological criterion for the acceptance of feelings and emotions, there is no doubt of the significance of physiological changes as clues to affective changes, even though evidence for the specificity of physiological patterns for affects has been difficult to obtain.

Behavioral Clues. A specific overt behavior may not be reliably linked with the onset of an emotion. This point has been stressed above. Civilized man, who accepts the social value of courage, does not run away from many feared objects. Most men in combat are in fear, even in terror, but do not run from the danger. Their social values of being brave have been incorporated into their self-concepts; they do not run under fire, but their emotional involvement is probably as great as or greater than that of those who run. Behavioral clues to emotions will become more useful as studies are increased concerning the typical emotion-inducing situations and the usual response patterns observed in different cultures.

Clues to the Presence of Emotions from Autistic Material. Projective reports as an avenue to inner activities called "emotional" have increasingly been studied and in many cases found to be valid. Only one study among many is presented below.

Fear increases the imagery of threats and related feared events. Soldiers in four conditions (three of them fear inducing and one a control condition) were asked to write imaginary stories concerning pictures in response to leading questions (634). The stories were written twice. The double testing permitted a comparison of results within the fear-inducing and control conditions. This fantasy material was scored for fear-related imagery. The general criteria for identifying a fear-related story were:

Somewhere in the story an external condition poses a threat to the physical welfare of a person(s). Evidence of threat can be provided by the appearance of one or more of the following kinds of imagery:

1. A direct statement of fear
2. Negative affect surrounding an external situation, such as tenseness
3. Statement of need to avoid the situation
4. Instrumental activity directed at avoiding a harmful situation, such as attempting to escape

If the imaged external situation posed a threat which did not clearly involve potential physical harm, an appearance of a statement of fear or negative affect was enough to justify scoring the story as having fear imagery. An example of this would be: "There is a storm coming up, and the mother and children are afraid." The storm mentioned by itself does not clearly involve potential physical harm, but in view of the statement of fear, the story would have been scored as a clue to the presence of the specific fear drive (634, p. 148).

The fear-inducing conditions under which stories were written by soldiers were the first three below:

1. In camps approximately ten hours before an atomic explosion. The men had participated in a rehearsal of the maneuver preceding the bomb test.

2. In trenches 4,000 yards from the point of the atomic detonation. These records were obtained immediately after the explosion.

3. Ten hours following the explosion when the soldiers were at a desert camp.

4. The neutral or control conditions were army posts many miles distant. These soldiers had not participated in the bomb maneuvers in any way.

Results of this study show that fear affected the amount and kind of imagery. *There were more imaginary events related to threat of physical harm in the fear-inducing conditions than when stories were obtained independently of any fear of an atomic explosion.*

Situational Clues to Affects. Emotions are situationally bound. Certain antecedents in the external physical or social field are observed as forerunners of emotional changes. Classifications have been attempted of the stimuli and/or of the situations in which different emotions may be expected to arise.

Fear. Watson and Morgan (638) early suggested that *fear* in infants was correlated with stimulation arising from loss of support, painful stimuli, or loud noise. Though the claim that the observable *fear pattern* of the infant could be identified was questioned (559), the suggestion that fear is evoked by certain stimuli without learning has continued to be influential. Miller (430) writes that fear is an innate response to painful stimuli.[5] He also cites various observations which would suggest that a fear is innately aroused by more than painful stimulation. Sudden and intense stimulation through any sense modality may produce what appears to be fear, as Jersild (317) and Cruickshank (135) showed in children and young animals. There are different innate fear stimuli (sign stimuli) in subhuman animals (608). Also, certain stimuli that do not spontaneously arouse fear may have a latent tendency to elicit it, with the result that (1) the subject will learn to fear these stimuli much more quickly than others, and (2) if he is already mildly afraid, these can intensify fear. In other words, fear may be high in the innate hierarchy of effects of some stimuli without the fear being dominant.

Relative frequency of fear in response to different situations varies with age (319). Children at ages one or two were observed by their parents to be more frequently fearful after a noise or in an unfamiliar situation than at ages four to six. Imaginary creatures plus darkness as fear inducing increased from early years to ages four to six. When older children are asked to list their worries (fears?), they report more culturally influenced fears.

Various lists of worries or fears of children have been made. Typical are those reported by Pintner and Lev (488) for fifth- and sixth-grade children. Boys and girls worry most about family and school items (including failing tests). Next in order come worries about personal adequacy, social adequacy, economic problems, and health problems. The socioeconomic status was of relatively little concern to the children, although there were considerable variations in socioeconomic level in the sample.

The situations in which arise the emotions of love, pity, jealousy, envy, and hate are linked closely to social interaction. The acts of others are perceived as in some way related to the perceiver. In his interaction with others his affects may range from extreme love to hate. And the feelings of success, failure, shame, pride, guilt, and remorse seem dependent on situations where there is some self-involvement and self-comparison with standards of some kind.

[5] Peripheral behaviorists like Miller describe fear as a response. The response is said to set up specific stimulus patterns which in turn act as one of the specific drives. The assumption herein is that emotions are central affective states. Response-produced afferent excitation patterns would be included as antecedents for setting up and maintaining emotions as central drive components.

Table 3. Fear-arousing Situations

Situation	Total frequency	Percentage frequency
1. Inferiority and loss of prestige.......	143	30.8
2. Illness and physical danger..........	80	17.2
3. School work.......................	187	40.2
4. Family relationships..............	28	6.0
5. Financial difficulties..............	13	2.8
6. Abstract problems.................	14	3.0

Source: A. Anastasi, N. Cohen, and D. Spatz, A study of fear and anger in college students through the controlled diary method. *J. genet. Psychol.*, 1948, 73, 243–249.

Situations arousing fear have been listed by college students who kept records for one week. School work represented the modal fear-inducing situation. As indicated in Table 3, other high-ranking origins of fear are the expectation of inferiority, loss of prestige, and illness and physical danger to the self and others.

Anger-inducing Situations. There is less diversity in the situations arousing anger than in those arousing fear, as reported by college men and women. The thwarting of self-assertion in one study accounts for 86 per cent of anger experiences, in which women react to persons more than men do (421). In a University of Florida study in 1960 (644), the same trend appeared, with women being more angered by men than men are by women. It was also noted that men are more bothered by mechanical failure than women. In the study of Barnard college women, anger also centers around thwarted plans (15). See Table 4.

What Are the Superior Clues to Identification of Emotions? The affect-initiating situations, if identifiable, can be linked to different activity

Table 4. Anger-arousing Situations

Situation	Total frequency	Percentage frequency
1. Inferiority and loss of prestige.......	125	20.9
2. Thwarted plans...................	311	52.0
3. School work.......................	76	12.7
4. Family relationships..............	59	9.9
5. Abstract problems.................	27	4.5

Source: A. Anastasi, N. Cohen, and D. Spatz, A study of fear and anger in college students through the controlled diary method. *J. genet. Psychol.*, 1948, 73, 243–249.

patterns described as physiological and behavioral, including verbal, changes. In other words, clues to affects are found in (1) the identified situations; (2) reported experiences; (3) the known degree and pattern of physiological involvement; (4) behavioral signs, including facial expressions and other responses; and (5) projections, including imagery.

FEAR AND ANGER AS SPECIFIC ENERGIZERS

Some observations of adult men in combat indicate that the fear of the possible loss of life, or of some part of the body, often stimulates a well-defined physiological pattern of reactivity, with some overt motor involvement. Men in combat fear the loss of an arm, a leg, eyes, face, or even of life itself. Or their fear may be that they will not be brave. The learned expectancies of what they have been told may happen, or what they have themselves observed, arouse a physiological pattern of reactivity correlated with behavior changes. Riflemen overseas who had recently experienced combat were asked to check a list in the order of frequency of certain bodily changes. A later scalogram analysis of the soldiers' replies showed that the order of nine of the reported reactions could be arranged as the following:

Less frequent but most severe	1. Urinating in pants
	2. Losing control of bowels
	3. Vomiting
	4. Feeling weak or faint
	5. Feeling stiff
	6. Feeling sick at stomach
	7. Shaking or trembling all over
	8. Sinking feeling in stomach
Most frequent but least severe	9. Violent pounding of heart[6]

Demonstrations with Nonhuman Subjects of the Activating Effect of Learned Fear. Demonstrations with animal subjects of the activating effects of learned fear were reported in Chapter 3. The reader will recall that the subjects, in an experiment by Miller, received in a white box painful electric shocks. When the shock was later removed, it was inferred from the animal's behavior that he had a learned drive component of fear; he continued to move away from the stimuli associated with previously received painful stimulation. In another study (92) the energizing role of learned fear was demonstrated: The vigor of the startle response of animals under a conditioned fear was found to be greater to a

---

[6] One item, "cold sweat," could not be fitted into the scale though it was checked. In this scalogram if a man reported the seventh item, "shaking and trembling all over," he also reported the eighth and ninth. If he checked the third, "vomiting," he then usually checked all others below on the scale: 4, 5, 6, 7, 8, 9 (From 588).

loud, sharp sound than that of control animals. Experimental and control animals were first matched on their magnitude of startle response to the sound of a toy pistol. The measure of startle was the depression of a platform of a small weighing scale from its normal position. (The animals were confined to a box with a grid fastened to the top of this converted stabilimeter.) On each of four days *following* the initial tests, the experimental animals received ten trials, seven of which were conditioning trials. The conditioned stimuli, a combination of light and buzzer, were presented for five seconds, with an electric shock being given for the last two seconds of this period. During the three-second waiting period, it was assumed that anticipatory learned fear would occur, reaching the greatest intensity at about the time the shock was normally applied. Then tests for the energizing role of the learned fear were made by *introducing the loud sound at the same time that the shock was usually given.* With the experimental animals, the vigor of their startle response increased as compared with control animals. The controls received the same number of light-buzzer stimulations and the same number of shocks but not in such a time order *that anticipatory conditioned fear could have developed.*

The above demonstration of an increase in the vigor of the startle response to a loud noise is evidence of the energizing effect of conditioned fear. Since the increase in vigor was obtained the first time that the loud, sharp sound of the toy pistol replaced the shock, the experimenters concluded that the marked increase in strength of the startle response was not due to a learned modification of the startle tendency but rather to a learned fear.

By the use of goads to action, learned fear has long been used to arouse men. The whipped slave who stopped working was aroused to action simply by the crack of the whip. The boy of the present age may mow the yard or perform other duties, though the crack of a whip is not the usual stimulus to arouse his fear. The stimuli arousing learned fear in children are few for some and apparently many for others. They vary from simple conditioned stimuli to more complex signals of possible harm. A child's drive may be affected in school by a learned fear, unverbalized yet real to him, aroused by threats that he will not pass his grade. There are other culturally imposed threats, as indicated in the lists above of children's fears.

Fear may change to anxiety, which ranges from reported slightly unpleasant feelings of uncertainty to a deep-lying, diffuse feeling of terror. Anxiety, in relation to arousal, seems to rise with the degree of involvement of the anxiety in the individual's self-organization. Anxiety as a specific tension state with motivational functions is further discussed in Chapter 13.

Anger, an Energizer

Expression of anger in the socialized human is much modified from primitive tooth-and-claw behavior. The social modification of anger in young college women is illustrated when they report their behavior under this emotion (215). A general rise in reactivity occurs, but there are also specific, culturally imposed anger responses. The most frequent bodily responses described by the college women were—as any careful observer of women might guess—verbal: "talking excitedly to others or making an angry exclamation"; "angry, sarcastic, sulky retort"; and "restless behavior of various kinds, pacing, tossing in bed, a shifting about in the chair, continuous singing, and that refuge of the offended maiden, refusing to speak or look at the offender." An unpleasant facial expression was described thirty times, and some change in breathing almost as frequently. A number of physiological disturbances were reported in the more violent experiences of anger: nausea, a hot feeling, and cold hands. Gates (215) writes in regard to women in the above study: "We might expect to find the impulse most frequently reported by the subjects to be a desire to perform those acts for which anger is supposed to be a preparation, i.e., to do physical injury to the offender; and this tendency is often described. More frequently appearing, however, is the learned impulse for which none of the internal response appears to be essential, i.e., to make a verbal retort, as to 'tell her what I thought about her,' to insult, and to scold." Meltzer (421) reported for both men and women the frequencies of various behaviors in anger situations. Percentage frequencies indicated in Table 5 show that men too have a tendency to

Table 5. Differences in Impulses Felt during Experience of Anger (In percentages)

Impulse	Women	Men	Men and women
To make verbal retort (tell her what I thought, etc.)	29.50	24.00	27.02
To do physical injury to offender (slap, kill, choke, push, etc.)....................................	12.74	20.66	16.51
To injure inanimate objects (tear up, bang, kick, etc.)	15.30	13.33	14.41
To cry, scream, swear, jump.....................	16.40	2.66	8.40
To give up efforts...............................	3.27	10.66	6.60
To run away, leave room........................	6.55	4.66	5.70
To "do what I wanted to".......................	1.09	0.00	0.60
To laugh..	0.00	0.00	0.30
To blame someone else..........................	2.18	0.66	1.50

Source: H. Meltzer, Students' adjustments in anger. *J. Soc. Psychol.*, 1933, 4, 285–309. (The most frequent reports taken from the lists presented by ninety-three college men and women.)

make a verbal retort, though not as frequently as women. Men tend rather to have the impulse to physical injury.

SURVIVAL NEED DRIVES

Present on any list of antecedents for specific drives are nonoptimal bodily conditions, tissue needs for survival substances as foods, water, oxygen. There are bodily needs for such acts as elimination, withdrawal from destructive agents, and, for the survival of the species, the reproductive act.

Why Has There Been an Emphasis on Tissue Needs as Origins of Specific Drives?

Bodily needs have long been of interest to philosophers, physiologists, and psychologists. Even before the physiologist Cannon (111) popularized the homeostatic principle, some attention was given to tissue deficiences as origins of a rise in activity. For example, Hobbes (288) in 1651 listed as basic tendencies hunger, thirst, sex, and fear arising from the perception of pain. Moreover, Hobbes had used Aristotle's *Rhetoric* (20), in which there appeared a similar list of tendencies that the orator must learn to appeal to in order to *move* an audience. It was, however, the evolutionary theory which led indirectly to an emphasis on tissue disturbances as movers of organisms. It was observed that survival, from simplest organisms to man, is dependent upon the structural "equipment" making possible either inherent and/or learned behaviors adaptive for reducing needs. Inevitably the phylogenetic comparisons increased an interest in the ways in which organisms learn to reduce their bodily needs, and thus psychology of learning and of motivation became entangled.

Tissue needs were and still are frequently advanced as basic motivational tendencies because their relief is so important to the survival of the organism. This survival significance of the reduction of bodily needs supports their claim for a high position in any hierarchy of energizing determinants. Maslow (404) in his attempted hierarchical list of significant moving determinants places the bodily survival needs first.

That tissue needs are strong determinants within the activity stream of men is easily illustrated by the many words of the English language concerning experiences. Men describe themselves as hungry, starved, ravenous. They speak of being fatigued, weary, tired, jaded, exhausted; they say that they are cold, chilled, frozen, or warm, flushed, hot; they have pain, they suffer, hurt, smart; they feel twinges, pinches, soreness. And they say that they are sleepy, drowsy, lethargic. They speak of being thirsty, dry; or stifled, suffocated, choked. And they know desire, itch, and lust, for there is the ever-present urge in the young healthy male (and female) for sexual libidinal release.

Bodily needs have also interested psychologists because they influence the cognitive world and hence the choices of men. That they may structure the cognitive field is illustrated in Chapter 11.

Another reason why tissue needs became so prominent, though it is a reason which does not support their significance for man, is the convenience of using them to control animal subjects, particularly organisms below the primates. The rat, for example, is usually more active when hungry. The hungry animal placed in a maze or similar training field is not so likely to remain motionless, go to sleep, or indulge in such acts as face washing and scratching. What we are saying is that the reason for inducing a bodily need in a subhuman subject and placing a reward in the field relevant to the need is that these serve as a means of communicating with such a subject. When a hungry animal responds and obtains food, so that there is a beginning of a relief of the bodily need, he is, as it were, "told" what he is to learn. He is to move through a path to a goal box, or jump where a specific sign is placed, or perform in that fashion which is followed by food. And he soon starts to behave *as if* he is learning what is defined by the need-reducing food.

Do Bodily Needs Move Civilized Men? To answer this question it is necessary to consider man (1) *as an individual,* and (2) *as a member of a group* of individuals who, in exchange for the products of work, obtain foods and other bodily essentials.

Long ago in the history of man—perhaps in the early Neolithic stage of development—he passed in his cultural and economic development from a condition characterized by pure food gathering to "one in which the accumulation of a social surplus made possible inter and intra-communal division of labor and the development of regular trade" (346, p. 208). And changes occurred in his motivation following this social reorientation. Today, as a cooperative member of a well-organized society, man contributes to its production by his work, and in turn he is provided with food (and other necessities for reducing his deficit needs). The social organization, of which today he almost inevitably becomes a part, prevents his individual survival needs from being the basis of his dominant drives. In other words, it appears that survival needs are not significant origins for moving individual men when there is a social organization whereby interchange of goods takes place on a fairly equal basis, and also where there are plenty of essentials. Bodily needs do not often, or not very long, trouble a healthy individual in modern society. Certainly man is not moved in daily work by hunger. How hard he works on the job is not determined by deficits of food, nor is his degree of energy expended in work based on the inciting effect of anticipated reduction of his *immediate* needs. In fact, the daily schedules of civilized men are so arranged that interruption to the day in order to reduce these needs will be minimal. Cultural schedules permit a regular reduction of most of the biological needs. By schedule—with a proper time to sleep, wash, eat, eliminate, exercise, make love—men are able to appease their bodily needs before they become extreme.

Are bodily needs no longer significant arousal origins for socialized men? A positive answer would imply too utopian a condition. True, a civilized man cannot be compared in his working and learning with a hungry rat running a maze for food. Man eats, then runs his maze. However, he may be activated by a *learned anticipation* that there might later be a time when, being hungry, he would need food. In other words, he does not have to be hungry to be stirred into activity; but he may be moved by an acquired anticipation of later hunger and later need for food.

Nor are the bodily needs absent in the lives of men. Though they may not often become extreme, they must be constantly anticipated. Though adult men in social organizations have learned to store and to distribute foods, they are at times hungry. Men protect themselves from excessive fatigue by the laws that they make, but they are far from being free from fatigue. And they have not conquered heat and cold, nor aging, nor disease with its pains, nor the pains and fear suffered in moving in this world of accidents, hurricanes, and tornadoes. Quickly do the bodily needs become strongly significant when there is a breakdown in the cooperative working of society. During disaster to a community—if it is prolonged—the bodily needs are the motivational determinants.

Demonstrations of Immediate Need Drives as Origins of Changes in Arousal

General Drive. Hunger and other need drives will step up the general activation of organisms. Though the well-established demonstrations of an increase in general drive have mostly used the rat and other subprimate mammals, there is evidence that human infants exhibit cycles in overall activity according to recurring need for food (306). Adult men are slightly restless under hunger (632) if not too long food-deprived.

Specific Need Drives. That children and men are more than restless under need drives is also observed. Specific responses to foods or learned "ways to food" appear. The energy release under hunger is specifically and appropriately channeled. That the evocation of the specific food- or specific water-related responses *may* be only dependent on internal cues is demonstrated in the following study (504). Rats were trained under alternating food and water deprivations to pull a lever one way when hungry and the other way to obtain an appropriate goal object. The to-be-responded-to stimulus, the lever, in the external field was the same from day to day, but the stimulating difference was in the internal environment. The hunger and thirst drives were the necessary differentiating central patterns to evoke an appropriate but different behavior on each day.

There are in addition many *specific food needs*. These qualitative needs follow deprivations of substances like protein and vitamins. The needs for specific food elements may arise with changes in food requirements due to maturation, aging, pregnancy, and lactation. Extremes of external environmental temperature and other stress conditions may create qualitative food needs. Structural insults to the body, such as removal of the pancreas, parathyroids, adrenals, or other organs, set up qualitative needs (74).

Even a wealthy group of men may suffer from specific food deficits. In the Orient in the old days, the rich family bought polished rice rather than eat the despised brown rice, and thus the wealthy suffered from specific food deficiencies.

Specific food needs are not as inevitably followed by a rise in activation as is deprivation from all foods. Animals observed under a need for some specific substance may show a rise in activity-level (73), or a decrease (633), or no change in the amount of activity.

That a qualitative food need will sustain a specific performance until learning occurs was demonstrated by Heron and Peake (272). Rats learned a black-white discrimination when they were deprived of protein, and they were rewarded by the reduction of this qualitative food need. Specific needs for food elements may sensitize the organism for what it needs. Its food selections are often appropriate. See p. 223.

Water Deficit. The systematic studies of the activity changes under conditions of water imbalance have usually been with subhuman mammals under water deprivation. An antecedent condition of water deficit produces a behavior pattern specific to this condition. With rats, the total intake of water in a given post-deprivation period is a negatively accelerated function of the length of deprivation time (584).

Adolph and his collaborators (2), using dogs as subjects, report that the normal drinking of these animals is proportional to their water loss measured in terms of per cent of body weight. "When no food is allowed during these tests, they take water at frequent intervals, in amounts proportional to the water they have lost. They do not, however, drink quite enough to make up their water losses completely unless they have access to food. If they eat as well as drink, they take amounts of water that are proportional to both the amount of solid food ingested and their previous water losses. With food and water ad libitum, therefore, perfect water balance is maintained over long periods of time" (2, p. 385).

Anoxia and Arousal. Regulatory responses, including a rise in activity-level, are usually evoked with the onset of need drives, but this is *not* true with respect to the need for oxygen. It is one of the most needed substances for the survival of organisms. Deficits, however, are infrequent, and there is not adequate built-in behavioral regulation. In other words, the anoxia state can increase in humans until death occurs, but few signs are present of increased activation. Increased arousal serves other drive states by moving the organism so that the probability of contact with the necessary deficit-reducing object or place is made. This adaptive energizing is low in cases of anoxia. However, *adaptive mechanisms* necessary to prevent death under anoxia are not entirely lacking. There are reports of irritability and fatigue, as well as noncritical states, though these do not inevitably lead to behavior relieving the anoxia. Of course, following any direct obstruction to respiration like a choking rope, there are behavior struggles to relieve the need for oxygen by freeing the respiratory mechanisms from interference. Also, the seconds of oxygen deprivation of rats before being placed in an underwater maze were positively related to an increase in running speed (84).

Nonoptimal Temperature as an Origin for Changes in Activation. As illustrated in Chapter 3, a cold environment is a nonhomeostatic condition for warm-blooded organisms. Observations of dog puppies of different breeds indicate more overt movements (and increased vocalization) on a cold and wet surface than in a warmer place. They relaxed or slept when the temperature was 108 to 110°. Fredericson et al. (199) suggest that the need for warmth is one of the basic variables determining social contact between parents and offspring. Whether one is justified in moving from dog puppies clinging together to the present-day emphasis on "togetherness" is doubtful. Such a suggested origin might raise doubts about the value of togetherness.

Specificity in Behaviors under Hormonal Changes. As reported in the preceding chapter, hormonal changes are correlated with variations in general drive. Should hormonal changes also be admitted into a list of antecedents for specific drives? For some motivational theorists, drive stimuli are assumed to be necessary for drives, and since hormonal changes influence through the bloodstream rather than via afferent tracts, these theorists question whether hormonal changes should be considered antecedents for specific drives. We assume that such changes are origins of specific components of drive so far as the excitation of neural areas also varies according to chemical differences in the bloodstream.

There is an observed correlation of variations in gonadal hormones and the frequency of sexually related responses. Administration of androgen to the male castrate increases specific sexual activity. Similarly, an increase in estrogen for the female castrate increases her sexual receptivity. However, the higher the organism on the phylogenetic scale, the less close is this association. With man, learning enters as a more significant variable in the specificity of his sexual responses (as well as for other primary drives), though *not as the sole determiner* of the degree of arousal. The sexual excitement, on a gonadal basis, remains as the main energizing variable in sex-related behaviors. Though there are a variety of learned behavioral methods of sex drive release, there is some identity in the behaviors, such as the final copulatory act.

Barriers to Expression of Sexual Drive in Man. The socialization of the human species increases the curbs on the release of sexual behavior, but even among the early primitive tribes, there was inevitably one potential barrier to complete sexual behavior: the refusal of a partner to cooperate. In the early history of the civilization of man, groups appeared in which the dominant male presented a barrier to the other males. His sexual rights came first. Subsequently, marriage customs (later laws) structured the male-female interaction, defining which females could be (or should be) sexual partners for which males. The rules (or laws) in regard to "correct" sexual drive expression were given strong "taboo" strength in the early history of developing cultures. In some societies violations of the sex codes were punished by death. Later they became "sins," and whether punished or not, the violations threatened the self of the violator. This inward moral censure was observed by Freud to be a source of serious conflict in both men and women. The reports of his patients suggested that early anxieties might start within the conflicts arising from the natural, but taboo, attraction of the boy to his mother. Freud gave less attention to the incest wishes of the girl for her father. The Freudian model, whether correct or not, recognizes the significant and obviously recurring conflict in civilized man arising from the fact that the sex drive is strictly regulated in its overt expressions.

Conflict is an antecedent for drive components. It sets up *frustration* and leads to *anxiety* and other tension states. The tension components in regard to sex arise not only from social censure of sexual behavior but from self-censure. The simplicity of these statements will not, it is hoped, conceal the complexity of the motivational and personality problems which center on sexual conflicts arising in social interaction.

DEENERGIZERS

There are a variety of antecedents correlated with decline in vigor of all activity. One significant deenergizer is muscular fatigue correlated with a decrease in activation. When fatigued, the individual may at first show a tendency to keep on being active, with a concomitant irritability. The child who has played too hard cannot relax and sleep, but the final quiescence is inevitable. Sleep is probably correlated with some kind of fatiguelike product.

Fatigue

Fatigue—a deenergizing drive condition—may at first depress only a small segment of the activity stream, though as fatigue increases, it is often widespread. It not only depresses the readiness to move an arm or other body part being used in a repeated response, but will finally spread sufficiently so that the individual's general drive is lowered, with a consequent depression in the readiness for arousal for any activity.

Fatigue is not a well-understood phenomenon. Or perhaps it should be said that it is not well understood because what is labeled fatigue is apparently a complex of several deenergizing conditions.

1. *Physiological fatigue.* With repeated responses, there is a loss in fuel and/or in oxygen. There is also an accumulation of waste products. These lead to cessation of specific muscular contractions, and as the tissue disturbances continue, there is a loss in general drive.

2. *Boredom* or *psychological fatigue* is reported by men. It apparently bears little or no relation to physiological fatigue. The same muscle system may be involved in a new nonboring task. A shift from drawing circles to drawing squares raises performance level. Even though the new task does not remove the muscular fatigue, task boredom is removed.

In order to remove psychological fatigue, or boredom, subjects set themselves subgoals in repetitive tasks. In a task of dropping a small block through a hole, retrieving the block, and dropping it again, boredom ceases temporarily when the subject tries to note how the block falls or what it sounds like. Karsten (327) reported ingenious attempts of subjects to introduce variety in simple but monotonous tasks. In drawing small vertical strokes with a pencil, the slant of the strokes might be varied. Boredom (psychological fatigue) is removed by variety, though physiological fatigue continues to accumulate as long as there are massed responses.

Fatigue, as noted in the industrial situation, includes more than one factor. There is evidence in physical changes of bodily dysfunctioning, and in some work situations there is boredom with a repetitious and/or nongoaled act. Probably contributing to indifference to work is the dislike of an unchanging stimulus field, as reported in Chapters 4 and 5.

The man who is working at a steady pace on a task that has a meaningful goal will experience less *psychological* fatigue than the same man when he is working much more slowly on a task which simply represents a meaningless repetition of motions. As the following observations by Whyte indicate, the worker who is making his quota on piecework generally experiences less fatigue than when holding back production on a job that does not offer quota attainment. On the face of it, this seems to be a paradoxical conclusion: The man works harder but is less tired. Man, however, is not naturally a passive animal who would do nothing if he were not stimulated toward activity through some sort of reward. Observations in industry indicate that man is naturally an active animal who is happier when he is doing something than when he is just standing around and doing nothing. "This does not mean, of course, that hard work just naturally has more appeal to employees than light work. It does suggest that complete idleness is not rewarding at all and that an unnaturally slow pace can be fatiguing" (654, p. 38).

Stimulus Satiation versus Reactive Inhibition

Two different interpretations—stimulus satiation versus reactive inhibition—have been advanced concerning the mechanism of cessation of specific responses after repetition.

Reactive inhibition is the hypothetical condition or negative drive state which is assumed by Hull to develop whenever any reaction is evoked in an organism and which has the innate capacity to produce a cessation of the activity which caused this negative state. Reactive inhibition is not independent of physiological fatigue, but it is not identical with the latter. Reactive inhibition is inevitable, accumulating with each response, though it can dissipate (disappear) quickly. Massed responses do not permit it to dissipate as do distributed responses, and hence there is quicker cessation of activity under massed responses.

Stimulus satiation is closely allied with boredom (and perhaps is another label for boredom). However, when an individual ceases responding to a stimulus, is it because he is sated with that stimulus or because there has developed an inhibitory response tendency? In a previous discussion (pp. 46–50) of why organisms tended to alternate between two paths (both of which lead to equal goals and both of which are equally long), an experiment by Montgomery (432) indicated that stimulus satiation was the factor significant in this alternation. When reversal of responses at a choice point could be traced either to avoidance of repeating a response pattern or to avoidance of the last-contacted stimulus, it was the latter (the avoidance of stimulus) which was found significant.

Though stimulus satiation may be significant in cessation of responses, it cannot account for all the relations observed between rate of responding and effort required. The greater the amount of effort required in a response, the slower is the rate of performance, not simply because of stimulus satiation but also because of response fatigue. In one study seventeen animals out of twenty pulling a 50-gram weight failed to meet a performance criterion in a standard time, while only one subject failed when the weight was 10 grams (19). Such findings, as well as many other observations, support the construct of response fatigue, i.e., when more muscular effort is required, a greater negative drive arises, and there is a consequent cessation of responses.

Blocking

When man is engaged in any continuous activity, there are observed fluctuations in alertness—rises and falls in readiness to respond. The more homogeneous the series of stimulus-response units, the more difficult it is to continue to be alert.

The temporary decrease of an individual's alertness has been called blocking. This blocking becomes more frequent during the work period. Blocking in color-naming responses in one study (217) was defined as a delay in a response when its latency was at least twice the median reaction time of responses occurring within the immediate minute. When so defined, there were almost 100 per cent more blocks per unit of time in the last five minutes than in the first five minutes of approximately an hour's work. This is characteristic of the effect of continuous, simply homogeneous, work.

There are two types of blocking in records obtained in this study: those associated with GSR (galvanic blocks) and those not associated with GSR. The first kind of block apparently resulted from momentarily shifted attention and reduced alertness. The subject is quite aware of type I blocking and is forced by the task pressure to reorient attention to the immediate stimulus (217, p. 27).

Type II blockings (faltering) are more automatic and spontaneous in their production. They occur quite frequently in the early period of mental work, but they also increase as the work period progresses. They seem to be automatic; the subject is unaware of their occurrence. The subject continues with the task without any altering of the effort required, as if the block were a normal variation. Exactly what these momentary, short, and frequent falterings represent is difficult to determine. They are similar to what has been called oscillations of attending, though the subject is not aware of the blocking. In such tasks as color naming, they may be due to brief failure of the receptor apparatus, to brief failure of the afferent system, or to variations in the recognitive mechanism (the selective mechanism). They may be due to competition among the response systems. It should be remembered that they increase with the work period; they may be outer signs of Hull's inferred accumulating reactive inhibition.

Loss of Set is Detrimental to Performance in a Learning Task

Decline in performance observed after rest in a learning task has been attributed to a loss of a readiness to learn due to dissipation of a postural set. Postural and attentive adjustments are acquired during warm-up practice and later facilitate performance. The loss of such a postural set brings a decrement in performance, and conversely, any condition which maintains or reinstates the muscular aspects of the set is beneficial to performance (12, 605).

Other Deenergizing Drives

Not only fatigue but also fear may be a deenergizer, at least of overt action. The "freezing" behavior of animals when alarmed suggests that behavioral *inactivity* is natural at times under fear. Fear may be concomitant with a rise in inner drive tension, though not inevitably with an increase in overt responses.

An increase in anxiety or fear-anxiety is at times correlated with a decrease in arousal, though the tension decline is more likely to be apparent than real. An inner tension rise without overt signs is reported for severe states of *combat anxiety*. The symptoms can resemble those of the condition of schizophrenia, in which, it is increasingly recognized, outer passivity may cover inner tension (231). The reports of chronic fear between air missions include "fatigue, a feeling of depression and a slowing down of movements and mental processes, restlessness, aggression, loss of appetite, trembling, being easily startled, not wanting to go on any more missions, insomnia, nightmares, interference with speech, making meaningless gestures, and maintaining peculiar postures" (430, p. 441).

Satiation with food may also lead to inactivity. However, when a food need drive is removed, some new determinant usually takes its place. Relaxation after cessation of an energizing specific drive component permits others to become dominant. Similarly, the attainment of one goal may be followed by the immediate rise of new goals and consequently by increased arousal. The cessation of activity is not general; it is specific to the responses which formerly led to the old goal.

LEARNED DRIVES

In the above discussion of the specific components of drive there was no systematic development of the role of learning in creating new drives. What moves an adult man and what leaves him "cold" are questions inadequately answered by the above review. Few observations have been successful in illuminating the role of learning in motivation, especially for the human species. Yet it is known to occur. Some of the representative theoretical positions are now briefly reviewed in regard to the unsolved problem of how socialization of a child leads to acquired drives.

Assumed Historical Link of Learned Drives to Primary (Unlearned) Components in Drive

Dashiell (138) suggested a historical link between learned drives and primary need drives, though without specifying in detail how this could occur. Freud had faced this problem even earlier in his assumption of cathexes, which referred metaphorically to energy charges (from the libido) with which the diverging activities of the growing child were presumably invested.

Tolman also historically links new drives to tissue needs. He assumes that specific drives arise out of biological needs. Tolman's views of motivation have undergone more revisions than other theorists', but there is a continuation from his earlier to later theorizing in regard to how he believes that biological needs are converted, during the development of the child, to greater and greater specificity of drives. Suggested in 1932 (614), and again developed in 1943 (617), Tolman assumes a conversion (derivation) of the "original energy from the basic biological drives

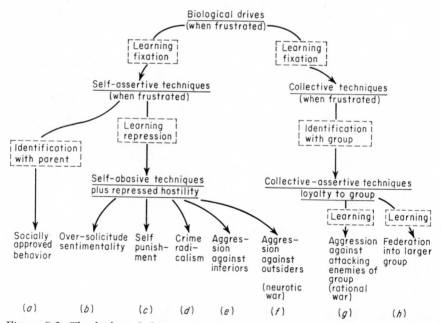

Figure 8-2. The biological drives, when frustrated, are said to lead either to self-assertive or to collective techniques. When the self-assertive techniques are themselves frustrated, their energy may be further converted, via identification with the parent, into socially approved behavior *or* into self-abasive techniques via instrumental learning accompanied by repression. On the right-hand side of the diagram is illustrated what is assumed to occur when the collective techniques are frustrated; on the left side, what is assumed when the self-assertive techniques are frustrated. Tolman (617)

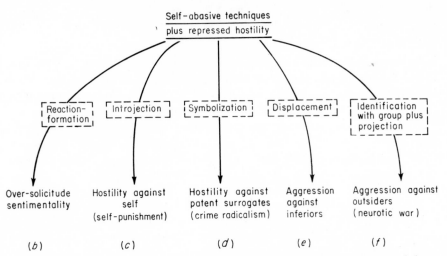

Figure 8-3. An enlargement of that area of Figure 8-2 projecting downward from self-abasement and the accompanying repressed hostility. It is the dynamism of *re-action formation* which is responsible for the channel whereby the repressed hostility is converted into (*b*), oversolicitude or sentimentality. And it is the dynamism of *introjection* which is responsible for the conversion channel leading to (*c*), self-punishment, etc. Tolman (617)

into drive mechanisms." He assumes a historical link between adult man's moving forces and the child's biological need drives. Tolman's con-versions are presented in detail in Figures 8-2 and 8-3. Note that what Tolman calls a specific drive mechanism, such as "hostility against self or self-punishment," is said to be derived via "introjection" following the blocking of "self-abasive techniques plus repressed hostility." Tolman further assumes that the latter arose from blocking of self-assertive tech-niques and originally from frustration of one of the biological drives. Figure 8-2 also indicates how Tolman appeals both to instrumental *learn-ing* and to *fixation* as suggested means by which *personal and social tech-niques are derived from biological drives after the latter are frustrated.*

He reasoned as follows: When a biological drive such as hunger is frustrated, the child first learns either (1) to be "self-assertive" by de-manding or soliciting food, or (2) to be "collective" by cooperating. Which the child would learn depends on which proves most helpful in removing the biological drive frustration. (Fixation of a successful tech-nique might occur so that it would appear even when it was no longer appropriate to the situation.) If the self-assertive or collective techniques are later frustrated, Tolman points to further modifications, as indicated in Figures 8-2 and 8-3.

If the child adopts the self-abasive techniques but they do not lead to satisfaction of the frustrated biological drives, then Tolman suggests that different Freudian mechanisms operate and may lead to *nonsocial* behavior of sentimentality, self-punishment, or crime. *Socially approved* behavior, however, is said by Tolman to arise if the child identifies with his parents. This is, of course, assuming that the parents' characters are above reproach; otherwise the identification might lead to nonsocial behavior. Thus we see that Tolman wrote of differentiation of drives by means of both instrumental learning and Freudian mechanisms.

Cathexis. In the 1949 version of his motivational system, Tolman (619) wrote of learnings including cathexis, an acquired relationship between drive and its object. Cathexes, both negative and positive, were very resistant to forgetting. Tolman writes:

> [By cathexes] I mean connections or attachments of specific *types* of final positive goal-objects, or of final negative "disturbance-object" to basic drives. (Note that I have coined the term final "disturbance-object" to cover what have sometimes been called negative goals.) I shall not argue the question as to how many, or what the basic drives may be. I shall assume, however, that you will agree that there are some. For example, none of you will dispute, I hope, the reality of hunger, thirst, sex or fright. By the learning of a cathexis I shall mean, then, the acquisition of a connection between a given variety of goal-object or disturbance-object—i.e., a given type of food, a given type of drink, a given type of sex-object or a given type of fear object—and the corresponding drive of hunger, thirst, sex or fright. That is, the learning of cathexes is the acquisition by the organism of positive dispositions *for* certain *types* of food, drink, sex-object, etc. or of negative dispositions *against* certain *types* of disturbance-object. (619, p. 144)

Canalization. To account for modifications during the lifetime of a man, Murphy (456) turns to a hypothetical mechanism called "canalization."[7] Many adult specific drives are assumed to develop by canalizations of an innate amorphous activity drive. Murphy's description suggests that canalization is roughly similar to Freud's "investment" or "cathexis."

> The process is one of progressive increase in the strength of the association between a specific object and a specific type of satisfaction, so that in subsequent behavior the satisfaction is sought by pursuing this particular object rather than some other object which might serve the drive just as well. The little child when hungry may be satisfied by milk, by strained carrots, by olive oil, by candle grease, by rice or by reindeer steak. But it is the function of the parents and of the broader culture to "teach" the child what are right or good ways of satisfying hunger, by presenting these objects repeatedly under conditions of hunger, so that a given food becomes

---

[7] How canalization occurs is not clearly delineated. There are no experiments demonstrating canalization as there are demonstrating conditioning. Young's (664, 669) experiments with choices of foods *may* be considered an exception.

the normal, right or appropriate food for the hungry individual. From such a point of view the child in one cultural area will come to accept reindeer steak as good food, and rice as a strange or alien stuff thrust into the mouth; the child in another area undergoes the reverse process. (456, pp. 611–612)

In other words, there are acquired tastes—types of satisfactions to be expected from certain objects which we see, touch, smell, or taste.

Conditioning. The learning theorist Hull and his followers, writing concerning the origins of learned drives, make use of principles established in conditioning experiments. Conditioning seemed, at first, an answer to how new drives might arise. Illustrated in Chapter 3 are some of the successful experimental demonstrations of the association of otherwise-neutral stimuli with escape responses aroused by painful stimuli. Fear, or fear-anxiety, are inferred as learned drive components on the basis of Miller's experiments (430) there reported.

Conditioning as the mechanism for accounting for the possible derivation of learned drives from more basic drives is at least subject to experimental testing. In contrast, the suggestions above of Freud, of Tolman, and of Murphy to account for the derivation of learned drives from earlier ones have not been subjected to definitive experimental proof or disproof.

It is not possible, however, to accept the conditioning of neutral stimuli to primary drives as responsible for all learned drives; hunger and similar need drives apparently cannot be conditioned as fear can. An organism does not "learn" hunger, though he acquires learned fear. Hunger-related *responses* are conditionable, such as moving into a restaurant when its sign is observed; but the evocation of these responses is rare or completely absent unless there is present some sensitizing primary hunger drive component, even if very weak.

Evaluation of the Significance of Learned Fear and/or Fear-anxiety as the Basic Drive Component. In the socialization of children does the learned drive of fear become the basis for *all* arousal?

Anxiety, or fear-anxiety, has been advanced as the origin of all learned drives: e.g., according to this assumption, the learned drive component called "love of mother" would be derived from fear of loss of mother. A child would respond, according to this view, to being separated from the mother with the drive of fear, and the child's reactions of approaching the mother would be rewarded by the relief attending her actual presence.

It is known that many stimuli can be conditioned to fear. Higher-order conditioning to a limited degree can also be formed with new neutral stimuli acquiring the property of inducing fear. Higher-order conditioning is, however, difficult to demonstrate beyond the second or third level.

The interpretation of anxiety as the basic arousal source may use the evidence of generalization along stimulus continuums. Early reported was the observation that the child conditioned to fear a furry animal also showed signs of fear when similar furry stimuli were in his external field (540).[8] After many fear-conditioning episodes in the life of a child, there might be a wide range of stimuli arousing fear or anxiety simply on the basis of stimulus generalization. This statement is also doubtful, both because of the impossibility of following all conditionings which may take place in the life of a child and because the use of stimulus generalization as a resultant of stimulus similarities is too often *ad hoc*. After the observation of generalization, *then* there is said to be similarity in the stimuli from which the generalization apparently arose.

Attempts to substantiate fear-anxiety as the basic component in any arousal have also implied that noxiousness is a necessary attribute of any activating source. It has been assumed that organisms are inert unless stirred into activity. This view has been discussed on pp. 118–119.

The acceptance of anxiety-tension as the basic arousal state, and its reduction as the basic reinforcer, will perhaps vary according to the degree of anxiety of the psychologist. Anxiety is a disturbing state, destructive and detrimental to normal development, a tension component usually correlated with disorganization in the activity stream. It seems absurd to assume that such a negative state is the basic source of arousal of men. See Chapter 13.

A Two-factor Theory of Learned Drives. McClelland et al. (413) advanced a modification of the anxiety-tension view as basic in the motivation of men. His two-factor theory of motivation stresses both the pleasure and the pain drives. He depends upon generalized conditioning save that in his theory the *early learning,* which is quite significant, is built upon acquisition of expectancies concerning whether stimulations will be followed by a change *to pleasure or to pain.* "Certain stimuli or situations involving discrepancies between expectation (adaptation level) and perception are sources of primary, unlearned affect, either positive or negative in nature. Cues which are paired with these affective states, changes in these affective states, and the conditions producing them become capable of redintegrating a state (A′) derived from the original affective situation (A), but not identical with it" (413, p. 28). An example is as follows: If a buzzer is associated with eating saccharine, the buzzer will attain the power to evoke (redintegrate) a state involving positive affective change. This state is appetite. And if the buzzer is associated with shock, it will acquire the power to redintegrate a negative

---

[8] Many studies (419) delineating conditions of generalization have followed but have not progressed sufficiently to substantiate the assumption that anxiety thus becomes a basic energizer.

affective state. The two redintegrated states are respectively *appetite* and *anxiety*.

Summary. The theories which assume that learned or social drives are *derived* from more primary ones include the views of S-R conditioning theorists; Tolman's attempt to set up a historical link by using drive divergences after interference of more basic drives; Freud's statement that basic libidinal energy is cathected to new objects; and Murphy's postulated canalization, a name for an unexplored possible mechanism for modification of early motivation of children. Experimenters in the field of conditioning are at present able to demonstrate learned fear in the laboratory, but no experiments show the steps in the acquisition of positive learned drives. The acquisition of goals is known, but much remains to be solved in regard to how such learnings occur. The next chapter briefly considers this learning problem. McClelland's two-factor theory demands more experimental support than as yet has been presented.

All the above theories are inadequate to explain how learned drives are historically linked to the primary need drives. Though conditioning gives a partial experimental answer, it is insufficient.

Taxonomy of Learned Drives without Attempting to Trace Their Origin

Perhaps drives arise without being linked historically to primary drives. Murray suggested in one of his writings (458) that man's motivational tendencies, such as the tendency to prevent a depreciation of self-respect, may be entirely learned and not derivatives of any other earlier tendencies. Murray's list (457) is based on inferences from general observations (and measurements) of the variety of behaviors of young adult males by a team of experts in the fields of clinical and experimental psychology. An adapted list of his psychological needs is presented in Table 6. Other catalogs of both primary and learned drives have also been attempted (388). Each cataloger views the problem in a slightly different manner.

Need-to-achieve. In Murray's list of social needs is *need-to-achieve,* one of the most studied of the culturally influenced dynamic tendencies (409, 411, 413). Man's social values strongly influence how sustained is a child's interest in achievement-oriented activities. What represents achievement may vary from group to group: e.g., achievement may be represented by collecting and shrinking the heads of enemies, by collecting wives, or by acquiring quite different symbols of success. Within the Western civilization, oriented toward valuing individual "progress" (onward and upward), there are even differences among subgroups in emphasis on achievement. The middle class, for example, stresses status striving more than other social classes (141, 119). When aroused, need-achievement as a latent dispositional tendency is assumed to change per-

Table 6. Murray's Tentative List of Psychological Needs

Need	*Brief definition*
Abasement	To submit passively to external force. To accept injury, blame, criticism, punishment. To become resigned to fate.
Achievement	To accomplish something difficult. To rival and surpass others.
Affiliation	To seek out and enjoy close and cooperative relationships with other people. To adhere and remain loyal to a friend.
Aggression	To overcome opposition forcefully. To attack, injure, or punish another.
Autonomy	To get free, shake off restraint, break out of confinement. To be independent and free to act according to impulse. To defy convention.
Counteraction	To master or make up for a failure by renewed striving. To overcome weaknesses. To maintain self-respect and pride on a high level.
Defendance	To defend the self against assault, criticism, and blame. To conceal or justify a misdeed, failure, or humiliation.
Deference	To admire and support a superior. To yield readily to the influence of others. To conform to custom.
Dominance	To control one's human environment. To influence or direct the behavior of others by suggestion, seduction, persuasion, or command.
Exhibition	To make an impression. To be seen and heard. To excite, entertain, shock, or entice others.
Harmavoidance	To avoid pain, physical injury, illness, and death.
Infavoidance	To avoid humiliation. To refrain from action because of fear of failure.
Nurturance	To give sympathy to and gratify the needs of weak and helpless persons. To feed, help, support, console, protect, nurse.
Order	To put things in order. To achieve cleanliness, arrangement, balance, neatness, and precision.
Play	To act for fun without further purpose. To like to laugh and make jokes. To seek enjoyable relaxation of stress.
Rejection	To separate oneself from a disliked object. To exclude, abandon, or remain indifferent to an inferior person.
Sentience	To seek and enjoy sensuous impressions.
Sex	To form and further an erotic relationship. To have sexual intercourse.
Succorance	To have one's needs gratified by the sympathetic aid of another person. To be nursed, supported, protected, loved, guided, forgiven, consoled.
Understanding	To ask or answer general questions. To be interested in theory. To speculate, formulate, analyze, generalize.

Source: Adapted from Murray (1938). David Krech and Richard S. Crutchfield, *Elements of Psychology.* New York: Knopf, 1958, p. 624.

174

formance according to the individual strength of this acquired disposition.

Does Need-achievement Function as an Energizing Drive Component?
Presumably a need-to-achieve (once initiated) would be correlated with
increased vigor of that performance which represents admired achievement. To achieve in school is generally admired in the Western culture.
To perform with greater vigor in school-learned acts, such as in working
arithmetic problems or in recalling words, should be observed in individuals scoring high on n achievement. Some studies by Lowell (383) support an apparent relation between n-achievement scores of individuals
and arousal measures in school tasks. As indicated in Figure 8-4, the

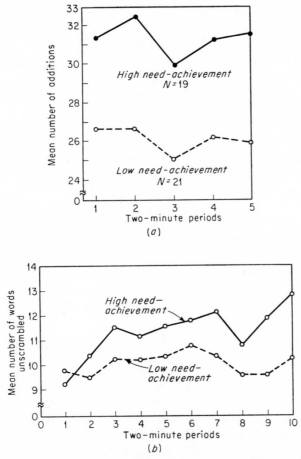

Figure 8-4. (*a*) Higher performance level is obtained in an addition task by individuals who have a high need-achievement score. (*b*) The higher need-achievement
subjects improve during the course of an anagram task, while the low need-achievement subjects do not. Lowell (383) as adapted by Brown (90)

number of addition problems performed and the number of words unscrambled were greater for subjects high in n achievement than for those with low scores. (The subjects were approximately equal in their capacity for the school task used.)

This correlation between need-achievement and arousal does not always appear. Parrish and Rethlingshafer (478) found that college students, all of high intelligence, divided into two groups of (1) school successes and (2) school failures, were *not* different in their scores on n achievement. McClelland (410) has questioned whether n achievement was aroused in this study, which employed individual administration of the test material. The negative results are attributed by McClelland to inadequate instigation of this latent tendency. However, college students, either successes or failures, are in a social climate in which scholastic n achievement is stressed. If it is a differential dynamic tendency of much importance, it should be ready, i.e., easily sensitized. And this should be true whether the administration of the achievement thematic test is in a group or alone. There is at present lacking any well-established method of *insuring* the instigation of n achievement.

Hypothetical Drive Components Supporting Social Interaction Patterns

Men are moved differently according to the social field; not only are the behavioral forms of individuals different within groups, as contrasted to being alone, but the degree of arousal may be affected. Examination of categorizations of social interaction patterns suggest that these patterns are supported by different drives, which are at different degrees of strength. An obvious example: The "mating pattern" is not based on the same drive component or components as is "giving signs of distress." "Aggressive or defensive fighting" would also demand a different component from other social patterns, as cited by Scott (544), in such categories as "imitating" and "investigating." The usual level of arousal (drive strength) would probably vary, being high in "attack" and low in other social patterns.

In order to understand drives significant in social interaction, we may, in contrast to the above approach, simply list assumed social drives and then study them individually. One frequently advanced drive component is gregariousness, the need to be with others. Understanding of the behaviors considered signs of gregariousness is slowly being attained by such studies as Harlow's analysis of the learned affectional patterns (248, 249, 252); e.g., infant for mother; child for child—peer for peer; heterosexual; maternal—and probably paternal. Harlow writes on the basis of observations of developing monkeys, some reared with surrogate objects as mothers (cloth mothers and wire mothers), that each of the above affectional patterns seems to progress through definable stages. He suggests, for example, four stages of the development of the neonate and infant monkey for attachment to the mother: (1) the reflex, (2) the attachment, (3) the security, and (4) the independence affectional stages.

In a different interpretation of the drives supporting social interaction patterns, Schutz (543) postulates for every individual three interpersonal needs: (1) inclusion, (2) control, and (3) affection. Inclusion is the need to establish and maintain a satisfactory relation to people with respect to interaction and association. Control is the need to establish and maintain a satisfactory relation to people with respect to control and power. Affection is the need to establish and maintain a satisfactory relation to others with respect to love and affection. To understand the breadth of meaning which these three needs carry for Schutz, the reader should consult *FIRO: a Three-dimensional Theory of Interpersonal Behavior* (543).

That the motivation of man's interpersonal behavior is subject to systematic observation is further illustrated in Inset 14.

INSET 14. SELF-ORIENTED NEEDS AS REVEALED IN DISCUSSION GROUPS*

An analysis of what might be considered symptomatic of self-oriented needs was made by a committee of psychologists at the University of Michigan (196). From data collected by means of Rorschachs, TATs, sentence completion, and intensive interviewing of fifteen undergraduates, the following description of needs was made. Since its immediate use was in the ratings of the self-oriented need expression of *individuals during group meetings*, the interpretations of the five general areas are from that point of view.

Dependency. (1) need for dependence on authority and (2) need for succorance. "A participant who demands rigid structuring of his group along the lines of parliamentary procedure when the occasion does not warrant such formalizing" is assumed to have a dependence on authority. A need for succorance is illustrated by such a statement as: "In regard to what Mr. X has just said, I feel it is very good because he is usually right about these things."

Status. (1) Status needs are exemplified by the individual who wants formal designations, the individual who makes bids to obtain a "title for title's sake," not because he wants primarily to serve the group. (2) An example of the need for status is a statement like, "I was a member of a coordinating committee once and we did some wonderful work in this field."

Dominance. (1) intellectual dominance and (2) dominance in social situations. Psychologists need no illustrations of the first. Social dominance in a group meeting is illustrated by an authoritative leader.

---

* Adapted from N. T. Fouriezos, M. L. Hutt, and H. Guetzkow, Measurement of self-oriented needs in discussion groups, *J. abnorm. soc. Psychol.*, 1950, 45, 682–690.

Aggression. (1) aggression against authority and (2) extrapunitiveness. Protests against any minor rules illustrates the first, and the latter in this particular approach refers to generalized aggression against any contributions to a group discussion by others.

Catharsis. Continual self-reference by a participant, particularly if emotionally aroused, is an example of expression of a need for catharsis in a group meeting.

Violation of Social Expectancies

Characteristic of a culture are common expectancies of how each individual should behave. As long as the individual remains a member of that group, there is pressure applied for him to behave according to the group's expectations. Moreover, such established social expectancies as mores, taboos, and fashions cannot be violated with impunity.

These expectancies are based on social rules which aid in defining the social expectancies and in stabilizing them. The presence of men in the same surroundings seems to set definite requirements for ordered relations between them. The first function of social rules is to establish paths of action and clear expectations. Social rules provide the necessary assurance that he who lives in a house today may also occupy it tomorrow and that the promise one has received yesterday will hold today. Rules "limit the area of the unknown and the unpredictable; they become the ground of stable orientation" (24, p. 350). They hold the individuals of a particular group or society in established and expected patterns of behavior. Any violations of these cultural expectancies, although quite slight, may irritate or even anger those around the violator.

When our cultural expectancies are not confirmed, we are irritated even as we are when a mechanical failure occurs. We expect the light to increase when we turn the switch on the lamp. A nonconfirmation of this expectancy is annoying. We expect children to behave (within reasonable limits) in certain ways. We are annoyed with them and their parents when our expectancies are violated even though we ourselves are not in any way harmed. There is a certain social pattern of behavior expected of a man or woman when together in public. (This expectancy is increasingly changing.) A soldier just returned from overseas was indulging in lovemaking with his wife in a public conveyance. Noting the censorious eye of the bus driver, the wife sat up and, straightening her hair, said, "I know that there is a law against unmarried people making love in public, but is there any law against married people?" "No law," said the public censor, "but the odds are against it."

Violations of social expectancies are apparently irritating in themselves even when no harm to an individual or to society seems to threaten. Why? Is the social censor envious? Does he feel frustrated because he has curbed his tendencies to violate the social rules? Is he more frustrated when he perceives someone who is getting away with an act which he has denied himself? Certainly the social censor, typified as the avid gossip, seems to be rearoused at any sign or imagined sign of violations of socially imposed codes. His irritations, his rise in drive tension, may be interpreted as resulting from frustration.

We turn now to the broad question of whether a performance, if well organized, must have some motivational support before it can occur. Further, must it have the original motivational support? The answer to the second question is no, but the answer to the first is more difficult to give.

FUNCTIONAL AUTONOMY OF BEHAVIOR UNITS

The question of whether an unlearned or learned behavior unit can ever function autonomously has been given a positive answer by Lorenz in regard to instinctive organizations and implied by Allport (8) in regard to some learned acts. What is meant by "functioning autonomously"? In Lorenz's view, as reported by Tinbergen (609), it refers to the appearance of an instinct in the absence of the intrinsic initiating external stimuli (the sign stimuli). The longer the time period from the last appearance of the instinct, the more probably would the instinct appear *in vacuo*, i.e., without the usual eliciting stimuli. Functioning autonomously, according to Allport (7, 8), refers to the appearance of a *learned* performance in the absence of the original motivation which sustained the performance when the learning occurred. Some new acquired system of motivation now sustains the performance. Allport assumes that when a unit of activity exhibits this functional autonomy, "some new function emerges as an independently structured unit from preceding functions." The activity of these new units does not depend upon the continuing evocation of the units from which they developed. The strength, the long duration, the apparent independence from the original drives that may characterize a behavior with this functional autonomy is indicated by his illustrations: "A workman feels compelled to do clean-cut jobs even though his security . . . no longer depends upon high standards," and the man who may have learned to value money when he needed it, later as a miser continues to "amass the useless horde" (8, p. 129). Some new motivational system sustains the collection of money.

Observations of the continuous activities of men and women reveal why the question of the autonomy of performance from any motivational source has continued to plague psychology. Though Heraclitus claimed that man never steps twice in the same river, observations of organisms from birth to death nevertheless indicate that there are recurring action patterns for which there seem to be no specific drive source nor any rewarding effects; even when there is nothing expected but unsatisfactory effects, man may be "caught" in the daily round of his usual and apparently nonsatisfactory habits. That such habits may however be supported by some unobservable learned drives and incentives is always possible. It is difficult to prove or disprove the hypothesis that habits may function autonomously of *any* motivational support (501). Allport (9), replying to the critics of his functional autonomy theory, pointed to the ego or self as a possible motivational support. Learned performances which appeared independently of their motivational origins (those present during learning) were, wrote Allport, never autonomous of the ego or self. In some way they served the self. In 1961 he continued to hold to this general position but only with respect to the higher level of the adult man's functioning (11, pp. 235–237).

The complexity of the meaning of the phrase "functional autonomy" is further illustrated in Inset 15.

INSET 15. RECURRING PERFORMANCE IN RELATION TO MOTIVATIONAL SUPPORT

In the variety of discussions of Allport's theory of functional autonomy, different questions have been asked. They are illustrative of the complexity of the hypothesis that the reappearance of well-established forms of behavior may become autonomous of the original or even of any motivational support.

1. Can a learned act become independent of the original eliciting situation? A habit of being polite in the home may transfer to the schoolroom (or the reverse may occur). The significant variables which determine when such transfer occurs and when it does not are being isolated in the psychology of learning.

2. Will a well-established performance continue to reappear independently of either internal or external stimuli, or of both? The intrinsic rhythms of activation, considered on pp. 64–66, suggest independence from what are traditionally called stimuli. Such recurring rises and falls in activation are not evidence, however, for stimulus independence of recurring specific forms of behavior, though the latter may be a real phenomenon.

3. Will a well-established act reappear without any general drive support? Since no organism is ever without some degree of excitation (nonspecific drive), this question cannot be answered, but it is observed that the probability of any reappearing act decreases as general drive declines.

4. Can a learned performance become autonomous of the *original* specific motivational support present during the learning? This is the question which Allport in 1937 answered positively (8) and again affirmed in 1961 (11). Allport, in regard to adult motivation, wrote in 1961 that an activity once extrinsic and instrumental may become intrinsic and impelling. An activity that once served a drive or some simple need "now serves itself,

or in a larger sense, serves the self-image (self-ideal) of the person (11, p. 229).

There are experimental demonstrations that a learned performance may appear in the same situation when the original specific drive component and reward are absent. For example, Elliott (173) reported that a maze learned under one of the drives and incentive would be performed with little change in effectiveness when the animals were put under another one of the drives and its appropriate reward.

Even the external field may be changed, but new drives and rewards can support the recurrence of a well-learned performance. Handwriting is well learned. It serves many drives in many situations, and is rewarded in many ways, including ways not present during learning.

5. A final question: Will a well-learned and specific form of behavior reappear independently of *any* motivational support? We consider this broad problem by asking other questions: (*a*) Will a habit appear independently of external energizing stimuli? (Possibly. See above.) (*b*) Will it appear independently of all specific components of drive? (If there is sufficient general drive to sensitize the performance, none of the specific drives are essential.) (*c*) Will a well-established activity unit continue to reappear independently of *any* rewarding effect? (Even a tentative answer cannot be attempted, since the mere evocation of an act may be intrinsically rewarding. Extrinsic rewards may be removed and even apparent punishing effects substituted, yet the specific behavior may continue to reappear. Is it "serving" the organism in some way? Because of the vagueness of the phrase "serving the organism," this question cannot be put to any definitive test.)

THE SELF

The Self: Its Functions

"What is this self inside us, this silent observer, severe and speechless critic, who can terrorize us and urge us on to futile activity and in the end, judge us still more severely for the error into which his own reproaches drove us?" (172)

Without attempting at this point to enter the maze of theories concerning the self, we simply state that various functions have been assigned to the hypothetical self. Among these are: (1) The knower, (2) the asserter, (3) the experiencer, (4) the organizer, (5) the pacifier, and (6) the social agent (382). Though each of these functions of the self may be involved in the dynamics of the individual, it is the asserting and pacifying selves which are of most interest in motivational psychology.

Later we are again concerned with the assertions advanced by personality theorists in regard to the self. Likewise the experimental studies on ego-involvement, arising from threat to the self-esteem, are presented in Chapter 12: The evidence is favorable to the hypothesis that attacks on the self-esteem are disturbing, in fact often so disturbing that the drive rise is nonoptimal either for performance or for learning. The present knowledge of the role of the self in drive rise or drive depression is, however, meager, though it is known that attacks upon the self-esteem lead to defensive behaviors and/or rising tension. A somewhat similar antecedent for arousal is briefly considered in the last section below on cognitive dissonance.

Cognitive Dissonance

Festinger (188, 189) has developed the construct of cognitive dissonance, which is disturbing to an individual and is correlated with a rise in activity directed toward eliminating dissonance. When an individual has two cognitions simultaneously which "do not belong together or fit together," he has a state of "dissonance." "If a person knows two things, for example, something about himself and something about the world in which he lives, which somehow do not fit together," this is cognitive dissonance. A person might know that he is an intelligent, highly capable person. At the same time, let us imagine, he knows that he meets repeated failure. "These two cognitions would be dissonant— they do not fit together. In general, two cognitions are dissonant with each other if, considering these two cognitions alone, the obverse of one would follow from the other" (189). An illustration of how cognitive dissonance was reacted to by a group is presented in Inset 16.

INSET 16. ILLUSTRATION OF REACTIONS TO COGNITIVE DISSONANCE*

Festinger in illustrating reactions to cognitive dissonance describes a group of people in the United States who predicted that, on a given date, a catastrophic flood would overwhelm most of the world. This prediction of the catastrophic flood had been given, so they believed, by direct communications from the gods, and it was an integral part of their religious beliefs. When the predicted date arrived and passed, there was considerable dissonance established in these people. They continued to believe in their gods and in the validity of the communications from them, and at the same time they knew that the prediction of the flood had been wrong.

For some time the people in the group had believed that those who would be chosen to survive would be picked up by flying saucers before the cataclysm occurred.

Tensely they waited for the final orders to come through—for the messages which would tell them the time, place, and procedure for the actual pickup. Finally, on the day before the cataclysm was to strike, the messages came. At midnight a man would come to the door of the house and take

* Adapted from L. Festinger, The motivating effect of cognitive dissonance from *Assessment of Human Motives*, edited by Gardner Lindzey et al., copyright (c) 1958, Holt, Rinehart and Winston, Inc., by permission.

them to the place where the flying saucer would be parked. The day was spent by the group in preparation and rehearsal of the necessary procedures, and when midnight arrived, the group sat waiting in readiness. But no knock came at the door, no one came to lead them to the flying saucer.

The dissonance was now established between their beliefs and actuality. From midnight to five o'clock in the morning the group sat there struggling to understand what had happened, struggling to find some explanation that would enable them to recover somewhat from the shattering realization that they would not be picked up by a flying saucer and that consequently the flood itself would not occur as predicted. It is doubtful that anyone alone, without the support of the others, could have withstood the impact of this disproof of the prediction. Indeed, those members of the group who had gone to their homes to wait alone—alone in the sense that they did not have other believers with them—did not withstand it. Almost all of them became skeptics afterward. In other words, without easily obtainable social support to begin reducing the dissonance, the dissonance was sufficient to cause the belief to be discarded in spite of the commitment to it. But the members of the group who had gathered together in the home of the woman who received the messages could, and did, provide social support for one another. They kept reassuring one another that the messages were valid and that some explanation would be found.

At fifteen minutes before five o'clock that morning an explanation was found that was at least temporarily satisfactory. A message arrived from God which, in effect, said that He had saved the world and stayed the flood because of this group and the light and strength this group had spread throughout the world that night.

The behavior of these people from that moment onward presented a revealing contrast to their previous behavior. These people, who had been disinterested in publicity and had even avoided it, became avid publicity seekers. For four successive days, finding a new reason each day, they invited the press into the house, gave lengthy interviews, and attempted to attract the public to their ideas. There were almost no lengths to which these people would not go to attract publicity and potential believers in the validity of the messages. If, indeed, more and more converts could be found, more and more people who believed in the messages and the things the messages said, then the dissonance between their belief and the knowledge that the messages had not been correct could be reduced.

CONCLUDING STATEMENTS

The purpose of this chapter was to untangle some of the specific drives as origins of fluctuations in activation. That man varies in the overall degree of activation was considered in the preceding chapter, concerned with general or diffuse drive. That man also varies in vigor in specific performances is observed. For example, at times he is highly energized in a withdrawal behavior, such as when there are antecedents for pain or pain-fear; at other times there is less vigor in the withdrawal. It is then said that his fear is not as "strong" as it was before. Fear is only one of many inferred specific drive components. Some of them are energizers; others are correlated with a lessening of arousal. This chapter was concerned with attempts to identify the antecedents of a few of the specific drives, both unlearned and acquired, and to present demonstrations of their correlations with the vigor of specific performances.

The next chapter will consider another significant energizer: learned anticipations of a to-be-attained effect, or goals.

CHAPTER 9

GOALS

Among the significant incitors of man are to-be-attained effects, or goals. Why some effects are more acceptable than others is often difficult to determine, but there is no doubt that whatever an individual anticipates as attractive may be inciting. Goals are learned to-be-attained effects. Not only do they incite, but they have other functions. Goals are also determinants at choice points, as is shown in Chapter 10.

What Mechanisms Permit a Goal to Influence before It Is Reached?

In the different answers of psychological theorists we will find that there is agreement on one point: Some kind of *symbol* of a past event represents a to-be-attained effect. What symbols permit time to be spanned? Man may use words to symbolize his past activities and their effects. "I had a fine time in Miami," he says. The effects are symbolized by the words "fine time." (Whether he did or not may be immaterial in determining whether the return to the vacationland becomes a goal.) And by word symbolization he can also state that he apparently wants to reattain that "fine time" in the future: "I would like to go back next winter." He has a goal of returning to Miami. He has acquired this goal, this to-be-attained effect.

The construct of expectancy, described more fully in the next chapter, includes goal expectancies, i.e., anticipated events may be satisfactory in varying degrees to the organism and may become influential as goals when symbolized as to be attained again. Goals, however, are not necessarily verbalized nor at the level of awareness. They may be symbolized by noncognitive activities. The peripheralists suggest that fractional anticipatory goal *responses*, acting as stimuli, are representative of the to-be-attained goal. A typical illustration of anticipatory goal responses of a hungry animal are salivating and swallowing. Such behavior is in Hullian symbols called r_g, which, it is assumed, gives rise to stimuli, s_g.[1]

[1] See Brown (90), pp. 176–180.

According to Spence (575) r_g-s_g incites (contributes to the general drive). Other theorists have frankly assumed some central event, which they may label "demand for" or "appetite" without specifying *how* these symbols incite and/or cue off relevant activity.

Clues to a Goal Anticipation

It is difficult to determine whether an organism like a rat or a man, moving rapidly toward what the experimenter calls a goal place, (1) is exhibiting a series of approach responses only evoked by external cues, (2) is being moved by an anticipated goal effect, or (3) is doing both.

What is evidence that an anticipated goal is moving an organism? Even very simple organisms are so structured that they are sensitive to stimulating objects or places which they need. Their responses to these cannot, however, be called goal-related behavior, nor is their restlessness when a need such as hunger arises, and there is no food, any evidence of moving toward goals. Nor, after they learn how to move rapidly and without error to needed objects, is the appearance of this well-formed behavior unit any evidence of anticipation of a learned goal. However, the following can be accepted as evidence that there is a learned antici- pated goal moving an individual: Assume that a particular place in the external field, marked by discriminable colors or other signs, is asso- ciated with a satisfactory event like need-reduction (eating food to a hungry organism). If he later moves toward the former stimulating place and if he varies the sequences of responses, such behavior suggests that he is being moved by an anticipation of an effect to be attained and not merely responding with a well-learned sensorimotor habit. Another il- lustration: Chimpanzees learn to work for poker chips, as if the neutral objects were liked objects such as peanuts, but first the poker chips and the peanuts must be associated. Also, the chips must be later exchange- able for the intrinsically liked object. The poker chips presumably ac- quire the satisfaction associated with the taste of peanuts. Another phras- ing (without the use of the subjective term "satisfaction") is that the animals behave as if they anticipated the liked objects associated with the chips. See pp. 207–208 in regard to how such animals will work for symbolic poker chips, even collecting and hoarding them for a time until the animals can go to a vending machine and exchange them for the intrinsically liked food objects.

Barriers may also be placed between a rat, monkey, child, or man when moving toward a former rewarding place. The behavioral signs of frus- tration, disappointment, anger are also clues to the presence of an in- ferred goal anticipation which, though blocked, is still active (610). Non- completion, as is indicated in Inset 17, is accompanied by more muscular tension than is completion of the task.

Identification of the goals of the child or man can be attempted by asking for verbal reports. A child or a man imagines what would be desirable and states that these are his goals.

INSET 17. MUSCULAR TENSION IN INTERRUPTION AND COMPLETION OF TASKS*

Evidence for goal orientations is the following study of muscular tension in interrupted and completed simple tasks.

Smith (564) found that muscular tension rose during tasks and was higher following interruption than after task completion. The tasks were mirror tracing of simple geometrical figures. Some of the tasks were completed, and some were interrupted by the experimenter. By means of continuous records of the bipolar EMG from five muscle groups, the degree of muscular tension was recorded (1) during a one-minute expectation (a period of waiting for the starting signal), (2) during the work on simple tasks, and (3) during one minute of no activity following interruption or completion. The electrodes were attached to the forehead, the back of the neck (over trapezius), the chin (above and below the point, over muscles of the lower lip and tongue), and to the extensor surfaces of both forearms.

The significant finding was that muscle tension dropped more after completion of the tasks than after interruption. Figure 9-1 indicates this fact: Tension in the active arm rises during the tasks and declines significantly more for the individuals allowed to complete the tasks than for those not allowed to complete.

This result is not attributed to the time factor, since the mean times for completed and interrupted tasks were not different. The possibility that the interruption, being unexpected or startling, led to slower decline of the tension was also considered as a conceivable explanation. As a control for this, half the subjects were told before they started that they were not to worry if they did not finish; the other half had no hint that they might not complete all the tasks. The suggestion that interruption is startling or anxiety producing, and hence more tension arousing, was not supported.

* Adapted from A. A. Smith, An electromyographic study of tension in interrupted and completed tasks. *J. exp. Psychol.*, 1953, 46, 32–36.

Figure 9-1. Tension in active arm as a function of distance from goal. The muscle tension drops more after completion than after interruption. Smith (564)

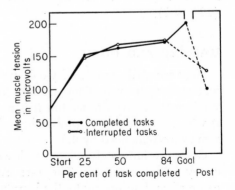

Smith suggests that the observed increase in muscle tension during the tasks reflects the developing organization of a central neural process, which controls and anticipates the overt activity and is yet relatively independent of immediate sensory stimulation (p. 35). That this increase in muscle tension is not simply the resultant of the task itself is suggested when task completion brings more tension release than task cessation without completion. There is a tendency to close the task (reach the goal), a tendency which remains unreleased and is responsible for the smaller tension decline when interruption occurs before the goal attainment.

Even more subjective than other central events, images are not by some psychologists considered acceptable clues to man's goals. Images do not necessarily follow the behavior signs of approach. It is possible, of course, that images of desired future events are more valid signs of a man's goals than are any other indices. (If one assumes the reality of an experience to lie in itself, then images of desired events are man's "real" goals whether he acts on them or not.) On this basis it is in the fantasies, the imaginative creations of a child or a man, that real desires can be revealed. If the expressions of the desires are socially prohibited, they may be imaged in symbolic form. Freud recognized this possibility, and in his model of a man he interpreted why the desires were not expressed directly, even to the man himself in his own silent musings.

It is noted by self-observers that in the dreams of day or night imaged events appear which, though quite fluctuating in details, reveal desires. Social success, for example, may be symbolized by imagining being received into a prestige social club, or being invited to "the dance of the year," or in many other ways. The goal of social success and the anticipated increase in self-evaluation remain unchanged through the different imaged events.

The methods of scoring imaginative stories to determine the individual's dominant needs and related goals include those of McClelland and his coworkers (410). Other methods of interpreting imaginative reports in order to identify desired events have also been developed (134, 401).

LEARNING AND GOALS

How are goals acquired? Goals are not inherited. Nor do they fall like manna from heaven. They are not given to us; we acquire them. (A reward may be given to us, but it is not a goal unless we have anticipated it with some degree of probability of attainment and have thus been in some way influenced by it.)

Goals are intimately related to learning. Learning of some kind is necessary to acquire goals. They are influential in the activity stream because of, and according to, the learning how to act so that the anticipated effects can be reached. However, learning how to reattain an effect is not the same as learning that an effect is to be attained. In other words, at least two learning problems exist here: (1) How do organisms acquire goals, and (2) how do they learn to reach them? These learnings sometimes are concomitant and sometimes are not.

Only the first will be considered here. Goals are learned at times by direct attainment of a satisfactory effect, which is later symbolized as a to-be-reattained effect. An attained satisfactory effect does not inevitably become a to-be-reattained effect, i.e., a goal. The determinants include opportunities of working toward the goal; capacity for work involved; necessity for abandoning other goals; "work escaped" if one goal is accepted rather than another; degree of anticipated satisfactory effect if the goal is reattained. The utility of a specific choice among other possible acceptable effects, including "not working," is a complex of many variables. This point is later reconsidered.

Goals can be learned vicariously by the human organism, i.e., by communication from others, either by words or by the cues given by emotional signs. Books, television, and movies demonstrate to the children "satisfactory events" in the lives of adults. Also, both children and men are constantly in contact with many events which by empathy they can to some degree enter. Children can perceive others receiving praise for a specific performance; then they say, "Let me do it." Boys may watch young men perform an act which is admired by others. The boys acquire a to-be-attained effect, as when a social value is assigned to the position of an "eagle scout." Goals common to a culture may be thus acquired.

Children acquire goals as verbal statements long before the goals can become satisfactory events. Children tell of what they are going to do when they grow up. Such daydreams may finally become reality; or at least they may lead to action, though the goals may not be ever attained. On the other hand, the contribution to behavior of merely verbalized goals may be absent or quite negligible, perhaps fitful or even bizarre.

Goals may be symbolized *before the individual has learned how to attain them.* Man may anticipate the satisfaction of freedom though he himself has always been repressed. He may set being a leader as his goal after watching leaders even though he has never been the center of a group and does not know how to attain such a goal for himself.

Two Illustrative Studies

In one study (120), children aged twenty-seven to ninety-six months responded with greater energy to reach a goal under *knowledge of success or of failure.* The specific goal was learned from the experimenter's direction. The children were told to make a bell ring by exerting pressure on a dynamometer. The addition of verbal praise or reproof increased the energy output. Such additional symbolic reward and punishment had a slight energizing effect. Note that verbal punishment did not stop the subjects or lower their drive output. In other words, any information, whether the children had reached the designated goal or not, increased the energy output. This fact suggests that we are dealing here with more than simple association of the stimulus (the bell) with satisfaction and increased drive. Whatever this higher mediating process is, it is aided by information to the children concerning the results on the environment of their own actions, i.e., the results of pressure on the dynamometer with respect to reaching the goal.

A neutral stimulus becomes a symbol of a correct response with human subjects. Hubbard (297) used college students in testing the effect of pairing a neutral stimulus with correct response. The learning task was to select the correct key from a bank of three whenever a number flashed in an aperture on a screen before the subjects. Hubbard attached satisfaction to the neutral stimulus (red light) by informing the subjects that *a red light would flash when they were correct.* By this information, they acquired a symbolic goal. The red light was a symbol of a rewarding effect, presumably because of a specific drive *to achieve* "being correct."[2] In addition, with one group an auditory stimulus—a tone—also sounded with the correct response and the red light. The subjects were not told that a tone would sound when they were correct, but they could associate the sound with the red light. (This association would be similar to the rat's associating a neutral stimulus, such as a sound, with food. The sound could become a symbol of a goal.) After training to thirty correct choices, the experimenter, without informing the subjects of the change in the experimental procedure, no longer used the light when the subjects were correct. With one group the tone, however, was continued with the correct response. With others there was neither tone nor red light.

The results indicated that the learned performance *was* supported by the red light and also by the tone symbol. The group with the tone continued significantly longer than the group without either red light or tone.

The red light acted as a signal that marked the correct response. All that was needed in order for these human subjects to acquire the goal of "seeing the red light" was the information that it was a signal of "being correct." (Whatever other learning was necessary had previously occurred.) However, the subjects who were never informed that the tone also sounded when they were correct were later sustained in performance by it alone. The tone stimulus apparently also became a goal symbol simply by association with the red light, a symbol of success.[3]

---

[2] "Being correct" may possibly continue to be a secondary (learned) reward and/or a goal when no longer dependent upon any one of the specific drives.

[3] In Chapter 14 there is a reconsideration of secondary rewards, i.e., of how neutral stimuli associated with rewarding effects possibly become rewards in themselves.

Some of the problems of *how* goal learnings occur are ignored in the discussion above. Space forbids any extensive attempt to discuss learnings significant in goal acquisitions, including perceptual learnings. The higher species—the primates, at least, and certainly man—may anticipate according to their perceptual structuring of the field.

Man, it is assumed, can make decisions concerning movements toward satisfactory effects in the future because of his capacity for inferences in regard to what will later be the situation in which he will find himself. Man can discover in objects properties that directly excite interest and exploration. Human action can grow out of insight into the relationship between object and need, or between action and consequence. In such instances there is no arbitrary connection of object with need or of object, need, and action. This is true even of the needs called primary; "we observe that a drink slakes our thirst and that the shade is cool." In the same way, men can find that other objects have properties that attract or repel. Goals thus can arise in direct response to the *perceived* properties of things and/or the perceived relationships between events and actions (24, pp. 339–340).

As indicated previously, the learning of goals may, however, be below cognitive awareness, even in man. An association between specific acts or objects and rewarding effects may be acquired irrespective of other aspects of the situation in which the association occurs. The goal may be normal or it may be abnormal: An example of an abnormal goal is a man with a compulsive act of touching females on the breasts irrespective of the social situation or of the females' acceptance.[4]

The energizing role of anticipated goals and the relaxing effect of attainment are of interest in this chapter. Experimental demonstrations reviewed here will concern the dynamic functions of symbolized to-be-attained effects. We must, however, first ask why some events are to be attained and other are to be avoided.

DETERMINANTS OF THE PERSONAL UTILITY OF EVENTS

One of the most significant problems ignored above will now be faced: What determines why some effects are to be attained and others are not? Unfortunately, to isolate the possible determinants of what is satisfactory (and the reverse, unsatisfactory), and in addition to interpret their

[4] In Allport's description of functional autonomy of motives (7, 8), he relates similar occurrences of specific *fixation of acts to goal objects* and of recurrence of the fixation in the absence of the original drive origin. However, automaticity of this compulsive action, supported probably by the reinforcement arising from increase in sexual excitement, is not like the automaticity of habits which are said to have a drive of their own. In this sense, the compulsion is not functioning autonomously of all motivational determinants.

changes in utility to an individual, is a long-term goal of motivational psychology itself and not yet even in sight. The following discussion is based both on some systematic studies and on speculative attempts to answer the problem of what determines the utility of events to a specific person.

In order first to identify the general variables which determine why some effects and not others are more likely to become goals for men, we start with a basic but unsolved problem of psychology, the problem of likes and dislikes. As indicated later, affective tone is not the only determinant of the personal utility of an event, but it cannot be ignored as a possible variable.

What Determines Why Effects Vary from Satisfactory to Unsatisfactory

1. First we point to the evidence suggesting that some sensory inputs are per se satisfactory and others per se nonacceptable. Sweet taste is not only satisfactory today, but also tomorrow. It is not only satisfactory to man but to the child and to most subhuman organisms. Pfaffmann, in his review of the "pleasures of sensation," states that though cats and birds do not show strong sucrose preferences, these organisms are exceptions to what appears to be a general rule (484). Nor is there convincing evidence that this liking for sweet is entirely acquired. The intake of nonnutritive saccharin solutions shows no signs of extinction, which should appear *if* the preference were acquired by association with need-drive reduction[5] (see pp. 329–330).

There are fairly stable preferences of animals and humans. Inherent liking of sucrose and inherent disliking of bitter-tasting substances are stable. Painful stimulations are in themselves never preferred, though they may be endured in order to attain satisfactory effects. In the studies of food selections it is found that influential factors are the characteristics of the foods presented and their background. Young's many studies have isolated factors which influence the choices of foods, including kind of food, concentration of any solution used, temperature, texture, and so forth. There are, as background factors, noises or lack of noises, distractions, and similar determiners which influence the selecting of food objects, apparently because of their contribution to the pleasantness or unpleasantness aroused by the stimulating foods (664, 666, 669).

2. Stimulus change (novelty) may be an inherently satisfying central event (see pp. 45–48).

3. The attraction of an activity may rise when it represents a successful development of an organismic capacity. In Woodworth's "behavior primacy" theory of what moves organisms (660), he hypothesizes that

---

[5] Other studies illustrating the role of the taste sensation in preferences are cited by Pfaffmann (484) and can also be found in Beebe-Center (48).

the use of capacities, as "to walk" by a child, is satisfying in itself. In addition, a sustained liking for an activity requires that it not be too familiar. There must be a challenge (slight or great). Walking, in other words, would be more satisfying during development of the skill than in its use after acquisition.

4. A stimulating event which is perceived as enhancing the value of the self can be satisfying, and attacks on the self-concept can be quite disagreeable.[6] There are specific social and individual standards incorporated into the self which affect judgments of events. These standards, however, may change as the situation changes, e.g., an individual alone behaves differently from an individual in a group. Standards (or values) change with the years. They may change from childhood through adolescence to adulthood. An individual's values may be the norms of the group. Or his values or social standards may be quite individual; a man may accept as satisfactory an event which by the values of others would not be acceptable. Successful stealing is a highly satisfactory outcome to a professional thief, since he values this nonsocial behavior.

5. Relief from irritation is per se satisfactory. Verbal expressions of man concerning relief after removal of painful stimuli, as well as other noxious stimuli, give strong support to this claim. Support is added by the behavioral signs of withdrawal and continued contact with other stimulation associated with removal of irritations. Reduction of the need drives (those that are irritating) is accompanied by satisfaction, as is the reduction of the learned drives of fear and anxiety.[7]

The inference that diminution of irritations is satisfactory is based on such common observations as that the greater the decrease in electric shock, the faster an organism runs to the place of decrease. In one study (78) at the starting place the animals received 250 volts of shock. At the goal place the animals, according to different groups, had 50, 150, or 200 volts for twenty seconds. They ran faster to the goal box with 50 volts. As an additional support to this, the amount of shock decrease was shifted (unexpectedly for the animals), and the organisms accordingly changed their speed, going slower, for example, if there was less shock reduction.

There is no simple interpretation, however, of what determines a satisfactory event. Is a rise in general drive ever satisfactory? If we use again the criterion that satisfaction is revealed if there is continuing sensory

[6] There are a variety of theorists who have developed the related concepts of self-enhancement, self-protection, self-actualization. Freud first recognized the significance of self-defense mechanisms. Rogers (519) posed self-actualization as basic in his theory of man. Others have followed or preceded him in their recognition of the development of the self. [See chap. 12 of (241).]
[7] It is *not* assumed that all drives are noxious to the organism. Nor is it assumed that reduction of the nonirritating drive components is nonsatisfactory.

contact, there are observations which suggest that the answer to the above question should be "yes."

6. An *increase* in excitation from the external field may be satisfactory if the drive source is not irritating. Increased sensory contacts with a rising number of stimuli, such as occur at carnivals with the bright and numerous lights and many sounds, are exciting *and* satisfactory. Men and women with laughing children move among noisy slot machines; the barkers cry their wares; the auctioneers sell their silver and their golden articles. The flashing lights prick the eyes; the taste of the foam candy lingers on the lips; there are the smells of humanity and of dirt. And these are exhilarating, exciting, satisfactory stimulations.

RELATIVITY OF A SATISFACTORY OR UNSATISFACTORY EVENT

Relativity of Decrease in Noxious Stimulation

Satisfaction following reduction of irritation, including relief from pain, is relative to the previous degree of pain. A high original level of pain requires a greater decrease to obtain a discriminated difference in decrease than if the original level of pain is lower. The reinforcing effect is relative to the degree of pain previously endured (109). Campbell (108) studied the reduction in another noxious stimulus ("white noise") in order to produce a preference in rats' choices of spatial location. Starting with an initial noise level of 95 decibels, a small decrease was sufficient to establish a 75 per cent preference for the spatial location of less noise. When the initial level of noxiousness was higher (115 decibels) it required a greater reduction to establish the 75 per cent preference for the less noxious place. It has been suggested that such reinforcement thresholds may be represented by Weber-Fechner fractions (105, 106).

When exciting stimuli (those *not* correlated with irritations) are increased, there may be increased satisfaction. However, there is no monotonic relationship between such increments in increased excitation and increments in satisfaction. When there are few stimuli in an external field, human subjects report boredom, even disagreeable feelings. In contrast, at a high level of stimulation, if there are no irritating components in the excitation flux, the high excitation may be exhilarating, except when some ongoing act requires careful and accurate movements. Then an increase in level of excitation may result in a nonoptimal drive and a nonsatisfactory state. Why? One interpretation which has had some support is that a high general drive level lowers the thresholds of many responses, some of which may be competing and hence interfering with ongoing acts (575).

Variability in Acceptability of Goal Objects

When we turn to the objective field and attempt to identify specific goal objects or events, we again observe how satisfaction is relative rather than absolute. What determines the desirability of food, money, or praise at the moment of the stimulation? In recall? And in successive reattainments? It is observed that the immediate acceptability, as well as the recalled acceptability, is relative to other variables. An event may shift in its degree of acceptability, becoming lesser or greater according to the ground (the situation). Hitting a home run is a satisfactory event to some degree to a ballplayer at any time. Its acceptability is always positive, but a home run with three men on bases is even more so. The "top" satisfactory event in a baseball career is, it is said, winning the last game of a World Series by hitting a home run in the ninth inning with three on bases.

The degree of satisfaction that most men find in the usual social rewards is relative to the satisfaction other men have with respect to such rewards. With human subjects the judgment of the worth of a socially valued object like money is based not only on its buying power but on the standard pay for the particular job. If most men get $50 for performing a job, then the degree of satisfaction a man gets for a $20 pay is dependent on this particular standard, or anchoring stimulus. The satisfaction is relative to the pay others receive for the same kind of work, as well as to previous pay received by the worker.

This seems to be in conflict with the suggestion by Edwards (171) that money is probably the most universally used and understood evaluative dimension in our culture. Is $1 twice as satisfactory as 50 cents? A $10 bill ten times as satisfactory as $1? Certainly most men learn a scale of subjective value corresponding rather closely to the numerical amount of money, but the individual's life situation, in terms of money available, inevitably affects his subjective scale of low-to-high value for a small-to-large amount of money. The subjective value scale shifts both as the economic conditions shift (especially for those most directly aware of the economic changes) and as the individual acquires more, or less, money. The scale of value attached to money in early life, however, seems most stable. The author finds it difficult to shift her subjective value attached to 5 cents in childhood to its economic value of today.

Satisfaction and Specific Drives, Immediate or Anticipated. The desirability of objects to be attained is relative to *immediate* drives and to *anticipated* drives. Probably the best known relationships in psychology of motivation are between immediate dominant need-drive components and what is acceptable or nonacceptable to the organism, i.e., what he approaches and contacts and what he avoids. These approaches or avoidances may be built into the organism; e.g., organisms respond positively to certain external stimuli (foods or other useful objects) according to their physiochemical condition. Learning is significant in establishing these relations in higher animals. The child learns that food is what he wants when hungry. He learns to associate aroused drives with external-in-origin events. The reverse also occurs: e.g., the sex drive is aroused by external-in-origin excitations.

Anticipated drives determine goals. Satisfaction of food is relative to the degree of hunger, but assume a man is *not* hungry. Will he then value food and will he increase his energy output to get food? The answer is no, but a significant point is that a food-satisfied man may work for a symbolic goal (money) *if he anticipates hunger which can be reduced by use of the money.*

Assume he is not sexually sensitized. Will a woman arouse him? The answer is no, but again, he may anticipate a sexual need.

Assume a man anticipates no danger. Then will secure places be goals? Yes, if he has a learned fear of the return of danger.

Let us say he is not status-seeking. Will offers of a prestige position attract him? Again yes, if he expects that he will later find the prestige satisfying.

Assume that he is not in a mood to achieve: He is relaxed, indifferent to any future success. Will he be attracted by attaining goals of which he is proud? Perhaps, if he anticipates the return of the need-to-achieve.

Though apparently infrequent or nonexistent in subhumans,[8] the anticipating of a goal effect is common in man. Moreover, man is capable of anticipating that certain drive conditions will recur and that the concomitant learned goals will be again desirable. Man not only learns that food is an acceptable object when he is hungry; he learns to anticipate hunger *and* to anticipate the satisfaction of food. In other words, he learns that he will be hungry again and that food will then increase in its desirability though at the moment he may dislike food. He can and does anticipate that drives will be later dominant though they are not at the present time.

One of the complicating factors in understanding why goals are relative to drives is that their satisfactoriness may be, and often is, relevant to more than one of the drives. "Going to an old home" (the phrase includes both the action and the objective goal) may be inciting both be-

---

[8] A possible exception appears in the studies of chimpanzees who held symbols (poker chips) of food rewards, suggesting that they too anticipated a later use of the poker chips. In simpler organisms, there are instincts which prepare them for later needs (e.g., the hoarding instinct), but these do not involve any anticipation of the later use of what is hoarded. Most nonprimate animals, at least as contrasted to man, are at the mercy of their immediate bodily needs and the immediate availability in the external field of what is essential for meeting the needs.

cause of anticipation of the relief of *primary* drives and because of novelty from changing the daily routine.

Goals within Social Interaction

Social interaction changes what is "satisfactory." What others around us admire is often what we admire. And what they work for is often what we perceive as satisfactory. An introspection of our "feelings" may, however, suggest that we do not always have personal satisfaction after attainment of admired social goals. If we are "good conformists," we may deny this observation and continue to work for the usual social goals. Rogers (519) emphasizes this incongruence between the feelings of hate toward a child by a mother and the verbal expression of love feelings which are socially admirable. This conflict is recognized in his discussion of what is "tension-producing."

Desirability of Later Effects Is Relative to the Moods of the Moment

The moods are one of the determinants of the expected satisfaction of events, including distant goals. A plan of action shifts in its acceptability if the mood changes from euphoria to depression. There is possibly a change in anticipation of success to anticipation of failure, or a change from high acceptability of the goal of the activity to a lower acceptability. The goal of increasing one's possessions by "good" business deals, for example, may be highly desirable when in a euphoric state and much less valuable when in another emotional condition. There may also be an entire shift in the goal directions within the activity stream. Under euphoria one may set out on a dangerous mission; with a change in mood, the direction of the overt behavior is reversed. The fluctuations in feelings, if extreme, may prevent the continuance to completion of goaled acts. What seems possible under one mood is impossible when the mood shifts. Though much of the above is speculative, it is not untestable. For example, under changing physiological bases for emotions, such as blood pressure changes, reported aspirations should shift accordingly.

Beebe-Center (48) wrote in 1932 concerning the close relationship of hedonic tone to moods. A common statement is: "So-and-so is in such a mood today that nothing would be pleasant to him." And Lehmann writes:

> As every mood (*Stimmung*) may be conceived as the perseveration (*Nachbild*) of an emotion, there are as many different moods as there are emotions. They fall, however, into two main groups, according to whether pleasantness or unpleasantness predominate. These groups are called in daily life good or bad frames of mind (*Launen*). If one is in a good frame of mind, sensitivity to unpleasantness is strongly decreased, minor bothers

are either entirely overlooked or throw but very passing shadows on the joyful condition to which they must quickly again make way. Entirely analogous is the manifestation of a bad frame of mind, of dejection (*Verstimmtheit*). In this condition all impressions normally provocative of joy are usually devoid of any effect or, at most, produce only a momentary cheerfulness. (362, p. 271)

And the reverse may also hold: Moods may change as goals are met.

Previous Success and Failures in Goal Attainment

Previous success or failure determines what is attractive. Filer (190) reports that when a toy was used as a goal and there was attainment, the attractiveness of the object increased for children (six to nine years). It decreased with nonattainment. Rankings of nine toys were first obtained. Then attainment or nonattainment of the middle-ranked toy was followed by a second ranking. The change in the second rating indicated that attainment of the toy was generally accompanied by an increase in preference for it and nonattainment by a decrease.

Satisfaction to Dissatisfaction as Related to Confirmation or Nonconfirmation of Goal Expectancies

Man's almost daily "ups and downs" in feelings of well-being may be the resultant of constantly being subjected to sudden shifts from what goals he expects to what he actually attains. In daily life, he learns to anticipate small pleasures in each day, and they may not be confirmed. Or if he is fortunate, they are confirmed, perhaps even in a more favorable way then expected. So his feelings of being "on top" or "in depression" come and go. More serious are the nonconfirmations of highly desired goals. Depression may long continue after such disappointments. In contrast, the elations which come with the unexpected windfall are not so long lasting, yet they are not quickly "submerged" by oncoming activities. We hold their memory and return to them to savor again their delight.

The origin of satisfactory to unsatisfactory affects is said by McClelland et al. (413) to lie in the degree of discrepancy between a sensory or perceptual event and the adaptation level (with the latter being similar to expectancy). Restated, the hypothesis is that the pleasure is maximal when an event, as perceived, is of a *moderate* discrepancy from the stable level of expectancy. Winning against odds like 1,000 to 1, however, can be a highly pleasurable experience, though, according to this discrepancy hypothesis, such a wide difference between the expectancy with low probability of attainment and the actual winning should lead to "shock" and no enjoyment. General observations of the emotional changes of men suggest that attainment of a goal highly desired but of low probability in attainment may lead to elation and apparent great satisfaction.[9] The experimental study reported later on pp. 208–209 suggests that the discrepancy hypothesis is more applicable when the anticipated reward is not greatly desired.

Morale and Degree of Strength of Confirmed and Nonconfirmed Expectancies in Regard to Promotion. An expectancy fulfilled should raise morale by increasing satisfaction with the events which surround the forming of the expectancy and the tasks which lead to a fulfillment. A nonfulfillment should lower morale. In one study (574) within the operations of the pseudomilitary situation, expectancy of a promotion, when fulfilled, was found to raise satisfaction. In the experimental directions to the different groups of subjects, contrasting probabilities of attainment were also established: e.g., expectancy of promotion was established by stating that only one out of four would be promoted. The less the probability of the expectancy's being confirmed, the more its fulfillment had an effect, but in a somewhat specific manner: e.g., the less the probability of expecting promotion, the greater the satisfaction if the expectancy was fulfilled. Such subjects, moreover, were more able to "take" the frustration of not being promoted.

Some Questions. Who can most easily adjust to nonconfirmation of expectancies? The intellectual man? The aggressive man? The man of strong curiosity? The authoritarian? The liberal? The conservative? The radical? There are two further questions: What are the criteria of adjustment to nonconfirmation? And how shall we delineate the different personalities? All such questions are significant in understanding the origins of differences in emotions among individuals under the same events, but no answers are attempted here. It can at least be stated that a degree of realism is necessary to adjust to the continuous nonconfirmation of goal anticipations.

The above discussion of variables which may be responsible for the shifts from satisfactoriness to more *or* to less, even to unsatisfactoriness, has so far avoided facing the criticisms of hypothesizing subjective states as psychological variables. We now turn to the doctrine of hedonism and the criticisms thereof.

HEDONISM

Hedonism is like a mischievous child who is told to stay home, but, insistent on going along, creeps into the car when no one is looking only

[9] Probability of attainment is subjective probability set by the individual. Expectancy may encompass the anticipation of an event to come and also the degree of probability that the event will occur.

to emerge later with a smile and a challenge, "Well, here I am." It has emerged at intervals in the history of psychological theory. From the time of the Greek philosophers to the twentieth century some form of this doctrine intermittently appears—the doctrine that the pleasures and pains are the "masters" of men.

Freud, in his early theorizing, assumed that all instincts "seek pleasure." Man's reality principle is in opposition to the seeking of pleasure, but in open or disguised form, according to the Freudian theory, pleasure is sought. Similar or modified views of the significance of pleasure have been held by a variety of philosophers and psychologists: Bentham (54), Spencer (578), Troland (623), McDougall (416). Today the assumption that drive (tension) reduction is the end state of all motives is a similar doctrine, i.e., the assumption that all drive increase (general or specific) is irritating and that drive decrease is satisfying. Mowrer (446) has made this the basic assumption in his attempts to untangle "fear" from "hope."

Today, hedonism is still a questionable doctrine, first because of its too broad claims in respect to the "cause" of man's activities, and second because of its use of such subjective terms as pleasant and unpleasant. We shall later consider how broadly applied may be a hedonistic interpretation, but we turn now to the second critical point: the subjectiveness of pleasantness and similar states. In our previous discussion was the assumption that the backlash effects of successive phases in the activity stream vary in affective tone, shifting according to many variables along a continuum from highly pleasurable to satisfactory through neutral to dissatisfactory or extremely noxious. Is such an assumption absurd?

Support for the Assumption of Differences in Affect of Phases of the Activity Stream

Studies of the Self-Stimulation in Subcortical Neural Areas. The hedonistic doctrine that man and other higher organisms are so constituted that sensory input is pleasant, unpleasant, or neither, is supported by recent studies of self-stimulation of areas in the limbic system (see Figure 9-2). Olds (471, 472) and others (98) have demonstrated that

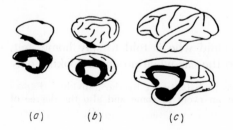

Figure 9-2. The limbic lobe, represented in black, forms a common denominator in the brains of all mammals. The lateral and medial surfaces of brains of rabbit (*a*), cat (*b*), and monkey (*c*), drawn roughly to scale. Reproduced from Pfaffmann (484)

(*a*)   (*b*)   (*c*)

if an organism self-stimulates (by an electric shock) certain neural areas (via an electrode inserted through the skull into a defined subcortical level), the animal will *continue* this self-stimulation. This fact suggests that the animal finds the stimulations satisfactory, perhaps pleasant. Similarly, other neural areas, when stimulated, are apparently unpleasant in their excitation since the animal *ceases* to give himself excitation in these areas. In addition, there are observations from men who have pathological lesions that this neural area is associated with a wide variety of auras involving all the body senses as well as a great number of feeling and emotional states (484).

Preferences for Stimulations. Further evidence suggesting that organisms are so constituted that they like certain stimuli per se and dislike others, comes from studies of acceptance and rejection of substances for further sensory contact (664, 666, 668). "Animals, surprising to relate, sip sugar and solve problems when they are not hungry. They explore their environment with no definite goal in view; they have preferences for salt which are inexplicable in terms of drive-reduction. In other words they seem to do certain things just for the sake of doing them" (482, p. 130). Young, on the basis of his experimental studies of food choices, considers the hedonic tone significant in the organization of behavior. Young writes: "When an animal makes contact with a foodstuff there is an immediate affective arousal that depends upon the kind of food, the temperature, texture, concentration of a solution, etc" (667, p. 253). In Young's theory, the affective processes are dependent however, on more than the characteristics of the food objects. Young (667) presents Figure 9-3, which indicates that affective processes are also dependent upon organic conditions. He does not deny the role of organic needs in determining the nature of the affective processes but makes the needs subsidiary to the general assumption that "neurobehavioral patterns are organized to relieve distress and to enhance (heighten, prolong) enjoyment" (667, p. 253). The evidence which Young gathered for support of his assumption of the role of hedonic tone in the organization of behavior lies essentially in his many observations that an animal such as a rat may prefer a food element like sucrose in spite of not needing it, or even in spite of needing another food substance which is presented along with sucrose. A food liking may continue to influence choices in spite of a bodily need for such substances as casein. Moreover, Young and his coworkers (669, p. 164) have illustrated that "liking" may be placed against a well-formed habit and may win. The food preferences may shift selections in spite of the frequency of previous choices.

As indicated in Figure 9-3, Young emphasizes the hedonic tone in the organization of behavior. He stresses three sources influencing the kind and degree of affect: (1) organic state (drive component); (2) the external object (food); (3) the situational context (surroundings). Young assumes acquired neural organizations which are the basis for appetitive and aversive behavior. They are preceded by the affective processes.

Evaluation of Hedonistic Theory

The suggestion that man's satisfactions and dissatisfactions are signifi-cant in determining performance is quite controversial. Mental processes need not, however, be assumed in order to incorporate satisfaction or similar subjective processes into psychological description. These are no different from any of the phenomena which psychologists accept. The difficulty of pinpointing their onset (and cessation) is necessarily acknowledged. If they can be inferred, the question remains of how they act upon the response-releasing mechanism. Moreover, the evidence that affective processes are aroused by stimulations is not extensive, though they can be inferred on the basis of Olds and others' findings suggesting that liking and disliking per se are determiners, at times at least, of choices.

The hedonistic doctrine in its most boldfaced form is more encompass-ing than the above would imply, and there are certain absurdities in any broad application of a hedonistic doctrine. One absurdity is the assump-tion that a man acts only to secure pleasure and to avoid pain. It is doubtful if a man ever seeks pleasure. Rather, the anticipated effects are objectified as goal objects or goal events. Second, pleasure is fleeting, an impalpable condition always yet to be attained. Moreover, man does not find pleasure even when he believes he is seeking it.

Why is man so unsuccessful in pursuit of pleasure? It is difficult to find pleasure, and certainly to maximize it in life. Perhaps man does not have the knowledge to maximize pleasure, even in his individual life and certainly not for all interacting individuals; and for *each* individual in social interaction to have maximum pleasure is even more difficult than

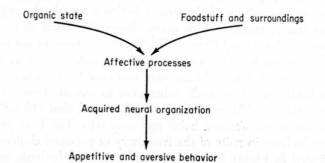

Figure 9-3. Central importance of affective processes in the organization of behavior. From Young (667, p. 252), in regard to *food* choices.

for the group to maximize it. Men *in interaction* cannot have maximum pleasure for all individuals, at least not with the present knowledge of how to interact so as to resolve the inevitable conflicts of men. Nor does the above imply that individuals alone can easily maximize pleasure. There is also little knowledge in regard to how, in the "alone situation," man can be maximally satisfied. Some satisfactions can only arise in interaction with others.

Men lack the innate capacity to, and often are unable to learn to, anticipate all possible effects of their actions. Moreover, all men in organized groups are to a greater or lesser extent bound by their daily schedules of living.[10] Habits acquired to adapt to group living hold them in activities in spite of weariness, disgust, and displeasures. And there is possible learned caution, or fear, or a more extreme anxiety, all of which restrict man's choices, restrict him from entering into attempts even to pursue what he anticipates as more satisfactory than his present goals.

In *summary,* organisms, at least at the higher level, can learn to anticipate the different effects of some of the constantly varying stimulating events. That some effects are more acceptable than others, either at the time of sensory contact or in anticipation, is inferred from the behavior of both the subhuman and human organisms.

However, pleasure is unpredictable and fleeting. Pleasure is like a drop of rain in the sun. It touches the central excitation for a moment and disappears. A goal attained may bring no pleasure, yet may be acceptable and even satisfactory. For example, the personal values which in a situation support the goal of attaining social status may give little pleasure but much satisfaction.

A superior description of a goal is the personal utility of events-to-come. Moreover, this phrase, as well as Lewin's similar description of plus or minus "valences" (365), avoids the implication that an event-to-come may be a goal solely on the basis of an aroused affective tone. Other than liking or disliking may determine the utility to a person of an event and its consequent attraction (valence). The more valid statement of why some events are goals is that they have some degree of personal utility.

[10] Maintenance schedules are dependent upon well-established expectancies of events, but their confirmations are not goals. The man expects the sun to rise, but its confirmation is not a goal. A man expects to have dinner at home, but its confirmation is not the reaching of a goal. He expects the work day to end at five o'clock, but the confirmation of the expectancy is not a goal reached. However, a man may set a goal of finishing his work so that he can leave at five o'clock instead of staying over-time.

The maintenance schedules can be goal influencing; they can control the direction into which the man moves throughout most of his twenty-four hours, but they do not present goals. They sometimes serve the individual to reach goals, or they sometimes prevent him from reaching them.

Goals have more than one function in performance. Their energizing role is now considered. In later chapters their role in the choices of men is reviewed, and the possible reinforcing action of their attainment is evaluated.

INCITING ROLE OF GOALS

Energizing is a significant motivational function of to-be-attained effects. Illustrative studies follow.

Attributes of Goal Objects and Inciting Function

The terminal goals may vary in many ways: e.g., food may vary in size, weight, volume, nutritional value, texture, number of consummatory responses required to ingest, color, shape, and even the container used. A larger quantity of food will, in general, increase the amount of energy expended. For subhumans this is true for food even when the hunger drive is held constant. Chickens moved faster through a simple maze when 6 grams of boiled rice could be eaten than when 1 gram was allowed them (230). Similar results were demonstrated by Wolfe and Kaplon (658), who added the evidence that the number of food pieces rather than the actual amount ingested was a variable. When one piece of popcorn was cut into four parts, the latter was more of an incentive than one. One whole grain was also more inciting than one-fourth of a grain. It was suggested that four pieces were more energizing because there were four consummatory responses. It is possible, however, that the larger number of parts so affected the perceptual field that size was the *learned* incitor.

Work Required and Expected Goal

Chimpanzees were observed to work harder for the larger of two visible pieces of banana (194). The animals were required to pull in their food from a distance of 18 feet, and the resistance encountered in pulling was varied by the use of braking devices or by an attached weight. If the work was too much and the piece of banana too small, the chimpanzee would not work.

The interacting influence of work required and expected goal effect are present in man's performance level. A frequent goal of man is money. How much it affects his drive level depends, in part, upon its buying power but also on the work required. In the industrial field, the dislike of a high rate of work may prevent a man from setting as his goal a large bonus, with a required high increase in energy output. In contrast, persistence in great effort expended when moving toward a highly valuable goal is observed in a few men who have overcome difficult barriers (see Inset 18).

INSET 18. PERSISTENCE TOWARD A GOAL*

That a man may ignore immediate bodily needs for a difficult-to-attain elusive goal is dramatized by a report from *Life* magazine on how Vernon Pick "fought storms, rattlers, poison water, death itself" to find uranium.

Pick finally moved to the place where the rewarding uranium lay, but he was not yet aware of having reached his goal. He had come laboriously through an arsenic-poisoned river running through a narrow canyon and had just failed in his attempt to purify the water.

He was very sick, he knew, and by now he lay three days away from reliable water. For the first time he allowed the thought to form that he might die. He examined the thought carefully, standing somewhat aloof from it. It was not terribly important, he found; not as important as he had imagined.

That night he only dozed, waking often from the wild racing of his heart. In the first light he checked his pulse with his watch and counted 130 beats to the minute. He could not recall what the rate was supposed to be, but he knew that his was much too fast. Soon, in the full light, he became aware that something was happening to his eyes. His vision seemed to go in and out of focus and now and then he was blinded by a hurtling flash of color. He told himself that he must rest for a while.

Although it had become conceivable to Pick that he might die, it was not conceivable to him that he could turn back. Even at this stage, what was still left in him that could think told him that he must keep going. He still is not sure why this was. Part of the reason, perhaps, lay in an obscure and rankling sense of destiny that had always bothered him, even when he was a boy and not doing well in school. Part of it may have been an irrational and, indeed, unconscious drive: he has said, "The river got in my way."

He had somehow become gripped by a "dumb obsession," as he has said, which made it absolutely necessary that he go on—not for the possible reward of money, since his mind no longer associated what he was doing with money, but to triumph against these hostile elements, to reach his goal (or die) for his own sake as a human being.

Interaction of Goal Object and Degree of Present Drive

Degree of drive influences the inciting function of the relevant goal. It is observed that, generally, speed of movements toward food rises with a hungry organism. Some of the earlier studies in motivation with subhuman subjects at the University of California demonstrated how performance level of rats in mazes rose as goals for primary need drives were introduced and fell when removed (621). The inciting influence of

* Adapted from Robert Coughlan's article, *Life* magazine, Nov. 1, 1954.

a goal of food was also demonstrated by delaying hungry rats in a series of wheels placed at regular intervals across a runway to food. The wheel-turning readiness was increased by giving a food reward and decreased by removing the reward (216). Another obvious illustration of the energizing effect of a goal object is in the action of most male dogs when there is a receptive female in the neighborhood. The lower the male sex drive, however, the less inciting is the female.

Preferred Food Goals

There is a greater inciting effect of a learned anticipation of a more preferred goal object than of one of a lesser preference. Hutt (303) found that both preferred taste and amount of food are significant contributors to the rate of bar pressing in a Skinner-type apparatus. Small, medium, and large pellets, saccharin-flavored, basic diet, and citric-flavored food were used. The rate of performance in Figure 9-4 is in the same order as found on independent preference tests. In another study (670) rats were trained to associate a particular degree of concentration of sucrose (a highly preferred substance) with the cues from a feeding place.[11] After this association was formed, the animals, neither hungry nor thirsty nor deprived in any known way, were placed in a new situa-

[11] The preliminary training was under two hundred reinforcements, so that performance was to some degree stabilized before tests of goals effects were made. The tests for the contribution of the variations in the goal were made in five successive daily sessions of thirty reinforcements per half hour. When tests for experimental extinction followed, resistence to extinction was found to vary with the previous quality and quantity of the goal object.

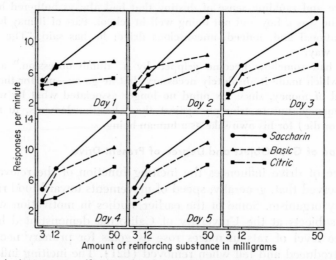

Figure 9-4. Activity rise (bar pressing) is a function both of taste and size of the food substance received after each bar press. Hutt (303)

tion where they could run to the feeding place. The animals which associated the feeding place with a greater concentration of sugar ran faster to this reward location. The preliminary training in the study did not include running toward the goal. Hence the greater inciting contribution of the learned anticipation for the more preferred sucrose concentration could not, on the first tests at least, be the resultant of a specific motor habit. Practice was continued in the running; speed further decreased under practice, and the effect of the preferences was no longer measurable.

Inciting Effects of Symbols of Goals

The inciting role of learned goal symbols for human subjects was illustrated on p. 190. A red light and an associated tone, both used as signals of the achievement of being correct, sustained performance. Also, children work harder with symbolic verbal praise or other information concerning their attempts to reach a goal. Experimental studies with subhuman subjects have likewise indicated that clicks, tones, white (black, striped, etc.) goal boxes, after association with rewarding conditions, can act for (represent) the more direct goals. And, if substituted for the more direct goals, they will, for a while at least, be a supporting source of continued performance (463).

The experiments with the chimpanzees by Cowles (130) and Wolfe (657) illustrate how the neutral stimulus (a poker chip) becomes a symbolic goal and is inciting. The chips are neutral at first, for after examining them briefly the animals were indifferent to them (not having been trained to play poker). But after they learned to use them in a vending machine to obtain a food reward, the tokens too had reward value. Chimpanzees once they learn that poker chips are symbols of grapes or peanuts will work for them. They will hoard them. They will compete for them (grab them from their cage mates), and if permitted to hold them, they will delay a longer time than usual before a barrier between them and the machine that will change the poker chips for food. The *energizing* function of anticipated attainment of the symbolic goal is indicated by an increased vigor in performance evoked from the chimpanzees when their action is followed by the poker chips. Such animals also learn where this symbolic goal can be attained. These symbols have an energizing function, as do the paper dollars for humans, presumably because they evoke learned anticipation of satisfaction.

One of the interesting behavioral tests of the energizing functions acquired by the poker chips was run by Wolfe (657) by putting two chimpanzees together in an experimental room. They were both already trained to "value" the neutral stimuli. These tokens were then thrown on the floor between the two chimpanzees. There was a scramble for the tokens. (Five minutes after the tokens were tossed on the floor, they could be exchanged for food.) In the pairing of two female chimpanzees, Bimba and Bula, Bimba got eighty-four of the symbolic rewards, while Bula had only forty-six. Thirteen sessions were run. When Bula was paired with a male chimp, Velt, she obtained even a smaller share of the tokens. However, Noos, another male, dominated the session when he was paired with Velt, and picked up or took from Velt all the tokens. (Velt had previously received some rough treatment from the other male.) Even for the chimpanzees, behavior is not a simple matter of responding to symbolic rewards.

The values of many of man's tokens rest on their exchangeability for other objects. But with man, there are learned satisfactions assigned to the symbols of his civilization which seem to grow out of the value which other men have for these tokens, rather than in their exchangeability for useful goods. What other men value, we value. This is sometimes called keeping up with the Joneses, but it is more complex than the phrase implies. There are "crazes" among adolescents—for certain kinds of clothes or matchboxes—and among adults, for old furniture or new furniture. These become goals.

That mothers may overaspire for their children and thus even threaten the children's adjustment is illustrated in Inset 19.

INSET 19. GOALS SET BY MOTHERS FOR THEIR CHILDREN*

That children's aspirations are fixed by their parents is generally acknowledged, even considered a proper duty of the parents. That goals set by parents may conflict with those desired by the children is again so easily observed that it has had little systematic study. To what degree such conflicts may be the source of psychosomatic difficulties is a question of interest in a study by Little and Cohen (376) comparing goals announced by normal and asthmatic children, as well as comparing those set by the mothers of these children.

The task was the usual dart-throwing performance. The results of a child's performance could be observed by the mothers. They wrote down what they thought their child would next attain. This was done before the child stated his aspiration score.

Both normal and asthmatic children stated positive goals, but the latter set reliably higher goals for themselves. Also, the mothers of the asthmatic children set reliably higher goals than the other mothers.

The Probability of Success in Goal Attainment

The probability of obtaining a satisfying effect as well as the amount of expected reward modifies the effort expended. In one study (Atkinson,

---

* Adapted from S. W. Little and L. D. Cohen, Goal setting behavior of asthmatic children and of their mothers for them. *J. Pers.*, 1951, 19, 376–389.

29) performance level (speed) was highest when human subjects were told they had a 50–50 chance of winning a small sum of money; in contrast, *a high or a low probability of success decreased the drive, as indicated by a decrease in speed of work.* (The measures were the amount accomplished in arithmetic problems and in a routine drawing task in twenty minutes. Female college students were used.) As indicated in Figure 9-5, the subjects worked harder when the probability of the reward was about 50–50. When the chance of losing was fairly certain, effort apparently did not seem worthwhile, at least with these subjects working for a *low* reward. And likewise, when the chance of winning was high, there was, so it seemed, little anticipated satisfaction and hence a decrease in effort expended.

A slight change in the experiment was made, i.e., there was an increase of the amount of the monetary reward. This change modified the curvilinear relation between probability of winning and effort expended. All subjects under a slightly larger money reward ($2.50 instead of $1.25) increased their efforts, doing this even when the probability of winning was low or was high. Figure 9-5 shows how the subjects' performance level increased under the larger money reward. The curvilinear relation between probability of winning and effort expended tended to disappear under the anticipation of a larger amount of money. In other words, with a greater reward anticipated, even if the probability of gaining it was low or the chances excellent, the individuals tended to step up their efforts. If offered a possible 5,000 dollars, this curvilinear relation would be even less likely to appear.

One variable in the test is disinclination to work. Atkinson (29) suggests that the "law of least effort" might be responsible for inhibiting work output. When attainment of a small reward is not probable, or when the probability of winning a small reward is quite certain, the indi-

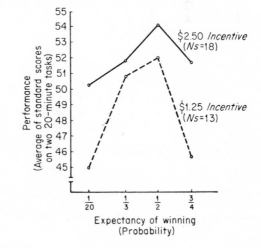

Figure 9-5. Effort expended is a function of the size of the monetary incentive and the expectancy of winning (probability). Female college students were the subjects. Atkinson (29)

viduals are disinclined to effort. The last condition offers no challenge. In the first, the reward attainment is too improbable to "risk" effort, especially for a low reward.

On the other hand, if a large sum of money can be won, even if the chances of winning are quite probable, quite improbable, or 50-50, effort is likely to increase in all situations. And differences among the situations in work output tend to disappear.

Proximity of Goal and Effort Expended

Among the early findings supporting the inciting function of goals were reports of the goal gradient: The closer the animal came to a learned goal place, the faster he ran (298). With practice, the gradient flattened. Man too is subject to the goal gradient effect. See Inset 20.

INSET 20. PROXIMITY OF GOALS INCREASES WORK PACE*

In work tasks, goals of differing proximity of attainment can be imposed upon human subjects. The closer the goal is approached, the higher the rate of work from men. In a study by Hauty and Payne (255) one group of young male adults (trainees in the Air Force) were told that they were to perform a perceptual-motor task for four hours; then they would be given a rest period. Another group were told to perform for seven hours. As indicated in Figure 9-6, the group with a more proximate goal (the rest

* Adapted from G. T. Hauty and R. B. Payne, Methods of mitigation of work decrement, *Project No.* 21-1601-0004, Randolph Field, Tex.: U.S.A.F. School of Aviation Medicine, *Report No.* 4, 1953.

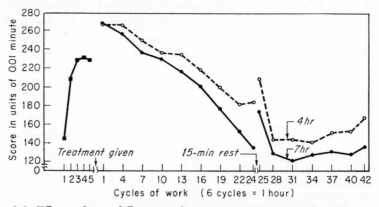

Figure 9-6. Effects of two different goal proximities upon rate of output in a perceptual-motor task. For one group (dotted line) the goal (rest period) was four hours distant. The other group was told that the rest period was seven hours away. Both groups were stopped after four hours. The work output was greater for the group with a more proximate goal, and this effect continued after the rest period. Eighty-four Air Force trainees in each group. Subjects were also being tested for different pharmacological treatments. Hauty and Payne (255)

period) worked at a faster pace. This finding is identical with that reported on pp. 16–17 in the discussion of a quantitative set. An assigned task which is not as long in time as another will elicit a higher work pace.

In addition, the rate of work increased when the goal was close. Moreover, after a fifteen-minute rest (given to both groups) the subjects who had originally maintained a higher work pace continued to do so.

The results suggest that goals and intermediate goals (subgoals) are beneficial to work output, though probably for more than one reason.

The interpretations of the goal gradient include an associative or learning explanation—that the responses preceding the goal are presumably better learned than those further back in the approach S-R unit. But the evidence reviewed previously that the rate of approach varies according to the size or other attributes of the goal object suggests that the goal gradient may be the resultant of a greater inciting (energizing) effect as the expectancy of attaining the goal increases. "Contrast effect" (reviewed below), moreover, supports this second interpretation.

Incitement as Related to Contrast Effect between Expected and Attained Goals

The degree to which goals are incitors is relative to the expected goal effect. Thus, anticipated satisfaction is anchored to the previous satisfaction obtained. When a hungry animal, however, obtains a piece of food which is *smaller than previously obtained,* he will show less vigor in his activity on the next trial. Why? The lesser effect from that which was anticipated seems to be a depressant of the drive level. And if extrinsic rewards are more than expected, the animals appear to be elated. This contrast effect has been noted with chimpanzees who exhibit behavioral signs of disappointment, anger, or both when the usual reward for some performance is shifted to a less preferred one. This same effect of shifting a reward was demonstrated by Crespi (133) and Zeaman (671). As seen in Figure 9-7, a shift in quantity of food reward to a smaller amount than had been received on many previous trials slowed down the animals. They were depressed in activation. Similarly, if the shift was to a larger amount of food, the rats were speeded up. They started faster toward the goal on the next trial. It is suggested that they were elated by the contrast between the old and the new reward.

Nor are the contrast effects under goal changes the exclusive characteristic of the subhuman organism. Man, that creature who is so unlike other animals in many ways and yet is often activated by what stirs the subhumans, is *incited* by goals; and he is also *depressed* when learned anticipated effects are not attained. And man, like the subhuman organism, shows signs of elation when the reward effect is greater than expected.

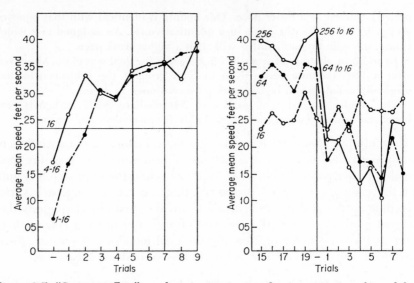

Figure 9-7. "Contrast effect": a change—increase or decrease—in size of usual food reward is correlated with a change in speed of running. On the left of the figure the change is from a small to a larger size (sixteen pellets). The animals run faster than controls, who are also rewarded with sixteen pellets. On the right side of the graph a decrease in size of usual reward is followed by a decrease in activity. The speed of the animals falls below the usual sixteen-unit level. Hull (301) as adapted from Crespi (133)

Goals—Are They Incitors or Reinforcers or Both?

Are goals, when anticipated, incitors to arousal and, when attained, reinforcers for learning? It has been shown that a real or symbolic goal energizes the organism. When attained, does it reinforce the learning how to reach it and/or reinforce the learning that the effect is satisfactory? The first question rephrased is as follows: Should the observed greater activating effect of a larger quantity of a goal, such as food for hungry animals, be interpreted as reflecting greater reinforcing (strengthening) of the learning "to move fast," or merely as indicating a greater *inciting*, or energizing, effect on the performance? There is no doubt that the performance improves in speed. Reynolds (506, 507) obtained higher performance levels with larger rewards. The rate of progress to the different levels of performance is the same, indicating that learning strength is not different under the varying sizes of rewards but that performance is different (661). Also support for the interpretation of performance change rather than of learning is the finding that a shift in the size of the reward *suddenly* shifts speed; learning is not so rapid in its appearance.

Maher and Wickens (389) added further support to the conclusion that different sizes of rewards affect performance levels rather than different degrees of learning. Groups of subjects were trained in a maze to different amounts of food reward. By the twentieth trial, running speed was significantly superior for the animals receiving a larger amount, but errors were not. A transfer test indicated that size of reward did *not* affect learning strength. Animals with small-sized rewards in their performance were tested two and a half months later for maze retention and were not inferior to the large-reward animals. (The transfer test for retention was on thirst, with no difference in amount of reward.)

This discussion has attempted to isolate general principles applicable to organismic activation, i.e., as related to to-be-attained effects. The following examines a more specific area of motivational interest: the goals of men in industry and the possible origins of the satisfactions therein. Both "spurt methods" and long-term incentives are briefly examined.

GOALS OF MEN IN INDUSTRY

Management has long been interested in having satisfied workers, apparently on the assumption that production would go up or, at least, costs would be reduced, since such factors as turnover or absenteeism would be lessened among "happy" workers. There is less correlation than might be expected between the satisfactions of men in their work and the gains to management, though some positive relationships are reported. And there is increasing recognition that more than the aims of management must be considered as justifications to increase satisfactions in work.

What variables in the work situations are correlated with reported satisfactory conditions? Two general origins are briefly considered: intrinsic and extrinsic rewards.

Intrinsic

The effect of an intrinsic goal, e.g., a goal to improve for the sake of improvement and not in order to reach an extrinsic reward, can lead to the intensification and the maintenance of efficiency over a long period of time. When, for instance, a subject is given an opportunity to check on the efficiency of his eye movements in reading every twenty-five minutes, the *length of time* that *he could read efficiently* increased (113). Pilots who had to read instruments at high speed and great accuracy could also maintain a consistent high level of skill *for long periods*, showing no bad effects whatsoever provided that they had at intervals *ways of checking on their performance*. It seemed as if something had been added to the original goal at the starting of the work. Workers in industry report greater satisfaction with stimulating (nonmonotonous) tasks, visible results, and opportunity for self-expression. A "feeling of accomplishment" in a factory situation is described by Whyte (654, p. 37) on observations of goals of industrial workers: "Repetitive factory jobs may seem to have no inherent meaning to the worker. He may think of his work as simply an endless series of meaningless motions. Piecework when quota appears to be attainable provides meaning to the job in the form of a goal to shoot at. But note that this goal does not seem to be present in every piecework job." When quota earnings seem clearly unattainable, the goal is not present for the worker and he abandons the game. "On the other hand, if the outcome is completely predictable and certain, then the work again can become monotonous and meaningless. Finally, if quota achievement or failure of such achievement depends predominantly upon chance factors outside of the worker's control, then he experiences frustration instead of satisfaction" (654, p. 37).

There is satisfaction in the industrial field that comes from signs of progress, slight though the progress may be. *If* goals can be set by the men themselves and *if* the knowledge that they are, or are not, meeting them is added, then the satisfactions of the day are affected. Men are concerned with progress for the sake of progress. That the progress is not at the rate which management might prefer may not interfere with the worker's satisfactions; though if the rate is above what is accepted as reasonable by the other workers, then conflicting social values may decrease the individual's satisfaction. In an industrial setting there may be fear of the other workers if a man sets a pace above the group norm, and the fear may be in open conflict with his own desire to make more money.

Extrinsic

Extrinsic factors can aid, or nullify, any *intrinsic* liking for a specific work task. Not all the variables that account for such differences have been adequately identified (607, p. 329). Among them are probably the following: working conditions, including the personality of the boss, and the social and cultural background of the employees. Reported as correlated with satisfactions are freedom from close supervision together with individual aid when needed.

A bonus is an extrinsic factor, but its significance to the worker changes with the probability of attainment and with other variables such as bonus amount, need for the money, work required. Extrinsic rewards, and there are many, are often "spurt methods" for increasing the rate of energy output and are of short-term usefulness. A contrast is drawn below between spurt incentives and long-term goals.

Long-term Goals

Bartlett (41), an English psychologist, writes in 1950, when England was concerned with improvement of industrial production after World

War II, that the use of spurt methods (short-term incentives) implies that in some fashion they can be made an almost magical cure for a large portion of our social discontents.

Definitely and decisively they cannot. They can operate in two ways only, by increasing effort or by prolonging efforts. The second is beyond question the steadier and the healthier way, but it is, equally certainly, the most unpopular. If incentives are to have a fair chance to achieve the wide social effects which are hoped for, there are two problems which people who know how to tackle them must be given reasonable opportunities to solve. First, we must know the normal limits of human tolerance for load, speed and particular environmental conditions of work. And secondly we must discover how to produce a socially responsible population in sufficient numbers. (41, p. 128)

The "socially responsible" population must have sources of long-term satisfactions in the workaday world over and above the fluctuating ones of each day. Not independent of rewards which come and go in the daily lives of men, yet basically more significant, are long-term incentives.

Among the characteristics of a job which make it appealing for a long-term acceptance are (1) its offer of advancement in some vocational aspiration and (2) the "feeling of security" gained by entering the particular line of work. In studies in England and in America (325, 518, 607) it was found that workers, especially those of the lower occupational groups, rated *job security* high on the different lists of factors affecting liking for a job. Bartlett (41) writes concerning workers in England in 1950 that, of the fundamental goals for releasing energy into work, the most important are a "foundation of a family which will go on from generation to generation, the slow accumulation of savings which will produce some future assured security, and, for the few, the gradual building up of power or reputation. In proportion as any society removes these from the range of everyday consideration for the bulk of its members, it must accept the external incentive as a condition of spurt only" (p. 128). In addition, jobs vary in degree of status given to the workers.

Status Symbols

Even on the job itself there are status symbols which are satisfying when attained. In one industrial setting new and slower workers were placed at the back of the workroom; status was later attained by being allowed to move up to the front and start on a new aspect of the job. The complexity of origins of satisfaction is revealed even by this simple illustration; moving up to the front could represent (1) individual progress, (2) implied promise of more pay, or (3) a rise in the "pecking order." Nor can the satisfaction from moving to the front be separated from the values (standards) of the society and specific groups therein with which an individual identifies.

The differences among societies as well as the absurdities of status symbols are illustrated in the following. (One's own peculiarities in this respect are often hidden from self-observations.) Viteles (631) reports an early observation that a change from the pick and shovel gang to the millwright gang (who could carry an oil can and wrench) "passed a man up" into a higher group of skilled laborers. This gave satisfaction, though the wage increase was only 2 cents an hour more. Linton (375) reports status symbols to be the row of *cooking pots on display* in the families of men in a primitive tribe of Madagascar. Men who had gone on contract labor and returned with these symbols of achievement had more status.

And the final illustration of a status symbol is not from extrinsic goods nor even from a fine display of cooking pots. A laborer, uneducated but with a good take-home pay, sent his daughter to college. When she had her degree, she found a position which had more prestige than money reward. The father was proud of his daughter, and proud of her professional standing. He said, "Of course, she's making $4,000 a year, and you know that's mighty good for an educated person."

CONCLUDING STATEMENTS

Goals are learned anticipations of events to be attained. Suggested as present action are learned anticipatory responses acting as stimuli. More central constructs have also been postulated as "demands for" or "goal orientations."

The clues by which an observer can identify the goals of others (as well as his own) include variable but continual movements toward a goal place (searching and persistent movements); frustration signs when an organism is blocked; verbal reports of goals; images of fantasies or dreams, or similar symbolic clues to "hidden" desires.

Goals are learned by direct attainment of a satisfactory event or by perceiving that some events would be satisfactory. Otherwise-neutral stimuli may also be associated with satisfactory events and become secondary (learned) rewards. These stimuli are rewarding; but if they are anticipated as to be attained, they are goals.

A most difficult question is what determines the personal utility of events, i.e., the degree of personal value attained or expected in an anticipated event. The value of a goal may in part be determined by anticipated satisfactions. Effects vary from satisfactory to unsatisfactory. Why? Some general factors influential in determining the affective tone are:

inherent or learned likes and dislikes; novelty; use of capacity; enhancement of the self and its values; decrease of irritation; rise in drive excitation if not nonoptimal.

To understand constant changes of affective tone of events along a continuum of satisfaction to dissatisfaction, the relativity of satisfaction must be considered. The degree of satisfaction of an event is relative to the ground in which it occurs. For example, the degree of relief from pain is relative to the original degree of pain. Desirability of objects to be attained is also relative to the immediate drives and anticipated drives, to present moods, to previous success and failure, and to the strength of the expectancies of reattaining the goals.

Hedonism as a general doctrine is denied. Pleasure and pain are not the mainsprings of all activity. Support for the assumption of difference in affects of events and of the role of these differences in behavior is, however, presented.

The personal utility of events-to-come, or Lewin's similar description of plus or minus "valences," avoids the implication that an event to come may be a goal solely on the basis of an anticipated satisfaction. Other effects than anticipated pleasure may determine the utility to a person of an event and its consequent value.

The inciting function of goals is well established. Variables that have been found to affect this function include attributes of the goal objects, the work required to attain a goal, the probability of success, proximity to goal, and the contrast between what is expected and what attained.

Industry is concerned with goals. The goals of men and management can be contrasted. A brief consideration of intrinsic and extrinsic origins of goals in industry indicates that social rather than primary rewards are extraordinarily potent.

CHAPTER 10

SELECTING—FROM
SENSITIZATION TO CHOICE

Unpredictability is greater for the higher animals, who are less stimulus-bound. There is more autonomous activity in the higher brain and more selectivity concerning which afferent activity will be integrated with the dominant ongoing activity. "Traditionally, we say that the subject is interested in this part of the environment, not interested in that; in these terms, the higher animal has a wider variety of interests and the interest of the moment plays a greater part in behavior, which means a greater unpredictability as to what stimuli will be responded to and as to the form of response" (260, p. 407).

Psychologists are constantly queried about such acts as theft, murder, suicide. Why do men steal? Or why did John Jones murder? Note that there are two questions: one concerning crime in general, but another concerning why John Jones committed the act in question. Similar questions are raised when a man goes against the mores of his social group and marries a woman of a different race. Why did he marry her? The query here is also concerned with the individuality of the man involved. Men generally marry, and questions are raised in regard to their choice. However, it is the violation of usual social expectations that brings the most "whys."

The violation of social rules is likewise behind a mother's questioning of her son: "Why did you hit little Johnny?" And neither the boy who does the hitting nor little Johnny agrees on what was obtained by the hitting. Nor are any verbal answers generally acceptable to the respective mothers of the boys, who probably also disagree with each other. So they may turn to a psychologist, if he is unfortunately present, and ask him. He must assume an air of wisdom which he does not possess in regard to such a difficult problem. He may murmur something about the natural aggression of boys, or he may make the sounder statement that psychologists need more information to answer such a question in regard to individuals. Each individual at a choice point with his specific selections among alternatives suggests new aspects of interwoven motivational and personality determinants, often in a pattern quite unique. However, observations which are slowly accumulating of behavior at choice points illuminate the selections of men in general.

Following is an illustration of selecting by a hypothetical adult man in Western civilization, where, we assume, he has already attained a particular position in a business organization. We must start at some place, that is, examine him at some point of time in his activity stream. We assume that the man is awake and engaged in some activity, such as waiting for his secretary to type a letter which he must sign. Now, since we may also assume that he would be active during this time, we will have him thinking about a puzzling problem which has challenged him. Assume further that he becomes deeply engaged in this thinking activity. We know that his relative thresholds of excitability are thereby raised in comparison with the time when he is not engaged in a problem; it would probably take a louder sound, or a brighter light, or a more unusual kind of stimulation to cross his threshold of excitation now than at some other moment. He loses, apparently, some sensitivity to the usual colors, touches, sounds, etc., in contact with him. Even though these external stimulations may register upon his receptors, their influence on selective orientations is restricted or not present. A loud bell rings. The physical properties of this particular stimulus source (e.g., the amplitude of the sound waves) are of such a nature that his auditory receptors are increasingly stimulated. He may then be overtly oriented. His ongoing activity is interfered with, and he turns his body toward the spatial source of the reception of the sound. Orientation is determined at first by the dominance of the auditory pattern; note how we assume that the sound is the *figure* against the ground furnished by all other afferent excitations. Selecting continues *after* this first primitive figure-ground relation arises. The auditory stimulation is recognized (selectively perceived) as a loud sound, a bell, and a telephone bell, and it may be responded to by further behavior or selectively ignored.

Motivational determinants may be present before the telephone bell rings. A man may be sensitized for specific stimulating patterns before the latter occur. One of the specific drives, a goal, a wish, or a set, may impose a specific perceptual structure on the sensory flux. If a man is set for a telephone call, he may quickly perceive any sound as a telephone bell, whether correct or not; but if incorrect, he is soon checked by his responses and the resultant feedback. If, for example, he answers the telephone and there is no one on the line, he has information which cancels his first but incorrect perception.

If a message is finally received, it may pose a significant choice: e.g., to buy some property or not; to accept an invitation or refuse; to join with others in a civic project or to spend more time in leisure. These and similar major or minor decisions are constantly demanded.

In order to consider the problems posed above, we will be first concerned with selecting as simple sensitization, then at a more complex level as evaluative choice.

Anticipated outcomes of various alternatives of possible action affect choices. There is a balancing of the utility of each alternative action. In Chapter 11 the discussion concerns the cognitive activities of focusing, perceiving, and remembering, which may be changed by the dominant motivational determinants. Selecting as a central process encompasses not only convergence without cognitive involvement, such as when drives sensitize differentially, but also choices via cognitive mediating activities.

Selecting is Manifest in Various Ways

Selecting is manifest among stimuli arising from the internal and external fields. First one, then another external aspect is the focus of orientation. All possibilities of afferent arousal are probably never realized even if the external origins of excitation are greatly reduced, thus limiting the sensory alternatives. If a bright light in the usual external field is the focus, there are also other potential stimulating sources. Simultaneously other receptors are being stimulated, resulting in sounds, feels, tastes, smells.

Many of the potential origins of stimuli are selectively eliminated. A man can turn his back, close his eyes, spit out a noxious-tasting substance. Adaptation also occurs to many sensory inputs.

Though the external stimulating field may not change, *response* evocation may change. A hungry child usually responds to food by eating, but as his hunger drive is satisfied his response may change to playing with his food rather than eating it.

Stimulus and Response Selecting. Assume that a child has been presented with two potential stimulating objects, let us say candy and an orange. The mere fact that these two objects are in his potential receptor field does not ensure that they will be stimulating agents to the child. However, assume both set up afferent inputs, i.e., the child senses both; then one may become the focus. In other words, one pattern of stimuli becomes temporarily dominant. The child, let us say, focuses upon the candy. Why? A learned anticipation of a sweet taste might turn him toward the candy. Or perhaps a temporary desire to resist social pressure constantly exerted against a choice of candy would affect his selecting of candy. Motivational psychology is concerned with such constant selective filtering among potential stimulations as well as with the temporary dominance of one perceptual pattern in the sensory flux over others.[1] Motivational psychology is concerned with the relationships observed between the perceptual organizations and the transient needs, wishes, longings, and temporary sets as well as with the more stable factors like the attitudes and values of an individual.

The *evocation of the response* is the final stage of selecting. The child of the above illustration may reach for the orange; then he may eat it or play with it. Motivational psychology is concerned with the selecting among the alternatives with respect both to (1) stimulations and (2) responses.

Stimulus and response selectings are usually concomitant. That the organism is sensitized for a particular external stimulus does not, however, mean that he will inevitably change his responses. An organism may shift in his focusing upon various stimulating sources in the external world even though his behaviors may not markedly shift. The common observation, however, is that whatever produces a change in the readiness of the organism for a particular stimulus also affects the selective releasing of behaviors. At the higher level of organisms, this may be phrased as follows: When the figure of the perceptual field changes, the responses usually do too.

Indices to Changes in Selecting

In previous chapters, measures of arousal variations were of the amount or rate of inner and outer reactivity. For indices to shifts in selecting from one alternative to another, there is the frequency of sensory contact and/or the number of recurrences of one response unit as contrasted to other potential ones. For example, when an organism is given a choice point of two paths (two alternatives), the percentage frequency of moving down path 1 versus path 2 is a measure of selecting.

Selecting Is Limited

Man is restricted in the potential alternatives among which selecting may occur. For example, man is restricted by his bodily structure. The selections on the input side are limited to the alternatives which he can *sense*: e.g., he is not as capable in his visual reception as is a fly or some birds. He cannot respond to stimuli for which he has no adequate receptors, and he may die as a result. Sunburn, for which he has no im-

---

[1] When it is said that an object is recognized (perceived), this assumes that there has been a differentiation of a sensory pattern (usually described as roundness and color, etc.) and moreover, that a meaning, such as "orange," has arisen in the perceptual activity.

mediate sensing, will kill; so will carbon monoxide, if breathed in sufficient quantity. His taste receptors are not completely adequate to discriminate poisons from nourishing materials (515). To the degree that he as an individual is inadequate in sense organs, this selecting is further limited.

The potential stimuli may be reduced by physical barriers; there may be restrictions (social or physical) upon movement. A homogeneous sensory field is highly restrictive to man, dependent as he is upon variation of stimulating patterns from external fields for variability in responses.

The aging process also curtails the selecting capacity because of lessened energy available to deal with a multitude of stimuli. The aging person excludes much from his awareness and thus decreases his opportunities for choice. Sleep, of course, is a refuge for both the infant and the aged against the clamor of the world, and death the final refuge.

Selecting by man is also limited by his feeble motor equipment. He cannot fly; he is slower and has less strength than many other animals. His superior intellectual functions, however, compensate for his poor motor capacities as well as for any sensory defects.

Selecting is limited when learning is inadequate. Any lack of discrimination between differences in the external field limits a child or man in what he can respond to. He can be limited by an inadequate repertoire of learned responses. Assume that a child has not learned to write, shake hands, or any of the other multiple socially necessary behaviors. These then cannot be selectively evoked.

Man's information may be incomplete in regard to possible outcomes of his action or the action of others or in regard to the occurrence of natural events. The prediction of the weather is one of man's obvious inadequate predictings. His choices of appropriate clothing for the day may be inadequate because of incomplete information. Or his choices may even be inappropriate because of personality-motivational determinants. The latter may be active when, not being a cautious man, he decides to leave his raincoat at home on the very day that there is rain.

SENSITIZATION

One of the simplest phenomena of selecting is the changing sensitization of an organism as its internal environment varies. At certain stages in growth, with internal tissue changes occurring, the organism responds to stimuli hitherto ignored and exhibits patterns of responses which had not been observed before. Elicitation of the complete sexual behavior is more probable when maturation has brought appropriate changes in the internal environment.

Also when the organism is under the influence of recurring tissue needs, a differential sensitization becomes manifest. The organism is then hypersensitive to some stimuli while it reduces or inhibits responsiveness to others. "It both focuses and filters the potential stimuli provided by the external environment" (466, p. 293). Dashiell's statement (138) that you can lead a horse to water but you can't make him drink *unless he is thirsty* illustrates the obvious role of need drives in the selectings of organisms, both on the stimulus and the response side.

Illustrations of Sensitization

Selections of food substances are in part determined by nutritional needs. Children select food elements according to their bodily needs, i.e., if they are offered all the foods which they require (142). "On any one day they may eat large quantities of butter or meat, for example, just as if they had an over-whelming hunger for some essential material in these foods. Over a long period of time, however, their selections shift from one kind of food to another so that they achieve a balanced diet and grow normally" (440, p. 395). A similar situation can be shown for rats and other subhuman subjects. If rats are presented with several foods each of which contains one element, such as salt, sugar, or fat, the rats will eat from each dish an amount which is just about correct for their needs. When they are given extra calories in their drinking water in the form of sugar or alcohol, they cut down the caloric values they take from solid foods (254).

Richter's investigations (512, 513, 514) have included studies of metabolic disturbances created by extirpation of different endocrine glands and the correlated changes in self-selection feeding. These changes have indicated, in general, remarkable self-regulation. The food selections of rats vary as their physiological conditions are changed, and this variation often permits the animals to survive by their own adaptive mechanisms. Among Richter's many significant studies is the following: If the parathyroid glands are surgically removed, rats develop tetany and die within a few days. When parathyroidectomized rats are given free access to a solution of calcium lactate, they ingest large quantities of it, keep themselves free from the symptoms of tetany, and survive indefinitely (516). This selection is not of a frequently practiced response; it appears with onset of extreme need.

Organisms vary in the capacity to select appropriately among needed substances (apparently such a capacity is in part inherent). Capacity to select food elements which are needed may be deficient because of insensitivity to differences in stimulating effects of tastes. It is reported that differences in sensitivity among individuals of the human species may reach such magnitudes that some individuals are said to be "taste-blind," e.g., sensitivity varies among humans to a group of substances like phenylthiocarbamide, which is bitter to some and, except in the highest concentrations, tasteless to others (71, 197). This insensitivity appears to be an inherited characteristic.

Sensitization by Nonneed Bodily Conditions. There are internal conditions which are not forerunners of drives, yet which sensitize in a manner similar to drives. Some supporting observations follow: (1) Pfaffmann (483) reports the influence upon tastes of such changed physiological conditions as arise from pregnancy, aging, and drugs. In women during pregnancy, the threshold of taste is elevated for sodium chloride and for acid (244). (2) Though aging may be correlated with reduced taste sensitivity, this is probably associated with a decrease in the number of *taste buds*. (3) Possible internal factors in the blood stream and body fluids are illustrated by Hartridge's study (253) of the effect of intravenous injection of certain drugs which give rise to taste sensations after a latent period attributed to circulation time. (4) In contrast, hypoglycemia following the injection of insulin apparently leads to reduced sensitivity for sugar. "Reduction of the blood-sugar level below 50 milligrams per cent appeared to render the sense of taste specifically less sensitive to sugar. Sensitivity to other substances was not affected" (483, p. 1155). (5) The auditory threshold may be lowered under alcohol with the result that sounds too faint to be detected under normal conditions become audible. In audition as in vision, discrimination is, however, decreased by alcohol. The change in discrimination threshold may amount to as much as 30 per cent (45).

Sensitization by a Learned Drive Component. Change in intensity of stimulation (external in origin) has been experimentally correlated with a learned anxiety. Hill et al. (281) obtained verbal reports of the intensity of pain (following electric shock) when subjects were and were not anxious. (These changes in reported experiences of pain would decrease further sensory contact.) An increase in the estimation of intensity of shock when the subjects were anxious about the experiment disappeared when their anxiety was relieved. Presumably the sense organs were excited to the same degree each time. It was the presence of a learned anxiety drive component that was related to the change in the reports of intensity of pain.

Need Drives in Response Selecting. Response selecting is in part determined by internal conditions for drives. The appearance of the *submissive response* patterns is related to the degree of hunger as well as to the sex hormonal level in chimpanzees. The dominance-submissive behavior patterns in pairs of chimpanzees shift according to degree of food deprivation. In line with this is an observation in the Minnesota study of semistarvation diet: Adult human males, quite hungry, were more easily irritated, more ready for aggressive responses. However, the social value of politeness or a respectful attitude toward the experimenters negated any direct expression of aggression against those who were withholding the food. (This social value does not protect the housewife from the hungry husband who finds no meal when he returns.)

Specific fighting behavior is likely to appear in the activity stream of nonprimates as the amount of male hormone increases in the organismic system. Fighting is increased in fishes, reptiles, and birds by androgen administration (44). Castrated male rats showed increased aggression under administration of large amounts of male hormone (44). Though there is a positive relationship between aggressiveness and level of sex hormones in primates, it is not so consistent a relationship as in the lower animals. Of course, the primates, especially man, are the most capable of indirect and subtle methods of expressing aggressiveness.

Changes in primary need-drive components also selectively influence the evocation of *learned* response patterns. It is easy to illustrate shifts in the multiple learned responses as drives change, e.g., kneeling in prayer within a church ceases when there is a fire. The learned behavior of moving out of the church appears when the fear of fire dominates.

An experimental study (503) illustrated a shift in the learned responses in a binary choice situation, a T-maze, as the drive component was changed on alternating days from thirst to hunger. After the animals had learned to run to one goal box when hungry and another when thirsty, then hunger and thirst drives were combined. The stronger of the two drives dominated and sensitized the learned correlated response pattern. For example, if twenty-two hours' hunger is combined with four, eight, or twelve hours' thirst, the learned behavior most frequently appearing is running the maze path which was previously followed by reduction of the hunger. Approximately 80 per cent of the choices are of the learned path which leads to food when the dominant drive is from twenty-two hours of food deprivation and the thirst is based on only four hours of water deprivation. But as thirst increases, the animals run more frequently the path that leads to water. If the twenty-two hours' hunger continues but the animals are also made thirsty for sixteen to twenty-two hours, neither hunger nor thirst is dominant in the combination of drives.

To rule out differences in habit strengths which might have influenced the selecting, a stringent criterion of learning was used in the study. In other words, the acquisition was carried to the same high level for learning to obtain food as it was for the different learning to obtain water. Hence, selection in this binary choice situation of one of the two alternative learned behaviors was attributed to the strongest of the combined drives and its correlated incentive, since the habit strengths to run either path were approximately equal. Another illustration follows of the sensitizing by a central motivational determinant of one response over another.

Moods Sensitize Responses Differentially. Shifts in word responses can be observed as mood changes are reported. A specific mood, as rated by human subjects, produces relatively more verbal responses *in line with the mood* than not related to it. Bousfield and Barry (76) found that subjects in a pleasant mood produced in free word association relatively more pleasant words. The verbal reports for subjects in an unpleasant mood were, in general, unpleasant words. Though it is difficult to produce in the laboratory intense mood states like the dejection and self-recrimination of the suicidal person, it is possible to induce moods with various drugs (468). Small doses of potent drugs have been administered to human subjects, and changes in their behavior have been studied. A checklist of adjectives was used against which the subjects rated their moods both before and after taking drugs. Dramamine produced an increase in the checking of adjectives like "tired," "drowsy," "detached," "sluggish," "disinterested," "dull," "lazy," "retiring," and "withdrawn." Amphetamine increased the checking of "businesslike," "talkative," "capable," "enterprising," "independent," and "jittery"; small doses of amphetamine plus seconal produced words like "generous," "cheerful," "industrious," "expansive," and "lighthearted"; larger doses produced words like "confident," "fearless," "forceful," "masterful," and "uninhibited." Osgood states that this is another demonstration of the "selective effect of motivational states upon language encoding" (474, p. 409).

MECHANISMS FOR SENSITIZATION

What are the mechanisms for sensitization? Does the *receptor* sensitivity change? Or is the selecting a central activity? We will first consider possible changes in the receptors.

Are Sense Organs Modified as Drives Change?

Sensitization of the organism changes with the specific drives. This is established. One suggestion as to how this occurs is that the *receptors are structurally modified* so that they differentially "register" external stimuli. Present evidence would negate this suggestion. A possible exception is, however, presented below.

The chain of intervening physiological events which Beach (45) has analyzed with respect to the loss of sexual behavior in rats following castration and to a decrease in androgen within the internal environment, illustrates how tissue changes following hormonal loss may modify afferent input via changed receptors. As a result of castration, "the number of (genital) papillae is materially reduced, the tactile sensitivity of the glans must be lowered. And marked reduction in this important source of sensory input might logically be expected to exert an inhibiting effect upon copulatory performance" (45, p. 90). Increased dosage of androgen is correlated both with an increase in the mean frequency of genital papillae and also in the proportion of the castrated rats who continue to copulate. Therefore, receptor modification is possibly involved in the decrease in sexual responses following castration.

Can changes in receptor structure account for other differential selectivity? The answer seems to be that if this occurs, it is rare. The next evidence presented supports the concept of more central selecting rather than that of peripheral receptor changes.

Central Editing in the Sensory Flux

The search for the mechanism or mechanisms of stimulus selecting is illustrated by a series of studies of changes in salt intake as need for it increases. Richter (511) and others (35) demonstrated that there is greater response intake of salt as the endocrine balance is disturbed and a need for the substance is increased. What is the mechanism of this selecting? In his early interpretations, Richter suggested that the threshold of the taste receptors was lowered for salt when the need increased. This interpretation has been questioned. The reasoning is as follows. As is well known, after adrenalectomy a strong need for salt arises. The animals under this specific need drive change remarkably in their sensitivity to salt. They detect even in water a very slight amount of salt. For example, in experimental tests one bottle of paired drinking bottles contains undiluted water, and the other has a slight trace of salt in the water; it is the latter which is more frequently selected by the adrenalectomized animals. Is this evidence of a lower receptor threshold for salt when the need is greater? The answer is no, since it is found by the electrophysiological method of determining excitation of taste receptors that the animals *not* greatly needing salt are also quite sensitive to a small amount in the drinking water (485). *The receptors of those animals not in need are as sensitive to a slight trace of the salt substance in the water as are the receptors of those animals who are in extreme need for salt.* The less intake of the slightly salty water by the normal animals is not due to a lesser sensitivity of their receptors. Receptor thresholds are *not* responsive to changes in needs. Rather, a more central editing is responsible for the increase in sensitivity and for the greater intake of the needed salt by the adrenalectomized animals.

Pfaffmann (484) adds evidence that rejection as well as acceptance is a central event. His studies were of nonacceptance of high intensities of salt and sugar. In Figure 10-1 the preference response for a salt substance with increasing concentration is plotted with the discharge of the chorda

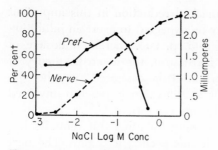

NaCl Log M Conc

Figure 10-1. Preference response to successive salt concentrations shifts from positive to negative without a change in the afferent input signal, i.e., a change that corresponds to the behavioral inversion. Ordinate on the left indicates preference responses of rats; ordinate on the right shows magnitude of integrator deflection (nerve discharge). Pfaffmann (484)

tympanum nerve of the rat. The behavior preference records of the animal for the salty solutions continue to rise until that salt concentration is reached which brings an inversion in the hitherto preferred substance. The significant observation is that the "stop" factor (the rejection factor) is *not* a change in the afferent input signal. Pfaffmann (484) writes that there is no change in the nerve discharge which corresponds to the behavioral shift from acceptance to rejection. Central rather than peripheral mechanisms are responsible for this rejection.

The hypothesis that there is a selective central inhibitory mechanism which might operate to filter sensory impulses has been further supported by such studies as the following. Records of responses in the cochlear nucleus were obtained from unanesthetized cats being bombarded by an auditory stimulus (click). Then visual as well as olfactory stimuli were presented. As long as the cat showed behavioral signs of selective attending to the visual (or olfactory) stimulus, the auditory potential in the cochlear nucleus was practically absent. The implication in this case is that a central inhibitory mechanism temporarily enhanced one afferent source at the expense of another (271).

Central selecting is not a new assumption. As is indicated in Inset 21, it is openly espoused or at least favored by such theorists as Tolman, Lewin, and Hebb.

INSET 21. THEORIES OF SELECTING

Central selecting is not a new assumption in regard to organisms. Organismic capacity for selecting is either implicitly or openly assumed in various psychological theories. Hebb (259) asks in regard to *stimulus selection:*

> Why has there been such a profound reluctance to postulate something going on within the animal that opens the door to one kind of stimulation and closes it to another? There is plenty of factual evidence that this sort of thing happens all the time in behavior, and plenty of physical models to suggest how, conceivably, it might come about. There is the modern dial telephone's selector switch, for example, or the catalyst idea from chemistry,

or the joint action of dust and water vapor to form rain or fog. It is not mysterious, therefore, to postulate attention as something that acts as co-chairman in charge of response, jointly with the present stimulus itself. Not mysterious, that is, unless one's thinking is controlled unwittingly by the picture of a nervous system in which such things are impossible. (259, p. 42)

Tolman (618) suggests that an organism possesses an active, selective capacity and emphasizes its manifestations on both the *stimulus and response* sides. The organism, it is assumed by Tolman, often has to look actively for significant stimuli. He "does not merely passively receive and react to all the stimuli which are physically present" (p. 201). In other words, a central selecting is assumed by Tolman. He writes that the organism is bombarded by stimuli, yet the "nervous system is surprisingly selective as to which of these stimuli it will let in at any given time." The following description indicates that Tolman *assumes* a central control.

> The central office itself is far more like a map control room than it is like an old-fashioned telephone exchange. The stimuli which are allowed in are not connected by just simple one-to-one switches to the outgoing responses. Rather, the incoming impulses are usually worked over and elaborated in the central control room into a tentative, cognitive-like map of the environment. And it is this tentative map, indicating routes and paths and environmental relationships, which determines what responses, if any, the animal will finally release. (618, p. 192)

The stimulus-response school of Hull (299, 301) has been accused of assuming that the organism responds helplessly and passively to the succession of external and internal stimuli. To what degree this accusation is correct is controversial. Certainly Hull pays little attention to selecting on the input side. However, in his last writings Hull considers the selecting factors governing whether approach or avoidance responses to objects in space would be released, and he even, perhaps inadvertently, writes of "choice." To the factors determining reaction potential—such as habit strength, drive strength, incentive, and the dynamism of the signaling stimulus trace—Hull adds such determining factors to "choice" as distance, barriers, and work involved. He states: " . . . in general where two adient fields are in competition, the organism will *choose* the nearer adient object; and the greater the difference in the distance between the two objects, the greater is this probability" (301, p. 269, italics added).

Within an entirely different theory, Lewin's topological psychology, "decisions" at choice points are attributed to forces acting in the field of the organism. The theoretical concepts of regions, barriers, valences, and vectors used in predicting the path of psychological locomotion in the life space of man are best obtained from Lewin's original writings (365, 366).

MOTIVATION AND EVALUATIVE CHOICE[2]

As discussed in the previous section, sensitization by drives is observed in simple animals. Sensitization is evident in man's activity stream, but man is also capable of evaluative choice. Openly and without shame, or at least without any apparent embarrassment, psychologists of today are interested in decision, with an assumption of choice by man. Ward Edwards (170), contemplating the human animal, writes that the central behavioral and introspective fact about thinking human beings is that they make choices. The phenomenon of choice is the key to the higher mental processes; if we know how to understand a person's choices, we know how he thinks. "Choices," adds Edwards, "are the end product of a series of processes which, collectively, have been called the higher mental processes. In spite of its vaguely 'turn-of-the-century' flavor, I know of no other phrase which so nearly describes this whole area of interest" (170, pp. 4–6).

A choice may not commit the man to any serious action. He may take no risk; he may even be indifferent to the outcome. Or again, a choice may commit him to consequences not only for the immediate future but for the rest of his life. Choices may be reversible or irreversible; the latter are usually more critical. Crucial choices affect many later choices. One crucial choice may involve not only the individual but others in many ways.

Cognitive evaluation of alternatives to action more frequently arises when the individual recognizes that he is at a crucial point, e.g., marriage or not, college or not, one vocation versus another. An amusing illustration of a crucial choice point is reported by Comdr. A. F. Blair. During that part of the Naval War College course known as Command and Decision, one instructor was stressing the importance and the difficulty of being able to make a sound decision under pressure. "A visiting officer from a small foreign navy spoke up, 'Decisions, you talk about decisions. I was 700 miles to sea in my destroyer when I received a dispatch from my country: WE HAVE JUST HAD A REVOLUTION. WHICH SIDE ARE YOU ON?'" (Adapted from *Reader's Digest*.)

Man's Capacity for Evaluative Choice

Man's cognitive superiority over other organisms arises in part from his capacities for perceiving complex relationships, for superior remembering, for evaluative judging. It is these superiorities which permit a cognitive balancing of alternatives to action. Man can cognitively span time

[2] Choice involves stimulus and response selecting, but no attempt is made in the studies cited to isolate these aspects for special observations.

periods of much greater length than the subhuman animals can. By the use of symbols, especially words and numbers, he "moves" into the past and into the future; always his anticipations of events in the future are based upon what has happened to him or to others in the past. Man is not a fortune-teller, but he is often and must be a seer who anticipates, sometimes wisely, in regard to the future outcomes of actions on the basis of the past events.

Man can analyze similarities in situations at a complexity greater than is revealed by studies of lower animals. He can act on relationships observed in the past and the present—relationships which he expects will hold in the future. Also because of his superior use of symbols, he can delay longer between the onset of anticipation of an end and the reaching of it.

Man, however, may not always act on the basis of his superior cognitive capacity. Fears, hopes, rage, need drives, likes, dislikes may rule him rather than cold reasoning. The purpose of this section is to illustrate how these and other motivational variables are involved in man's choices.

Expectancies, Their Strength and Personal Utility

In order to consider the significance of motivational variables in man's choices, it is first necessary to consider the construct of expectancy. Choice is made on the basis of learned anticipations or expectancies. For example, a man predicts (anticipates) the behavior of a race horse on a muddy track and chooses to bet or not. If he bets, he expects with a certain degree of probability to win some money. The personal utility of the expected outcome may be quite significant to him, even though the expected payoff may not be a large sum of money. Man acquires various expectancies of what will happen, not only in regard to race horses—and they are often unpredictable—but also in regard to the behavior of other men and of physical events. His choices are also made on the basis of learned anticipations of his own future actions. All choices depend on learned expectancies of events, though there may be great uncertainty in regard to some of these events.

Each expectancy has a certain strength, i.e., man learns the probability of an expectancy's being confirmed. However, the man's subjective probability that an expectancy will be confirmed may be high though the objective or actual probability, as determined by observations of others, may be low. A child may have a high subjective probability of obtaining a pony on his birthday, but all the observations of others indicate that the probability is low, or practically zero, that his expectancy will be confirmed. If a child or an adult has many high subjective probabilities of expected events which do *not* match the objective probabilities of the events occurring, the individual is nonrealistic.

In Chapter 9, Goals, the construct of goal anticipation or expectancy was employed. A goal expectancy is a learned symbolization of an event to be attained. That it will be attained can be predicted on the basis of its attainment in past trials or of observation of others who have attained a similar goal effect. This learned subjective probability may be low or high in regard to reattainment of a goal. And the utility (the personal value) of the goal may range from a low to high degree of desirability. In the treatment in Chapter 9 of goals as satisfactory outcomes, there were considered certain stable factors which determine the desirability of events. The relativity of the degree of anticipated value (personal utility) of goals was also indicated.

Not all expectancies of events to come are goal anticipations. Some events are to be avoided, as was indicated in Chapter 3. Other expectancies have no personal relevance, positive or negative. That 2 plus 2 adds to 4 is an established expectancy, but it may have no personal relevance unless $2 is being added to 2 more and the expectancy of 4 is not confirmed when we are given only $3.

General Description of Formation of Expectancies

Information is useful to establish expectancies. Drops of water fall upon our face. "It is raining," we say. The amount of information from the immediate stimulation of our sensory avenues is limited, but in our past experience a fairly consistent relationship between a few drops of water coming from above and then a downpour of many similar drops permits, in fact forces, the judgment: "It is raining." We not only state what is happening, but we indicate an expectation that rain, a much greater amount of water than a few drops, is coming. And interestingly enough, this provisional expectancy or hypothesis will function selectively, so that we perceive what was present in our external environment but to which we had not previously responded in any organizing fashion. Now we bring to the support of our tentative expectancy other sensory data by observing the clouds, the temperature, the humidity. This further sensory data is immediately organized with the already present hypothesis that "It is raining." This further information will support or deny the provisional expectancy of rain.

For a young child, probably few events are strongly predictable, except that (if the child is fortunate) he expects the older individuals around him to protect him from harmful unexpectedness. Even he, however, early sets up more or less tentative predictions of what will occur. He continues with increasing confidence (higher probability) to set up more and more predictions as his tentative expectancies are confirmed or nonconfirmed by outcomes of his own behaviors or by observations of events around him.

Frequency of confirmation of the expected increases the subjective probabilities of the anticipated actually occurring, but a reversal of an expectancy may occur on one nonconfirmation. For example, strong expectancies are established in regard to the path of the stars, but even one nonconfirmation would raise questions, since it would indicate that the relations between cosmic events might have been incorrectly predicted.

ILLUSTRATIVE CHOICE SITUATIONS

In a simple classification, choice situations can be divided into (1) those in which there are well-learned signals or cues of what events to expect and well-established probabilities of the frequency of the actual occurrence of the events after the signals; (2) those in which there are no signals and/or no known probabilities. However, there are gradations from category 1 to 2.

As is illustrated in Choice Situation I below, there may be knowledge of what events will occur, i.e., established expectancies of events, but probabilities of the frequencies of the events are at first unknown, though they can be learned.

The personal value or utility of the expected events to the individual changes his choices among alternatives. As is illustrated in the studies outlined below, the personal utility of the expected events following different possible alternatives affects choices of men.

CHOICE WHEN THERE ARE NO CUES
CONCERNING THE ONSET OF EVENTS

Choice Situation I: Guessing Situation

In some choice situations in life there are no relevant signals or cues identifying the onset of specific events. All that is known is that an event will occur. Men learn what may happen and learn the frequencies of the events, but in this guessing situation it is not known exactly *when* the events will occur. The bombardment of a town by gunfire, for example, may be correlated with an established expectancy of the bombardment's occurring at night, and the general frequency of the bombardment may be learned. However, the exact time of its onset may be unknown. A choice to remain or not remain on any night is a guessing game. A similar situation in life occurs in interaction of men and women. A man learns the approximate frequency with which his wife will greet him pleasantly when he comes home from work and the approximate frequency with which she will not. However, the cues which would enable him to predict exactly when he may expect a warm greeting are not isolated by him. Other life situations include partial or more adequate learning of signals concerning the exact time and place of specific events.

Experimental Demonstration. The following experiment (229) illustrates the learning of probabilities of events when *no cues* are given in regard to *when* the events occur. The experimenter, however, informed the human subjects that there were two events (light on–light off), though he did not state when or how frequently they would occur. The human adult subjects in this experiment were given sixty opportunities to guess whether a second light would flash. The lights were on a board in front of the subjects. The left light flashed; then the subjects guessed whether the right light would or would not flash. The subjects recorded their bets, or guesses. The interval between the trials was about ten seconds. As the trials continued, the subjects adopted a rate of guessing that matched the actual proportion of the appearance of the second light[3] (see Figure 10-2).

This experiment is an illustration of the learning of probabilities of expected events. The subjects acquired subjective probabilities which matched closely the objective probabilities of the two possible events, i.e., the second light (1) flashed or (2) did not.

Summary. As is indicated above, expectancies of events and subjective probabilities of the events are not identical though both are acquired. In the experiment the subjects were told what events to expect by the experimenter, but they had to learn more slowly, i.e., by a series of trials, how frequently the events occurred. It is also important to remember that in this experimental guessing situation, no cues were given indicating when the light would occur and when it would not. It has been observed by Jarvik (312) that the subjects may attempt to use as cues the number of preceding positive (or negative) trials: e.g., after five trials of the light flashing, then the subjects hypothesize that the light will not appear on the next trial. Such hypotheses are never consistently confirmed in these guessing situations, since the sequence of the events is so arranged by the experimenter that it is essentially random. The problem-solving approach, however, appears in such experiments.[4] As is suggested in

---

[3] There were five different groups predicting under the objective conditions of 100, 75, 50, 25, and 0 per cent of the actual appearance of the second light following the first. All the groups acquired by the sixtieth trial a subjective probability of the appearance of the event that they were predicting. This subjective probability, as indicated by their guesses, closely matched the actual (objective) probability, i.e., the proportion of times that the experimenter flashed the second light. The two groups who were shown the light 100 per cent and zero per cent of the trials were the quickest learners.

[4] See (95, 525) for a discussion of the problem-solving attitude.

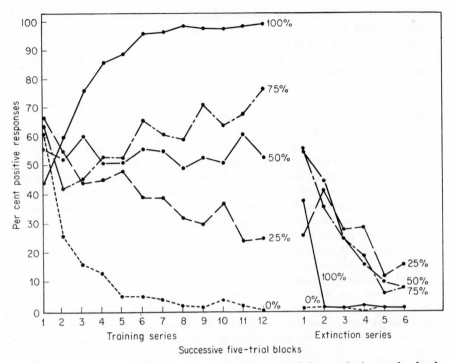

Figure 10-2. Human subjects acquire subjective probabilities which match closely the objective probabilities of two events (light-on or light-off). Change in frequency of positive reports is plotted against trials in training and then in extinction, when light no longer comes on. Grant, Hake, and Hornseth (229)

Inset 22, the "trying out" of responses in some situations can aid the subject in learning the probabilities of the occurrence of events or of any changes therein.

INSET 22. RESTRICTING INFORMATION*

A study by Rogers, Webb, and Gallagher (521) tested human choice behavior in a form which experimentally represents an often-occurring paradigm of human behavior: The individual has the option of trying a response or not, but he can achieve information about the correctness of a response only by making it.

All subjects in this study were told that they must guess whether or not a light would come on after a buzzer had sounded. After this guess, if they thought the light would come on, they were to press a key. If they thought it would not come on, they were not to press the key.

* Adapted from Owen E. Rogers, Wilse B. Webb, and Thomas J. Gallagher, Effect on extinction of restricting information in verbal conditioning. *J. exp. Psychol.*, 1959, 57, 219–223.

One group always had an immediate and complete knowledge of whether they had guessed correctly or not. For others such information was only obtained if they pressed the key. This second group had only partial information unless they deliberately tested what they guessed would be wrong responses.

After the subjects in both groups learned the approximate frequency of the onset of the light, the experimenter, without telling the subjects, stopped flashing the light on any trial. The only correct answer now was to say, "No light will come on." Those subjects who had always been given complete knowledge quickly learned that the light had stopped. However, the individuals who had only partial information continued to guess on some trials that there would be "light onset." Their cessation of incorrect guesses was more gradual, since the feedback after their guesses was inadequate. *If* they had tested each prediction by responding, they would have soon learned that the light had ceased.

Significant points of this study are that handicaps in predicting events correctly include not only incomplete information but also lack of responding, even if the response is in error. In choice terms, the subjects under partial knowledge conditions were asked to choose between responding and finding out whether they were correct, *or* not responding and not knowing if they were correct or incorrect. The subjects with partial knowledge extinguished more slowly, persisting in their incorrect guesses longer than those who had complete knowledge of the results of their choices.

Motivational and personality determinants may modify the probability matching, e.g., the matching by subjects of the objective frequency of an event (the light in the above study) with their subjective probabilities for it.

One of the motivational determinants is now considered: the desirability to an individual of successful prediction. Various studies (399, 132, 305, 320) report fairly consistently that men are more likely to predict the occurrence of an event if it is personally desirable than if it is undesirable. In one study (155) young male undergraduates persistently overpredicted personal success, i.e., they predicted it far more often than they were told that they obtained it. This overprediction was greatest for the least successful men, though it was rare for anyone to predict all successes or all failures. Only one man in the entire experiment gave the same prediction on all trials; this subject predicted failures throughout. He represented the exact opposite of the usual choices.

In contrast, when these male subjects were predicting the success of *another* man, their predictions were close to the actual successes of this man. Their reports were more realistic concerning the frequency of an event which had no personal relevance to them than concerning an event which was personally desirable.

CHOICE IN LEVELS OF ASPIRATION

Choice Situation II: Levels of Aspiration Set by Individuals

Choice Situation II is not simply a guessing game. In other words, limited cues are present on which an individual may predict, and hence he can choose with increasing certainty on specific trials. The subjects are asked to perform in a task for which they assume that their capacities for skillful performance or intelligent responses are required. In these level-of-aspiration investigations, which arose within Lewinian theory (368), the subjects are asked to state successive goal expectancies or aspirations, such as whether they will succeed during dart throwing in hitting the center of a target. After each trial, the subjects are told their scores. These reports of scores from the experimenter may not be the actual scores obtained; they may follow a prearranged number of successes and/or failures. The subjects, however, assume that the reported scores are the actual results and use them to decide whether they will perform more or less successfully on subsequent trials. A subject judges his success or failure by the difference between his statement of his goals and his actual performances as reported to him. A man may also be compared, or compare himself, with an average performance of some group with higher or lower status than he has.

Motivational and Personality Variables and Levels of Aspiration

In their statements of levels of aspiration the subjects are reflecting their successes and failures in the immediate performance and also their personalities. For example, their own estimates of their capacities, skills, strength, intelligence, or whatever is required in order to perform at different levels of achievement will affect the extent of their aspirations and the likelihood that they will change their successive goals to match their reported performances (545).

In a number of studies, variables of motivational interest have been isolated as affecting goals set by individuals. These variables include (1) the difficulty of the task for an individual, (2) his previous successes or failures in other or similar tasks, and (3) his usual self-esteem, including his degree of confidence in his ability to attain goals. These and other variables have been either established or suggested as significant in various studies of levels of aspiration (122, 368). Success generally leads to a raising of level of aspiration, and failure to a lowering. Success and failure are relative, however, and not simply determined by the absolute amount of progress. An illustration of the relativity of failure is a man who has reached a high degree of achievement in his life according to usual social standards but who considers himself a failure because his level of aspiration was originally higher than he attains.

Among personality variables which have been studied as possible determinants of level of aspiration are (1) anxiety tendencies, (2) strength of need to achieve, (3) general adjustment, and (4) as indicated above, self-esteem.

General adjustment as a variable in level of aspiration was tested by Gruen (232). He compared the levels of aspiration of adolescents who differed in personality adjustment as determined by a general adjustment inventory (Rogers), teachers' ratings, and observations in classrooms. The subjects were asked to estimate their level of performance in a familiar task. The results indicated that the group of maladjusted boys and girls made more *extreme* overestimates and underestimates of what scores they would obtain on successive trials compared with the more adjusted children. An interpretation of these results is that the maladjusted were not able to face possible failure; hence they tended to vary what they stated that they would be able to do. An extreme underestimate protected them from failure. An extreme overestimate, if not attained, could be easily rationalized as an impossible goal.

In another study (582) the problem of how the self is viewed was investigated as a possible parameter in stated levels of aspirations. Self-ratings were obtained under different instructional sets so that the role of certainty-uncertainty or optimism-pessimism attitudes could be determined. Then levels of aspiration were recorded. Results were as follows: Uncertainty about the self tended to accompany high goal setting and an expectation that one's performance would be variable. Pessimistic self-appraisals were related to low goal setting. The above studies indicate that the self-concept is of consequence in choices of levels of aspiration.

Another personality tendency is need to achieve. High *n*-achievement subjects have a greater subjective probability of goal attainment (328). During repeated trials on a digit-symbol task, individuals with high as contrasted to low *n* achievement had greater difference scores between what they attained and what they stated was their level of aspiration. However, when these high *n*-achievement subjects were given knowledge of the results of their performance, they moved the level of their stated aspirations closer to their actual performance. They became more realistic with knowledge of the results in their predictions of what they could attain.

Level of Aspiration in Pathological Groups. There is a "tendency for anxious groups to show much greater variability in level of aspiration, setting their goals either very high or very low, relative to less anxious persons" (27, p. 370). Persons with affective disorders (neurasthenia or dysthymia) typically set extremely high goals for themselves; hysterics, on the other hand, show a minimal level of aspiration, often setting their future goal even below the level of past performance (179, 287, 425). Normal control groups have fallen between these two extremes.

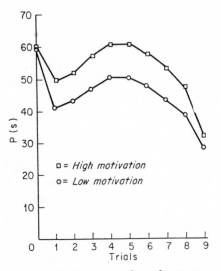

Figure 10-3. Estimation by subjects under different degrees of motivation of their chances of reaching a goal set by the experimenter. Diggory, Riley, and Blumenfeld (158)

CHOICE WITH A FIXED GOAL

Choice Situation III: To Continue or Not Continue toward a Fixed Goal[5]

When men are observed in life situations where there is a fixed goal toward which they are working, they may choose to continue to the goal or not to continue. Often individuals who drop out of college or of some other achievement-oriented situation report that they have no "chance" of graduating. Their subjective probability of attaining this goal of graduation is not strong. Of interest in one study (158) was the relation of the subjective probability of reaching a fixed goal to (1) the subject's rate of progress, (2) the proximity to goal, and (3) the deadline for reaching the goal. When adult men were given knowledge of their rate of progress in a simple task, they estimated (at different levels of actual progress) the probabilities that they would reach the fixed goal. The results indicated that the closer they were to the goal, the greater was their subjective probability of reaching it. A definite deadline of so many remaining trials was also announced in one part of this investigation. Every successive trial reduced the remaining opportunities under this deadline condition. There was a decline in reported subjective probabilities of goal attainment when the deadline was close.

The higher the value of the goal to the subjects, the greater was the estimated probability of reaching it. The high motivation by which the utility of the goal was increased was experimentally induced by a promise that a good performance meant being placed on a national roster of students who would be given special training by the government in physical sciences. In Figure 10-3 the high-incentive group is shown to be

[5] This is a variant of the level-of-aspiration situation.

significantly higher than the low-motivation group in estimates of chances to reach the fixed goal. High subjective probability of goal attainment is one of the factors determining persistence toward a fixed goal with high utility. Though not tested in this study, the individual's self-esteem aroused by the task is no doubt a variable in determining persistence to a fixed goal.

CHOICE AMONG GOALS WITH DIFFERENT PAYOFFS

Choice Situation IV: Choice Is on the Basis of Balancing Personal Utilities of Outcomes to Action. The Skill of the Chooser Is Not Involved, Nor Is There Any Question of the Certainty of the Payoff

Choice Situation IV is distinguished from the preceding two situations in that there is no question of the skill of the chooser in determining whether an expected outcome will or will not occur. Choice Situation IV differs also from the "guessing" situation in so far as there are now signals or cues which indicate what events will occur and when they will occur. It is known, for example, by the chooser that one "path" (one alternative) will lead to a certain end effect or payoff and that other paths will lead to other effects. In other words, the payoffs are known and inevitable. Choice Situation IV often occurs in life. As a child develops, he learns at home, in school, and elsewhere that different outcomes of different actions can be expected. He learns that some expected events are negative in value for him. Some have positive utility for him; others have no personal relevance. The child also learns the cues which precede certain outcomes. These cues for a variety of possible events are slowly and at times imperfectly learned but in many life situations are well established. The learned expectancies of the events are evoked *whenever* certain signals or cues appear. These signals may be as simple as conditioned stimuli which indicate the later onset of a noxious or other affective-toned unconditioned stimulus, or the signals may be more complex patterns of stimuli perceptually meaningful only within certain situations. When these cues or signals of some oncoming event are well learned, the subjective probability of the event approaches certainty. This choice situation presents (1) discriminated alternatives for action; (2) fixed outcomes of each action; (3) high certainty of the occurrence of the expected outcomes of each possible action; and (4) payoffs which vary in utility among alternatives.

To test experimentally for motivational variables in Choice Situation IV, an experimenter announces the outcomes of the alternatives for action from which the subjects are to select. The expected effects of one choice over another will not change from what is announced, whatever is the capacity of the individual to perform ably or not. The choice in such an experiment is a balancing of the utilities of the outcomes: e.g., if a man chooses alternative A, he obtains $10, but if he chooses alternative B he gets to look out of a window after being in a monotonous environment for many hours. Or he may marry Susie *or* Helene. Or he can buy for a fixed sum of money one of four different goods. Or he may spend only part of his money (one alternative) or all his money (another alternative). A child with 25 cents may be standing in front of a candy bar and considering two alternatives: If he spends all his money, he has a lot of candy but no money left; if he spends ten cents, he has some candy and 15 cents left. The economic theory of decision making is a theory about how to predict such decisions.

Typical Conflicts

The conflicts among alternatives with different payoffs in Choice Situation IV may become extremely disturbing. Lewin (365) in 1935 outlined conflicts: (1) When alternatives for choice all have satisfactory outcomes, i.e., all positive utilities or, as Lewin described utilities, all positively valenced; (2) when a possible alternative has both positive and negative valence; (3) when alternatives for action all have negative valences. These respective approach-approach, approach-avoidance, and avoidance-avoidance conflicts are illustrated in Figure 10-4. Hovland and Sears (295) elaborated the third conflict to make a fourth, i.e., the double approach-avoidance conflict. For example, a college boy is offered in his junior year an attractive job, but for him a college degree is also positively valenced. The choice of either alternative carries a penalty; if he chooses the college degree, he

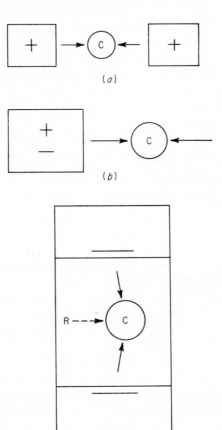

Figure 10-4. Typical conflicts: (*a*) approach-approach; (*b*) approach-avoidance; (*c*) avoidance-avoidance. ⓒ represents an individual in conflict. In the avoidance-avoidance conflict the individual may leave the field as indicated by R --→. Adapted from Lewin (365)

loses the attractive job opening; and if he takes the job, he loses the college degree.

These typical conflicts may be increased in complexity when the probabilities of expected events after choice do not approximate certainty, as is true in Choice Situation V below.

CHOICE WHEN BOTH PAYOFFS AND PROBABILITIES OF ATTAINMENT VARY

Choice Situation V: Probabilities of Outcomes of Alternatives May Vary

Risk is increased if an individual must choose among alternatives when the probabilities of attainment of the payoffs vary. Consider the interesting choice when an individual must select among alternatives A, B, and C (preferred in that order). He knows that he can attain B for certain (the "certain option") or take a chance on A or C, since the probabilities of their known payoffs vary.

Davidson, Suppes, and Siegel (140) present a similar situation. Assume that a man is faced by a choice between two alternatives. He will either gain 5 cents or lose 10 if he chooses alternative 1. There are equally probable outcomes for alternative 1. Similarly, if he selects alternative 2

	Alternative 1	Alternative 2
If heads of a coin comes up........	Obtains 5¢	Obtains 16¢
If tails comes up................	Loses 10¢	Loses 22¢

he may obtain 16 cents or lose 22 cents. The subject is asked to select one of the two alternatives. If he chooses alternative 1, a throw of a coin determines whether he obtains 5¢ or loses 10¢. If he chooses alternative 2, he may win 16¢ or lose 22¢ depending upon whether the coin comes up heads or tails.

What a man chooses in this and similar situations may be affected not only by what he may gain but also by what he loses. The relativity of possible losses and gains in choice situations remains in large part to be investigated.

INDIVIDUALITY IN CHOICES

Let us assume that a man is told that after selecting alternative A, a sword will inevitably cut off his head, but that the other alternative B will end in satisfactory results to him. Even in this binary choice situation there may be variability among individuals in what they choose. One person may hesitate, may even select alternative A and lose his head.

Why? Assuming that the man understood the outcomes of the alternatives, there is no simple answer to the question. From an analysis of the personality of the individual, there may be hypotheses which must remain untested, at least in regard to the beheaded man. Guilt, weariness, sorrow may shift death to a positive-valenced event.

As indicated in Chapter 9, the personal utility of events is dependent upon the motivational variables significant at the moment of choice or anticipated as possibly being significant later. For example, a man may know that later he will be hungry, and he therefore has a high utility for food. Stable individual differences also determine what is personally valuable. Men acquire stable likes or dislikes of various places, objects, acts, people. The specific likes and dislikes of individuals are recorded by interest inventories, by scales of values, and by vocational preference records. Market research, when directed at what consumers like or dislike, records stable preferences. Attitude scales record favorable or unfavorable reactions to a variety of social stimuli. Choices of men for specific vocations, avocations, and marriage partners are guided by such stable likes and dislikes. Though the reliability (stability) of the individual scores on such general likes and dislikes varies to some degree, they represent fairly stable variables in man's choices.

In spite of evidence of the stability of preferences they may not be arrangeable along a continuum from highly preferred to least preferred. If men are asked in binary choices whether they prefer honesty to gaining money, they may select honesty. If gaining money is placed against gaining their children's love, they may choose money; thus the continuum appears to be as follows:

A	B	C
Honesty	over	gaining money	over	gaining children's love

But when C is matched against A, then C is preferred; i.e., the men may prefer their children's love rather than honesty. This example is hypothetical but illustrative of shifts in preferences; prediction is difficult in regard to man's choices.

LIFE CHOICES

In daily life, many decisions cannot be pigeonholed in one of the choice situations reviewed above. To illustrate this statement let us examine a choice that ambitious men often must make: a choice in regard to dividing their time between their family and their work. In this decision are involved some of the motivational variables of each of the choice situations above.

The man who is making such a decision may be largely guessing concerning what will follow his choice. He may have few cues on which to predict. He may have learned from past observations that the probabilities of divorce are high when men spend more time on their jobs than with their families, but he does not know exactly why some men can do this and keep a secure family life. Nor does he have much opportunity to learn even the average frequencies of divorce as correlated with time on the job. What he greatly desires may, moreover, shift his subjective probabilities.

The studies of level of aspiration are also of interest here in understanding a man faced by two such alternatives: spending more time with his family or more on his work. He may, for example, have an unrealistic level of aspiration concerning future success in his work.

His employers may set for him a fixed goal with a deadline. Now his choice is complicated by the variables considered above in Choice Situation III, in which to continue or not to continue to a fixed goal was studied.

Let us assume that the outcomes of each of the alternatives with which the ambitious man is faced are known by him with certainty. He may be told by his employer that he will be fired if he does not spend more time on the job, but his wife may say that she is leaving if he neglects her. Assuming he believes that these are inevitable outcomes, he is in Choice Situation IV, where he is merely balancing personal utilities of outcomes of possible action.

Let us assume, however, that he believes there is a chance that his wife will not leave him. In other words, his subjective probability concerning that outcome is not what is called certainty. In this case he has moved into the complicated Choice Situation V, where more uncertainty in regard to payoffs exists.

One final illustrative situation is now presented, the distinguishing characteristic of which is that the decision of an individual will affect the lives of others. In the above illustration of a man faced by a choice in regard to division of his time between a job and his family, there is the effect upon other individuals of whatever he does. Without attempting to consider all that is involved in choices in social situations, we now present Situation VI, where decisions immediately affect the lives of others.

CHOICE IN THE SOCIAL FIELD

Choice Situation VI: Decisions Which Affect the Lives of Others

Social, ethical, or moral problems are most obvious when a decision is made in a social situation that demands immediately counteracting or aiding the welfare of others. One simple illustrative study is presented (627).

Children four to sixteen years of age in Istanbul were asked to decide how to divide nine nuts with another child. Some children took as long as ten minutes to decide. In general, regardless of age, sex, economic status, or family size, the children could be classified into three groups as indicated below.

	Per cent	No.
Those who give less (selfish)	14	40
Those who share equally (equalitarian)	42	123
Those who give more (generous)	44	128
Total	100	291

As the age of the child increased he was more likely to divide equally. In general, the poorer children were as often generous as the rich, more often equalitarian,[6] and less often selfish. The larger the family, the more the child was generous in his division. No sex differences were found. Comments of the children on their own behavior are classified in Table 7. As the age of the children increased, they moved from egocentrism to judgments of their own behavior based on their concept of justice. Further evidence of changes with age in social values, as represented by altruism, is added by developmental studies of ethical insight (290) and of interiorization of moral norms (53).

A disinterested concern for others is developed through childhood. The question remains open in regard to its basic origin.

Disinterested Concern for Others: Its Origin. What is the origin of a disinterested concern for others? One study cannot answer this question, but the study discussed above emphasized the environmental factor of size of family, with the implication of the significance of *learning* to share. As the children grew older their verbalized attitudes included more comments on abstract concepts such as justice.

In contrast to seeking an environmental origin of ethical values is another line of research. After reviewing observations of higher animals, including dogs, chimpanzees, and porpoises, Hebb and Thompson (264) concluded that, though disinterested action reaches its greatest potential in man, it is not something which is entirely imposed on the growing child by reward and punishment. A similar position was suggested by Müller, a distinguished geneticist. The provocative question was raised of whether there may be a genetic basis for those social feelings and behaviors which are collected under the term "brotherly love." Such

[6] The children who divided the nine nuts equally might give the extra one to the teacher or to someone else.

Table 7. Relationship of Moral Customs to Moral Behavior

Moral and religious rules and customs	Frequency of rules cited by			Total	
	Gener- ous	Equali- tarian	Selfish	N	%
You give more to your friend..............	18	...	...	18	28
The older one gives more (or an equal amount)...............................	8	1	5	14	22
The younger one gives more (or takes more)	5	...	1	6	9
It would not be fair to keep the bigger share.	4	...	2	6	9
It is necessary to offer to guests...........	5	...	...	5	8
He who is given the nuts to divide must give most.................................	3	1	...	4	6
Sharing between brother and sister.........	2	...	1	3	5
If you eat in front of another, you must give (share equally).........................	1	1	...	2	3
Unkindness should be replied to with a kind act....................................	2	...	...	2	3
One should always think of others, of the poor...................................	2	...	...	2	3
Generosity is a good action before God.....	1	...	...	1	1
Boys give to girls........................	1	...	...	1	1
Girls give to boys........................	1	...	...	1	1
Total...........................	53	3	9	65	99
Percentage frequency of all rules cited....	81	5	14	100	

Source: Refia Ugurel-Semin, Moral behavior and moral judgment of children. *J. abnorm. soc. Psychol.*, 1952, 47, no. 2, 463–474, supplement.

behavior tendencies might have had survival value and might have been transmitted along family lines. Müller's hypothesis brings genetic influences back into the picture as important variables in social response. At least, writes Thompson (602) in a review of developmental psychology, the "prospect must be faced that much of the variance among individuals in aggressiveness, dependency, nurturance, and so on may be due to differential genetic factors. Moreover, these genetic effects may have variable timing in different individuals. Müller's suppositions make man's hopes for a brighter new world through environmental control of experiences less tenable."

Whatever the origin of disinterested concern for others or of any of the ethical values, they do affect decisions, as was indicated in the reported observations of children. Whether genetically based or not, ethical values and/or conscience owe much to learning.

Three criteria for recognizing the functioning of conscience in young children were advanced by Sears et al. (548): (1) resistance to temptation, (2) self-instructions to obey the rules, and (3) evidence of guilt when transgression occurs. Sears et al. regard conscience as representing internalization of control, which is fundamentally different from external control whether by force, fear of punishment, or hope of material reward. Hill (285), however, illustrates in Inset 23 how resistance to temptation, at least, may be simply viewed as avoidance learning.

INSET 23. LEARNING AND CONSCIENCE*

Hill turns to learning theory to interpret conscience as defined by Sears, Maccoby, and Levin.

The first criterion of conscience, *resistance to temptation,* may be viewed simply as avoidance learning; many experimental data are available concerning it. Sidman's studies (561) of avoidance behavior without a warning signal and Dinsmoor's analysis (159) of punishment show how feedback from an individual's own acts can become a cue for avoidance and how persistent such avoidance may be. Although children can presumably learn to respond to more abstract characteristics of cues than can animals, there is no reason to regard a child's learning to avoid certain behaviors as fundamentally different from a rat's learning to do so. The fact that the child avoids the forbidden acts even in the absence of the parents is presumably due to the parents' having in the past discovered and punished (in the broadest sense of that word) transgressions committed in their absence.

A second criterion of conscience, *self-instruction,* obviously makes the human case different from the animal case, but it does not introduce any new motivational principle. One of the advantages of membership in the human species is the possibility of using verbal symbolization in dealing with one's problems. It is natural that a person learning an avoidance, like a person learning any other difficult response pattern, should give himself verbal instructions, especially since verbal coaching by others is so important in the learning of social prohibitions. Moreover, such self-instruction is an imitative act which might be learned.

The third criterion of conscience, *guilt* at violations of the prohibitions, is itself complex, with many verbal, autonomic, and gross behavioral aspects. However, the striking paradox about guilt, which has seemed to some students to set it apart from the ordinary laws of learning, is that it often involves the seeking of punishment. The person who has transgressed, rather than trying to avoid punishment or even waiting passively for it to come, actively seeks out the authorities, confesses, and receives his punishment with apparent relief. He may also—or instead—go to great

* Adapted from W. F. Hill, Learning theory and the acquisition of values. *Psychol. Rev.,* 1960, 67, 317–331; R. R. Sears, E. E. Maccoby, and H. Levin, *Patterns of Child Rearing.* Evanston, Ill.: Row, Peterson, 1957.

lengths to make restitution. Were it not for these phenomena of punishment seeking and self-sacrificing restitutions, it would be easy to dismiss guilt as merely the kind of fear associated with anticipation of certain sorts of punishment. As it is, the existence of guilt serves as an argument for regarding conscience as something more than the sum of all those avoidances which have moral significance in one's culture.

HOW REASONABLE IS MAN IN HIS CHOICES?

Emotionally Supported Choices

Man is not coldly rational in choices. In emotional arousing situations —for example, when there is danger or a threat of danger to the body or even simply to his self-esteem—his choices are more emotionally affected. A young student suddenly faced with loss of his wife by divorce goes berserk, committing injuries to his wife and child which he himself holds in horror once he views them with lessened emotion.

A common assumption is that a man in an "insane rage" is not responsible for his actions; and this has been accepted in courts of law, even if the insane rage is considered only a temporary state preventing "rational" behavior. Experimentation (372, 34) supports this opinion. By operations upon dogs and cats, the cerebral cortex was removed while the thalamus and all lower neural structures were left intact. In some animals, the thalamus as well as the cortex was sectioned, but the hypothalamus and midbrain structures were left alone. In other animals a section of the brain stem was made below the hypothalamus or below the midbrain. The findings which are of most interest in understanding choice are:

(1) The threshold of rage response was lowered after the removal of the cerebral cortex. There is apparently some mechanism in the cerebral cortex, or forebrain, which normally restrains the hypothalamus.[7]

(2) Though the hypothalamus can mediate the complete patterns of rage, the animal without cortical control shows behavioral deficiencies in his emotional expression. There is loss of inhibition ("voluntary" control), particularly in regard to the emotion of rage. The hypothalamic animals lack normal direction in their rage responses. In their fury, responses are *not* directed toward the source of the stimulation which is arousing them. This is perhaps the result of removing the cortical control which is necessary for the basic perceptual equipment, thus interfering with the usual directed emotional responses. Blind rage, when an animal

---

[7] Further support for the belief that the cortical areas exert a restraining influence upon the emotional response comes from studies isolating certain cortical areas as significant in the cortical "control."

or man runs amok, destroying everything irrespective of whether it is related to his rage, illustrates a temporarily hypothalamic organism.

(3) A third finding is that the decorticate animal recovers more quickly than the normal animal from an emotional response. Though the cerebral cortex has some kind of "braking" or inhibiting control on emotional responses, the cortex also seems to contribute to their normal persistence.

Bodily Survival Versus Social or Human Values

Individual survival in this world has a high value for most men. The survival of the groups to which he belongs—his family, his friends, his country—has likewise a high value. Since the survival of the human species is now threatened by atomic warfare, men are discovering that they value the human species quite highly.

The high survival value of the body to the individual man can be easily illustrated. Assume that a normal man is given a choice between two acts, one of which, he is informed, will lead to his death and the other of which will not. What will he do? Most frequently, he will choose the act which will permit his individual survival, though not always will his choice lie in that direction. At least we can speculate that there are some values for men greater than their own survival. If given the choice between killing his own child—or even the child of someone else —in "cold blood" and dying himself, a man may well choose to die himself. And to some degree this is true of the lower animals, for they will fight for their young and in so doing may die. However, the choice to stand and fight is not what we are attempting to illustrate. "Aggressive defense" is common among all animals. Rather, we are pointing to *human values* (a few) which can be placed against *individual and group survival* and which will usually win. Many men, though by no means all men, would choose to die rather than torture anyone. Most would not betray their country but would rather die; some would not live in submission; some would not "sink into vicious slander"; most would not rape their own daughters. However, the social values which will completely dominate individual survival are few. Activities which protect and maintain the bodily self so that it survives as an intact, living system are highly prepotent.

We now turn to the construct of intention, which may subtly twist evaluative choice into new directions.

INTENTIONS

Man, and perhaps only man, is capable of intentions. Man has diverse intentions. Mr. Jones says that he intends to take his vacation next week;

or he says that he intends to finish some task that he has started; or he tells us that his intention is to help his friend who is in trouble.

Intentions are not expectancies. An intention of a man may be in conflict with, independent of, or supportive of his expectancy of the outcome of a decision. Intentions may arise independently of a frequently confirmed expectancy. In human conditioning when electric shock is used as the unconditioned stimulus, subjects report that the expectancy of the onset of stimulus shock can be differentiated from the intention to do something about it. The intention, once the expectancy of a noxious event is well established, may be to take the shock. The intentions vary according to the expectancies, but the two are not identical. Expectancies grow strong with confirmation, but the strength or weakness of intentions is dependent on supporting self-systems.[8] In the discussion of level-of-aspiration studies, it was indicated above that men "bet" on how well they will score on some test or perform some skill. Such bets may even be against confirmed expectancies of failure. Having failed fifty times even to hit the target, nevertheless, some men state that they *intend* to hit the center the next time. A student whose past performance has been at a low level of achievement says his next semester grades will be good. His intentions may be supported by his self-defenses; for example, his belief that he is really capable of being a good student. That he does not study he will grant, and perhaps he will even grant, if forced to face his own established habits, that he will again not study; but his intentions as reported by him are excellent. Thus he is relieved of tension, feeling that he has solved his problems by the statement of his excellent resolutions.

It Is Easier to Describe What an Intention Is Not than What It Is. Intention is not a habit, though only through learning can man have intentions. The specific form of an intention may be traced to past experiences, even to former rewards and punishments, yet the intention per se is not fixed, as is a habit. Nor is it a dynamic dispositional tendency, such as to be hostile in *any* situation. And intention is not a learned sensorimotor skill, as is driving home along a certain route every evening. Nor is it an even more simplified automatic skill such as may be seen in industry. In fact, it is not always a performance; it may not ever be released into performance. We often have "good intentions" in regard to others, but they may never be acted upon. Or we have "bad intentions" which we act upon and then deny that we had these intentions.

An intention is not a need drive. It is not an emotion. It is also not a

---

[8] Hebb (263, p. 744) writes that even a simple kind of intention (to repeat a series of nonsense syllables), set up by the experimenter's instructions before any of the syllables has been presented, may involve the imagined action of the self making certain sounds.

value, a social role or an interest; but intentions *may* reflect the needs, emotions, values, roles, and interests of man. Allport (10), who has emphasized the necessity of considering the intentions of men ("directing schemata," as he describes them), protests against linking them either with Hullian fractional anticipatory goal response or with central expectancies of goals. Intentions are not stencilled copies of man's previous rewards. A man with an intention is not oriented toward specific goals. Man may have a consistent direction of striving, but the goal, if any, is either transient or else undefinable.

Intentions of men are certainly not so concrete as goals to satisfy need drives. Physiological drives become attached to this or that needed object. This is demonstrable in the laboratory, but human motivation is more than drives, more than goals. An intention "reaches forward hungrily into the future like a tip of scarlet-runner bean groping for a goal that it does *not know* about" (10, p. 58).

Is an Intention of a Man Necessarily at the Level of Awareness? The answer is no. There are intentions both at a conscious and unconscious level. Psychology has generally accepted the emphasis by Freud of determinants operating below awareness and of man's rationalizations or other self-defenses, *the intent of which is below his awareness.* An individual does not always know precisely what his intentions are. Consciously or unconsciously he may misinterpret the line of his own endeavor. Insight is either lacking or partially lacking. Rapaport (496) illustrates the complexity of the psychoanalytic inferences involved in interpretations of unconscious intentions. In his illustration, a man makes a slip of the tongue. After listening to a chairman's explanation of mismanagement of a group's affairs, a man, a member of the group, "consciously" intending to praise the chairman by saying, "now things are becoming clear," actually says "queer" for "clear." He is not aware of his mistake, but when told about it, he is outwardly embarrassed.

An intention may be revealed by overemphasis on possible alternatives other than the one selected. A man may state that he plans to catch a certain train, but he adds detailed instructions about what he will do if he misses the train. Such careful preparation for failure may be considered a sign of a cautious attitude. Or it may indicate that the man does *not* intend to get on a train. Moreover, he may not be aware of this intention, and it cannot be controlled; his careful planning in regard to alternatives if he misses the train suggests the presence of an active unconscious intention not to go. A similar phenomenon is recognized in Freudian mechanisms like reaction formation.

Intentions reflect the inner rather than the expressed desires, hates, loves; they reflect the basic rather than the stated likes or dislikes; they may be in conflict with the announced ambitions, plans, and aspirations.

Intentions may also be in conflict with reported goals, verbalized values, and roles, even if they are outwardly played.

When the Victorian father asked the suitor of his daughter whether the suitor's intentions were honorable, apparently the father assumed the young man knew his own intentions. Or perhaps the father was issuing a warning against acting on dishonorable intentions, given some pleasant opportunity.

The intentions of men can be symbolically formalized, though by no means are they always formalized. Men verbally discuss their intentions as if they were dealing with an objective referent. They often report what they intend to do or that they did not accomplish their intentions, or they argue against imputing "bad" intentions to their actions even though their behavior is not socially acceptable. Their intentions thus seem (to them) not in conflict with social values.

Intentions may not be based on reasoning or differentiated by evaluations, but nevertheless they may be reflected in the choices of men. They may determine the choices without being in focus and without being subject to examination. Reason may be called upon to support them rather than reason determining them.

Men "Read" the Intentions of Others. The socially clever man not only shapes intentions in others but "reads" the intentions of others. Neither the suspicious nor the cautious are free from the machinations of the clever, though some men are more easily led than others. In the words of Iago, the Shakespearean villain, some men are as tenderly "led by the nose as asses are." Is psychotherapy (client-centered therapy) a method of "leading" the clients?

Fortunately, or perhaps unfortunately, our intentions may be easier to identify by those around us than by ourselves, and hence we cannot "fool" all the people, or often even a part of them, all the time. Of course, we ourselves are among those whom our own intentions may fool. The cry of the murderer: "I didn't intend to kill him (or her)," is sincere. It was that unknown intention which ignored the fact that a gun, when pointed in anger, somehow often goes off. The hidden intention was the murderer.

Can Intention Be Subjected to Experimental Testing? In order to determine the parameters which may be influential on the elusive intentions of men, more insight into central events is needed than psychologists have at present attained. A beginning can be made in experimentation by using as a definition of an intention the verbal directions given to subjects. The experimenter says to the subject, "You are to listen for the buzzer and respond by pressing this key." This presumably imposes a determining tendency upon the subject, though since it is arbitrarily imposed, it may be quickly nullified by the subject wondering, "Why am

I to listen for the buzzer?" In examining possible answers to his own question the subject may forget the intention to listen. Or another intention which he had verbally phrased for himself that morning may arise: To call his girl at a certain hour. In spite of such difficulties, nevertheless, experimentally imposed directions may be used and studied, thus throwing some insight upon this construct.

In *summary*, (1) emotions in conflict with reason can be rephrased as the hypothalamic versus the cortically controlled man; (2) bodily survival may be in conflict with social values, the latter being learned and accepted according to the training received in a particular group; and (3) the intentions of men may override all their verbalized reasons for actions.

CONCLUDING STATEMENTS

In the activity stream of an organism there is convergence both among potential stimuli and upon one response unit among the organism's repertoire of potential responses. This selecting varies from simple sensitization, according to the organism's dominant drives, to the evaluative choice of man.

Selecting is a central event. Present evidence indicates that the mechanisms for selecting and rejection are primarily central rather than peripheral in locus. Central selecting is not a new assumption. Hebb, Tolman, and Lewin have presented models of man based on the assumption of central selecting.

The illustrative studies of choice situations which were presented demonstrate that motivational determinants, such as personal utility of the payoffs of different alternatives, are significant in affecting decisions and in resolving conflicts which may become serious before decisions. The role of motivational variables in the selective mediating activities of focusing, perceiving, and remembering is developed in the next chapter.

CHAPTER 11

COGNITIVE ACTIVITIES,

MOTIVATIONAL DETERMINANTS,

AND SELECTIVITY

There are in the usual environment of men multiple sources of potential stimuli. There are among the many potential a few which become adequate stimuli. With each man when he is awake there is a central focusing which constantly shifts from one aspect to another of the total potential field. Perceiving, the organizing which occurs in the sensory flux, is in part on the basis of past impressions. The selective recall of some impressions and the forgetting of others affect how the present is perceived.

These three mediating activities—focusing, perceiving, and remembering—are central cognitive activities which permit selecting at higher levels. Their role in learning is not considered in the discussion below, and the question of how they are dependent on learning is necessarily ignored. This chapter is concerned with a few of the studies which demonstrate that these cognitive activities are affected by motivational determinants, i.e., by the transitory states as well as by dynamic personality variables. Though these three cognitive activities are interdependent, they will be briefly considered separately.

FOCUSING[1]

Organisms selectively focus only a part of the total stimulating origins of excitation; then they shift to another aspect. The focusing of organisms

[1] Related topics have been previously developed: (1) vigilance, Chap. 5; (2) stimulus dynamism, Chap. 7; (3) exteroceptive drives, Chap. 8; (4) satisfactory to unsatisfactory stimulations, Chap. 9; and (5) sensitization by drives, Chap. 10. For extensive and intensive reviews of selective attention, see Berlyne (62) and Woodworth and Schlosberg (661). Easterbrook (169) presents a theory concerning emotion and cue utilization.

refers to attending, or orienting. Organisms may be prefocused for on-coming stimuli. Or the attributes of the stimulations—such as intensity—may force the organism to focus these over others. The determinants of what is focused include both temporary and transient variables as well as long-term readinesses, such as an established interest in the field of history, space travel, or other areas. We first consider how temporary pre-focusing may be established.

Prefocusing

Temporary Preparations (Short-term Sets). A set (a temporary readi-ness) may be established for a specific stimulus such as being ready to focus a red light when it appears. Preparation to make a specific move-ment may also be established, such as to respond with the right hand but not with the left hand. Preparations for movements to be released are called motor sets. There may also be "mixed sets," such as to respond with the left hand if a red light appears and not to respond if there is a blue light.

Such preparatory sets, once adopted, control the focusing of the organism as well as the release of responses. Sets serve the central select-ing process. The selecting process is temporarily in abeyance when there is a well-established set. Making a choice and being set are not identical processes. Rather, selecting, or choice, precedes and determines the establishment of a particular set. An illustration of prefocusing follows.

An Illustration. Being ready to focus upon one of two or more incom-ing messages may be facilitative of recognition of the one prefocused. Broadbent (83) was interested in the problem of selective attention to two auditory verbal messages which started at the same point in time but of which one was irrelevant to the ongoing task of the subject. A subject (an adult) was required to answer incoming messages on a radio-telephone about a visual display. It was found that the subjects bom-barded by two voices were able to answer correctly less than 50 per cent of the special messages directed to them. When, however, a further direction specified which of the two voices had priority, the subjects made fewer errors. This focusing upon the relevant voice was not so use-ful when it was done toward the end of the message as when it was done at the beginning. It is often necessary to discard some inputs and center on others. Selecting can be more easily attained if the focusing mecha-nism is at work before the receptor is aroused rather than afterwards.

The Period of Waiting for an Oncoming Stimulus

The relationship between the length of time spent in waiting for something to happen and the degree of readiness for an event has been little investigated. Though periods of waiting certainly vary and are of much significance in our lives, even their classification has not been attempted. Waiting may start with a signal, or there may be no exact cue signifying the onset of an event.

Experiments have varied the foreperiod in the classical reaction time studies where there is a *ready signal*. In general, the optimal waiting time is around one to two seconds. Observations also indicate that the subject will adjust his preparation according to the length of previous periods of waiting.

The reaction time studies with a ready signal do not duplicate those life situations where quickness of reaction is frequently required but there is no ready signal. There are, however, a variety of problems which should be investigated by measuring reaction time *when no ready signal is given*. For example, light could be thrown on differences among individuals in their reaction to the unexpected by obtaining the latency of a choice response among simultaneous stimuli for which the subject is either unprepared or only prepared for "something." There are such problems as the following: Would a man waiting for a signal of an event from which he must defend himself be less likely to fluctuate in readiness than if he were waiting for the signal which would indicate that he might approach and examine? Would the personal value of the oncoming stimulus influence reaction time? Such questions could be approached in the laboratory situation by measurement of latency of response, together with other measures of organismic changes, during the period of waiting before choice.

An individual may be prepared for a stimulus while he continues in other tasks during the waiting period, but the strength of his preparation may vary. Rethlingshafer (502) found that a prepared focusing could be maintained while other tasks were performed but that the degree of readiness of the subjects shifted according to the nature of the concomitant tasks engaged in during the waiting period. The subjects in this study were first prepared by verbal directions to respond to a buzzer as quickly as possible whenever they heard it. Then they were started on one concomitant goal task such as a stylus maze or solving a puzzle. Another task used in the study was nongoaled—dropping a marble in a box, removing it, dropping it again, and so on without any completion being designated. As indicated in Figure 11-1, the reaction time to the buzzer (the index to the strength of the preparation) was faster when there was no goal in the concomitant task. Reaction time to the buzzer was also faster at the beginning or after completion of a goaled task. And, as indicated in Figure 11-1, the readiness for the buzzer lessened when the extra task required was difficult. The persistence and strength of a preparation to react to an oncoming stimulus is decreased whenever an individual is moving toward a nonrelated goal in some concomitant task and further decreased when the moving toward the goal is difficult.

Drives as Related to Focusing

As indicated in Chapter 10, specific drives sensitize the organism to relevant stimulations. Learning to discriminate various aspects of the external field must however precede any orienting toward different stimulating sources; it is also observed that given equal previous learning, they are focused according to their relevance (significance) for the dominant drives.

Each drive component narrows the range of cue utilization. Moreover, as specific drives increase in strength, the subject's span of apprehension further narrows. This is observed when hunger narrows the individual's focus to foods alone. If a man is attempting to find food, such narrowing of the range of stimulus cues is facilitative for his observing food. If, however, he is engaged in a problem *not* related to food, an extreme food sensitization is nonfacilitative of the problem solving. He cannot see anything but food or objects which remind him of food. Another il-

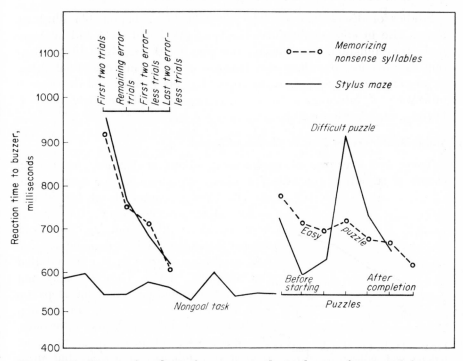

Figure 11-1. Degree of readiness for an expected stimulus is a function of the concomitant task: memorizing nonsense syllables; learning stylus maze; solving puzzles; or working on a nongoal task. Rethlingshafer (502)

lustration: As the intensity of anxiety increases, there is evidence of reduction in range of cues utilized in focusing. Lucas (384) reported for anxious subjects low scores in immediate memory span compared with nonanxious subjects.

The narrowing of the focus of human subjects by a strong incitor was demonstrated by Bahrick, Fitts, and Rankin (31). The central task was continuous tracking, but subjects were also required to report the occurrence of occasional lights on the periphery of the stimulus display and to respond to the occasional deflection of a needle on a peripheral dial. Strong and weak incentives were used. The subjects decreased in the proficiency of their reports concerning changes in the periphery of their focus when bonuses were introduced to improve both on the target and the peripheral stimuli. Similar results were reported by Bursill (97) when the air temperature was increased from 60–70°F to 95–105°F. The high temperature—an antecedent for a drive component—was correlated with increased errors in responding to peripheral stimuli. The proficiency of focusing on the central cues increased but at the cost of the range of cues.

Increase in Emotionality Interferes with Discrimination

Studies of discrimination (later developed in Chapter 14) illustrate how a rise in emotionality may reach a nonoptimal level and interfere with discrimination. This interference may be the resultant of a reduction in capacity to utilize cues because of increasing emotional drive. Supporting this hypothesis is the report by Jones (322) of a decrease in utilization of information from visual displays when electric shock is introduced. See Figure 11-2.

Stable Readiness for Specific Classes of Stimuli

There are ever-present readinesses, inborn or learned, for certain classes of stimuli as contrasted to others. Wild animals, for example, are said to have a continual set for danger signals. Even during sleep, the central nervous system filters out the innocuous sensory messages while remaining responsive to danger signals. It is reported that the sleeping captive elephant may not awaken when another elephant steps on him, but the sound of a human footstep brings the giant beast to his feet in seconds. The grazing gazelle never feeds for more than a few minutes at a time but must raise its head and inspect the surroundings at frequent intervals. The sleeping human mother with a sick child hears the slightest

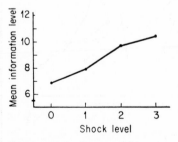

Figure 11-2. Emotionality interferes with utilization of visual information. (High information level represents less efficient utilization of information.) Jones (322)

sound which may signal a need for aid. The "trouble shooter" of industry is ready to note slight changes in well-learned sensory patterns of machine sounds.

Vigilance and Anxiety

Liddell, as reported by May (406), links vigilance in animals with anxiety. Liddell believes that animals do not have anxiety as the term is applied to human beings, but that they have a "primitive, simple counterpart, namely *vigilance*." When an animal is in a situation that involves a possible threat—such as a sheep in a laboratory expecting an electric shock, or a seal asleep in its natural habitat waking every ten seconds to survey the landscape lest Eskimo hunters sneak up on it—the animal exhibits an alertness and an expectancy of danger. "It is as though the animal were asking, 'What is it?'" This vigilance is characterized by generalized suspiciousness with tendencies to act but without any clear-cut direction for acting. Such behavior is the parallel in the animal to the vague and generalized apprehensive behavior of the human being in anxiety (406, p. 97).

Attitudes and Interests

Attitudes are learned readinesses to react favorably or unfavorably to such stimuli as race, the church, and other stimulating sources. Attitudes reliably prepare individuals to react to certain stimuli in a fairly stereotyped fashion. They are stable prefocusing mechanisms. Interests are also prepared readinesses to focus differentially. A man interested in old cars is constantly ready to focus any such cars and is not as ready for other cars. A woman interested in fashions is usually ready to pause and stare at windows displaying the new styles. Interests as identified by factor analysis are presented in Inset 24. Interest patterns vary according to occupational groups (589).

INSET 24. INTERESTS IDENTIFIED BY FACTOR ANALYSES*

Interest is a generalized behavior tendency of an individual to be attracted to a certain class of incentives or activities. This conception of an interest is sufficiently broad to include negative as well as positive attractions.

Studies of interests have frequently used self-reports of what a man likes or dislikes or what he prefers to do or not do. Such studies have culminated in standard interest inventories, including *Strong's Vocational Interest Inventory* and the *Kuder Preference Record*.

Factor analyses permit categorization of the large number of likes and dislikes which are reported by human subjects on such inventories. One

* Adapted from J. P. Guilford, P. R. Christensen, N. A. Bond, Jr., and M. A. Sutton. A factor analysis study of human interests. *Psychol. Monogr.*, 1954, 68, 1–38.

of the factor analyses reported the usual vocational interests and other interests which affect the choices of individuals.

Guilford et al. (234) factor analyzed scores on approximately 1,000 items selected in part from interest inventories. The subjects were young adult males in the Air Force and were divided into two groups. Centroid factors were extracted from an airman correlation matrix and from an officer matrix.

Of the twenty-eight interpretable factors from the two analyses, six, and possibly seven, were regarded as definitely directed toward vocational stereotypes or occupational classes.

> Under a broad definition of interests, nineteen additional factors may be regarded as basic interest factors, some of which have vocational implications of a very broad nature. Thus the vocational factors that have been found in other studies by factor analysis do not disperse among more basic factors when the analysis is very comprehensive. The structure of the domain of interests, therefore, seems to include a limited number of vocationally oriented variables superimposed upon or differentiated from a broader base of general interest variables that have non-vocational implications as well. (234, p. 36)

The well-known factors related to vocational interests were found: mechanical, scientific, social welfare, aesthetic appreciation, aesthetic expression, clerical, and business. Only the linguistic or verbal-interest factor is missing from the well-established list of vocational-interest factors. The analysis added another factor to the vocational interest list: the outdoor-work-interest factor.

The nonvocational-interest factors identified included adventure versus security, cultural conformity, self-reliance versus dependence, need for diversion, autistic thinking, need for attention, resistance to restriction, physical drive, aggression, thinking, expressiveness versus restraint, sociability, need for sympathetic environment, precision, social initiative, cultural interest, orderliness versus disorderliness, physical fitness interest, ambition, and need for variety.

PERCEIVING—A SELECTIVE ACTIVITY

We have stated that there are many potentialities for stimulation but that from these only a few become adequate, and among these few there is only one focus at a time. We now add that only one organization (figure against a ground) may become temporarily dominant. Then in the next phase of the activity stream, a new structuring (organization) may emerge.

Different Views of Perceiving

Perceiving is selective. This is granted no matter what particular approach is made to the successive organizations within the sensory flux.

However, in several of the views of perceiving presented below, there is *no* recognition of the selective influence of motivational determinants.

1. Perceiving has been approached by *analyzing* the external stimulus field (external to the central nervous field) and the concomitant reported perceptional change. The analytical approach in vision is illustrated by the reviews of Judd (324) on the physical parameters, of Bartley (42) on the physiological parameters, and of Graham (227) on the psychophysical parameters. Little or no attention is given to the possible role of temporary organismic variables as they affect psychophysical relations.

2. Another approach, the *phenomenological* approach to perceiving, came into psychology when the Gestalt movement "forced abandonment of the view that perception is a composite of sensations and images" (269, p. 3). Wertheimer insisted that perceptual phenomena be taken at their face value without reducing them to elementary units. Thus the phi-phenomenon (perception of movement when there is physically none) was regarded as no less real psychologically than perception of physically moving objects. "Wertheimer also asserted that brain processes underlying phenomenally similar perceptions (e.g., real movement and phi) must also be similar in spite of their different stimulus origins" (269, p. 3). (Genetic and historical antecedents play little or no role in this specific view.) "Every experience exemplifies an essence and carries its own validation. Distinctions such as real vs. illusion, perceived vs. imagined, remembered vs. sensed, are of no importance unless the immediately given experience carries marks by which the distinctions may be made." It is assumed that *meaning, value, purpose, and significance are inherent in experience as well as sensory qualities which correlate with stimulus dimensions. "The way in which an individual perceives the world constitutes his reality, and no external validation is needed to tell him that he is sad or happy, frustrated or satisfied"* (269, p. 3, italics added). The phenomenological view developed by Wertheimer and other members of the Gestalt school (342) describes the laws of figure-ground structure. Probably the most primitive, innate modes of perceptual organization include contrast, continuity of surface or lines, reduplication of elements, and the like. These and other "perceptual laws," such as closure, determine the perception of "objects" against a less definite ground.

It should, however, be added that the Gestalt psychologists have been aware of central directive determinants, including those which cannot be predicted from the stress of the perceptual field moving toward optimal organization.

Approaches 1 and 2 are primarily concerned with perception in and of itself, without regard for the manner in which it is imbedded in the other ongoing activities of the perceiver. In experiments arising from these views, the individual is asked to be neutral, wishing "neither to eat, destroy, caress or in any manner to use the stimulus presented to him." Such experimentalists have been called formalists.

3. Another group of experimentalists in the field of perceiving has been labeled functionalist. These men are interested in the influence of temporary organismic states as well as individual differences in perceiving. Such investigators, concerned with problems relating the motivational factors to perception, have assailed the psychophysical and the Gestalt schools for concentrating on structural or stimulus-bound aspects of perception and neglecting the influences of differences among men arising from effects of individuality in motivational determinants. The Gestalt psychologists, for example, employ tachistoscopic exposures of stimuli to show that perception is ordered, dependable, and much the same from person to person. They illustrate its functions according to dynamic principles common to physics and psychology. However, it has become increasingly clear that in various ways (unknown) inner factors may change perception in the direction of personal ends. It is this third approach to perceiving which has generated studies of the role of motivational variables in perceiving.

INDIVIDUALITY IN PERCEIVING

Man's perceptual organizations may reflect the drives based on his immediately active emotions, his physiological conditions, and his goal orientations, intentions, and sets. His personality affects how *he* perceives the external sources of stimulations as contrasted to how other individuals perceive—even individuals of his own culture, age, sex, education. Perceiving, it should be remembered, is not entirely individual nor is it solely subject to the immediate transitory organismic conditions or traceable to the personality of the individual perceiver, including his socially acquired values, norms, or attitudes. In structured external fields perceiving is highly controlled by the pattern of the incoming sensory excitations from that field. Any well-defined relations (spatial, temporal) within the objective world permit firm rather than fluid percepts, with general agreement among reported perceptions of several observers. On the other hand, the unstructured fields are more likely to permit the influence of organismic determinants, including motivational determinants.

It is necessary to consider briefly the meaning of *structured* and *unstructured*. If one is looking at a cloud, the "forms" within are vague and undifferentiated, but even when there is no movement of the physical cloud field, the observer can perceive variation in forms and even perceive their movement from one to the other. A cloud or a similar non-formed field like a Rorschach ink blot is called an unstructured stimulus field. However, there is no marked dichotomy between an unstructured field and a structured one. The structured external field permits more consistency in reported attributes of that field.

Almost every student in psychology has attempted to report the attribute of a physical object, e.g., to report the length of lines, or heaviness of weights, a comparison being made sometimes to a standard. The degree of correspondence between the physical measures and subjective percepts as reported by one subject, as well as by several subjects operating under the same set of conditions, has permitted reliable psychophysical relationships to be revealed. In such cases it is customary to call the stimulus field structured.

PERCEIVING AND MOTIVATIONAL DETERMINANTS

An early study showing the effect of prefocusing on perceiving was by Külpe (349) in 1904. Working in the now historic Wurzburg school, he found that what his subjects reported after tachistoscopic presentation of colored letters might be strikingly different from the actual colored letters presented. If, for instance, the subject was *set* to count the number of letters, or *set* to reproduce their spatial arrangement, the colors apparently were not perceived, or at least not reported. Perception is not simply a copy of the external field. The imposed organization reflects organismic variables. We now turn to some of the evidence which supports this general statement.

Misperceptions Correlated with Need Drives

Osgood (473, p. 286) is responsible for noting the following typical illusions which owe their origins, in part, to temporary needs. "I pass each day," he writes, "an office numbered 400-D. Inevitably, when the hour is near mealtime, I perceive this as FOOD. The car I used to drive had the euphemistic label SILVER STREAK on its dashboard; inevitably, when the hour was near mealtime, I would read this as SILVER STEAK." Perceptual distortion illustrates "the well-known, but little understood, fact that perceptual processes are readily molded to fit an individual's momentary needs. It also recalls Tolman's notion of how demands *sensitize* the particular means-end-readinesses and expectations with which they are associated" (473, p. 286). In Osgood's illustrations in a structured field, increased sensitization from hunger was responsible for the repeated illusions. In the following studies concerning the role of need drives in perceptual organization, the external field is less structured.

Some early experiments specifically tested the effect of hunger upon perceiving or related processes. Sanford (532) studied the effect of food deprivation upon word association and the reported perceptions of ambiguous pictures. Ten children were given tests both before and after meals: Twice as many food-related responses were made before as after meals. In another study (533) the time without food was more carefully delimited, so that groups which had undergone food deprivations through one to five hours and one group which had been deprived for twenty-four hours were studied. Other tests used included chain associations, drawing completion, and word completion. Again the results indicated that the physiological state affected the test scores. Levine, Chein, and Murphy (364) obtained similar results in regard to the effect of hunger on the perceiving of ambiguous figures. McClelland and Atkinson (412) measured the effects of hunger upon the projective productions in a "subliminal visual perception" test. A very faint image was first projected upon a screen, then the subjects were given the impression that other faint images would be projected, but there were actually none. In most of the tests the experimenters made such comments as: "There are three objects on the table. What are they?" The three groups of naval trainees were hungry in varying degrees, having been deprived of food for one, four, or sixteen hours. The reports of the subjects on what they had perceived varied according to the number of hours of food deprivation which they had suffered. In general the number of food-related responses for both the structured and unstructured situations increased progressively with need. Also, the reported food objects which the subjects said they perceived on the blank screen grew somewhat larger in relation to neutral objects as hunger increased. The general emphasis, however, in their results was upon food-related objects rather than actual food objects. The number of such objects as forks, plates, etc., was found to increase with increasing food deprivation, but food objects did not. Also, differences between the one-hour and either the four-hour or sixteen-hour groups were generally significant, but differences between the four-hour and sixteen-hour groups were not.

What Function Is Served by Misperception, Whether It Corresponds or Not to a Temporary Deficit Condition? Possibly changes in perception may aid in reducing a dominant need drive. If I perceive a box as a chair when I am fatigued, I can rest on it and reduce the fatigue. Related to this is a study finding improvement in recognition accuracy of pictures of foods in a quick-exposure device by subjects under three to four hours of food deprivation (359). The perceptual errors under needs generally tend to aid the recognition and memory for the need-related forms. In one study (219) the subjects were asked to recall the brightness of colored slides of need-related objects and neutral objects. Thirsty subjects overestimated the brightness of the recalled need-related stimuli as contrasted to water-satiated subjects. Moreover, the tendency to overestimate increased for the need-related forms as the need increased. (Such sensitization is adaptive to man when in need.) When need was reduced, the subjects no longer enhanced the brightness of former perceived forms. This was true for both need-related and non-need-related stimuli as indicated in Figure 11-3.

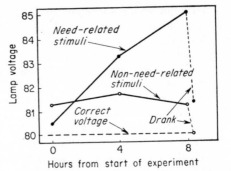

Figure 11-3. Subjects increased in overestimation of the luminance of need-related stimuli during increasing hours of water (and food) deprivation. The positive error was also present, but less so, for non-need-related stimuli. The effect disappeared when subjects were permitted to drink. Gilchrist-Nesberg (219) as adapted by Brown (90)

Values

Social values are group-accepted standards or norms of the worth of something (see Inset 25). Values of men are in sharp contrast to transitory need drives. Values are acquired and are usually ready to be influential. There is no necessary period of deprivation, though that which the organism is deprived of may grow in value for him when it is needed. Values are attached to many objects, including those necessary for the reduction of need drives. Social values may transcend values based on individual needs. The significance of a social value may be greater in weighting an alternative at a choice point than the value attached to some individually needed goal (166).

terms of wider and more enduring goals. "A football player wants desperately to get drunk after his first big game, but this impulse conflicts with his values of personal achievement and loyalty to his teammates, coach, and university" (339, p. 399).

Values are operative when an individual selects one line of action, or thought, over another to the degree that the selection is influenced by generalized codes rather than determined simply by impulse or temporary expediency. The selection is not necessarily at the level of awareness of the individual involved in the selection. It simply happens; but the generalized codes may be operating. Not only the goal but the way of carrying out a valued goal can be evaluated. There is no wrong way to obtain a right goal, provided that values are operating both in the choice of goals and *also in the modes of attainment.*

Values in Relation to Perceiving

Ansbacher (18) found in 1937 that the value of stamps pasted on cards affected the perception. The estimate of the number of stamps on a card was decreased if the stamps had more value, and he concluded that the larger the denomination of a stamp, the larger its physical size appeared to the observers.

Bruner and Goodman's well-known study (94) of the effect of the value of perceived objects (coins) used ten rich children from a school in a superior economic area, ten poor children, who were selected from a settlement house in one of Boston's slum areas, and ten control children whose economic status was presumably average. When the real coins were present, all children significantly overestimated their sizes, the amount of overestimation increasing with the value of the coins (with the exception of the 50-cent piece). And with the poor children, there was more overestimation than with the rich children. These findings suggest that the socially valued objects—the coins—are perceived by all children as larger than they actually are and that the greater the need for these coins, the more they are overestimated.

Similar studies have been reported, some of which support and some of which question the hypothesis that the value of an object enhances its perceived size. Carter and Schooler (115) repeated the experiment of Bruner and Goodman above, and found that there was less overestimation than previously reported. The real size, rather than simply the value of the object, seemed to be affecting the overestimation found. And this time there were no significant differences between rich and poor children when the coins were present, but when working from memory, poor children showed significantly greater overestimation than rich children.

Other experiments are pertinent to this problem of how, or if, values affect perceptions. Bevan and Dukes (65) compared judgment of distances from the observer of a valuable object (money) with a non-valuable piece of cardboard. Two groups of undergraduate psychology students were matched on the basis of twenty records of their adjusting a movable object to the same distance from them as a stationary object which had been placed 360 centimeters away. The stimuli used were two light-green cardboard rectangles, 3 by 6 inches in size, which approximated the size of a valuable stimulus object later to be introduced, a 20-dollar bill. A Howard-Dolman distance-perception apparatus was used with slight modifications. Both right and left positions, as well as "from" and "toward" the subject, were equalized in the method of average error.

The experimental variable was, as stated above, an increase in the value of the stimulus objects used. On the second session, several days after the session with the cardboards, both groups made twenty more judgments, with the experimental group now using two 20-dollar bills as the stimulus objects, one bill being fixed at a standard position. The results: The group who used the money made fewer errors in adjusting the stimulus to the standard.

Two reasons were suggested for the diminished average error when subjects were to adjust the valuable money to a fixed spatial distance from them. "(1) The perceiver, in the face of valued objects, becomes more *alert,* responding with sharpened sensitivity, finer discrimination; and (2) by *accentuating* size, enhanced value in effect, reduces distance, thereby *increasing accuracy* of judgment" (65, p. 584).

Again, Dukes and Bevan (167) asked children to estimate the weights of "valued" small jars of candy and neutral small jars filled with sawdust. Valued stimulus objects appeared heavier than neutral objects of the *same* actual weight. When both were valued, the response variability was less.

An interesting attempt to control all influences upon the subjects except the value attached to money was made by Ashley, Harper, and Runyon (25). Using college subjects from middle-class homes, they suggested under hypnotism for each subject at different times a rich family background and a poor family background, and then tested for his estimation of the size of coins. The judgments made under the two induced value systems were then compared with the subject's normal judgments.

The method of estimation of the size of coins was similar to that of Bruner and Goodman. The subject adjusted a variable-sized spot of light until it appeared to be the size of a specified coin. The hypnotized subjects were told that they remembered nothing about their past. Then one of the "life histories" shown below was suggested under hypnotic trance. Every subject made estimations of coin size in the "rich," "poor," and "normal" states.

The outline of the life history given for the "poor" man was:

He had been born of poor parents and his childhood had been spent in poverty; his father had never had an adequate income and consequently could not afford many of life's necessities; his clothes had been rags, his diet meager, and his allowance negligible; he could not go to high school because he had to help support his family; he was still very poor; he had no regular job; what money he did earn was used to help support his family and to pay some of his many debts.

The life history given for the "rich" man was:

He had been born of very wealthy parents; he lived in a large mansion in the best and wealthiest neighborhood; he had attended the very best schools; he had always had a large allowance and never had to wish for anything; his father had given him a car and a large expense account when he had entered high school; his clothes had always been of the best quality and very expensive; he had never had any financial worries; at present he had an extremely large income that was further supplemented by his father. (25, pp. 566–567)

The experimenters add two significant points in regard to their procedure. (1) Though half of their subjects were from psychology classes, none were aware of the experimental results and of the theorizing in this field. (2) Furthermore, no mention was made of the particular size, value, or worth of coins.

The subjects who under hypnosis believed that they were poor adjusted the light so that a larger spot was judged equal to the coins than when these same subjects believed that they were rich. This confirms some of the previous work which indicates that the value of money for an individual influences his perception and memory of coins; the poorer he is, the larger he perceives the coins to be. When in the normal state, these subjects judged the size of the coins to lie between the two hypnotic states. In the normal state, they were somewhat closer to reality when the coins were *not* present than when present. This seems rather paradoxical, but it is interpreted by the experimenters as due to illusory effects. The subjects were also shown a slug from an electrical terminal box and were told under hypnosis that it was made of lead, silver, white gold, or platinum. The subjects perceived the size of the object as larger the greater its reported value, with the "poor" individuals doing this to a greater degree. The contribution of these results under hypnotic states to an understanding of individuals under normal conditions can be questioned, but the justification for such a study lies in the difficulty of obtaining control, in the usual experiments, of the significant variables influencing perceiving. For instance, in the Bruner-Goodman type of experiment investigating the role of values of rich and poor children in perceived size, it is difficult to control the experiences of the subjects with money. Their varying life histories are uncontrolled. Under hypnosis, presumably, it is possible to induce only the relevant attitudes, as of rich or poor.

Personal value systems have been investigated by defining them from scores on the Allport-Vernon scales (theoretical, economic, esthetic, social, political, and religious scales) (630). The following experiment (491) tested the hypothesis that personal values, so defined, will affect recognition thresholds for words. The words were chosen to represent the six values: e.g., for theoretical value the words were "theory," "verify," "science," "logical," "research," and "analysis"; for social value, "loving," "kindly," "devoted," "helpful," "friendly," "sociable"; etc. According to the hypothesis, subjects would recognize more quickly those words which were related to their personal values. And the results, in general, were in line with this: a selective sensitization by the individual's value system upon the individual's recognition thresholds. Although this experiment was immediately subjected to criticism on the basis of its lack of control of familiarity and usage of words, the general conclusion continued to hold.[2]

Perceiving Changed as Moods Shifted under Hypnosis

Leuba and Lucas (363) suggested three different moods—happy, critical, and anxious—when the subjects were under deep hypnosis and directed the subjects to describe six different pictures. Amnesia was suggested for the pictures between each induced mood. The perception of the structured pictures was influenced by the induced moods. With respect to a picture of "young people digging in a swampy area," one subject reported in the happy mood: "It looks like fun; reminds me of summer. That's what life is for," etc.

Perceptual Defense

Common-sense statements often made are that "we see what we want to see," or "we note what we are told to see." In these statements we have a hint of the many problems involved in understanding the perceiving activity. Do we not perceive something which is threatening us? Or do we perceive and at times ignore or repress what we perceive? Or do

[2] Solomon and Howes (572) repeated the experiment of Postman, Bruner, and McGinnis (491) on the perception of words associated with specific values. Groups of familiar and unfamiliar words (based on frequency of Thorndyke-Lorge word count) were selected for each value. There was a considerable difference of reading time between familiar and unfamiliar words, but very little difference between those of little and great "value." Extreme range on the Allport-Vernon scale increased this reading difference between valued words. Postman and Schneider (492) reported a close relationship between reading time and value rank for relatively unfamiliar words but not for the more familiar.

we forget selectively according to ego defenses, remembering only certain parts of the total perception? The relationships among selective attending, selective perceiving, selective remembering, selective reporting are not yet clearly perceived by psychologists (see Inset 26).

INSET 26. AUTONOMIC DISCRIMINATION WITHOUT AWARENESS AND PERCEPTUAL DEFENSE*

McGinnies (418) in 1949 performed an experiment which suggested that human subjects differentiated taboo from nontaboo words before they reported the words presented in a quick-exposure device. In brief, McGinnies presented his subjects with a set of words some of which were neutral in affect and some of which were taboo and presumably anxiety-arousing. Identification thresholds were measured by increasing the exposure duration of a word until it was correctly read by the subject. At the same time that these thresholds were being measured, there was a recording of the subject's GSR.

There were two major results: First, the taboo words had higher thresholds than neutral words, an effect which is considered a demonstration of perceptual defense. Second, during the preidentification trials, subjects gave higher GSRs to the taboo words than to the neutral words. In other words, on these trials on which a subject could not correctly verbally report the words, he still gave a differential GSR to the two kinds of words. This result has been interpreted as evidence of "autonomic discrimination without awareness." It was assumed that somehow enough information was transmitted to the autonomic nervous system to yield a differential GSR to the two classes of words; but supposedly, insufficient information reached the brain centers responsible for correct verbal classification. These assumptions have been criticized adversely.

As is the case with many of the experiments in this controversial area, alternative explanations are possible. Perhaps the simplest suggestion is given by Howes and Solomon (296), who argue that the subjects' higher thresholds for the taboo words resulted from their reluctance to utter these words without more confidence in their guesses than they required for neutral words. If this were so, it would account not only for the elevated thresholds, but also for the differential GSR during the "preidentification" period.

Another suggestion offered by Howes and Solomon is that the taboo words have a lower frequency of occurrence in the written language than do the neutral words; this difference could explain the threshold difference, but it would leave intact the discrimination-without-awareness aspect of the results. However, further experimentation (128) has indicated that neither of the two factors suggested by Howes and Solomon can account for the higher thresholds of the taboo words.

* Adapted from W. N. Dember, *Psychology of Perception*. New York: Holt, 1960, pp. 318–320.

Lazarus and McCleary (358) experimentally created traumatic and neutral stimuli. Five nonsense syllables were paired with shock during a training period, while five others were presented but not paired with shock. After a sufficient number of trials, the shock-paired stimuli became threatening to the subjects, but there was no threat involved in their being uttered by the subjects. Thus, the problem of response withholding was circumvented in this experiment. At the same time there was no problem of differential familiarity, since the two classes of nonsense syllables were equally unfamiliar.

Following the training period, recognition thresholds were measured in the usual way, and the GSR was also recorded. On those trials when the subject's guess was incorrect, there was a higher GSR to the shock-paired than to the neutral syllables. These data write Dember (152) constitute strong support for the notion of *autonomic discrimination without awareness.*

This last finding does not establish but does suggest than an individual might exhibit perceptual defense without awareness, e.g., defend his self-concept by selectively rejecting below awareness perceptions such as of words taboo for him. See Jenkin (314) for a review of the experiments pertinent to the concept of perceptual defense.

Summary

In general, the results of the preceding studies indicate an accentuation in the perceiving activity as need drives increase, as valued objects are sensed, and as moods rise in pleasantness. It is *possibly* adaptive that needed objects or valued ones are accentuated in the perceptual field. This interpretation is close to that presented above by Bevan and Dukes (65).

That motivational determinants act selectively upon recall has long been noted. We now turn to a few of the relevant studies substantiating this fact.

SELECTIVE RECALL

Freud popularized the belief that forgetting may be an activity which serves the individual rather than merely the resultant of loss of learned impression.[3] We may be fearful, for example, that the recall of a former event will destroy our equanimity or worry or grieve us; hence we attempt to forget it and even may deny that the event ever happened. Certainly as far as we can recall at the conscious level, the memory is ab-

---

[3] The interference theory of forgetting is the best which has been established by experimentation. Osgood (473) points out that "repression into the unconscious" *can* be translated into "substitution of an interfering response" (see p. 599). How the learned "impression" is made, how it remains in the individual—as "associations," "reorganizations," "schemata"—is not of concern in this discussion of motivational manifestations in forgetting.

sent. (Whether it is actually any "weaker" is unknown.) In the Freudian theory, repression is considered the principal defense of the infantile ego, which does not have the capacity to withstand temptation or to postpone or modify by compromise the gratification of an impulse. Whatever impulse appears in consciousness has to be converted into action immediately. Repression remains, therefore, the only effective defense. Repressed impulses, however, do not cease to exist merely by exclusion from consciousness and thereby from motor expression. To deal with the tension of these pent-up impulses the ego, according to this theory, has to resort to further defenses, classified into two groups: "(a) further reinforcements of repression, or (b) substitute vents by which the original impulses can find at least a partial modified ego syntonic release and by which their pressure is decreased" (3, p. 12). Thus there is suggested in Freudian theory both selective forgetting of threatening material and selective recall of what supports the ego, including modification in the recall of what occurred in the past.[4]

Observations Supporting Defensive Forgetting (or Ego-supporting Recall)

Clinical observations of individuals who have suffered from traumatic experiences suggest that mild to severe memory losses occur with respect to former noxious situations. A *fugue*, for example, involves loss of all memories which would bring an individual back to a former traumatic situation. That the unpleasant memories are repressed rather than lost is further supported by studies using hypnotic technique to obtain recall under trance. Improvement in recall during hypnosis is greater for anxiety-linked material (473, p. 577).

The clinical facts of amnesia, a memory loss for which there may or may not be later recovery, indicate a defensive forgetting. An illustration of amnesia for self-identification, which was followed by recovery, is the clinic history of a young married girl who forgot her name and other identifying self-clues: She was able to recover these memories, including her own name, quickly when her fear of an unwanted pregnancy was found to be incorrect. Since her desire for a divorce apparently was going to be blocked by the unwanted pregnancy, she attempted to escape by forgetting. The rapid recovery of her memories by removal of her fear indicated that in this clinical patient the repression was not due to more serious and less conscious dynamic tendencies. Nor was there any organic impairment of the cortical areas involved in forgetting.

A variety of attempts have been made to bring the Freudian theory of repression to an experimental test. Early studies of recall of affectively

---

[4] Various studies are attempting to relate repression to personality attributes and to social class (426).

toned events or of words have shown a positive trend (39, 420, 552 and many others), i.e., subjects recalled experiences of verbal materials judged unpleasant less well than those they judged pleasant. Though there was no evidence presented in such studies that the ego strength was threatened in any direct way and that there was repression of the unpleasant, these results are interesting in themselves even if not directly supportive of the Freudian assumption of ego-defensive forgetting. The absence of any proof that the former pleasant and unpleasant experiences of individuals were equal in frequency and in strength of learning raised, however, a critical question concerning the validity of the studies.

That forgetting may be greater for anxiety-tinged events is suggested in the following illustrative studies. Sharp (552), using normal subjects and clinical patients, tested for recall after they had learned word pairs taken from clinical case histories of the abnormal patients. There were three lists: one of acceptable, another of neutral and another of anxiety-producing words. The last proved to be less well recalled as well as harder to learn.

To involve the ego (or self-esteem) is operationally defined in various ways in the next chapter. In general, a threat to some value, such as achievement, is used. In an early experiment Koch (340) had students rate their feelings on receiving a score in ten true-false quizzes. When asked five weeks after the last test to recall the scores, the high (rated pleasant) scores were remembered best. In 1960 Coopersmith (126) also found with children in the fifth and sixth grades a greater recall of successes in a series of simple tasks. Previous studies have in general supported these findings. Coopersmith advances the interesting hypothesis that two factors are necessary for the recall of a failure: (1) the ability to tolerate failure and (2) the striving to overcome its effects.

As indicated in Inset 27, Pascal (479) has experimentally demonstrated the facilitative effect of relaxation on the act of recall.

INSET 27. INTERFERING EFFECT OF TENSION UPON RECALL*

James wrote concerning the frequently observed experience of failure to recall when an active memory "search" is attempted. Then when the individual has gone to a new activity, the name, word, or event pops into awareness. "Something we have made the most strenuous efforts to recall, but all in vain, will soon after we have given up the attempt, saunter into the mind, as Emerson somewhere says, as innocently as if it had never been sent for" (W. James, *Psychology*, 1892, p. 681). The clinical observations of Freud led him to the hypothesis that interference in recall was generally an active defense against unacknowledged desires. Clinicians

* Adapted from G. R. Pascal, The effect of relaxation upon recall. *Amer. J. Psychol.*, 1949, 62, 32–33.

have assumed that recall is aided by relaxation and that a "blockage" represents repressed material with its accompanying tension.

Pascal compared recall of nonsense syllables under a normal face-to-face situation with recall under relaxation. The five minutes of relaxing instructions were given as the subjects were reclining on a couch. The degree of relaxation attained was not measured, but the interested reader might have himself subjected to the directions for relaxation that Pascal reports (p. 36). No doubt a cooperative subject would lose a large amount of the feeling called tension. After relaxation, the recall of the thirteen nonsense syllables was requested with the following direction: "Now I want you to remember the syllables I gave you an hour ago (or twenty-four or forty-eight hours ago). Try to remember as many as you can, but don't worry about them. Try to keep relaxed. All right. Go ahead."

Figure 11-4 shows that the percentage of syllables recalled under relaxation is superior to the recall in the face-to-face situation of the control period with subjects sitting quietly in a chair. This is true whether one, twenty-four, or forty-eight hours intervened between the learning and the test for recall. In Figure 11-4 there is a significant difference in favor of the relaxed condition between each comparable pair of points.

Experimental Tests of the Hypothesis of Repression

If the assumption is accepted that repression is an active process, then it should be possible to demonstrate experimentally the recovery of repressed material following the removal of the motivational determinant responsible for the repression. Zeller (672, p. 46) states the point as follows: "No test of repression can be considered adequate until the removal of the repression factor has resulted in the restoration to consciousness of the repressed material. Any experiment which does not include this crucial step is not complete and the results can be attributed to other factors such as set, differential learning, differential motivation, practice, etc. rather than to active repression." As he also points out, it is difficult to demonstrate experimentally that the nonrecalled material is first repressed. Several experiments by Zeller (673) demonstrated that the introduction of an "ego threat" in a task depressed the performance; and when the ego threat was removed the performance improved.

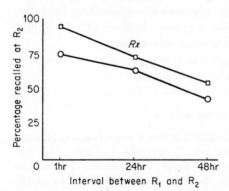

Figure 11-4. Percentage of syllables recalled after relaxation as compared with control. Rx is relaxation. The lower curve is the control. The intervals between the recall immediately after learning (R_1) and second recall (R_2) were one, twenty-four, and forty-eight hours. Pascal (479)

Aborn (1) systematically observed the effect of stress on memory for material (1) for which the subjects were set to learn and (2) for which they were not set, i.e., memory for incidental learning. He found no effect of stress on memory for the first kind of task but a depression in recall for incidental learning and a slight recovery following the removal of threat. Though these improvements may be attributed to removal of repression by removal of the threat, they may also be the resultant of increased interest or a lessening of indifference. In other words, any deterioration in memory following ego threat may be the resultant of (1) repression, or (2) possibly mere indifference (inattention?).

Activity-in-progress as Significant in Perceiving and Recall

The contribution of memory traces to perceiving is not questioned by the varieties of perceptual or cognitive theorists, but there is much controversy concerning how "contact" is made with the memory trace. Of interest are: what mediates the necessary recall, how it is focused, how it is used during perceiving. Assuming that we recognize an object such as a hammer, what mediates the necessary recall of the former handling of a hammer, or of seeing others use it in one or more situations? When the memory traces are contacted, how is the perceiving influenced so that the object is recognized in the immediate situation, though it differs (inevitably) to some degree from all other previous situations? For example, if a man is hanging a picture, this activity-in-progress in some way determines what is isolated in recall and how the sensory input contacts the memory trace. The man sees, perhaps, a metal bookend, and he says to his wife, "Give me that hammer." Moreover, he uses the bookend appropriately to drive a nail into the wall so that the picture can hang. If his wife protests that the bookend is not a hammer, he says that it is a hammer for him. In other words, the sensory input of metal and its associated hardness is in contact with a memory of such objects being useful for driving nails. The particular source of drive behind the activity-in-progress of hanging a picture is unimportant in this case. The activity itself is an influence upon the perceiving and recall.

CONCLUDING STATEMENTS

The influence of motivational determinants upon cognitive activities is by no means facilitating in all ways. True, the personal ends of an individual are often served. What is anticipated as to be attained by an individual, for example, will accordingly focus him on what is relevant to the attainment of this goal. On the other hand, strong motivational determinants may nonadaptively constrict the sensory field. Even more detrimental effects of strong drives, goals, and sets upon cognitions are observed in misperceptions. In other words, what an individual perceives may be what he wants to perceive, not what is veridical. The distortions in social perceptions are easy to make, since the social field is ambiguous (unstructured). Prejudices and stereotyped attitudes are formed, and misperceptions follow. And the results are misunderstandings, quarrels, and more serious conflicts.

Man selectively attends to that which is relevant for him. His successive perceptual reorganizations are structured according to his drives. His recalls are of what concerns him. Facilitative as this often is in the sense of aiding to solve his problems, there is the ever-present danger of biased focusing—personally oriented perceiving as well as inaccurate recall. That which is unpleasant is forgotten, though it might be helpful at times, at least, to remember former unpleasantness.

Perceptual-motivational correlations will not be understood until there is more insight into individual differences in what is perceived in the external fields, particularly fields of ambiguity. Individual differences have been demonstrated, investigated, and reinvestigated in such areas of projections as Rorschach and TAT cards. Though of interest to motivational psychology, the clinical findings are in general left unreviewed in this volume. See Inset 28 for a consideration of the concept of projection (462).

INSET 28. THE CONCEPT OF PROJECTION*

The word "projection" stems from the Latin verb *projectus*, meaning "to cast forward" (51). In the field of personality one would be hard pressed to find a concept so capable of multiple interpretation and so varied in meaning as the concept of projection. Surely, this concept has had more interpretations than the smile of Mona Lisa.

The research literature seems to indicate four possible categorizations of the concept of projection: "classical," "attributive," "autistic," and "rationalized" projection.

Classical Projection

The concept of projection was known several centuries before the appearance of Freud. Thus Thomas a Kempis stated, "What a man is inwardly that he will see outwardly" (117). The *Malleus Maleficarum*, written in the Middle Ages, gives a clear example of projection.

For fancy or imagination is as it were the treasury of ideas received through the senses. And through this it happens that devils so

* Adapted from B. I. Murstein and R. S. Pryer, The concept of projection: a review. *Psychol. Bull.*, 1959, 56, 353–355.

stir up the inner perceptions, that is the power of conserving images, that they appear to be a new impression at that moment received from exterior things (674, p. 54).

At the close of the nineteenth century, Freud gave the following definition of projection: "The psyche develops the neurosis of anxiety when it feels itself unequal to the task of mastering (sexual) excitation arising endogenously. That is to say it acts as if it had projected this excitation into the outer world" (52, p. 353). With this definition, the use of the concept soon became quite widespread.

The view of "classical" projection held currently by many psychologists is: "A situation in which the ego feels threatened is likely to result in the ego's refusing to acknowledge the trait and in the subsequent attribution of the trait to the outside world" (460, p. 418). Adherents to this view are many, though they differ in the wording used.

Attributive Projection

Attributive projection has been described by many psychologists, including Cameron (107). A recent definition is: "The ascribing of one's own motivations, feelings, and behavior to other persons" (461). It is perhaps the most popular of the uses of projection today in the field of personality. The concept's popularity rests on its broadness; i.e., unlike classical projection, there is no concern with the subject's unconscious, or self-concept. It is often sufficient merely to note that there is a correlation between some characteristic of the subject and some statement or prediction he makes concerning other persons.

Autistic Projection

Perception which is strongly influenced by the needs of an individual, in that the figural aspects of the perceived object are modified so as to be consistent with the need, may be referred to as autistic projection. Murphy (455, pp. 338ff.) wrote, "So wherever our needs differ we literally *see* differently. Much of the process of individual perception depends upon the force of past wants, the person's need to disentangle and restructure in terms of the situations with which he has had to cope." Sears (547, p. 121) has written, "It may be said in general, that the presence of a need or drive provides the antecedent condition for the perception of objects related to that need or drive."

Rationalized Projection

This type of projection is similar to "classical" projection in that the projective *process* is held to be unconscious. The projector, however, is conscious of his behavior. He attempts to justify it by inventing a rationale. Thus, the person caught buying on the black market says in self-justification, "Everybody else is doing it." Here, the attempt is to convert neurotic anxiety about doing something wrong into objective anxiety about not getting enough to eat (460, 461). Baldwin (32, p. 498) states:

> Finding a child disobedient and unloving justifies resentment. This introduces us to another sort of defense against guilt—namely to justify the rejection so that it no longer evokes guilt feelings. This attribution of blame to the people toward whom we feel hostile is a defense mechanism called "projection."

From this and the preceding chapter on selecting, we conclude that the selecting capacity of organisms is broadly influential and is manifest in more than one way: It varies from the simplest changes in increased sensitivity of the surface of an amoeba when its need for food increases, to quickened recognition of food-related objects—even to misperceptions of abstract shapes and forms as foods—by man when he is hungry. Selecting is manifest in the greater readiness (increased vigilance) of the fearful subhuman animal, in the focusing on stimulus signs of danger, and in size accentuation by man of his valued objects.

We note variations in choice ranging from the rat selecting his needed vitamined foods to man's quicker reaction time in recognizing words which symbolize his social values.

We ask at least if the "freezing" of animals when fear signals arise in their field is similar to man's possible perceptual defenses (his denials to his recognition of taboo words)?

Beyond suggesting that motivational determinants (as well as personality differences) must be taken into account in attempts to understand evaluative choices of men, we make no attempt to interpret how personally biased cognitive activities are therein at work. We simply accept that they are, subtly, quietly, and at times harmfully—at times in social conflicts even threatening the survival of man.

Factors not considered in detail in this chapter are forcing veridical perceptions and recall; without these compensating factors, motivational variables would lead man into greater absurdities than they do. That transitory drives and goals, and the stable attributes of individuals as well, are at times adaptive in their influence on cognitive activities should also not be forgotten. Though man forgets easily what is unpleasant, he may show excellent recall for what is needed. What is an adaptive goal may be more of a determinant of veridical perceptions than any defense against reality.

CHAPTER 12

TENSION

Tension is not a new concept, not a term only for the twentieth century. Shenstone (557) wrote in 1756: "When a fancy's vivid spark impels the soul to scorn quotidian scenes . . . what nostrum shall compose its fatal tension?" And many nostrums for tension have been advanced, but as yet there is no reliable cure. Tension is not today described as necessarily fatal. It may be assumed that everyone must bear some tension, yet often the implication is that man desires to be relieved of it.

Tension is not a well-identified construct. It is not unusual in psychology to discover that a verbal label is but a mask that covers different meanings and thus fools the unwary reader. Tension, however, frequently refers to nonfacilitative general drive, the meaning accepted in this chapter. Tension is nonoptimal excitation, either because there is a drive overload or because of certain specific origins of drive. Tension is negative in its effects on the activity stream, either immediately with its onset or later. Tension is diffuse, but it encompasses specific components such as frustration and anxiety. In other words, tension onset can be traced to (1) nonoptimal rise in *general drive,* (2) any of the *specific drives* if nonoptimally increased and/or blocked in immediate release, (3) a few specific drives, such as anxiety, whether at a low or high level of intensity.[1]

Tension and stress are identical terms. They both describe dysfunctioning of the organism when the onset of an interfering, sometimes noxious, dangerous, or threatening event cannot be adequately adjusted to by the organism.

Clues to the Onset of Tension or Stress

Clues to the onset of tension or stress include excessive emotionality with a decrease in cognitive control, quick and irrelevant reactions, ex-

[1] Tension is *not* identified by a nonhomeostatic state, disequilibrium, tissue tension, or simply muscle tension. These conditions may exist without nonoptimal drive excitation.

cessive or odd behavior, and other physiological or behavioral signs of disorganization in the optimal functioning of the living system. Other clues are being empirically determined. Two illustrative studies of tension clues from verbal responses follow. Osgood (474) reports a study of verbal behavior of individuals who presumably were in tension, since these individuals later committed suicide. Their suicide notes were significantly stereotyped and less diversified in vocabulary than the control writings used.

One interesting observation was that the emotional stress apparently forced the writers of the suicide notes toward extremeness of polarization in judgment and assertion, as indicated by a significantly greater frequency of "allness terms" ("everything," "nothing," "everybody," "nobody," "always," "never").

In another approach to clues of tension, Mandler, et al. (397) used a rating scale for verbal responses to threatening and neutral verbal phrases. The threatening phrases from Heath's Phrase Association Test included those with aggressive content like "He spit in his mother's face," rejection content like "His roommate would not lend him money," and phrases with competition and sex content like "His girl friend is very promiscuous." The rating scale, in scoring the degree of tension revealed by *verbal responses* of the subjects to the threatening phrases, used five categories. These categories can be considered verbal signs of stress-tension. Briefly described, they are an *avoidance* when the subject succeeded in not directly responding to the context, such as when he simply repeated the stimulus phrase; *interference*, such as laughing, sighing, or not finishing an answer; *recoding*, such as evasive responses or misinterpretations of the stimulus phrases; *rationalization*. (Other ego defenses are also said to represent stress-tension.) *Personalization* was scored if the stimulus phrases evoked verbal responses of a personal nature, such as references to the self or family.

In addition, Mandler et al. obtained physiological scores like skin resistance and peripheral blood flow. These scores differentiated the responses of the subjects to the threatening from the responses to the neutral verbal items. Physiological changes when stressors are present are further illustrated in Inset 29.

Physiological Dysfunctioning as Clues to Tension. Exposure to *physical* stressors of space flight has increased interest in studies of what the body can take. Physical stressors include extreme noise, heat, light, cold, pain, absence of stimulation, continual darkness, weightlessness, and others. An illustration of one of the important stressors of the jet age, the g exposure, is reported by Brozek (93). Accelerative stress induced experimentally in the human centrifuge is g exposure. Profound changes take place in vision, from dimming of peripheral vision to its loss (so-called grayout) and, at a higher level of the stress, from a progressive constriction of the visual field to loss of central vision (so-called black-out). Many other studies of physical stressors have recorded bodily dysfunctioning (292, 495).

Selye's work and his theory (550, 551) in regard to the adaptation syndrome is concerned with the *physiological costs* of stress. Selye has suggested three distinct stages in the bodily changes when stress continues: alarm reaction, stage of resistance, and stage of exhaustion. These three stages are presented in Inset 29.

INSET 29. SELYE'S PHYSIOLOGICAL APPROACH TO STRESS*

Selye has written more about stress than any other individual. For Selye stress refers to bodily changes differentiated from the factors which produce these changes and which he calls stressors.

Adaptation syndrome. Selye (550) interested in stress from bodily disease, has suggested three distinct stages in what he calls the general-adaptation syndrome (GAS). Following the onset of a disease (or any damaging agent) the general syndrome evolves in three distinct states: alarm reaction, stage of resistance, stage of exhaustion. Selye, a doctor of medicine, writes:

> My very first experiments showed that upon continued exposure to any noxious agent capable of eliciting this alarm reaction (unless it killed immediately), a stage of adaptation or resistance followed. In other words, no living organism can be maintained continuously in a state of alarm. If the body is confronted with an agent so damaging that continuous exposure to it is incompatible with life, then death ensues during the alarm reaction within the first hours or days. If survival is possible at all, this alarm reaction is necessarily followed by a second stage, which I called the "stage of resistance." (550, p. 31)

The stage of resistance is characterized by bodily regulatory attempts to combat the noxious agent. The manifestations of the second stage are reported as quite different in form and in many instances the exact opposite of those which characterized the alarm reaction.

> For instance, during the alarm reaction, the cells of the adrenal cortex discharged their microscopically visible granules of secretion (which contain the hormone) into the blood stream. Consequently, the stores of the gland were depleted. Conversely, in the stage of resistance, the cortex accumulated an abundant reserve of secretory granules. In the alarm reaction, the blood became concentrated and there was a marked loss of body weight; but during the stage of resistance, the blood was diluted and body weight returned toward normal. Many similar examples could be cited, but these suffice to illustrate the way one can objectively follow resistance-changes in various organs. (550, p. 31)

* Adapted from H. Selye, *The Stress of Life.* New York: McGraw-Hill, 1956.

Negative tension or harmful tension arising during the first alarm reaction is also in the stage of resistance, but its effects are most clearly observed in the stage of exhaustion.

Selye adds: "I call the entire nonspecific response the *general adaptation syndrome*." This whole syndrome evolves in time through the three stages just mentioned, namely: (1) alarm, (2) resistance, (3) exhaustion. After prolonged exposure to any noxious agent, any acquired adaptation is eventually lost. In the "stage of exhaustion," the symptoms are in many respects strikingly similar to those of the initial alarm reaction. At the end of a life under stress, this is a kind of premature aging due to wear and tear, a sort of second childhood which, in some ways, resembles the first phase. The deterioration from prolonged tension would resemble this last stage.

ACTIVITY CHANGES UNDER CONTINUED INTERFERENCE

We divide into three general phases the activity of an individual under *continued* thwarting. (1) Nonfrustration phase: There is drive rise but *no* tension. There is at first adaptive behavior focused on overcoming the barrier. (2) The second phase is strongly marked by emotional behavior (often aggressive). In this phase the tension is best described as frustration. (3) In the third phase there is anxiety-tension. A man before a barrier usually passes gradually from one phase into the second and perhaps into the third. Again, the man, if permitted by the situation (or by his own personality), may leave the field and never enter into a state of tension-frustration nor ever exhibit signs of anxiety-tension. Or a man may be in the first phase of adjustive problem solving, then suddenly indicate by his aggressive behavior and/or other emotional signs that he is in a state of frustration, only to return to adaptive instrumental attacks upon the problem presented by the barrier. The description which follows is concerned with hypothetical tension states as inferred from the activity of individuals under *continued* interference.

Phase One in the Activity Stream after Interference

Immediately following interference, there is usually an increase in energy expenditure. The increase in drive may be inferred from the overt behavior as well as from physiological indices to greater arousal. Solley and Stagner (570) report that increases in palmar sweating were statistically reliable when a barrier (delay) was introduced in solutions of anagrams. The individual blocked in a goal-directed activity will generally orient toward overcoming the barrier and reaching his original goal. *He has a rise in general drive.*

Normally an organism becomes more alert after interference. His behavior stream may *not* at first be characterized by poor quality of performance. Reasoning, planning, and creative solutions are reported. Strategy may be at a high level with no signs of emotional disorganization. Problems which the interferences pose are the occasions for creative activity. This fact has been recognized. There are theses in regard to society as a whole, such as Toynbee's that the protracted existence of a challenge, often in the form of a difficulty in meeting the needs of bare subsistence, is the condition for the activity that produces a new civilization. Dashiell (139) in his early analysis of adjustive learning illustrated the normal problem-solving behavior immediately after the introduction of a barrier.

Both human and subhuman subjects, after interference, may remain in a problem-solving attitude and never enter into frustration-tension or anxiety-tension. This was illustrated in a study reported by Tolcott (612) who was interested in the behavior of a simple organism when there were the simultaneous pressures to obtain food and to avoid a flashing light. Since the food was obtained by bar depression and avoidance of the light was accomplished by the rat's standing on a pedal some distance from the food magazine, both needs were simultaneously aroused. The solution to the problem was as follows: "The rat would sit on the pedal for a brief period, keeping the light off, then would slowly edge off, holding the pedal down with his legs as long as possible; suddenly he would make a dart toward the bar (often stopping for an instant as the light came on), press the bar for food a few times very rapidly, eating each pellet as he released it, then turn and run back to the pedal, sometimes carrying the last pellet back and eating it on the pedal" (612, p. 101). Figure 12-1 shows the rise in rate of bar pressing during conflict sessions. When a comparison is made of the rate of bar pressing to obtain food during the twelve conflict sessions with the rate when only need for food was present, we find an increase. Such an increase in speed of reaction is adaptive in overcoming interference. This increase in speed is also illustrated in the study of interference when rats were trained to run a straight-away with two successive goal boxes in which food was found. After running speeds had stabilized, the rats were then blocked in their first goal box; on half their trials they had no food. They ran faster and showed lower latencies in leaving this box on the blocked goal trials. Speed is only one of the adaptive changes that can be made to the problem presented by an interference of some kind (pp. 208–223 of 90).

Phase Two: Tension-frustration Following Continued Interference

A tension state called frustration may arise immediately with the onset of a barrier or, more usually, after *continued* interference. It is characterized by aggressive responses. Assume that a child who is blocked in

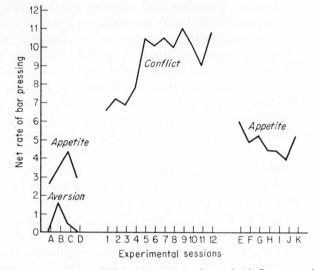

Figure 12-1. Increase in rate of bar pressing to obtain food during conflict between light aversion and need for food. Tolcott (612)

his plans for a holiday starts aggressive attacks upon the interfering agent or upon surrogates, i.e., scapegoats. He is now in the frustration phase. There can be no completion of the original activity, but the individual remains oriented to the blocked goal and shows signs of nonoptimal drive rise. The form of the aggression may be direct or indirect. The barrier may be directly attacked, or subtle forms of aggression may appear for which social punishment is not inevitable.

The well-know theory associating aggressiveness with continued interference is the frustration-aggression hypothesis (162).[2] This hypothesis most broadly stated suggests to the student of human nature that when he sees aggression, he should turn a suspicious eye on possibilities that the organism or group is confronted with frustration, and that when he views interference with an individual or group, he should be on the lookout for, among other things, aggression. Aggression varies from direct physical attack on the interfering agent to self-destruction or self-punishment. The interference which produces frustration may not be great, or it may be a threat to the organism's existence. Another individual may be the agent which brings about the blocking of the activity of the frustrated person, or the interference may be an inanimate object. As indicated in Inset 30, the origin and degree of interference affect the degree of the aggression.

Always there is the possibility of a substitute outlet for the blocked

[2] See (91, 99, 402, 537, 55) for the development of and changes in the frustration-aggression hypothesis.

goal. Substitute acts vary in their effectiveness in accomplishing the reduction of the original drive and of the additional "pressure" (tension) added when the frustration-tension arises: "Eating raisin pie when there is no mince, reading romantic stories when real romance is unavailable, producing amateur theatricals when having a professional career prevented" may, or may not, be adequate substitutes for the original denied activities; they may, or may not, reduce the rising tensions. Substitute responses can be less or even more effective in terminating the tension than the original response. To the extent that they are equally or more effective, they put an end to the frustrations preceding them and to the aggression produced by these frustrations.[3]

INSET 30. DEGREE OF INTERFERENCE AS RELATED TO AGGRESSION*

The degree of interference is positively related to the degree of aggression. However, the specific source of the interference is a contributing variable. In one study (228) boys and girls, all white, around fourteen years of age, and in the ninth grade of schools in New York City, were instructed to complete various statements in regard to aggression. Examples: "When John's mother hit him, he _____." "The colored kid called him names, so Ricky _____." "When her mother bawled her out like that, Thelma _____." The subjects were instructed to complete each statement according to "what you think would be the most likely way for a person to act in such a situation."

Five origins of interference were used in writing the statements to be completed: parent (mother or father), sibling (brother or sister), friend or classmate, authority ("cop" or teacher), and inferior ("colored kid" or "pesky little neighbor's kid").

Five strengths of external forms of aggression could be used by the children in completing the statements: hitting or slapping, bawling out or making dirty cracks, talking about the offender behind his back or carrying tales about him, making faces or giving nasty looks, and not liking.

After the children had completed the sentences, their selections were judged according to the degree of their expressed aggression: (1) per cent frequency of aggressive response; (2) average scale value (on a ten-point scale) for the intensity of the aggressive responses, called amplitude; (3) average intensity of all responses (magnitude).

For all three measures the greater the aggressiveness of the attacker (the specific source of interference) the stronger, or more intense, the description of what these children believed would be most likely to happen. If slapping or hitting occurred, then in return slapping or some

[3] Freudian theory has generated a number of "defense mechanisms" such as rationalization, etc. These are also means of reducing tension-frustration.

* Adapted from F. K. Graham, W. A. Charwat, A. S. Honig, and P. C. Weltz, Aggression as a function of the attack and the attacker. *J. abnorm. soc. Psychol.*, 1951, 46, 512–520.

similar bodily injury would be expected from the person attacked. "An eye for an eye and a tooth for a tooth" was the rule *if* expectancy of punishment was low.

The teacher, the "cop," or the parents do not, however, evoke the same intensity of aggressive responses. And the overt aggression expressed is of such a mild nature as "not liking," so that it is even difficult to consider it as aggression. It is, however, possible that latent aggression may be very intense against authority though no overt signs appear. Or it is possible that attack from authority is not so emotionally disturbing as from an equal or inferior.

The general conclusion: The greater the aggressive attack, the more vigorous is the *reported* aggression by adolescents. Authority figures with the right to punish do not evoke the same degree of aggression as do equals or *inferiors*.

Energizing of an Organism in the Frustration Stage. There is an increase in arousal following interferences, but it is difficult to differentiate that rise in drive which initiates phase one (the problem-solving stage after interference) from the drive rise with the onset of tension. Increase in arousal is observed in both phase one and phase two. When a chimpanzee presses harder on a water spigot if the flow of water is stopped, this increase in vigor of response may be an attempt to solve the problem presented by the absence of water. However, such behavior has also been considered a sign of frustration. *If* the chimpanzee would, in addition, bite or show other aggressive and nonadaptive behaviors with respect to the barrier or to a substitute, frustration-tension could then be more validly inferred.

Aggressive behavior after interference is a better clue to frustration than simple arousal. Aggression takes many forms. It may range from hitting an irritating insect to wars among nations, from laughter when others are hurt to cold planning for destruction of enemies. It may be self-punishment which culminates in suicide. Aggression may be indirect, as are dreams of murder or enjoyment of the tragedies of Shakespeare. Aggression is clearly observed in young children under interference. Records of preschool children's agitations when interfered with during a rewarded task indicated aggressive patterns: e.g., shouting, hitting the apparatus, etc. (629). No observer of children will doubt these results. The degree of aggression is related to the degree of interference from anyone who represents a barrier. Hokanson (289) reported that college students administered significantly more shock to the frustrater (the experimenter) in high as contrasted to low thwarting situations.

In regard to the question of whether frustration has motivational functions, the obvious but positive evidence cited above is the observed increase in arousal which, in its most direct expression, is behavioral attack. The goal most apparently dominant in the frustration-tension stage is to return to the original activity, but in addition there may be signs of a need to relieve tension, with indirect release such as on a scapegoat also being observed. There is, however, no goal object, place, or condition specifically related to frustration, as is food to the hunger drive component.

Phase Three: Anxiety

With continued interference there may be signs of the onset of tension-anxiety. Tension-anxiety is *not* always distinguishable from tension-frustration or even from the first phase of increased drive when the individual is attempting to solve the problem presented by the interference. The man's inner excitation may change gradually from drive alertness to frustration-tension, to anxiety, and finally to extreme anxiety.

The general index to the onset of extreme anxiety is the appearance of self-defeating behaviors. The merely frustrated individual will use the learnings acquired in his attempts to solve the problems presented by a barrier, and he will return to the original activity when the barrier (or interference) is removed. *In contrast, the man afflicted with anxiety, if extreme, will not show such a normal adjustment.* The characteristics of the behavior pattern in phase three are repetitious, self-defeating—in general, nonadjustive.

Summarizing the above, we have said that at first general drive rises with interference. When the subject is first blocked in an ongoing act, he generally reacts as if he had a subproblem to solve before he can return to his original act. The drive components in phase one are curiosity, or even wonder, with increased alertness. The rise in drive is facilitative of the problem-solving attempts. When, or if, the man passes into frustration, the general drive rise is nonoptimal. Frustration, a component of the drive-tension flux, leads to overreactivity, incoordination, or other signs of disorganization. However, the nonoptimal drive-tension increase is most obvious when anxiety is extreme. The anxious man may even decline in overt activation but not because of relaxation. There may be apparent apathy, indifference, and submission, but if the subject cannot withdraw from the field, anxiety-tension continues to rise. Extreme stress symptoms increase, until finally the body can no longer function adequately. Convulsions in rats are recorded when they are forced by a blast of air to continue in insolvable problems (391, 392). Coma and death may follow.

Significant Variables in Rise of Central Excitation to Nonoptimal Level

Variables probably significant in determining the successive changes in the total activity stream during interference include:

1. The nature of the interfering agent, e.g., whether it is a barrier raised by another man, and if so, whether he is of the same, of a higher, or of a lower place in a dominance hierarchy.

2. The possibility of substitute activities which may relieve the rising tension to some degree or even to a greater degree than the original task. This possibility is important in determining whether the effect of an interference passes into frustration and anxiety-tension.

3. The dominant drives *before* the interference occurred. The drives supporting the interrupted act, including the inciting original goal, if any, are important in determining the effect of an interference in that act. The stronger the original support, the more the barrier is stress producing.

4. The length of time the interruption continues. This variable is related to No. 3 above and is dependent, in part, upon how the subject perceives the interference. In some cases, in spite of the presence of even a physical barrier, there is no interference since the subject perceives none. A noise to one individual is interfering; to another it is not even heard. The physical form of the external interfering agent is also significant. An extreme painful stimulation is interfering to almost everyone.

Sometimes an interference does not continue long because the subject withdraws from the original activity. And there can be no interference in an activity which no longer exists for the subject. Lewin (367) early described "going out of the field" as a response to conflict.

5. The identification of the source of the barrier and the anticipated effects if attacks are made on the barrier. The anticipated effect refers to fear of possible punishment if direct attacks are made upon the source of interference. Man behaves differently if he anticipates punishment for efforts to overcome the barrier than if he anticipates praise for his attacks.

6. The expectedness or unexpectedness of the interference. An unexpected insult is responded to differently from an expected unfriendly communication. Berkowitz (56, 57) reports that the hostility which arose following a violation of *expected* friendly behavior from a partner was more likely to increase hostility than the sequence of expected hostility and received hostile comments.

TENSION AND THE SELF

This discussion of the three tension phases following interference or thwarting did not consider any involvement of the self. There was, however, no denial that self-involvement might be a significant factor in tension rise. Certain experimental methods of setting up interference specifically threaten the self-esteem, i.e., ego-involve the individual.

Conventionally any degrading of the self-esteem is described as ego-involving. The individual whose self-value is threatened often moves immediately into frustration or even into anxiety. The first phase described above—the problem-solving stage—is then less often observed.

Theories in Regard to Relation of Self and Tension

Within the Freudian model of men, tension and the libidinal energy are used as synonymous terms. With conflict—an inevitable event, in the Freudian model, between the demands of the id and the social pressures of the superego—tension is said to rise. Repression, if it occurs, of an id impulse leads to increased tension *not* because of the repression but as the result of anxiety that the repression will not be controlled by the self (ego). Nonassimilated conflict is assumed to lead to various symptoms, all of which are tension signs. The defense mechanisms, the projections, the rationalizations, and others are assumed to be tension releasers, though they also represent signs of unsolved problems. Conflict, continuing at times below the level of awareness, is assumed to be responsible for tension, which then may be released in direct or indirect ways.

Tension and the Self-concept. Rogers (519) suggests that the origin of psychological tension is any discrepancy between "significant sensory and visceral experiences" and the conscious self-concept. He illustrates by citing the mother who feels dislike, distaste, or even hatred of her child but who denies to her conscious self that such experiences exist in *her, a mother who loves her child.* She has as part of her concept of self a whole constellation of attitudes which may be summed up by saying, "I am a good and loving mother." This conceptualization of herself is based in part upon distorted symbolization in which the values held by others are introjected *as if* they were her own experiences.

> With this concept of self she can accept and assimilate those organic sensations of affection which she feels toward the child. But the organic experience of dislike, distaste, or hatred toward her child is something which is denied to her conscious self. The experience exists, but it is not permitted accurate symbolization. The organic need is for aggressive acts which would fulfill these attitudes and satisfy the *tension* which exists. The organism strives for the achievement of this satisfaction, but it can do so for the most part only through those channels which are consistent with the self-concept of the good mother. Since the good mother could be aggressive toward her child only if he merited punishment, *she perceives much of his behavior as being bad,* deserving punishment, and therefore the aggressive acts can be carried through, without being contrary to the values organized in her picture of self (519, pp. 511–512, italics added).

Self-consistency is adjustive in Rogers's theory, whether the self-concept is socially admirable or not. We defend ourselves not from attack but from any suggestion that we are not what we believe ourselves to be. Tension, according to Rogers, results from the failure of an individual to incorporate into his self-concept all the organic cravings and social demands which he may have. Thus in the above illustration of the mother who both loves and hates her child but who believes herself capable only of loving her child and refuses to acknowledge any dislike of her offspring, the mother has an inner tension. *If* the mother perceived her total self, including her dislike of her child, then this inner tension would decline, according to Rogers.

This illustration of the origin of tension is said by Rogers to be indicative of most maladjustments in which the organism is striving for certain satisfactions in the field as organically experienced while at the same time the concept of self is "constricted and cannot permit in awareness many of the actual experiences."

There are, however, clinically two somewhat different degrees of this tension. There is first of all the type just illustrated, in which the individual has a definite and organized self-concept based in part upon the organic experiences. For example, while the concept of a good mother has been introjected from social contacts, it has also been formed in part from some of the sensations actually experienced by the mother and has thus become more genuinely her own. "In other instances, the individual feels as he explores his maladjustment that he has no self, that he is a zero, that his only self consists of endeavoring to do what others believe he should do. . . . Since the values held by others have no necessary relationship to one's actual organic experiencings, the discrepancy between the self-structure and the experiential world gradually comes to be expressed as a feeling of tension and distress" (519, p. 512).

The Construct of Tension in Interpersonal Theory. Within Sullivan's interpersonal theory of personality man is described as a "tension system." Tension varies from absolute relaxation accompanied by euphoria to absolute tension, such as exists in extreme terror. One origin of tension is needs. Needs are *not* primarily the resultant of instabilities in an organism as an isolated entity. Though Sullivan suggests that needs include the physiochemical instabilities, they also include those states arising in the interaction of individuals in the process of acculturation. For example, the need for "good feeling," for euphoria (based on security) is developed "primarily from one's experiences of approval and disapproval of others, especially the mothering one" (452, p. 52). Another general origin of tension in interpersonal theory is anxiety. Within Sullivan's theory one of the important tasks of psychology is to discover basic vulnerabilities to anxiety in interpersonal relations (591).

Methods of obtaining categories of interpersonal behavior aid in supporting or denying the hypotheses implicit in Sullivan's theory: that tension rises or is reduced according to interpersonal relations. A scoring scheme for interpersonal relations, described as relatively comprehensive by its authors, is presented in Inset 31. When scores were obtained on six hyperaggressive boys in residential treatment, it was found that the major change from the treatment was in the interpersonal relations of children to adults. There was primarily a decrease in hostile-dominant behavior and an increase in friendly-passive behavior. The appropriateness of behavior increased both in relations with children and with adults.

INSET 31. A SCORING SCHEME FOR INTERPERSONAL RELATIONS*

The search for methods for describing human interactions and the problems involved in extant approaches have been reviewed by Heyns and Lippitt (276). Raush et al. (497) present a scheme (1) applicable to a wide variety of situations, (2) relevant to the study of personality and individual behavior patterns, (3) suitable for dealing with the behavior of both children and adults, and (4) relatively comprehensive. The approach initially described by Freedman et al. (200) and discussed in detail by Leary (360) was used.

The scheme indicated in Figure 12-2 is based on two polar coordinates. One is along the dimension of affection: from love (affiliate, act friendly) to hate (attack, act unfriendly). The other axis is concerned with status: from dominate (command, high status action) to submit (obey, low status action). Each action of one person toward another is coded by letter into one of sixteen categories along the periphery of the circle in accordance with its blending of the two coordinates. The words below the letters are simply examples of the kinds of actions that might be coded at that position. In practice, coding was generally a compromise between the words representing the categories and the position relative to the two axes, but in cases of doubt the position was utilized rather than the words.

As in the Bales scheme (33), the attitude taken by the coder is that of the "generalized other." The question he attempts to answer via his categorization is, "What is this person doing to the other? What kind of relationship is he attempting to establish through this particular behavior?" (276, p. 91). For example, when a child says, "Wasn't that a good movie we saw last night?" he is generally not coded J, although J can include asking someone's opinion; he is rather coded M, which is simple affiliation. Or when a child says to another, "I can kick better than you," rather than simply stating an opinion P, he is usually establishing a dominant, slightly hostile relationship B, although within some contexts such a statement might involve more of an aggressive element than one of status differentiation and so might be coded D. The statement, "I don't want to play with you," may represent active rejection C, whiny complaining F, or very passive withdrawal H, depending on the context and on the quality with which it was said.

* Adapted from H. L. Raush, A. T. Dittmann, and T. J. Taylor, The interpersonal behavior of children in residential treatment. *J. abnorm. soc. Psychol.,* 1959, 58, 9–26

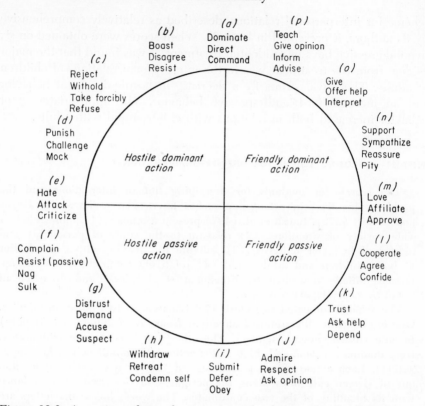

Figure 12-2. A scoring scheme for interpersonal relations. Raush, Dittmann, and Taylor (497)

The observers write: "In relations with peers, the children received about the same amount of aggression as they expressed. They received less aggression from adults than they expressed toward them. Changes in patterns of behavior toward others were accompanied, in general, by reciprocal changes in the behaviors of others, both adults and children" (497, p. 25).

Methods of Ego-involvement

Man learns to esteem his self-image. In general he defends it if attacked, though he can accept himself as inferior to others in some characteristics but not all—at least, not without detrimental effects to him. He is normally startled, alarmed, angered by an attack on his own self-concept. He becomes emotionally aroused, ego-involved, when there is a degrading of himself. Ego-involvement is generally nonfacilitative of performance.

There are a variety of studies which attempt to ego-involve subjects by means of attacks on the self. These studies are closer to the Freudian theory of the origin of tension than the other theories reviewed above. However, they should be viewed simply as experimental observations rather than as tests of Freudian theory. Among the experimental methods of ego-involving men are those outlined below.

1. The feeling of *failure* is in some way induced in the subject. For example, before he has finished all of a series of problems, he is interrupted and told that his time is up. Another technique for the production of failure is the introduction of false norms which imply failure even if the performance has actually been adequate. The use of this technique may incorporate other aspects. For example, an individual may be interrupted before he has completed all of the items on a test and then told by the experimenter that anyone who has *not* finished has done poorly. The subject may also be told at the outset of the experiment that anyone with normal intelligence (or who expects to be successful in college, or to have a career in the Air Force, etc.) ought to be able to complete the task within the time limit. In the latter case, failure to complete the problems automatically tells the subject that he is failing.

Any attempts to induce a feeling of failure present certain difficulties: (a) Skepticism on the part of the subjects about the reality of the failure situation (it is simply interpreted as another one of those "tricks" of psychologists). (b) There may be little or no involvement by the subject in the original task. The task is not significant *to him*. Suppose he does fail in it; so what?

2. *Difficult tasks.* The situations called *task-induced stress tension* involve a difficult task which makes excessive demands upon the subject.

There may be also continuous external distraction. For example, a person learning to drive a car has many distractions; nor is the task simple. The subject has the capacity to do the task, but he must not be distracted. Failure is interpreted as ego-involving the subject.

3. *The individual overchallenges himself.* A man knows he can do the task. It is not even difficult and there are no excessive demands or distractions, but he attempts to meet high standards of speed, accuracy, or persistence which he sets for himself. If his level of aspiration is greater than his capacity for performance, there may be excessive demands upon him, even upon his physiological functioning. His increased efforts may improve his performance, but the stress is exhausting.

There are other ways by which the self-esteem may be involved with a resulting rise in tension. Holtzman and Bitterman (292) have reviewed a variety of "stress tests." One warning: Individuality in the reactions to interferences is to be expected. If any experimenter believes he can involve the ego of *all* his subjects by the same objective methods, the experimenter's own self-esteem may suffer from failure.

Detrimental Effects of Ego-involvement on Performance

Ego-involved failure stress when there is a drive rise to nonoptimal tension leads frequently to disorganized behavior.[4] The nonfacilitating role of failure is reported by a variety of experimenters. See Lindsley (371), Easterbrook (169), Lazarus and Eriksen (357), and Lazarus et al. (356). Disorganization under tension from ego-involvement has been interpreted in various ways. It may result from a loss of inhibitory control due to increased emotionality. Or attention may be focused on failure rather than on how to overcome it. The disruption to the self may be so severe that emotionality, including anxiety, overcomes all productive thinking. The stress interview by the OSS assessment staff during World War II used ego-involved threat, which led to severe anxiety attacks in some individuals (475). Another observation has shown that failure at first increases variability in behavior and, as tension load increases, ends in disorganized performance. Speed may be increased but at the expense of accuracy (356).

The differences in observed performance between interferences when there is and when there is not a threat to the self suggest not only that the tension load is immediately greater with ego-involvement but that a goal appears, self-protection. Moreover, activity directed at maintaining the self-esteem often prevents the effective continuance of the original performance. Normal problem solving may cease. Wessman et al. (651) report on the basis of records of moods by college women that a consistent factor present in a drop from elation to depression is a loss in self-esteem.

Any of the well-known ego defense mechanisms may appear after failure, including regression to earlier forms of behavior (36) and other mechanisms (542) like rationalization.

STRIVING FOR PRESTIGE, SOCIAL-CLASS STATUS, AND TENSION RISE

In social interaction there are often challenges to the self-concept. Such challenges are said to lead to tension, as does the competitive "rat race" of the business world, which includes the striving to move upward in prestige status. The push upward in the United States is primarily from the middle class for inclusion in the upper "country club" group (or

---

[4] If failure stress (or any stressor) aids performance (635), a nonoptimal level of drive has probably not been induced.

Emotionality rise in some subjects (such as nonanxious individuals) is not so rapid as in others after interference, and hence the onset of disorganizing tension is not so quickly observed. Intellectual level is also a significant variable in determining whether failure is followed by a decrement in performance.

similar upper-upper groups). This goal as an incitor increases the efforts of the man (and his wife) to attain symbols of upward movement. Vance Packard, author of *The Hidden Persuaders*, writes that before the present era of great material abundance in America, it was assumed that prosperity would eliminate or greatly reduce class distinction. In other words, all men were presumed created equal and so would remain equal in a society with plenty of goods. However, this proved too optimistic a view. In the social structure from hamlet to city, the attempts to move upward continued to set up distinctions among groups. Though the means of signifying social status change through the years, the pursuit of class prestige does not waver (476).

The systematic observations of the sociologically oriented surveys of communities substantiate the reality of class lines (119). To what degree upward class striving is a source of tension in individuals is not easy to establish. The hypothesis, however, seems reasonable that striving for class status might be preventive of sufficient relaxation and thus at times bodily dysfunctioning would occur. The physiological effects of prolonged competitive activity have been established, though certainly all the conditions are not known which would produce ulcers and other physiological clues to an extreme tension load from status striving.

Characteristic of an American male is high aspiration in regard to his own future. It has been claimed that the young white American male believes that his future permits the attainment of almost any ambition which he may have: to become president of a bank, head of his own business, head of a corporation, president of the United States; to accumulate the traditional millions; or to achieve accomplishment in some other line for which his interests or capacities fit him (or even in one for which they do not fit him). It is possible that such individual aspirations are now less prevalent than before the fearful experiences of the last great depression and the long years of hot and cold war. The young male of America may today consider security more significant than great "accomplishment with risks," but the prestige hierarchies are still prominent in American culture, and statuses of different kinds are sought.[5]

The position of a man in a group, particularly a group with some semblance of hierarchical organization, is an index to his status *in that group*. One group, however, may be higher in a general prestige scale than another. The varying business, civic, and social clubs in any com-

---

[5] Status may be defined simply as position, or place, in the social order. Woman is a name for a status; so are man, child, father, lodge member, Republican, president, general, or sergeant. The "prestige" of the status, or place, occupied is usually a significant aspect of the meaning of the status and of the importance of the role that it demands from the individual who has attained or been given the status.

munity can be arranged in hierarchies of prestige value as groups. Even to belong to one country club is not as socially prestige laden as to belong to another. High position in the organization of janitors carries little, if any, prestige status in the eyes of a professional man.

One specific hypothesis that has been tested is that men seek to attain high level in all groups (184). In other words, if status for an individual is high in one group, he will attempt to equal that position in all other groups to which he belongs. Prestige in one group, or a few groups, is not sufficient. High position in other social hierarchies must also be sought. The hypothesis was put to a test at one university. The selected groups, the most important of the college groups, were rated according to a preliminary study as follows:

1. The particular "house" group to which the student belonged (social club)
2. Other school groups or outside groups
3. The general student body
4. Friends or acquaintances
5. The family (immediate and/or relatives)

The subjects, male sophomores, rated their *present* general standing and their *desired* position in each of the reference groups. (The subjects indicated their positions on an eleven-point percentage scale.) The difference between the two ratings was called the individual's status striving.

The results indicate a significantly larger striving in the groups in which the individuals reported that they were at that time in low position than in the groups where they had a higher status. (This finding was also true for a group which generally represented the middle range in all their present positions.) Thus the tendency was observed for these college sophomores to strive to move upward in those particular groups in which their status was the lowest, and moreover, to strive to a greater degree in the groups in which they occupied a low status. In terms of personality stability, the above results are suggestive of a reference point for the individual which permits him to maintain a constant self-image. Murphy states that "when (a young adult's) status is higher in one sphere than in another, he anchors the self at a point that permits a rather constant degree of self esteem" (455, p. 513). Hoppe (293) similarly points out that aspiration levels (reference groups in this study) in different tasks are part of a constant "Ichniveau." The fundamental property of the ego level, according to Hoppe, is that it tends to be held high at all costs.

Though positive status striving exists, some individuals have zero status strivings or neutralized status, and some even have negative status strivings. Over 20 per cent of the ratings in the above study indicated the desire to have less status within certain groups. This last finding might be interpreted as a belittling of the group and thus indirect protection of one's own self-image. If the group is not important, no position in that group would be important. The zero and negative strivings might also indicate a desire to escape the responsibilities and demands that arise from a high position in certain groups like a family or social club.

PERSONALITY AND REACTION TO STRESSES

The reader should be warned that the relation of personality to tension is difficult to untangle. When two such complex concepts as tension and personality are examined in order to see what relation, if any, might be found, complexity is compounded.

Personality traits no doubt are important in determining whether a stressor will have a small or large tension effect. The highly tense individual is likely to overestimate the difficulty of any task and starts off at a high level of tension. Success may not relax him. The confident individual can start with less and endure a greater tension load. Failure or threat of failure in the less confident man may decrease drive tension to a nonoptimal amount, and thus he may not finish the task. Such possible events are not at present predictable with any certainty. Personality differences may be so great with respect to tension load that lumping together the results from different subjects will give ambiguous or misleading conclusions in regard to such variables as induced failure.

A suggested personality dimension which has had some study as it affects the reactions of individuals following failure is the capacity to endure frustration. Rosenzweig (522) pointed out that individuals vary in their frustration tolerance, a suggestion which implies that there are stable differences in the degree of emotionality aroused by interference. Duffy (163) reported correlations of tension measures with the ratings on excitability of nursery school children, a finding which would support the personality dimension of frustration tolerance.

A relationship between degree of need-achievement and reaction to failure has been suggested (26). Persons who are low in any need-to-achieve tend not to recall failures, but those high in need-achievement tend to ruminate over their past failures and keep them active in their recalls. Caron and Wallach (114) add supporting data for this relation of the personality attribute of n achievement to the degree that failure is frustrating.

Individuals may also be scored on test inventories of anxiety signs. As is indicated in the next chapter, individuals who score high on such tests are more sensitive to disruption from stressors than are those who have low test scores on anxiety.

CONCLUDING STATEMENTS

Tension or tension-stress is indicated by nonoptimal changes in the activity stream when there is a continued interference or thwarting. Tension is negative in its effects on performance.

Three stages of reaction to continued interference were suggested, each stage being characterized by a slightly different effect on performance. In the first stage, normal attempts to overcome the barrier are observed. There is no tension. There is at first merely a rise in activation after the thwarting of an ongoing act.

Frustration-tension which adds to general drive appears in the second phase of the changes which occur with continued interference. Frustration is characterized not only by a rise in drive tension but by maladaptive, often aggressive, behaviors.

In the final phase with continued interference, extreme anxiety is most obvious. There may even be a fall in overt activation. Signs of apathy or indifference may appear. Disorganization is acute. Selye's last stage (550) in his adaptation syndrome is approached or reached in this final phase.

Attacks on the self-esteem are significant interferences in the lives of men. Threats to the self-esteem or the actual degrading of the self is a stress antecedent correlated, in general, with ineffective performance. Extreme anxiety may develop under threats to the self if they are continued.

The relations of personality dimensions to the degree of disorganization under stressors has had limited study.

CHAPTER 13

ANXIETY—A SPECIFIC

TENSION STATE

As adults we are threatened by future wars not of our own making, by fluctuations in economic factors that are unaffected by our own individual efforts, by the possibilities of sudden death inherent in our mechanized way of life, and by a host of variables that we cannot identify or call by name, but which nevertheless have great possibilities of vitally influencing our lives. In short, our society forms an environmental background well calculated to create the necessary conditions for anxiety, i.e., threat of danger with poor identification of its source and poor orientation of effective avoidance response.[1]

"And which of you by being anxious can add one cubit to his span of life?" We may know the answer to this question, but yet our tension increases and our anxieties grow strong. Whether future historians will name the twentieth century "the age of anxiety" is yet to be known.[2] We may be entering only the first years of an age of fearful fears. Man has engaged in a long struggle with the forces of nature, and now that he has successfully conquered many of them, it appears paradoxical that he now fears what he himself created. He has beaten, or is holding his own, with many of the plagues that were once his torment. And his early, his primitive fears are almost gone. Man once feared the fires that swept the forest, the lightning that started the fires, the wild animals that were both

[1] L. I. O'Kelly, *Introduction to Psychopathology*. Englewood Cliffs, N.J.: Prentice Hall, 1949, p. 80.

[2] The *Shorter Oxford English Dictionary*, 1933 edition, reports that the use of the word "anxiety" dates from 1525, "anxious" from 1623. In the King James version of the Bible (1611), "these terms were therefore either new or unknown, their meanings being rendered by such expressions as 'wild with care,' 'take thought of,' etc. In modern versions of the Bible, the words 'anxiety' and 'anxious' appear relatively frequently" (445, p. 533). Mowrer (445) states that he was unable to find the word "anxiety" in the King James version of the Old Testament.

his enemies and his food, the floods that he could not always escape, the earth itself that might stir and engulf him in its pits of fire. His great fears of the present age are of the condensed power that he has learned to unleash, the atom bomb and all the similar destructive agents with which he is so skillful. And he fears himself, for he knows that man is now his own great enemy.

Anxiety is not a simple condition. There is normal as contrasted with neurotic anxiety. The latter is not inevitable and perhaps even what is labeled normal is unnecessary in a life space for the optimal functioning of a man. But this optimistic view is not acceptable to many. Increasingly the existentialists turn psychologists to an acceptance of the inevitability of anxiety.

Anxiety is not something we "have" but something we "are," or so say the existentialists. It is the center of our being. "The uncertainty of when death may come is an evitable source of inevitable anxiety." "And do not all men experience the threat of nonbeing?" (407, p. 1354). In a less all-inclusive position, but one which still accepts the innateness of anxiety, William James earlier called anxiety an instinctive reaction to certain objects or situations which might represent danger. If the danger is real, then the anxiety reactions have a biological usefulness and can be considered an evolutionary product in the struggle for existence. He also assumed that some anxiety reactions were altogether senseless and represented "nature's imperfect wisdom." However, he considered any anxiety phylogenetically fixed and unlearned. This belief in inherent anxiety permeates certain approaches to states of stress from conflict. And Freud too assumed the inevitability of anxiety, which arises in the "helpless state of affairs" at the birth of the child. The infant had few (if any) ways of dealing with this helplessness, but he later learned to anticipate "danger" (painful stimuli) and also learned preventive measures.

DIFFERENCES AMONG FEAR, NORMAL ANXIETY, AND NEUROTIC ANXIETY

What are the differences among (1) fear, (2) normal anxiety, and (3) neurotic anxiety? It is observed that they shade into each other. It is difficult to distinguish even in adults when one starts and when another has ceased. Nevertheless, distinctions can be drawn: (1) between no fear and onset of fears, (2) between fear and the onset of normal anxiety, and (3) between normal and neurotic anxiety. Combinations of situational and behavioral observations aid in distinguishing among them. Summarized below are some of the suggested distinctions among these negative tension states in human adults, as commonly described by observers of their own tension states and as inferred from the behavior of others under similar antecedent conditions. These distinctions are not provided within any specific theoretical framework. Though they thereby suffer from some inconsistency, they are more inclusive of the variety of observations which in one way or another suggest that these inferred states are not identical.

Anxiety—even normal anxiety—is not identical with fear. Anxiety is more like a mood in that its onset is sluggish and it lingers, while a fear is quicker in its coming and going. A fear is a quickly passing cloud that moves across the sun; anxiety is the cloud that lingers and truly beclouds the man. This analogy should reveal two essential differences between fears and anxiety: (1) the fears are more specific in regard to what is anticipated as threatening than is anxiety; (2) the fears are more quickly dissipated than is an anxiety, even a normal one. May (406) reports an illustration of normal anxiety in Inset 32.

INSET 32. AN ILLUSTRATION OF NORMAL ANXIETY IN AN ADULT MAN*

A prominent Socialist was living in Germany when Hitler came to power. Over a period of some months he knew that some of his colleagues were being imprisoned in concentration camps or taken off to other unknown fates. During this period he existed in the continual awareness that he himself was in danger, but he never could be certain *if* he would be apprehended, or, if he were, *when* the Gestapo would come, or, finally, *what* would happen to him if he were arrested. Throughout this he experienced the diffuse, painful, and persistent feelings of uncertainty and helplessness. And the threat confronting him was not merely that of possible death or the inconvenience and discomfort of the concentration camp; it was a threat to the meaning of his existence as a person, since the freedom to work for his beliefs was a value which he identified with his existence. This individual's reactions to threat had all the essential characteristics of anxiety, yet they were proportionate to the actual threat and could not be termed neurotic.

Normal anxiety (1) is not disportionate to the objective threat, (2) does not involve repression, and (3) does not require neurotic defense mechanisms. It "can be confronted constructively on the level of conscious awareness *or* can be relieved if the objective situation is altered" (406, pp. 193–194).

Fear may lead to normal anxiety and then to neurotic anxiety. Assume that a child is afraid of a dog next door, because he knows that this dog bites almost everyone. This is a specific normal fear, and his expectations of what will happen are to a large degree quite specific: If he meets the dog, it will bite him. But he may also have some normal anxiety, for he is not always certain when he may meet the dog or exactly what to do if he does meet him. Also, the dog does not bite everyone, just "almost everyone." It is possible to escape, but how? He has an unsolved problem, involving a threat to the existence of the self. Not only is his bodily

* Adapted from R. May, *The Meaning of Anxiety.* New York: Ronald, 1950.

self threatened but his self-concept may be. He may have various possible answers to the problem, but he is in a conflict. His conflict has concomitant fearful uncertainty (anxiety) about an event in which a threat or danger is foreshadowed. Note that we first assumed that the child is afraid of a specific dog. This is a normal fear which, however, can become general. He may come to fear not only the neighbor's dog but many dogs. This diffuseness of fear is the beginning of normal anxiety. Assume, moreover, that there is added shame from the laughter of others. The child may now "act brave." The whole episode may possibly be denied: He insists that he is not afraid.

Neurotic anxiety (in Freudian theory) is linked with repression (see Inset 33). Though repression does not inevitably lead to neurotic anxiety, according to the Freudian view, anxiety increases when there is a repression of an *unresolved* conflict, with a fear that the ego will not succeed in resolving the conflict. In the illustration of the boy and the biting dog, *neurotic* anxiety might arise after repression, not because of the repression but because of the boy's fear of loss of control of the inhibiting or repressing capacity. To complete our illustration we can assume that anxiety arises in the child's conflict between his wanting to go into the external world and his fear of going. The neurotic anxiety arises when the child denies the conflict and then moves into the external field where vicious dogs may lurk. The neurotic anxiety arises not because he denies his fear but because he has not resolved the conflict but merely denied it. There may remain, therefore, a diffuse anxiety; memory of its origin may be "lost." Feelings of helplessness and dread return to him at intervals, but their origin is not understood by him. The dread may increase and become more diffuse and disturb him in many ways.

This illustration, though in part based on Freudian assumptions, should be compared with the description in Inset 34 adapted from a more extensive report by Freud (204) in *The Problem of Anxiety*.

INSET 33. ANXIETY NEUROSIS*

The following case as presented by Alexander (4) illustrates the dynamics and clinical picture seen in anxiety neurosis. It particularly highlights the etiology and demonstrates how the anxiety neurosis can be the initial phase of a breakdown in ego functioning which can then lead into the development of a clinical picture characterized by phobic and depressive features as the ego's defenses become operative.

A thirty-four-year-old married white woman, following a serious quarrel with her mother-in-law, developed an acute attack of anxiety. Her free-floating anxiety, obviously a reaction to repressed hostile impulses, became manifest in tachycardia, palpitation, loss of appetite, and weakness and

* Adapted from F. Alexander and L. B. Shapiro, Neurosis, behavior disorders, and perversions. In F. Alexander and Helen Ross (eds.), *Dynamic Psychiatry*. Chicago: University of Chicago Press, 1952.

tremulousness of both upper and lower extremities. The anxiety soon became attached to the idea that she had heart trouble and that she was going to die. This phobia persisted for several months and finally led to hospitalization and cardiac study. After six weeks she returned home to her husband and three children, relieved of the thought that she had heart trouble. However, the unconscious hostility toward her mother-in-law and marriage now became displaced by obsessive thoughts that her husband and children would die or that he would divorce her. By the time she was referred to the psychiatrist, she was deeply depressed and full of remorse and self-accusations (p. 123).

INSET 34. THE ANXIETY OF HANS, AS ADAPTED FROM FREUD'S INTERPRETATION*

Relation of Anxiety and Symptom Formation

Little Hans refuses to go out on the street because he is afraid of horses. He fears that they will bite him. This is the raw material of the case. An analysis has furnished the basis for this phobia. The horse is representative of the father whom the boy both fears and hates.

The Origin of the Neurotic Symptom

The child is in the jealous and hostile Oedipus attitude to his father, whom, however, in so far as his mother does not enter the picture as the cause of the dissension, he loves devotedly. Thus we have a conflict springing from ambivalence—a firmly founded love of his father and a not-less-justified hatred, both directed toward the same person. His phobia is an attempt to resolve this conflict.

Significance of Repression in Development of Neurotic Anxiety

The instinctual impulse which the phobia represents is a hostile one directed against the father. One may say that this impulse is repressed by a process of transformation into its opposite; in place of aggression against the father, there appears the father's aggression—retaliation—against the individual himself. Since such aggression is rooted in the sadistic stage of libido development in any case, there is necessary only a certain degree of degradation thereof to the oral level, such as is intimated in the case of Hans by the fear of being bitten. But in addition, analysis makes it possible to establish beyond any doubt that simultaneously still another instinctual impulse has succumbed to repression—one of opposite signification, namely, a tender passive impulse towards the father which had already reached the threshold of the genital (phallic) stage of libido organization. This last seems even to be more significant as regards the end result of the repressive process; it undergoes the more extensive regression and obtains the decisive influence upon the content of the phobia. Therefore, where we before traced the repression of but a single impulse, we have now to recognize the conjunction of two such processes, the two instinctual impulses concerned—sadistic aggression against the father, and a tender passive attitude toward him.

* Adapted from S. Freud, *The Problem of Anxiety*. New York: Norton, 1936.

Castration Anxiety Is Said to Be the Source of Repression and of Transformation from Aggression to a Phobia

The motive force behind the repression is fear of a threatened castration. It is because of castration anxiety that little Hans renounces aggression against his father.[3] And the content of the anxiety—being bitten by a horse —is a distortion of a substitute for another content, that of fear of being castrated by the father. It is precisely this content which has undergone repression as such. But the anxiety affect of the phobia, which constitutes its essence, does not arise from the process of repression or out of the libidinal cathexes of the repressed impulses but from the repressing forces themselves; the anxiety of zoophobia is transformed castration anxiety and therefore a real anxiety, a reality fear—fear of a danger actually threatening or believed to do so. *Here it is the anxiety that causes the repression, and not, as I earlier stated, the repression the anxiety.*

THEORIES OF THE ORIGIN OF ANXIETY

Anxiety and Conflict

As indicated above, Freud was concerned with the role of repression in anxiety. Using his model of man with an id and a superego, he assumed a conflict between the two which results in anxieties and possibly in repressed conflicts. An anxiety arises, Freud said, from any threat that a conflict between the superego (conscience) and the repressed id (primitive impulses) might be resolved in favor of the id.

Why is man, the Freudian man, afraid of direct expression of his id? Is it from fear of punishment? Certainly Freudian theory permits self-accusations, but it also stresses the tyranny of the superego's introjected social prohibitions as repressive measures. Mowrer (445), in what has been labeled neo-Freudian theory, suggests that there are anxieties when man loses "moral control," i.e., when the id "really wins" over the superego. Then arises a guilt anxiety. This moralistic position implies that anxieties arise in the conflict between what a man has done and what his conscience (superego?) "tells" him that he *should have done.* Mowrer's view proposes that anxiety comes, not from acts which the individual would commit but dares not, but rather from acts which he has committed but wishes he had not. It is, in other words, "a 'guilt theory' of anxiety rather than an 'impulse theory'" (445, p. 537).

Interpretation of Neurotic Anxiety as Noncoping (Nonadequate) Behavior

Goldstein's observations of brain-injured patients (223, 224) lead him to an emphasis on inability of men to cope with their environment as the

---

[3] The term "castration" is often used as equivalent to punishment, loss of favor, or loss of a parent's love. If fear of the loss of the penis is seen both as a fear of loss of favor from the parent and as an origin of anxiety, the critical questions are: Why is the child afraid? What is threatened? What is the relationship of the parent and the child?

basis for anxiety. His patients devised innumerable ways of avoiding difficulties. Compulsive patterns of orderliness were interpreted by Goldstein as reflecting a patient's desire to evade anxiety that arose when he could not react adequately. Since life constantly presents new situations, in Goldstein's theory anxiety would be inevitable, and to avoid anxiety, the individual's withdrawal from all uncertain situations should be inevitable. However, since man enters constantly into new and uncertain situations, withdrawal from uncertainty to escape anxiety is characteristic of only a few—those who are unable to confront anxiety and move ahead despite it.[4]

Anxiety in Interpersonal Theory

Horney's emphasis (294) is that the threats leading to anxiety arise within the interpersonal relations which the individual holds vital to his existence as a person. The individual may recognize a crucial unconscious conflict without yet seeing a way out, and there would be aroused deep feelings of anxiety and helplessness. "The anxiety produced by such insights is the person's response to a dawning vision that he must eventually change something in his foundations if he wants to become free. But the factors that must be changed are still deeply entrenched, are still vitally important as a means of coping with himself and others. He is therefore afraid to change, and insight produces not relief but panic" (294, pp. 115–116). A negative reaction to insight may, however, become transformed into a positive one, and this may even happen quickly in some individuals according to their capacity for self-evaluation.

Anxiety has been said to arise within the frame of a need for security. It develops as an inevitable consequence of the child's fear of loss of his security as represented by his mother or other significant adults. Sullivan (590), who is responsible for this view, also relates anxiety to the self. "With the appearance of the self system or the self-dynamism, the child picks up a new piece of equipment which we technically call anxiety. Of the very unpleasant experiences which the infant can have we may say that there are generically two, pain and fear. Now comes the third (anxiety)."

The Self and Anxiety

In the above theories concerning the origin of anxiety there was implicit or explicit an acceptance of the significance of a self-development and a self-awareness. Rogers (519) early singled out as the origin of

[4] May (406), reporting Goldstein's views, states that Goldstein returns to Kierkegaard's development of self-realization as normally involving anxiety (331). Selfhood depends upon the individual's capacity to confront anxiety and move ahead despite it. Any failure to move ahead involves neurotic anxiety.

anxiety any discrepancy between "significant sensory and visceral experience" and the conscious self-concept.

In most general terms, Rogers' view in regard to the end point of personality development is a "basic congruence between the phenomenal field of experience and the conceptual structure of the self—a situation which, if achieved, would represent freedom from internal strain and anxiety, and freedom from potential strain; which would represent the maximum in realistically oriented adaptation; which would mean the establishment of an individualized value system having considerable identity with the value system of any other equally well-adjusted member of the human race" (519, p. 532).

Conditioning and Normal Anxiety

The Freudian assumption of a transition from an early helpless state to normal anxiety as preparatory for overcoming pain has been interpreted as conditioning. The reasoning is as follows: The helpless state of the neonate is accompanied by automatic anxiety reactions, but with growth and new and repeated experiences a transition takes place. Increasingly, the anxious reaction no longer occurs automatically to a dangerous (painful) situation which is already present, but instead somehow comes to occur in modified form *before* the onset of the painful stimulation; and anxiety is thus said to take on a signaling or warning function followed by learned behavior to avoid intense pain. "This transition," write Sarason et al., "seems to come about through some sort of learning or conditioning process which probably depends jointly on the maturation of the motor and nervous system and upon occurrence of certain kinds of specific experiences" (536, pp. 30–31). Mowrer's early translation (444) of Freudian interpretation of anxiety into S-R conditioning constructs is presented in Inset 35.

INSET 35. MOWRER'S TRANSLATION OF ANXIETY INTO THE LANGUAGE OF CONDITIONING*

Mowrer "translated" a Freudian description of anxiety into stimulus-response language. We place together the two passages: first Freud's and then Mowrer's "translation" of it into S-R language. The "translation" seems pertinent in regard to normal anxiety.

Freud noted that there may arise a feeling of helplessness when we estimate our strength in relation to the magnitude of a danger that confronts us. (This danger may be real or not: It may be in the external world, or it may be within ourselves, "instinctual danger.") This feeling of help-

---

* Adapted from S. Freud, *The Problem of Anxiety*. New York: Norton, 1936, pp. 149–150; O. H. Mowrer, A stimulus-response analysis of anxiety and its role as a reinforcing agent. *Psychol. Rev.*, 1939, 46, 553–564.

lessness is a traumatic experience. In anxiety we expect this trauma (this helplessness) to recur, or we may relive the feeling of helplessness that we actually had in some period of the past. In any case the anxiety acts as a warning, a signal of danger to come. Freud wrote:

> Now it is an important advance in self-protection when this traumatic situation of helplessness (discomfort) is not merely awaited but is foreseen, anticipated. Let us call the situation in which resides the cause of this anticipation the danger situation; it is in this latter that the signal of anxiety is given. What this means is: I anticipate that a situation of helplessness will come about or the present situation reminds me of one of the traumatic experiences which I have previously undergone. Hence I will anticipate this trauma; I will act as if it were already present as long as there is still time to avert it. Anxiety, therefore, is the expectation of the trauma on the one hand, and on the other, an attenuated repetition of it.

Translating the Freudian hypothesis of learned anxiety into stimulus-response terminology, Mowrer (444) writes:

> A so-called "traumatic" ("painful") stimulus impinges upon the organism and produces a more or less violent defense (striving) reaction. Furthermore such a stimulus-response sequence is usually preceded or accompanied by originally "indifferent" stimuli which, however, after one or more temporally contiguous associations with the traumatic stimulus, begin to be perceived as "danger signals" i.e., acquire the capacity to elicit an "anxiety" reaction. This latter reaction, which may or may not be grossly observable, has two outstanding characteristics: (1) it creates or, perhaps more accurately, consists of a state of heightened tension (or "attention") and a more or less specific readiness for (expectation of) the impending traumatic stimulus; and (2), by virtue of the fact that such a state of tension is itself a form of discomfort, it adaptively motivates the organism to escape from the danger situation, thereby lessening the intensity of the tension (anxiety) and also probably decreasing the chances of encountering the traumatic stimulus. In short, *anxiety (fear) is the conditioned form of the pain reaction*, which has the highly useful function of motivating and reinforcing behavior that tends to avoid or prevent the recurrence of the pain-producing (unconditioned) stimulus.

We now turn to the findings of *experiments* in conditioning as an aid in understanding development of anxiety.

Anxiety as a Conditioned Strong Fear. At intervals throughout this volume various problems suggested with respect to learned fears have been raised (see pp. 28–30). We now have another. *When does a con-*

ditioned fear become anxiety? This is a more difficult question to answer than is often recognized. Though the well-established conditioning studies illustrated in Chapter 3 have greatly aided understanding of learned fears, there are fewer attempts to determine *when* learned fear is present and *when* learned anxiety occurs. For example, beyond stating that fear is anxiety "when its source is vague," Miller (430) ignores this problem in his well-known development of "Learnable Drives and Rewards." He deals, however, with a related problem: why some learned fears are stronger than others. He implies that (1) the objective intensity of the unconditioned stimulus is correlated with the strength of the learned fear; (2) also, if two neutral stimuli both acquire fear-arousing responses, the combination of stimuli evokes a higher level of arousal. One answer, therefore, to the question of when learned fear becomes learned anxiety, is as follows: When the conditions are such as to establish strong fear, anxiety may arise. This is not a sufficient answer to the question concerning the origin of anxiety from fears. One suggestion is that a precipitating condition for anxiety is a generalization of a learned fear to stimuli other than the conditioned stimulus. The diffuseness of the spread of fear to a variety of similar stimuli was early reported by Watson and Rayner (639) when they found that a child conditioned to fear a furry animal also showed fear of similar stimulating objects. That stimulus generalization is often an *ad hoc* interpretation limits its predictive significance. It is observed, however, that the greater the generalization of the fear response to a variety of stimuli, the more the fear resembles anxiety.

Summarizing the above and other observations of fear conditioning which suggest how anxiety might develop from fear, we have the following events. During the "waiting period" between the onset of a learned warning signal (conditioned stimulus—CS) followed by painful stimuli (unconditioned stimulus—UCS), the individual "tenses" (physiological reactivity). This increased excitation is likely to change into anxiety *if* during the time of waiting, one, or more than one, of the following occur: (1) Strong fear is aroused, (2) there is irregularity in the intensity of the unconditioned stimulus, (3) little or no preparatory action is possible, (4) a "strong" unconditioned stimulus is *prolonged* and widespread physiological involvement is recorded, (5) the correct signals of possible "danger" (noxious UCS) are difficult to discriminate from the incorrect.

Summarizing the theories in regard to the origin of anxiety, we find diverse interpretations which range from a simple acceptance of anxiety (1) as the center of our being (the existentialists); (2) as inevitable and as present at birth but changing from a diffuse helplessness to a signaling function (Freud); (3) as based on conditioning, at least normal anxiety (Mowrer, Miller); (4) as originating from any incongruence between the self as is and the self as desired (Rogers); (5) as developed upon the fear of loss of the "mothering one," i.e., fear of loss of security (Sullivan); (6) as increasing when "coping" is difficult, e.g., in brain-injured individuals (Goldstein). Mowrer in a neo-Freudian theory challenged the notion that neurotic anxiety arises from threat of loss of ego control. He suggests that it is linked to guilt for acts already committed.

METHODS OF IDENTIFICATION

There is no standard method for identification of the presence of anxiety (normal or neurotic) in men. Methods include:

(1) Placing individuals in continued experimental stress situations, which often involve the self, and inferring that the subjects are anxious.

(2) Studying clinically diagnosed anxious subjects to determine whether their physiological functioning is in any way different from normal controls. They may also be put under further stress. Since psychiatric judgments vary concerning the clues used for diagnoses of anxiety, it is possible that identification of anxious subjects may not be similar from one clinic to another. For example, anxiety may be inferred in an individual on the basis of his defenses against anxiety, but the presence of a defense (a successful one) might be more appropriately considered a clue that anxiety had been eliminated or at least greatly lessened.

(3) Using self-reports on standard inventories, called tests of anxiety. As Sarason (534) points out in his review of anxiety scales, however, there is no reason for believing that the various measures of anxiety are all tapping the same thing.

PHYSIOLOGICAL CORRELATES OF ANXIETY

Attempts have been made to give corporeal substance to the construct of anxiety by studies of physiological changes when anxiety is inferred by any one or more than one of the above methods.

The variety of physiological changes reported with anxiety is no doubt due to the differences in the methods used to identify the presence of the anxious state and/or of anxious subjects, and also to the differences in conditions under which the physiological measures are obtained. As indicated above, records may be obtained under some immediate stress or during relaxation, such as when a subject is resting quietly.

One early identified and usually substantiated physiological concomitant of anxiety is cardiac change, both an increase of usual level and a rapid change under stimulation. Heart rate and cardiac output increased in medical students before an oral examination as compared with a more relaxed condition a month later (277). Neurotic subjects after criticism had increased heart rate as compared with a decrease after praise (395).

The heart rate is prognostic of movement *about to be executed*. In human patients the heart rate goes up before, rather than during, a movement, such as a shift in position. Here is some evidence of the possible internal cardiac activity that would appear in an anxiety state where action is not yet possible. White and Gildea (652) reported that patients in whom anxiety was a predominant symptom showed greater heart-rate increases to cold stimulation than did the normals. The records were obtained during (1) a rest period, (2) a brief anticipation period when the dish of ice water was moved closer to the subject, and (3) the period of stress stimulation. The anticipation period was correlated with the greatest increase in heart rate with both normal and anxious subjects.

Accelerated gastric activity has been attributed to anxiety states, while hypofunctioning of the stomach is found during periods of fear. This was also early reported in the "classical" studies of "Tom," a man whose fistulated stomach was observed over a seven-month period. The gastric fistula was a direct opening into the stomach made to permit feeding after an accident had closed his throat. The experimenter employed Tom as a technician and had an opportunity to observe the vascular and other changes in the lining of the stomach under different conditions. In desire to escape, the mucosa became pale, and both stomach motility and digestive secretion were inhibited. But states described as hostility or resentment gave a red lining, with an increase in stomach motility and in acid secretion (656).

The studies of peptic ulcer patients by Mittelmann, Wolff, and Scharf (431) indicate increased stomach acidity, increased peristaltic motility, and hyperaemia *when* conflicts involving anxiety were discussed with patients. Mahl (390) reported that *chronic* fear increased the stomach acidity. He produced ulceration in dogs by conditioning chronic fear in response to shock. Gastric acidity was found to increase even when the primary stimulation of shock was omitted, suggesting the appearance of a learned anxiety.

Comparison of Physiological Correlates of Fear-anxiety with Anger and Pain

If there is any unique physiological pattern for fear-anxiety, it should be in some ways distinguishable from the changes recorded during such inferred states as anger and pain. Martin (400) has compared in Inset 36 the results from four studies investigating physiological changes during fear-anxiety, anger, and pain. In Table 8 it appears that, in spite of some inconsistencies among the studies, there are distinguishable patterns that can be tentatively called correlates of the constructs of fear-anxiety as

Table 8. Comparison of Physiological Measures Associated with Different Emotional Arousal States in Four Studies

Measure	Ax (1953) Fear	Ax (1953) Anger	Schachter (1957) Fear	Schachter (1957) Anger	Schachter (1957) Pain	Lewinsohn (1956) Fear	Lewinsohn (1956) Pain	Funkenstein et al. (1957) Fear, %	Funkenstein et al. (1957) Anger-out, %
Systolic blood pressure	20.4	19.2	22.5	21.1	17.8	......	......	19.6*	13.1*
Diastolic blood pressure	14.5*	17.8*	13.7	14.5	11.8	......	......	9.7	22.8
Heart rate (+)	30.3	25.8	18.7*	10.8*	0.3*	5.4*	0.9*	33.3*	7.4*
Heart rate (−)	4.0*	6.0*							
Cardiac output	......	......	6.7*	3.0*	−0.25*			61.9*	−3.2*
Peripheral resistance	......		−1.10*	0.04*	1.28*			−19.3*	32.9*
Hand temperature (−)	0.045	0.050	0.036*	0.030*	0.024*				
Palmar conductance	14.8*	9.4*	−1.99*†	−2.18*†	−2.33*†				
Largest deflection in stress, GSR	......		......			2.52	2.15		
No. GSRs	4.7*	11.6*							
Respiratory rate	6.0*	2.3*	2.8*	2.1*	0.7*				
Frontalis muscle tension	3.34*	4.35*	1.30	2.26	1.65				
No. muscle potential peaks	13.2*	10.5*							
Finger tremor	......		......			87	118		
Salivary output	......		......			−0.9	7.9		

* Significant at the 0.05 level; for Schachter this is based on an overall analysis of variance for the three conditions.

† Schachter used the transformation, $\log 1/(R_1 - R_2)$, where R_1 = initial resistance and R_2 = lowest resistance during stress. The smallest negative number, −1.99, for fear accordingly refers to the largest decrease in resistance.

Source: B. Martin, The assessment of anxiety by physiological behavioral measures. *Psychol. Bull.*, 1961, 58, 234-255. The results of four studies are summarized in Table 8. Most scores in the Ax and Schachter studies represent prestress resting level and the highest (or in some cases the lowest) level reached during stress. The scores in the Lewinsohn study represent differences in the mean during rest and the mean during stress, with the exception of the GSR score, which represents the largest deflection during stress. All scores reported from the Funkenstein study are percentage changes from prestress levels.

311

contrasted to anger. These four studies used both normal and anxious subjects as well as adding stressors. The results in general indicate that a person in fear or fear-anxiety does not have so great an increase in diastolic blood pressure as he does in anger. He has more of an increase during fear in heart rate. His palmar conductance increases more in fear-anxiety than in anger, though the number of discrete GSRs is higher in anger than in fear. Rise in respiration rate and muscle tension peaks are greater in fear-anxiety than in anger.

Further evidence concerning possible unique physiological correlates of fear-anxiety as contrasted to anger is found in records of the effects of epinephrine as contrasted to the hormone norepinephrine, both being secretions of the adrenal medulla. Fear merging into anxiety, as defined by situational stressors and clinical diagnoses, is correlated with the same or similar physiological reactions which follow the injection of epinephrine (400). Not all evidence, however, is positive. Injection of epinephrine, for example, does not reliably produce reports of anxiety feelings (343).

INSET 36. FOUR STUDIES OF PHYSIOLOGICAL REACTIONS WHEN FEAR (FEAR-ANXIETY), ANGER, AND PAIN ARE INDUCED*

Four studies reported by Martin (see Table 8) attempt to distinguish between two or more experimentally induced arousal states where one of these is considered to represent a fear or anxiety reaction.

Ax (30) reported a study in which a variety of physiological measures were obtained from *normals* under conditions presented in counterbalanced order that were designed to elicit fear and anger respectively. The fear condition was ingeniously contrived to make the subject think that the apparatus was faulty and that he was in real danger of receiving a severe, perhaps even fatal, electric shock. Anger was aroused by an obnoxious assistant who generally insulted and belittled the subject." Schachter (538) repeated Ax's study using hypertensive, potential hypertensive, and normotensive subjects, and added a pain experience (cold pressor test) to the fear and anger situations. All subjects received the treatments in the same order: pain, fear, and anger. Lewinsohn (369) obtained three physiological measures plus a measure of finger tremor on groups of normals, anxiety-reaction patients, ulcer patients, and hypertensive patients, all subjected in counterbalanced order to the *cold pressor* test and a *failure experience* accompanied by criticism and electric shock. Another study which is highly relevant to the issue but which employed a somewhat different research strategy is that of Funkenstein, King, and Drolette (212). After subjecting their college-student subjects to stress, they determined in a poststress interview whether a subject had tended to experience anger

* Adapted from B. Martin, The assessment of anxiety by physiological behavioral measures. *Psychol. Bull.*, 1961, 58, 234–255.

outwardly directed, anger inwardly directed, or anxiety. The scores obtained were limited to blood pressure and ballistocardiographic measures.

The results, though suggestive of differences between fear (fear-anxiety) and anger, nevertheless need further clarification in regard to distinguishing physiological signs of fear (fear-anxiety) from those concomitant with other activation sources like extreme hunger.

Factor Analyses of Physiological Scores

One approach to the physiological correlates with anxiety is by factor analyses of intercorrelations of physiological measures of individuals generally anxious and/or under stressors presumably correlated with anxiety onset. The results of a series of studies are summarized by Cattell and Scheier (118) in Table 9. In the anxiety state, they report, there is an increase in systolic pulse pressure, an increase in heart and respiration rate, a decrease in electrical skin resistance. These physiological signs of

Table 9. The Physiological Pattern Inferred for Anxiety as a State

Physiological associations are listed in approximate order of degree of association and degree of confidence in confirmation. The sources of evidence can be found in Cattell and Scheier (118). Anxiety is not identified by the same operations in all the studies used.

Associated with Increase in Anxiety (State)

Increase in systolic pulse pressure
Increase in heart rate
Increase in respiration rate
Increase in basal and current metabolic rate
Increase in phenyl hydracrylic acid in urine
Decrease in electrical skin resistance
Increase in hippuric acid in urine
Increase in 17-OH ketosteroid excretion
Decrease in alkalinity of saliva
Decrease in cholinesterase in serum
Decrease in neutrophils and, less clearly, eosinophils
Increase in phenylalanine, leucine, glycine and serine
Increase in histidine in urine
Decrease in urea concentration
Decrease in glucuronidase in urine and in serum

At lower levels of association and/or with less confidence, we can add to the above: *Increase* in body temperature, general corticosteroid excretion, sodium in serum, red cell count, volume of saliva secreted, and, possibly, palmar sweat. *Decrease* in blood glutathione, alkalinity of urine, phosphorus and potassium in serum, staff neutrophils in white corpuscle count. *Increase* of hand tremor and of tension in trapezius (EMG), but *decrease* in involuntary muscle tension in arm and in handwriting pressure exerted.

Source: R. B. Cattell and I. H. Scheier, *The Meaning and Measurement of Neuroticism and Anxiety.* New York: Ronald, 1961, p. 208.

anxiety are not contradictory to the results reported above. In addition Cattell and Scheier call attention to the increase in basal and current metabolic rate and other physiological changes during an anxiety state.

Physiological Correlates of High and Low Anxiety Scores

No specificity in physiological correlates of anxiety can be obtained when anxiety is measured by such paper-and-pencil tests as Taylor's Manifest Anxiety Scale (594) and Sarason's Test Anxiety Scale (535). Attempts to establish a specific physiological pattern distinguishing high from low scorers on anxiety inventories have not as yet been successful. Sarason (534) states, however, that high- and low-anxious individuals identified by anxiety inventories may differ in physiological responses to perceived threat but not to nonthreat conditions.

ANXIETY AS A MOTIVATIONAL DETERMINANT

In order to illuminate the functions of anxiety in the total activity stream, we now ask whether it has any motivational role. It is apparently not a goal or a reward. It is not a satisfying state or one anticipated as to be attained.

Its onset can be shown to be correlated with changes in arousal and, more frequently, with a rise in arousal, though behavioral apathy may be found with extreme anxiety. The physiological changes, as shown above, indicate that an anxious individual is an aroused person.

High and Low Anxiety Scores and Correlated Drive Changes

A series of studies have centered on the role of anxiety in an anxious individual, who is identified as such by his score on the Manifest Anxiety Inventory (MAS) devised by Taylor (594).

Taylor (593) and Taylor and Spence (596) raised important problems. (1) Were the scores on the MAS reflecting the general drive level of the subjects? (2) And if so, would predictions (based on Hullian theory) concerning the effect of general drive on performance be confirmed when MAS scores were used as measures of individual differences in levels of general drive? The most general prediction was that the higher the MAS score (the higher the drive), the more sensitized would be all responses of an individual. This prediction has had some support. Taylor selected individuals with high and low MAS scores and conditioned their eyelid blink. As stated, it was assumed that differences in scores of individuals indicated different levels of general drive and that the high-scoring individuals would condition more rapidly than the low-scoring individuals. This was found in classical defense conditioning of eyelid blink. The difference in rate of conditioning was interpreted as a resultant of general drive-level differences between groups of high- and low-anxiety test scores. In extinction the more anxious group took more trials and gave more responses than the nonanxious group, but the differences were not significant. Spence and Taylor (577) further demonstrated the effects of strong and weak intensities of an unconditioned stimulus (puff of air) on the conditioning of anxious and nonanxious subjects. Again the anxiety level of subjects was determined by the scores on anxiety items from the MAS, high scorers representing high drive, low scorers low drive. Anticipatory eyelid responses were then recorded during one hundred conditioning trials to light as CS and to UCS puffs of air. The results indicated that the more anxious subgroups were consistently superior performers to the nonanxious groups, with the difference being statistically significant. Again drive-level differences based on levels of emotionality (anxiety) scores were said to determine the performance differences. These two findings have been substantiated by further studies. Both the intensity of the UCS as well as the level of the individual's manifest anxiety facilitated the performance in classical defense conditioning.[5]

A further prediction within the Hullian theory in regard to learning by individuals with high and low anxiety scores, considered as drive measures, was that subjects with high-scoring anxiety (high drive) would not perform or learn as well as low-anxiety individuals in a task in which interfering responses were already associated with stimuli used (596). An example: If paired words were to be learned, then each stimulus word might be already associated with a response word, as "short" is associated with "long"; and if in the learning task a new response word, like "old," was to be associated with "short," the high-anxious individual (high drive) would not learn as well as the low-anxious individual. This prediction was based on the assumption that high-anxious individuals had a higher general drive. Hence such subjects would be more ready for all responses including the wrong or interfering ones, such as saying "long" instead of "old."

A related prediction was of superior learning for the high-anxious individuals *when* the task included few or no established interfering responses.

These predictions were confirmed in some studies when the anxious and nonanxious individuals were identified by the MAS inventory (180, 595). However, other studies which have followed have questioned the interpretation that a score on a paper-and-pencil anxiety test represents

[5] This superiority of anxious subjects in classical conditioning was not found by Bindra, Paterson, and Strzelecki (68). They used a nondefensive response to be conditioned. Negative results have been obtained in other studies of conditioning with high- and low-anxious subjects (70, 280, 335).

the drive level of an individual and/or that the above predictions hold (530, 534, p. 406).

DETRIMENTAL EFFECTS OF ANXIETY

Woodworth (660) has asked: Is not anxiety always to be avoided? This question assumes that anxiety is not the "center of our being," nor is it inherent, or inevitably acquired. Why should anxiety be "scorned" as an energizing determinant? Simply because it is unpleasant? In the practical world, this is no answer, but there are attributes of anxiety which suggest that it should be placed low or eliminated in any "acceptable" hierarchy of sources of drive. The attributes of anxiety which warn against its use as an arousing source are: (1) It is diffuse. (2) For many children and adults it is not only exhausting but also likely to structure the personality in rigid, futile reactions. (3) There is a tendency for a man dominated by anxiety to turn inward, with rising tension leading to ineffective performance (50). (4) High anxiety individuals are reported more sensitive to experimental stress than those with low anxiety scores. Sarason (534, pp. 404–405) states that the bulk of the evidence indicates that subjects highly anxious on inventories are more detrimentally affected by failure or similar threats than are the individuals scoring lower on anxiety inventories. (5) Removal of anxiety is difficult once it is induced, more so than is the extinction of fear.

Anxiety is self-perpetuating. It becomes more frequent in occurrence until it permeates the whole self like a cancer which comes slowly and yet devours. The deviousness of the invasion by anxiety is aided by all which prevents discrimination of the origin of the anxiety, so that it may become diffuse terror. There is no easy relief for anxiety. In contrast, there can be avoidance of a specific feared event. In anxiety there remains the dread of that which cannot be avoided since it is not known clearly.

The self-perpetuating character of anxiety may be the resultant of the concomitant widespread physiological changes. The slow-moving physiological activity (as contrasted to the quicker skeletal movements) is, so it has been suggested, the basis of the continuance of anxiety. This statement needs elaboration, for it suggests different possibilities. (1) One possibility implicit in a report by Mahl (390) is that a chronic physiologically disturbed state (perhaps rising and falling as stress varies) becomes autonomous of the original stressful situation producing anxiety and is the basis for continued anxiety. (2) Another similar interpretation is that the self-perpetuating character of anxiety is the resultant of the following events: The diffuse pattern of neural, muscular, and glandular activity appears with the onset of stressful unconditioned stimulating events and is conditioned along with withdrawal movements to a new stimulus. Then with the onset of the conditioned stimulus (warning signal), the subject performs movements to avoid the oncoming danger. The conditioned physiological reactivity, being slow in onset (as compared with skeletal movements), does not occur until after the avoidance responses. In other words, there can be no avoidance of the heightened physiological reactivity, since it does not occur until after the animal removes himself from the situation. The heightened physiological reactivity lingers and is the basis for continuance of diffuse anxiety (573). [In line with this are the reported observations (214) on the difficulty of extinguishing cardiac conditioning.] (3) A third and quite different interpretation (520, p. 322) of lingering anxiety is that it prevents the discriminations which permit self-examination, an activity necessary, in Rogers' personality theory, for the relief of anxiety.

Each of the personality theorists previously reviewed also would have a slightly different view of lingering anxiety. Freud, for example, would trace lingering anxiety to unresolved *early* conflicts.

What can be said with any certainty concerning this elusive construct called anxiety? Some of the difficulties of interpretation arise from the complexity of referents of the term. It will only be understood as studies increase of its origin or origins and of its various manifestations. Enough is known of its harmful effects to justify studying ways of reducing it.

CHAPTER 14

MOTIVATION AND LEARNING

More than thirty-seven hundred years ago in Lower Meso-
potamia, a Sumerian scribe stated some sage advice on clay
tablets. He begins with a dialogue between father and son:
"Where did you go?"
"I did not go anywhere."
"If you did not go anywhere, why do you idle about? Go
to school and stand before your school father [professor],
recite your assignment, open your school bag, write your
tablet."[1]

Today, in the twentieth century A.D., millions of dollars are spent for
teaching in private and public schools, in industrial training programs,
and in the armed services training units; yet resistance to learning is still
met by instructors. Even a willing student who has chosen his school and
his course and is paying his own way may resist learning. And the adult
who lays out for himself a program of study may find a resistance within
himself to his own self-imposed study.

One is tempted to compare the concept of resistance to learning with
that of the inertia of organisms, were it not for the fact that often the
student resistant to learning in the classroom is by no means hampered
by inertia in other learnings. The learner and the nonlearner may be
reversed outside the classroom. Moreover, students can be found who
offer no resistance to learning, who learn difficult, uninteresting material,
even when it is poorly presented; such a person may learn when his
personal life is so "fouled up" that many another would be unable to
continue. Extreme as this may appear, it raises the problem of the motivational variables in learning—those variables which aid or harm the
performance necessary for learning.

[1] Adapted from a report by Dr. Samual Noah Kramer, Professor at the University
of Pennsylvania, as reported by the *New York Times*.
318

Two Motivational Problems

We will be able to review only those studies which will possibly illuminate two motivational problems: (1) the relation of drive level to learning and (2) the relation of effects after a response to its repetition and thus possibly to its retention.

Definition of Learning

Learning is a modification—a nontransitory modification of the organism which usually permits more effective performance.[2] (However, organisms also learn to be *less* effective than chance performance.)

Psychologists who attempt a definition of learning agree that maturational or other structural modifications may be confused with learning. The past history of the organism, however, permits the observer to determine whether a change in performance is the resultant of learning or of maturation and/or of a structural change.

Performance versus Learning

Performance must be distinguished from learning. Learning is revealed in performance, but the latter is sensitive to more than learning changes. It reflects, among other variables, motivational determinants.

Performance, moreover, may not reveal the learning which has taken place or is occurring. The well-known latent-learning studies have shown that an organism may be learning but that the modification is not immediately manifest in his performance.[3] Blodgett's early experiment (72) called psychologists' attention to latent learning. A hungry animal placed in a maze or a similar situation is allowed to explore for several trials. Later, given a food reward when he reaches the end of the maze, he may show sudden improvement in running the true path. Learning, it is assumed, was previously occurring in the exploration period, but it was not manifest in performance until the reward was given to the animal.

Man also shows evidence of latent learning. A student may note where books may be purchased and later use this learning when he must buy his texts for a course of study. This learning is latent until later when it is used. Latent learning is easily illustrated with children. Young Johnny recites his poem perfectly at home, but on the stage at the PTA program he cannot recite. That his learning of the poem is latent but not lost is substantiated when he returns home and again recites it perfectly.

[2] An important problem is ignored in this definition of learning: What is modified? R-R, S-S, or S-R associations? Expectancies? Probabilities of payoffs? All of these? Only one of these?

[3] See Thistlethwaite (601) and other sources (333, 385) for an elaboration of latent-learning studies, including those which have failed to demonstrate such learning.

Learning may be confused with the change in performance which is the result of temporary motivational variables such as specific drives or goals. The best clues to *motivational* changes in performance are time scores. These scores are sensitive to motivational shifts. The best clues to *learning* are signs of modifications in the activity stream which *continue* to reappear with increasing probability. In other words, decrease in errors and the retention over time of this change in performance best represent learning.

The above discussion has distinguished between time-dependent and time-independent scores (errors). We now consider in more detail these two kinds of scores.

Time-dependent versus Time-independent Measures. Time scores as compared with errors are not as valid indices to learning, for time scores are too sensitive to motivational variables. In one study (131), reported by Bugelski (96), it was found that time (speed) scores in a maze were a significant function of degree of drive but that errors were a function of number of trials. With rats under varying periods of food deprivation, the error score gradually decreased with trials, but throughout the training, speed retained a close relationship to the different degrees of food deprivation. In other words, errors were the best clues to learning, and speed the best clue to drive-level shifts.

In the discussion below, as far as possible the clues employed as evidence of learning will consist of decreases in errors and stability in that error elimination. Stability can be measured in immediate repeat performances, or a superior index of stability can be obtained after a lapse of time. Reliability of a learning modification may also be tested by transfer as well as in relearning. The test conditions should not introduce new motivational variables, i.e., those not present in the original learning. An exception to this statement: Several retention tests may be run with a variety of motivational shifts. To the degree that the performance does not change according to the changes in the motivation, the strength of a learning is thereby substantiated. For example, handwriting, a well-learned performance, remains approximately the same throughout a variety of different motivational conditions.

DRIVE LEVEL AS RELATED TO LEARNING

The problem which is of interest in this section concerns one of the common beliefs, in fact a popular fallacy, that a rising drive inevitably aids in learning. If a school child receives poor marks, his parents may urge him to work harder. They say, "Try, and you'll learn." One possible reason for the fallacy is that the higher the drive level, generally the more frequent are performances, and thus there are more opportunities for learning. However, when frequencies of performances are controlled in experimentation so that groups under different drive levels can be compared, the results are not so definitive as would be implied by the common-sense view. We will now consider drive level as it is related to conditioning, instrumental training, discrimination, problem solving, and/or testing for insight.

Varying Drive Level during Conditioning

In classical conditioning, the intensity of the unconditioned stimulus serves as one drive source. That the UCS represents a drive source useful to maintain performance and thus aid in the progress in conditioning was early suggested by Culler and his associates. This hypothesis arose from their failures in obtaining higher-order conditioning. Since the UCS must be removed in attempts to obtain higher-order conditioning, it was hypothesized that the failure might be due to the removal of this drive source. A constant energizing source (shock) was, therefore, applied to the thoraxes of dogs during the trials to establish higher-order conditioning. The experimenters report that higher-order conditioning was facilitated by the use of the shock as a general energizer (191).

Direct variation of the intensity of UCS has been tested in several experiments to determine its relation to learning strength. Passey's study (480) is illustrative of results in classical aversive conditioning when the intensity of the UCS is varied. He reported that the stronger the UCS, the more rapid the progress of conditioning. Extinction scores, however, less reliably differentiated the groups who learned under different intensities of the unconditioned stimulus (see Figure 14-1).

When drive level is raised during classical defense conditioning by introduction of hunger or other drive components, some results support facilitation of the frequency of conditioned responses from the increasing drive. Pavlov (481) reported superior salivary conditioning for dogs if they were hungry. Eyeblink conditioning with human subjects, however, was not affected by submitting the subjects to food, water, and tobacco deprivation (198). As cited on pp. 314–316, scores on anxiety inventories have been used to obtain high- and low-drive subjects for conditioning studies. In some studies but not all, classical defense-conditioning progress is superior with high-drive (high-anxiety) subjects, but resistance to experimental extinction may not be significantly stronger. Support for the facilitative effect on conditioning progress of increased general emotionality was added by Runquist and Ross (528) and Runquist and Spence (529). High- and low-emotional subjects were selected on the basis of physiological indices such as pulse rate, skin conductance in response to a noxious stimulus, or magnitude of muscle action potentials from the neck muscles. The number of conditioned responses increased with a

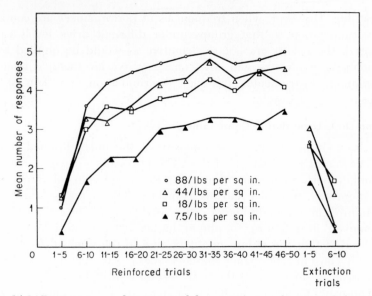

Figure 14-1. Progress in conditioning eyelid responses is a function of the intensity of the unconditioned stimulus (air puff). The intensities of air puff tested are 7.5, 18, 44, and 88 pounds per square inch. Passey (480)

rise in the emotionality as identified by these physiological measures of inner excitation.

Varying Drive Level during Instrumental Learning

Studies investigating drive level as related to learning may use training devices such as mazes or Skinner boxes in which performance is instrumental in obtaining a reward. Results from varying studies do not definitely support any position concerning the role of drive level in learning with such instruments. Higher drive level may, or may not, aid progress in instrumental learning. Nor is any such learning inevitably more permanent under higher drive. Evidence is contradictory, as is indicated below.

When drive rise was set up by an increasing deprivation of needed substances and errors consisted of entering blinds in a maze, increasing drive level did not facilitate error elimination with rats as subjects (597, 21, 286). When the drive level was varied during acquisition and retention was later measured under the same or a different drive level, the results of three studies suggest superior retention of mazes when learning was with higher drive. MacDuff (386) reports superior retention. Heyer (275) and O'Kelly and Heyer (470) report easier relearning when the original learning was under high drive. In contrast, Maher and Wickens (389) found no superior retention for rats who learned a maze under a large food reward as contrasted to those who learned for a smaller reward. The larger goal object had more inciting effect, but the maze retention was not superior when learned under the more inciting goal as contrasted to a lesser one. The lack of definitive support of a relation between high drive and retention brings into question the common-sense belief that rising drive level is beneficial to instrumental learning. The contradictory evidence on this subject continues to grow.[4]

Discrimination

Since most learnings involve discrimination, the effect of a rising drive on its development is of central interest. One of the first of the pertinent observations, made by Yerkes and Dodson (662) in 1908, compared a strong versus a weak noxious source of drive. It was found that the optimal level of drive for acquisition of a discrimination was dependent on the difficulty of the discrimination. Progress in forming a difficult discrimination was more quickly disrupted by an increasing noxious drive source (electric shock) than when the discrimination required was easy. Similar results were reported by Broadhurst (84) using air deprivation. Noxious sources of rising drive may at first aid progress in discrimination; then as drive increases, it is nonoptimal for learning progress.

These findings are not inevitably duplicated when studies of discrimination use other origins of drive differences than noxious sources. Dodson (161), using increasing food deprivation with rats, found a nonoptimal level for discrimination at 48 hours' food deprivation. Food deprivation up to 47 hours with monkeys as subjects neither interfered with nor aided in their forming an easy discrimination (423). When Miles (424) used both easy and difficult discriminations, the significant variable in acquisition was not food deprivation but rather the difficulty of the tasks. As the problems increased in difficulty, the per cent correct per trial decreased. Though, presumably, intense hunger is noxious, it does not quickly become nonoptimal for acquiring a discrimination, as does painful stimulation.

These results, together with the studies reported previously in regard to nonfacilitative effects of stress in learning difficult tasks, may be summarized as follows: A rise in drive may become nonfacilitative of formation of discriminations. The disorganization from rising drive is observed more quickly in difficult discriminations. Results in a few studies

---

[4] Various problems of significance are necessarily ignored in this volume: e.g., (1) the interaction of drive level used in acquisition with that employed during retention tests; (2) the interaction of associative strength (habit strength?) and drive level in tests of retention; (3) the possibility that high drive sensitizes more interfering responses than low drive.

suggest that increasing food deprivation does not, however, as quickly lead to a nonoptimal level of drive for formation of discrimination as when other means to increase drive are employed.

Insightful Learning

In insightful or perceptual learning the number of trials is not related to the strength of the learning. If a man gets an insight into some problem in one trial, he seems to know it as well as if he had twenty trials, nor is the twenty-trial man likely to retain his insight into a problem any longer than the one-trial man. Whether greater drive (from whatever origin) would lead to quicker insight and longer retention has not been tested systematically as far as the writer knows. It is known, however, that the drive level may be increased to a nonoptimal level for learning during exploration or during problem solving which involves perceptual changes. Johnson (321) reported that rats, given a preliminary opportunity to explore under low thirst drive, later behaved more appropriately at a choice point in a T-maze than did rats whose previous exploration was under high thirst drive. The perceptual learnings were presumably superior under a low drive. Previously shown (pp. 257–258) is evidence that the range of cues used narrows with increasing drive. Birch (69) found medium degrees of hunger optimal for problem solving in chimpanzees. Too little hunger seemed to fail to direct these animals toward the goal of food. Too much hunger directed them toward food to the exclusion of perceiving the surrounding objects necessary for problem solving.

Summary

The following general conclusion is inevitable: The present studies of the relation of drive level to the degree of learning progress do not suggest any general and invariable relationship between the two. Some specific statements, however, can be made: (1) There is a trend toward quicker progress in conditioning under higher drive. (2) Discrimination is *not* facilitated when drive becomes excessive, particularly if the drive is noxious. (3) Moreover, the nonoptimal level of drive is more quickly reached if the discrimination is difficult. (4) High drive narrows the range of cues, and it may interfere with perceptual learnings. (5) Contradictory results exist in regard to the role of drive level in instrumental learning. No conclusion, even tentative, concerning drive level and instrumental learning can be made.

One of the difficulties of obtaining definitive results may be inadequate experimentation. An experimental design for separating the effects of drive level on performance from the effects on learning is outlined in Inset 37.

INSET 37. EXPERIMENTAL DESIGN FOR SEPARATING EFFECTS OF DRIVE ON
PERFORMANCE FROM EFFECTS OF DRIVE ON LEARNING*

| | | \multicolumn{2}{c}{Later test drive} | | |
		High	Low	
Initial training drive	High	Measures obtained in test condition	Measures obtained in test condition	Means reflecting habit differences
	Low	Measures obtained in test condition	Measures obtained in test condition	

Means reflecting performance differences

Kimble outlines in the revision of *Hilgard and Marquis' Conditioning and Learning* the experimental design which has been used to separate the effect of drive-level variations on learning as contrasted to performance.

Different groups of subjects are trained initially under two or more different levels of drive. Then at some point in the training each of these groups is subdivided. Some of the subjects continue under the original drive condition; others switch to the alternative drive levels. For the simplest situation, where only two test drive levels are involved, this procedure generates the 2×2 factorial design in which the rows represent the conditions of original training and the columns represent conditions after drive levels have been switched for some of the subjects. Differences in the column means represent performance differences, and differences in the row means reflect learning differences, that is, differences due to the original training drives are now reflected with drives equated.

Results from studies show, in general, that the column means are reliably different, with the higher drive level during the testing sessions being correlated with more effective performance.

When the row means are compared, it is essential that the measures used be of the immediate performance of the subjects. In other words, if an individual is trained under a high drive and then tested under a low one, evidence that the drive level during the training was facilitative of learning can only be obtained from the immediate performance after the drive shift. Otherwise the *testing drive level* may itself become a variable of significance in further learning. The best evidence that learning is affected by drive level would be as follows: Subjects trained under a high drive and shifted to a low one would *continue* to be superior in performance over those subjects trained under low drive and shifted to a high level during the testing session. The studies do not show such clear-cut results.

Not all of the experiments attempting to answer the question of drive

* Adapted from Gregory A. Kimble, *Hilgard and Marquis' Conditioning and Learning* (rev. ed.). New York: Appleton-Century-Crofts, 1961, pp. 411–412.

level as related to learning have employed a complete factorial design. Particularly in the earlier studies, the procedure sometimes was to train subjects under a variety of drive levels and then to test with drive equated for all groups. This creates problems, because shifting from a high drive to an intermediate one may not be the same as shifting from a low drive to an intermediate one. There sometimes seems to be a residual effect of the earlier drive level which enters and complicates the interpretation of the results in the second phase of the experiment.

THE RELATION OF LEARNING TO THE EFFECTS AFTER A PERFORMANCE

Rewards and Punishments

Rewards are defined as satisfactory events which follow a performance. The question of what events are possibly satisfying and the indices used to infer their acceptance was previously considered in Chapter 19 on Goals.

Goals are learned, to-be-reattained effects. When attained, they are rewarding. As anticipated, they are inciting. The drive level is raised, as was shown on pp. 204–212. We are interested in this section in the rewarding effects on learning; in other words, we are now interested in the possible reinforcing (strengthening) effects of any rewards, whether they were goals attained or not. (Not all rewards received are anticipated as goals.)

Some sensory events are per se more predictably acceptable than others. These are called primary rewards. As antecedents for rewards there are reductions in irritations, changes in monotonous environment, certain attributes of sensory inputs such as sweetness. Not only are there such conditions for primary rewarding effects, but there are antecedents for primary nonsatisfying or punishing effects such as follow the arousal of pain receptors. That the onset of affective states of satisfaction (or the reverse) is *relative* to other variables was earlier emphasized (pp. 194–199).

To unlearned rewards and punishments may be added learned (secondary) rewarding or punishing conditions. For example, secondary rewards such as the words "right" or "good" are symbols of rewards. Secondary punishments such as "wrong" represent or symbolize the possible onset of former noxious conditions.

Such symbols may possibly become directly rewarding in themselves without any revival of anticipated primary rewards. Symbols may be punishing without the onset of fear that a noxious stimulation will recur. These last statements are quite speculative, however.

Effect of Different Schedules of Rewards on Performance

Performance is quite sensitive to the aftereffects of responses. Using an apparatus (bar pressing followed by an immediate food pellet) which permitted fairly quick association between a specific response and a reward, Skinner and his coworkers (187) have established close relations between rate of responses and schedules of the reward. The schedule of a presented reward, such as food to a hungry animal, is highly significant in the rate of evocation of that response preceding the food pellet. Different schedules of reinforcement have been used. Some of the well-known findings are briefly summarized below.

A *fixed-interval reinforcement schedule* represents the condition when periodically a reward is given after a fixed time interval. When the animal has learned to expect the pellet after an interval of time, his *rate* of response is higher for shorter intervals than for long ones.[5] The rate of responding is inversely proportional to the interval between rewards.

A *variable-interval schedule* represents the giving of a reward at random times, as after one minute, then after twenty seconds, etc. This schedule produces a performance which is quite stable in rate.

On a *fixed-ratio schedule* the animal receives a reward after a predetermined number of responses. The animal, after learning approximately how many responses must be made, sets his pace accordingly. Just after a reinforcement it is slow; then it rises rapidly.

A *variable-ratio schedule* of rewards, typically yielding a high elicited rate, is similar to life situations. Our rewards come intermittently; they come after different numbers of correct responses. We may perform correctly, for example, a few times and be rewarded; then we continue for many responses until finally there is another reward obtained. Of course, in life situations the performances, of men at least, are not in such highly controlled external fields (or in internal fields) as it is possible to obtain for a pigeon or a rat in a Skinner box. Hence the findings in these control conditions are more valuable, but at the same time they cannot be applied indiscriminately to performances of men.

The purpose of this section, however, is not to consider when performance is sensitive to what follows it. Our purpose is to consider the relation of the aftereffects of performance to *learning*. We therefore turn to a brief review of theoretical positions on the role of aftereffects in those changes in performance which signify learning.

Rewards as Strengtheners of Learning

Theoretical Positions in Regard to the Role of Aftereffects in Learning. One early view by Thorndike (603) was that a satisfying effect "stamped in" associations. The "bonds" between stimulus and response were said to be stronger after rewards. The responses "accompanied or closely followed by satisfaction" were, other things being equal, more

[5] Skinner does not assume the animal learns to "expect" the reward. But this is one possible interpretation of what is occurring inside the organism.

firmly connected with the situation. This particular interpretation, called the law of effect, is within the specific theory called connectionism.[6] Learning in this theory was assumed to be the strengthening of associations (bonds) between stimuli and responses. Within a similar theory, Hull's assumption (299) was that the backlash effect which was essential to strengthen S-R associations (learning) was a drive reduction, or drive-stimuli diminuation. The basic "relief" or reward was reduction of primary drives based on bodily needs. Neutral stimuli, if associated with primary reinforcing conditions, could acquire secondary reinforcing property.

Other theorists assumed that learning was made possible if the performance was repeated, but their answers to how learning was aided by rewards were different from those of Thorndike or Hull. Two theorists (Tolman and Guthrie) suggested that rewards were facilitative of performance and hence indirectly of learning. Tolman (616), for example, suggested that rewards might inform organisms of "what-actions-lead-to-what." Guthrie (240) approached this problem by suggesting that rewards were facilitative for learning to continue *if* the aftereffects prevented attachment of new responses to the stimulations.

Is Drive Reduction Essential for Learning? In the theory of Hull there is the assumption that essential for the acquisition of associations is a specific adaptive change, described as primary need reduction, drive decrease, or drive stimuli diminuation. Since empirical observations suggest that learning may occur without such a drive stimuli diminuation, Hull postulated that otherwise neutral stimuli associated with established reinforcers acquired reinforcing or strengthening property.

There is no question that a primary drive reduction is among the variables in increasing the probability of a recurrence of a performance which preceded this drive decrease. But it is still an unsolved problem what role such an afterevent has in the learning itself. We will now ask whether learning can occur independently of any drive decrease.

In contrast to Hull's theory of reinforcement by drive reduction is the view of Tolman. He early stated that learning could occur without drive reduction. His view was supported by the latent-learning studies, in which learning occurred even though there was in the early trials no drive reduction. As indicated previously, latent learning essentially refers to acquisitions which do not immediately appear in performance. One significance of latent learning is that it may be acquired without need-drive reduction. In other words, after trials in a maze *without* food

---

[6] Various problems were posed: (1) How could any effect strengthen associations of the past? (2) How much "spread" of effect was there? (3) How did nonsatisfying effects "work"? See Postman (490) and learning texts (279, 333) for a development of experimental studies related to these questions.

reward, hungry animals will later indicate that they were previously learning the maze paths. This learning is inferred because their performance is superior to that of control subjects who do not have the opportunity for such previous learning. After introduction of food, the experimental animals enter fewer blinds on the way to the goal box than do the controls. Learning without drive reduction is thus inferred because of the *later* performance.

Learning as inferred from *immediate* performance can also occur without any apparent drive diminuation. Beach (46) found that rats will learn to prefer a goal box *associated* with postmorphine-injection euphoria. He suggested that this euphoria is not a drive-reduction process. Learning may occur when what follows a performance is a stimulus increase in the external field. Butler (103), as developed on pp. 42–43, found that monkeys perform longer if a change in external field follows. They perform more frequently if what follows is a novel event. This aftereffect is not apparently a decrease in drive; in fact, it could be classified as a rise in drive.

Another method of testing for learning when there is no apparent drive reduction includes studies of the effect of saccharine, a nonnutritive sweet substance and one, presumably, that does not reduce hunger. These studies (553, 554) report repetitions of a performance which end in the taste of the saccharine. This finding does not establish that learning occurred or that the taste was the necessary variable for the learning, but it *suggests* that learning *can* occur without drive reduction. Sheffield and Roby (553) report that rats would exhibit a choice performance more frequently if it was followed by a saccharine solution than if it was followed by tap water.[7] A sweet taste, it can be concluded, is an adequate effect to elicit continued performance and, apparently, learning.

Is it *known* that preference for sweet is entirely independent of any drive relief? A negative answer is given in Inset 38.

INSET 38. IS PREFERENCE FOR SWEET TASTE ENTIRELY INDEPENDENT OF ANY DRIVE RELIEF?

That the preference for sweet can arise independently of any drive relief has not gone unchallenged. It is possible that the liking for a sweet taste may be innate, but with drive relief associated with sweet taste, the liking for it increases. Miller (429) states that rats eat less after ingestion of saccharine than would be expected, suggesting that in some way saccharine reduces a need drive for nutrition. Mice are said to be more

---

[7] The anticipated consummatory response is emphasized by Sheffield, Roby, and Campbell (554) as a significant variable in obtaining the continued performance.

likely to survive insulin shock if fed saccharine after the injection with insulin. These observations suggest that saccharine has some effect on need for nutrition. Pfaffmann (484) suggests that the liking for a sweet taste may increase as a result of postingestive factors. Moreover, it is possible that liking for saccharine is entirely acquired, the secondary (learned) rewarding property being traceable to associations with former hunger drive relief in eating sweet foods.

Punishment as an Aid in Extinction of Learning

The purpose of punishment is to bring about extinction of a response. How? Possible interpretations follow. (1) The withdrawal following punishment may remove the organism from the situation eliciting the designated response. Thus there is no further strengthening of the associations to be eliminated. It could be assumed that new learnings then interfere with the older acquisitions. (2) Withdrawal responses themselves may be associated with the situation, and there is an immediate interference with the older association—the one to be eliminated. (3) If the organism cannot physically withdraw from the noxious stimulus, he may nevertheless cease the preceding response. In other words, he now learns "to not respond." (4) Another possible interpretation of cessation of the response which precedes a noxious event is that there is suppression of the punished response but not a loss in learning. The assumption is that organisms tend temporarily to cease performing any responses followed by noxious stimulation because fear aroused by the stimulation suppresses responses (177). (5) The cessation of a response which is followed by a noxious stimulus may be traced to the alerting or focusing on the relevant cues by the organism *before* the response is evoked again. The alerting function of noxious stimulation has been suggested by Muenzinger and his coworkers in a series of studies of rats learning to make a correct choice in a T-maze (447, 448, 449, 451). The results of these studies, in terms of cumulative error curves and tests of significance between means, suggest a division of motivating conditions into two classes: (*a*) as producers of fast learning would be listed studies which had shock or a barrier immediately *after* the choice point, and (*b*) as conditions which lead to less rapid learning would be studies which had either *no* shock or shock *before* choice. Muenzinger's interpretation is that the superior learning when there is an obstacle such as shock *after* choice is due to the delay which the animal makes at the choice. A barrier like shock after choice forces the animal to delay before choice. *He is thus longer exposed to the cues to be learned.* Other interpretations of why punishment brings a cessation (at times) of the responses which it follows appeal more directly to cognitive activities (see Inset 39).

INSET 39. PUNISHMENT AND COGNITIVE ACTIVITIES*

The idea that one may "discover" in a genuinely cognitive sense the undesirability of a course of action that appeared superficially to be desirable is, so far as I know, writes Prentice (493), an unexplored one. But the cognitive approach might conceivably clear up the present mystery and confusion about the role of punishment. Let us, in a purely speculative way, consider the possibility that punishment produces three distinguishable results.

In one case, punishment may deter the attractive response. A child, knowing that he will have his hands slapped if he steals the cake, eyes it greedily from afar but does not touch it. Continued contemplation does not diminish the desirability of the forbidden object. Indeed, in some cases, deterrence may result in just such opportunity for contemplation as will bring out hitherto unforeseen attractions in the forbidden response.

In the second case, punishment having deterred the response itself, study and contemplation of the total situation may follow and have the opposite result. That is, a child punished for playing in the street may live to understand the situation as his parents understood it and thus find it no longer inviting. The punishment may serve primarily to focus attention on the problem and provides a respite from the activity that was indulged in so automatically that suitable contemplation never occurred.

The third case, that in which a relatively strong response tendency seems to be permanently destroyed, may come about not through the discovery of unsuspected properties in the original situation, but more directly by the addition of punishment to that situation. Perhaps there, too, hypothetical answers can be proposed in terms of cognitive structure. At least two aspects deserve investigation. To what extent is punishment made to appear intrinsic to the situation? Touching a hot stove or walking into areas posted for dangerous radiation provides a deterrent very different psychologically from the intrinsic fear of detection and punishment by a policeman. If an activity can be made to appear *inherently* painful or destructive or sinful, that may in itself be sufficient to produce permanent withdrawal and distaste. Secondly, the structural characteristics of the punishment itself, already hinted at above, deserve the most careful investigation. To be scolded by Mother and to be scolded by Teacher are two different matters. Mother's scolding when angry is itself different from her scolding when she is apparently otherwise in a good mood. A punishment accepted as personal rejection is different from mere retributive payment of a symmetrical kind such as blows or angry words exchanged by boys on a playground.

Obviously we do not have the theoretical tools for dealing with such differences in cognitive pattern, and we must begin to forge them. I have seemed to describe all motivation in terms free of self-reference, and many of you will be uneasy about the seeming disappearance of the self from

* Adapted from W. C. H. Prentice, Some cognitive aspects of motivation. *Amer. Psychologist,* 1961, 16, 503–511.

the motivational stage. There is not time to develop the thesis fully, but I want to suggest that the self too is a cognition and that it appears as a single factor in relation to others in experience. The kinds of relationship between self and others or between self and objects that lead to particular kinds of action simply need the same kind of careful descriptive account that we need in dealing with other cognitive facts. "Self-realization," "self-esteem," and similar words describe cognitions. When we recognize certain kinds of failure or opportunity or threat involving ourselves we behave in particular ways. We must seek the regularities in such self-involved behavior as we would seek those in more objective situations.

Neutral Stimulation Following a Response

If a neutral stimulus follows a response, it has been claimed that this aftereffect is also facilitative of learning. Some early studies (378, 379) of affectively neutral aftereffects reported slight success in increasing learning by using nonsense syllables, meaningful words, flashes of light, and clicks after a performance. These stimulations were neither rewarding nor punishing nor, presumably, informing, since they were not systematically varied according to whether the responses were correct. They merely happened after a response. Stephens suggested that the mere fact that *something* happens after a response aids in that the connection is "attended to" (586). Studies with the rat and the monkey further support the assumption that a neutral stimulus (nonaffective, non-need-related stimulus) is facilitative of learning (243, pp. 60–61).

INFORMATION

Learning may be simple or complex, bringing only a slight modification or a complete change—a revolution in man's activity. Let us assume that a man perceives significant errors and reverses his whole approach to a problem. His life style might even be reversed. A passive role in a social situation based on wrong information may shift to an entirely different role when "facts" are known.

Learning *is* information if both are broadly defined. Information is not simply conveyed by verbal or other symbols concerning the correctness or incorrectness of a response. A rat (or a man) that moves in a maze and perceives the "blinds" has nonverbal information. He perceives that he cannot continue on this path.

Experiments studying the effects of knowledge of results vary the degree of information ranging from incomplete to exact knowledge needed. The learner, let us say, is told that he responded to an incorrect stimulus among many presented. The greater the number of stimuli to which he could have responded, the less information he has. Moreover, if alternative responses are many, and the learner is only informed that the one he made is incorrect, the information does not greatly facilitate his progress. He knows what is wrong but not what is correct. In other words, informing feedback may permit error identification but not immediate error correction. This statement poses an old and very much discussed problem today in training by teaching machines (442). How much guidance should be given the learner, and in what ways should he be informed?

Noxious Stimuli as Informing. Subjects are likely to react to any noxiousness after a response, such as an aftereffect to be avoided. On the other hand, if a man learns that shock is a signal of a correct response, then the noxious stimulus informs him that his performance will be effective if he repeats this response.

A shock stimulus can be informing to rats (377). In one study animals were given a shock preceding food reward on half the trials in running to a goal box. On other trials neither food nor shock were used. The rats seemed to learn quickly that "no pain" was correlated with "no food," and thereafter did not even look under the food cup when there was no shock. Presumably they learned conversely that shock was a signal that food would follow.

Human subjects may interpret a noxious stimulus immediately following a response as information. If human subjects are told, or learn, that shock which follows a response is a signal that the response is correct (gains a reward), then painful shock is not only noxious but also informing.

Achievement Information. Information given to subjects may not inform them concerning their specific correct or incorrect responses but does inform them concerning the degree of their overall achievement in the task. Smode (566) reports on results of giving a large and small amount of achievement information to subjects working on a tracking task. Since the information in any of the feedback methods that he used was not so presented that it could be very useful in specific error correction even if it was useful at all, the motivational effects of the achievement information were emphasized by Smode.

Information that Smode used increased interest in the task, as was indicated by the protocols from each subject on answers to "What is your reaction to this type of task? How does it strike you with regard to interest, monotony, or fatigue?" The subjects with the high amount of achievement information had a greater interest in the task. Three reported bases for the increased interest were as follows: (1) Interest was greater because of the feelings of tension under the high-level information condition. Some individuals reported a general *increase in attentiveness* to the task, together with feelings of increased tension and pressure to perform well. (2) *Self-competition* increased interest. The subjects cited the competitive value of achievement information and its high incentive value and gave statements framed in terms of trying for a high-score goal. (3) There was a *game-playing* attitude. Some subjects reported that the continuous progress feedback made the task easier and more fun, engendering a better attitude toward the task, so that they viewed it as a game like playing a pinball machine.

It is important to remember that achievement-information feedback tells a subject how the results of his responses conform to some norm, including possibly his own standard of performance. Other studies indicate that achievement-information feedback (1) increases the level of performance in tasks that are highly overlearned (23, 75, 398), (2) increases the rate of improvement early in practice on a new task (174, 494), and (3) increases the frequency of reports that tasks are more interesting and less fatiguing (13, 494), as compared with conditions in which achievement information is withheld.

Knowledge of achievement may have an inciting effect on behavior. However, it is not at all clear whether the more rapid improvement resulting from such progress feedback during the early practice trials on a task is indicative of more rapid learning, or only of a heightened level of performance attributable to greater motivation and effort. Again we have the question whether we are dealing only with performance or with both performance and learning.

The complexity of the role of information in performance and in learning is revealed in a review by Ammons (13) in Inset 40.

INSET 40. KNOWLEDGE OF PERFORMANCE*

Ammons, in a survey of studies of the effects of knowledge of results on the effectiveness of performance, presents eleven generalizations. Each was based on experimentation, which is described below for the first five generalizations. Ammons considers both achievement-oriented information as well as feedback useful in correction of specific responses.

1. The performer usually has hypotheses about what he is to do and how he is to do it.

In an experiment requiring blindfolded subjects to draw three-inch lines, four-fifths of the subjects reported the use of cues of one sort or another in attempting to learn to draw the lines, the principal ones being kinesthetic cues from arm and hand. Other cues were the sound of the pencil, the number of counts required to draw the line the correct length, and visual images of a ruler (624).

2. For all practical purposes there is always some knowledge of his performance available to the human performer. There are at least subjective impressions of what is correct or incorrect.

Objective tests were given to a college class which was divided into groups receiving different amounts and kinds of information about their

---

* Adapted from R. B. Ammons, Effects of knowledge of performance: A survey and tentative theoretical formulation. *J. gen. Psychol.*, 1956, 54, 279–299.

progress. The largest differences were not between the group with no knowledge and the group with full knowledge, but between the group with partial knowledge and the group with full knowledge. However, the group referred to as having "no knowledge of progress" actually had subjective knowledge in the form of personal impressions (523).

3. Knowledge of performance affects rate of learning and level reached by learning.

Pressey (494) reported in 1950 on the use of a punchboard self-scoring device used by his students in taking quizzes. The learning was of Russian vocabulary, difficult English vocabulary, and the subject matter in psychology. Students using the device did superior work with a saving of sixty per cent or more in number of class hours. In short, self-instructional tests with immediate knowledge of results made it possible to learn more in less time. To this study can be added the increasing number of new lines of investigation on teaching machines.

4. Knowledge of performance affects motivation.

Four kinds of goal-setting techniques were compared in a block-turning task. Subjects were placed in four groups corresponding to four kinds of motivating conditions: (a) knowledge of results, (b) self-set, (c) externally-set norm, (d) externally-set improvement. The results indicated that none of the three more complicated goal-setting techniques produced greater motivation than simple knowledge of results (268).

5. The more specific the knowledge of performance, the more rapid the improvement and the higher the level of performance.

Various groups were given different degrees of information concerning successes and failures. The task was the estimation of a twelve-second time interval. The results showed that the improvement in judgment was roughly proportional to the degree of information given (636).

6. The longer the delay in giving knowledge of performance, the less effect the given information has.

7. In the case of discontinuous tasks where knowledge of performance is given, small intervals between trials are generally better for learning than longer ones.

8. When knowledge of performance is decreased, performance drops.

9. When knowledge is decreased, performance drops more rapidly when trials are relatively massed.

10. When subjects are no longer being given supplementary knowledge of performance by the experimenter, the ones who maintain their performance level probably have developed some substitute knowledge of performance: e.g., the increased efficiency without knowledge of performance in an ergographic task was accounted for by visual and kinesthetic imagery.

11. When direct (supplementary) knowledge of performance is removed, systematic "undershooting" or "overshooting" may appear in motor tasks.

See Ammons's original review for experimentation supporting the generalizations from 6 to 11.

SYMBOLIC REWARDS AND LEARNING

Acquisition of Secondary Rewards

An otherwise-neutral stimulus may acquire the property of being rewarding.

1. For example, a neutral stimulus is present simultaneously with, or immediately before, an already established reward. A sound or a light is presented immediately before or concomitant with a satisfying event like eating food.[8] The otherwise-neutral stimulus then becomes a secondary reward.

2. Another method: The subject manipulates the otherwise-neutral object, such as money. He exchanges it for a primary reward. In studies with chimpanzees by Wolfe (657) and Cowles (130) the animals first associated the poker chip with liked grapes by *using* the tokens to obtain the grapes in a vending machine. Coins for children in everyday life become symbolic rewards in somewhat the same way. Children use the coins in exchange for liked objects such as candy. A child early learns that the way of obtaining satisfaction from objects *later needed* is via money. "You will need lunch, so take this dollar." The association of money and satisfaction of later wants is a continual event in life.

3. Social symbols may acquire reward value for human subjects who observe the admiration that follows the symbol attainment by others. The child cannot exchange a high grade in school for any primary reward, nor has the grade necessarily preceded or been concomitant with any other satisfaction, yet when a child receives an A, it is an immediate reward for him. He has learned before his attainment of the high grade that it is a social reward. He knows that he has received a reward. And as long as *his* group *values* school achievement and he has accepted this value, high grades remain a reward for him.

Functions of Secondary Rewards

1. The *inciting* function of a symbol of a former reward was demonstrated by Estes (176). Rats in a Skinner box were trained to pull a bar, an action which was followed by the primary reward of food. Then the bar was removed and a tone introduced for sixty seconds prior to delivery of food. When later the animals were tested for experimental extinction of the bar pressing, the sounding of the tone increased the rate of re-

---

[8] Beck (47) writes, after reviewing studies using shock termination as a means of establishing a secondary reinforcer: "There is almost no evidence to show that secondary reinforcement can be established by the association of a neutral stimulus with noxious drive reduction" (p. 43).

sponding as compared with a control group for which there was no tone. The tone, which was presumably symbolic (a signal) of the later food reward, was inciting. Other evidence for this energizing role of a symbol representative of a former reward was reviewed in Chapter 9, Goals.

2. A neutral stimulus, after it becomes representative of a former reward, will act upon the selecting process, and learning can occur. Saltzman (531) placed a former goal box as a symbolic reward at the end of one path in a U-maze. The rats had been first trained in a runway to associate the distinctive goal box with a food reward. After this training, the symbolic reward (the distinctive goal box) was placed at the end of one arm of a U-maze. No food was now given. The animals selected more frequently than chance the path to the symbolic reward, that is, to the goal box where they had previously received food.

That a neutral stimulus associated with a former liked object acquires a function of increasing the repetition of a specific S-R unit is also illustrated by Cowles (130). After training chimpanzees to work for poker chips and then to spend them for food in a vending machine, he took the animals into another room and presented them with two boxes. If they opened the one on the left, they found a poker chip; if they opened the one on the right, they found nothing. They quickly learned to open the box with the symbolic reward, though they were not allowed to exchange the tokens for food until the end of the session.

With animals below man the secondary rewards (if the primary reward is omitted) are not long lasting in their control of performance, but this does not seem to be true for man. Interpretations are now considered for the continuance with humans of the motivational functions of symbolic rewards. When the former primary rewards are no longer given to man and apparently not even expected, symbols of "right" or "good" continue to act as if they were the original satisfying events.

Autonomy of Secondary Rewards and Punishments in Controlling the Performance of the Human Species

For men, learned rewards become more autonomous of the original conditions under which they were acquired than for animals. They are thus far more effective for men. For a man verbal praise, whatever was the specific history of its acquisition of a rewarding effect, may be later transitutional. For example, a man may act on the need-to-achieve, or on an interest in stamps, or because of values attached to religion, but one symbol, such as the word "good," following each of the performances will function like a reward irrespective of the original or present instigator of the performance. Similarly, the verbal symbol of "wrong" is a punishing agent leading to the cessation of many acts. These punishing symbols affect performance in a variety of situations for children and adults.

Verbal praise and punishment seem to become independent of the original situation in which they were acquired and even to become autonomous of the individual's immediate drive components. They affect behavior in many situations irrespective of what drives initiated the behavior. Symbols like verbal "right" and "wrong" may apparently become independent of former rewarding events even though there are no expectancies of such recurring events. Why? A child learns to value social acceptance by others, and a symbol gives information to the child that he is behaving in keeping with the value attached to "conforming." This is a possible answer to the question of the value of the symbols. The young child at first enjoys his acts of aggression, stealing, telling lies, or other nonsocially accepted behaviors. He at first questions both the symbolic "right" and "wrong" when his parents attempt to nullify his intrinsic satisfactions. Later he may decrease his questioning as *he accepts conforming*. How society possibly induces conforming in its individuals is discussed by Murdock (454) in Inset 41.

INSET 41. CONFORMITY*

To understand social conformity it is necessary to understand the pressures to respond to stimuli in the same or a very similar fashion as do others. These stimuli may be from any source and may arise when the individual is dominated by drives that would not support the conforming behavior. For example, even if quite angry, a man smiles in certain situations; this behavior is what others of his age, social group, and culture exhibit in these situations.

Murdock comments on the question: Why is there conformity?

A culture consists of habits that are shared by members of a society, whether this be a primitive tribe or a civilized nation. The sharing may be general throughout the society, as is normally the case with language habits. Often, however, it is limited to particular categories of people within the society. Thus persons of the same sex or age group, members of the same social class, association, or occupational group, and persons interacting with others in similar relationships commonly resemble one another in their social habits though diverging behaviorally from persons in other categories.

The social sharing of habits has several causes. The fact that the situations under which behavior is acquired are similar for

* Adapted from G. P. Murdock, How culture changes. In J. E. Nordskog, (ed.), *Social Change*. New York: McGraw-Hill, 1960, pp. 86–87.

many individuals conduces in itself to parallel learning. Even more important is the fact that each generation inculcates on the next, through education, the cultural habits which it has found satisfying and adaptive. Finally, the members of any society exercise pressure upon one another, through formal and informal means of social control, to conform to standards of behavior which are considered right and appropriate. This is particularly true of behavior in interpersonal relationships, where the success or failure of an action depends upon the reaction of another person to it, rather than, for example, upon its adaptiveness to the innate qualities of natural objects. Once one has acquired a limited number of stereotyped patterns of social behavior one is equipped to cope successfully with widely diversified social situations, and one is also provided with a body of reliable expectations regarding the probable responses of others to one's own behavior. This gives confidence and spares the individual an immense amount of individualized learning which is ever a painful process. It is with good reason, therefore, that every society lays great stress on social conformity.

Another interpretation of the permanence of symbolic rewards is traced to intermittent associations of symbols with actual rewards. Experimental evidence indicates that learning is more permanent if there is intermittent association of a specific response with a rewarding effect. And in general the verbal symbols of "correct," "right," and "good" are in the early life of a child associated, but only intermittently, with directly rewarding events. This is partial reinforcement method and is known to be a superior method of training to obtain retention (316, 370).

SUMMARY

The above review concerns two significant areas in which motivation and learning overlap: the roles of drive level and of aftereffects in performance.

There is no question that variations in drive level and aftereffects can interfere with, support, or facilitate *performance* of many kinds and under variable conditions, but in relation to the main interest in this chapter—their role in *learning*—the generalizations which can even be tentatively advanced are few in number.

Acquisition of conditioning using a noxious unconditioned stimulus is greater under stronger unconditioned stimuli, but a ceiling on this would no doubt be reached if extreme shock, for example, were used. The disruptive effects are observed of strong noxious stimulation, particularly in establishing difficult discriminations.

There is no established relation between drive level and instrumental learning. Problem solving is likely to be ineffective when the drive rises to a nonoptimal level. This was likewise indicated in the earlier chapters in considering how performance became ineffective when a nonoptimal drive level was reached.

Effects after Performance and Their Relation to Learning

Performance can be easily shaped according to the aftereffects and their schedule of appearance in the activity stream. This statement is well supported, though only limited evidence was presented above.

The theories concerning aftereffects in relation to those modifications of performance indicating *learning* include (1) the theory that S-R associations are strengthened by drive reduction (Hull) or by satisfying aftereffects (Thorndike), and (2) the theories that aftereffects may be significant in facilitating learning but not by directly strengthening S-R associations. Contiguity and frequency are appealed to by Tolman and by Guthrie as the strengthening conditions.

Evidence reviewed concerning Hull's original assumption that drive relief was *essential* for learning was not conclusive. Drive *increase* may be an aftereffect, and yet there will be signs of learning occurring.

There are a variety of aftereffects which may have some role in learning. For example, information is a broad category for aftereffects. It includes those effects called information which in some way isolate the correct stimulus or stimuli as well as the adequate response or responses. In addition, achievement information for a human subject may be inciting because it permits comparison of his own performance with a *norm*. This norm may be his own average performance or the progress of some comparison group. For the individual who is being moved toward a "good" performance, such information is energizing. If the information indicates that he is below the progress expected either by himself or by the experimenter, he will increase his efforts. However, this whole area of investigation is complicated by individuality in responding to information concerning so-called success and failure.

REFERENCES

1. Aborn, M.: The influence of experimentally induced failure on the retention of material acquired through set and incidental learning. *J. exp. Psychol.*, 1953, 45, 225–231.
2. Adolph, E. F.: *Physiological regulations.* New York: Ronald, 1943.
3. Alexander, F.: Development of the fundamental concepts of psychoanalysis. In F. Alexander and H. Ross (eds.), *Dynamic psychiatry.* Chicago: University of Chicago Press, 1952.
4. Alexander, F., and L. B. Shapiro: Neurosis, behavior disorders, and perversions. In F. Alexander and H. Ross (eds.), *Dynamic psychiatry.* Chicago: University of Chicago Press, 1952.
5. Allee, W. C.: *The social life of animals.* New York: Norton, 1938.
6. Allen, C. H., H. Frings, and I. Rudnick: Some biological effects of intense high frequency airborne sound. *J. acoust. Soc. Amer.*, 1948, 20, 62–65.
7. Allport, G. W.: The functional autonomy of motives. *Amer. J. Psychol.*, 1937, 50, 141–156.
8. Allport, G. W.: *Personality.* New York: Holt, 1937.
9. Allport, G. W.: The ego in contemporary psychology. In C. L. Stacey and M. F. DeMartino (eds.), *Understanding human motivation.* Cleveland: Howard Allen, 1958.
10. Allport, G. W.: *Personality and social encounter.* Boston: Beacon Press, 1960.
11. Allport, G. W.: *Pattern and growth in personality.* New York: Holt, 1961.
12. Ammons, R. B.: Acquisition of motor skill. I. Quantitative analysis and theoretical formulation. *Psychol. Rev.*, 1947, 54, 263–281.
13. Ammons, R. B.: Effects of knowledge of performance: a survey and tentative theoretical formulation. *J. gen. Psychol.*, 1956, 54, 279–299.
14. Anastasi, A.: *Differential psychology.* New York: Macmillan, 1958.
15. Anastasi, A., N. Cohen, and D. Spatz: A study of fear and anger in college students through the controlled diary method. *J. genet. Psychol.*, 1948, 73, 243–249.
16. Anderson, E. E.: Interrelationship of drives in the male albino rat. I. Intercorrelations of measures of drives. *J. comp. Psychol.*, 1937, 24, 73–118.
17. Anonymous: An autobiography of a schizophrenic experience. *J. abnorm. soc. Psychol.*, 1955, 51, 677–689.

341

18. Ansbacher, H.: Perception of number as affected by the monetary value of the objects. *Arch. Psychol., N.Y.*, 1937, no. 215.
19. Applezweig, M. H.: Response potential as a function of effort. *J. comp. physiol. Psychol.*, 1951, 44, 225–235.
20. Aristotle: *Rhetoric.*
21. Armus, H. L.: Drive level and habit reversal. *Psychol. Repts.*, 1958, 4, 31–34.
22. Arnold, M. B.: *Emotion and personality*, Vols. I and II. New York: Columbia University Press, 1960.
23. Arps, G. F.: Work with knowledge of results versus work without knowledge of results. *Psychol. Monogr.*, 1920, 28, no. 3 (Whole no. 125).
24. Asch, S. E.: *Social psychology.* Englewood Cliffs, N.J.: Prentice-Hall, 1952.
25. Ashley, W. R., R. S. Harper, and D. L. Runyon: The perceived size of coins in normal and hypnotically induced economic states. *Amer. J. Psychol.*, 1951, 64, 564–572.
26. Atkinson, J. W.: The achievement motive and recall of interrupted and completed tasks. *J. exp. Psychol.*, 1953, 46, 381–390.
27. Atkinson, J. W.: Motivational determinants of risk-taking behavior. *Psychol. Rev.*, 1957, 64, 359–372.
28. Atkinson, J. W. (ed.): *Motives in fantasy, action, and society.* Princeton, N.J.: Van Nostrand, 1958.
29. Atkinson, J. W.: Towards experimental analysis of human motivation in terms of motives, expectancies, and incentives. In J. W. Atkinson (ed.), *Motives in fantasy, action, and society.* Princeton, N.J.: Van Nostrand, 1958.
30. Ax, A. F.: The physiological differentiation between fear and anger in humans. *Psychosom. Med.*, 1953, 15, 433–442.
31. Bahrick, H. P., P. M. Fitts, and R. E. Rankin: Effect of incentives upon reactions to peripheral stimuli. *J. exp. Psychol.*, 1952, 44, 400–406.
32. Baldwin, A. L.: *Behavior and development in childhood.* New York: Dryden, 1955.
33. Bales, R. F.: *Interaction process analysis.* Reading, Mass.: Addison-Wesley, 1950.
34. Bard, P., and V. B. Mountcastle: Some forebrain mechanisms involved in expression of rage with special reference to suppression of angry behavior. *Res. Publ. Assoc. nerv. mental Dis.*, 1947, 27, 362–404.
35. Bare, J. K.: The specific hunger for sodium chloride in normal and adrenalectomized white rats. *J. comp. physiol. Psychol.*, 1949, 42, 242–253.
36. Barker, R. G., T. Dembo, and K. Lewin: Frustration and regression: an experiment with young children. *Univ. Iowa Studies Child Welf.*, 1941, 18, 1.
37. Barmack, J. E.: The length of the work period and the work curve. *J. exp. Psychol.*, 1939, 25, 109–115.
38. Barnes, G. W., and G. B. Kish: On some properties of visual reinforcement. *Amer. Psychologist*, 1958, 13, 417.
39. Barrett, D. M.: Memory in relation to hedonic tone. *Arch. Psychol., N.Y.*, 1938, 31, no. 223.
40. Bartlett, F. C.: *Remembering: a study in experimental and social psychology.* New York: Cambridge, 1932.

41. Bartlett, F. C.: Incentives. *Brit. J. Psychol.*, 1950, 41, 122–128.
42. Bartley, S. H.: *Vision: a study of its basis.* Princeton, N.J.: Van Nostrand, 1941.
43. Bartley, S. H., and E. Chute: *Fatigue and impairment in man.* New York: McGraw-Hill, 1947.
44. Beach, F. A.: *Hormones and behavior.* New York: Hoeber-Harper, 1948.
45. Beach, F. A.: Body chemistry and perception. In R. R. Blake and G. V. Ramsey (eds.), *Perception: an approach to personality.* New York: Ronald, 1951.
46. Beach, H. D.: Effect of morphine on the exploratory drive. *Canad. J. Psychol.*, 1957, 11, 237–244.
47. Beck, R. C.: On secondary reinforcement and shock termination. *Psychol. Bull.*, 1961, 58, 28–45.
48. Beebe-Center, J. G.: *The psychology of pleasantness and unpleasantness.* Princeton, N.J.: Van Nostrand, 1932.
49. Beebe-Center, J. G.: Feeling and emotion. In H. Helson (ed.), *Theoretical foundations of psychology.* Princeton, N.J.: Van Nostrand, 1951.
50. Beier, E. G.: The effect of induced anxiety on flexibility of intellectual functioning. *Psychol. Monogr.*, 1951, 65, no. 9 (Whole no. 326).
51. Bell, J. E.: *Projective techniques.* New York: Longmans, 1948.
52. Bellak, L.: The concept of projection. *Psychiatry*, 1944, 7, 353–370.
53. Beller, E. K.: Two attitude components in younger boys. *J. soc. Psychol.*, 1949, 29, 137–151.
54. Bentham, J.: *An introduction to the principles of morals and legislation.* Oxford: Clarendon Press, 1879. (A reprint of a new edition published by Bentham in 1823.)
55. Berkowitz, L.: The expression and reduction of hostility. *Psychol. Bull.*, 1958, 55, 257–283.
56. Berkowitz, L.: Repeated frustrations and expectations in hostility arousal. *J. abnorm. soc. Psychol.*, 1960, 60, 422–429.
57. Berkowitz, L.: Some factors affecting the reduction of overt hostility. *J. abnorm. soc. Psychol.*, 1960, 60, 14–21.
58. Berlyne, D. E.: Novelty and curiosity as determinants of exploratory behavior. *Brit. J. Psychol.*, 1950, 41, 68–80.
59. Berlyne, D. E.: Attention to change. *Brit. J. Psychol.*, 1951, 42, 269–278.
60. Berlyne, D. E.: The arousal and satiation of perceptual curiosity in the rat. *J. comp. physiol. Psychol.*, 1955, 48, 238–246.
61. Berlyne, D. E.: The influence of complexity and novelty in visual figures on orienting responses. *J. exp. Psychol.*, 1958, 55, 289–296.
62. Berlyne, D. E.: *Conflict, arousal, and curiosity.* New York: McGraw-Hill, 1960.
63. Bernard, C.: *Leçons sur les propriétés physiologiques et les altérations pathologiques des liquides de l'organisme*, Vols. I and II. Paris: Ballière, 1859.
64. Berrien, F. K.: The effects of noise. *Psychol. Bull.*, 1946, 43, 141–161.
65. Bevan, W., Jr., and W. F. Dukes: Value and the Weber constant in the perception of distance. *Amer. J. Psychol.*, 1951, 64, 580–584.
66. Bexton, W. H., W. Heron, and T. H. Scott: Effects of decreased variation in the sensory environment. *Canad. J. Psychol.*, 1954, 8, 70–76.

67. Bindra, D.: *Motivation.* New York: Ronald, 1959.
68. Bindra, D., A. L. Paterson, and J. Strzelecki: On the relation between anxiety and conditioning. *Canad. J. Psychol.,* 1955, 9, 1–6.
69. Birch, H. G.: The role of motivational factors in insightful problem-solving. *J. comp. Psychol.,* 1945, 38, 295–317.
70. Bitterman, M. E., and W. H. Holtzman: Conditioning and extinction of the galvanic skin response as a function of anxiety. *J. abnorm. soc. Psychol.,* 1952, 47, 615–623.
71. Blakeslee, A. F.: Genetics of sensory thresholds: taste for phenylthio-carbamide. *Proc. Nat. Acad. Sci.,* 1932, 18, 120–130.
72. Blodgett, H. C.: The effect of the introduction of reward upon the maze performance of rats. *Univ. Calif. Publ. Psychol.,* 1929, 4, 113–134.
73. Bloomfield, A., and M. L. Tainter: The effect of vitamin B deprivation on spontaneous activity of the rat. *J. Lab. clin. Med.,* 1943, 28, 1680–1690.
74. Bodansky, M., and V. B. Duff: Effects of parathyroid deficiency and calcium and phosphorus of the diet on pregnant rats. *J. Nutrition,* 1941, 21, 179–192.
75. Book, W. F., and L. Norvell: The will to learn: an experimental study of incentives in learning. *Pedag. Seminary,* 1922, 29, 305–362.
76. Bousfield, W. A., and H. Barry: Quantitative correlates of euphoria. *J. exp. Psychol.,* 1937, 21, 218–222.
77. Bowen, H. M., and M. M. Woodhead: Royal Air Force Research Unit interim report FPRC 955. Cambridge, England: Applied Psychology Research Unit.
78. Bower, G. H., H. Fowler, and M. A. Trapold: Escape learning as a function of amount of shock reduction. *J. exp. Psychol.,* 1959, 58, 482–484.
79. Bragiel, R. M., and C. C. Perkins, Jr.: Conditioned stimulus intensity and response speed. *J. exp. Psychol.,* 1954, 47, 437–441.
80. Brandauer, C. M.: A confirmation of Webb's data concerning the action of the irrelevant drives. *J. exp. Psychol.,* 1953, 45, 150–152.
81. Brayfield, A. H., and W. H. Crockett: Employee attitudes and employee performance. *Psychol. Bull.,* 1955, 52, 396–424.
82. Bridges, K. M. B.: Emotional development in early infancy. *Child Develpm.,* 1932, 3, 324–341.
83. Broadbent, D. E.: Listening to one of two synchronous messages. *J. exp. Psychol.,* 1952, 44, 51–55.
84. Broadhurst, P. L.: Emotionality and the Yerkes-Dodson law. *J. exp. Psychol.,* 1957, 54, 345–352.
85. Brody, E. G.: Genetic basis of spontaneous activity in the albino rat. *Comp. Psychol. Monogr.,* 1942, 17, no. 5, 1–24.
86. Brody, E. G.: A note on the genetic basis of spontaneous activity in the albino rat. *J. comp. physiol. Psychol.,* 1950, 43, 281–288.
87. Brody, S.: *Bioenergetics and growth, with special reference to the efficiency complex in domestic animals.* New York: Reinhold, 1945.
88. Brown, J. S.: The generalization of approach responses as a function of stimulus intensity and strength of motivation. *J. comp. Psychol.,* 1942, 33, 209–226.
89. Brown, J. S.: Problems presented by the concept of acquired drives. In *Current theory and research in motivation: a symposium.* Lincoln, Nebr.: University of Nebraska Press, 1953.

90. Brown, J. S.: *The motivation of behavior.* New York: McGraw-Hill, 1961.
91. Brown, J. S., and I. E. Farber: Emotions conceptualized as intervening variables with suggestions toward a theory of frustration. *Psychol. Bull.,* 1951, 48, 465–495.
92. Brown, J. S., H. I. Kalish, and I. E. Farber: Conditioned fear as revealed by magnitude of startle response to an auditory stimulus. *J. exp. Psychol.,* 1951, 41, 317–328.
93. Brozek, J.: Physiological psychology. *Annu. Rev. Psychol.,* 1958, 9, 71–98.
94. Bruner, J. S., and C. C. Goodman: Value and need as organizing factors in perception. *J. abnorm. soc. Psychol.,* 1947, 42, 33–44.
95. Bruner, J. S., J. J. Goodnow, and G. A. Austin: *A study of thinking.* New York: Wiley, 1956.
96. Bugelski, B. R.: *The psychology of learning.* New York: Holt, 1956.
97. Bursill, A. E.: The restriction of peripheral vision during exposure to hot and humid conditions. *Quart. J. exp. Psychol.,* 1958, 10, 113–129.
98. Bursten, B., and J. M. R. Delgado: Positive reinforcement induced by intracerebral stimulation in the monkey. *J. comp. physiol. Psychol.,* 1958, 51, 6–10.
99. Buss, A. H.: *The psychology of aggression.* New York: Wiley, 1961.
100. Butler, R. A.: Discrimination learning by rhesus monkeys to visual-exploration motivation. *J. comp. physiol. Psychol.,* 1953, 46, 95–98.
101. Butler, R. A.: Incentive conditions which influence visual exploration. *J. exp. Psychol.,* 1954, 48, 19–23.
102. Butler, R. A.: The differential effect of visual and auditory incentives on the performance of monkeys. *Amer. J. Psychol.,* 1958, 71, 591–593.
103. Butler, R. A.: Acquired drives and the curiosity-investigative motives. In R. H. Waters, D. A. Rethlingshafer, and W. E. Caldwell (eds.), *Principles of comparative psychology.* New York: McGraw-Hill, 1960.
104. Butler, R. A., and H. F. Harlow: Discrimination learning and learning sets to visual exploration incentives. *J. gen. Psychol.,* 1957, 57, 257–264.
105. Caldwell, W. E.: The mathematical formulation of a unified field theory. *Psychol. Rev.,* 1953, 60, 64–72.
106. Caldwell, W. E.: Field theory. II. Some mathematical applications to comparative psychology. *Psychol. Rev.,* 1954, 61, 271–275.
107. Cameron, N.: Perceptual organization and behavior pathology. In R. R. Blake and G. V. Ramsey (eds.), *Perception: an approach to personality.* New York: Ronald, 1951.
108. Campbell, B. A.: The fractional reduction in noxious stimulation required to produce "just noticeable" learning. *J. comp. physiol. Psychol.,* 1955, 48, 141–148.
109. Campbell, B. A.: The reinforcement difference limen (RDL) function for shock reduction. *J. exp. Psychol.,* 1956, 52, 258–262.
110. Campbell, B. A., and F. D. Sheffield: Relation of random activity to food deprivation. *J. comp. physiol. Psychol.,* 1953, 46, 320–322.
111. Cannon, W. B.: *The wisdom of the body.* New York: Norton, 1932.
112. Carmichael, L.: Ontogenetic development. In S. S. Stevens (ed.), *Handbook of experimental psychology,* New York: Wiley, 1951, chap. 8.
113. Carmichael, L., and W. F. Dearborn: *Reading and visual fatigue.* Boston: Houghton Mifflin, 1947.

114. Caron, A. J., and M. A. Wallach: Personality determinants of repressive and obsessive reactions to failure-stress. *J. abnorm. soc. Psychol.*, 1959, 59, 236–245.

115. Carter, L. F., and K. Schooler: Value, need and other factors in perception. *Psychol. Rev.*, 1949, 56, 200–207.

116. Cattell, J. McK.: The influence of the intensity of the stimulus on the length of the reaction time. *Brain*, 1886, 8, 512–515.

117. Cattell, R. B.: Principles of design in "projective" or misperceptive tests of personality. In H. H. Anderson and G. L. Anderson (eds.), *An introduction to projective techniques.* Englewood Cliffs, N.J.: Prentice-Hall, 1951.

118. Cattell, R. B., and I. H. Scheier: *The meaning and measurement of neuroticism and anxiety.* New York: Ronald, 1961.

119. Centers, R.: *The psychology of social classes.* Princeton, N.J.: Princeton University Press, 1949.

120. Chase, L.: Motivation of young children. *Univ. Iowa Studies Child Welf.*, 1932, 5, no. 3, 1–119.

121. Child, I. L.: The relation of somatotype to self-ratings on Sheldon's temperamental traits. *J. Pers.*, 1950, 18, 440–453.

122. Child, I. L., and J. W. M. Whiting: Determinants of level of aspiration: evidence from everyday life. *J. abnorm. soc. Psychol.*, 1949, 44, 303–314.

123. Cofer, C. N.: Motivation. *Annu. Rev. Psychol.*, 1959, 10, 173–202.

124. Coghill, G. E., and R. W. Watkins: Periodicity in the development of the threshold of tactile stimulation in amblystoma. *J. comp. Neurol.*, 1943, 78, 91–111.

125. Combs, A. W.: *Individual behavior: a perceptual approach to behavior* (rev. ed.). New York: Harper, 1959.

126. Coopersmith, S.: Self-esteem and need achievement as determinants of selective recall and repetition. *J. abnorm. soc. Psychol.*, 1960, 60, 310–317.

127. Corso, J. F.: The effects of noise on human behavior. *WADC Tech. Rept.*, 1952, no. 53-81.

128. Cowen, E. L., and E. G. Beier: Threat-expectancy, word frequencies, and perceptual prerecognition hypotheses. *J. abnorm. soc. Psychol.*, 1954, 49, 178–182.

129. Cowen, E. L., J. Landes, and D. E. Schaet: The effects of mild frustration on the expression of prejudiced attitudes. *J. abnorm. soc. Psychol.*, 1959, 58, 33–38.

130. Cowles, J. T.: Food-tokens as incentives for learning by chimpanzees. *Comp. Psychol. Monogr.*, 1937, 14, no. 5.

131. Coyer, R. A.: The effect of magnitude of reward and degree of deprivation on the acquisition of a complex maze habit. Unpublished doctoral dissertation, University of Buffalo, 1953.

132. Crandall, V. J., D. Solomon, and R. Kellaway: The value of anticipated events as a determinant of probability learning and extinction. *J. gen. Psychol.*, 1958, 58, 3–10.

133. Crespi, L. P.: Quantitative variation of incentive and performance in the white rat. *Amer. J. Psychol.*, 1942, 55, 467–517.

134. Cronbach, L. J.: Assessment of individual differences. In P. R. Farnsworth (ed.), *Annual review of psychology.* Palo Alto, Calif.: Annual Reviews, 1956.

135. Cruikshank, R. M.: Animal infancy. In L. Carmichael (ed.), *Manual of child psychology*. New York: Wiley, 1946.
136. Crutchfield, R. S.: The determiners of energy expenditure in string-pulling by the rat. *J. Psychol.*, 1939, 7, 163–178.
137. Dashiell, J. F.: A quantitative demonstration of animal drive. *J. comp. Psychol.*, 1925, 5, 205–208.
138. Dashiell, J. F.: *Fundamentals of objective psychology*. Boston: Houghton Mifflin, 1928.
139. Dashiell, J. F.: *Fundamentals of general psychology*. Boston: Houghton Mifflin, 1937.
140. Davidson, D., P. Suppes, and S. Siegel: *Decision making*. Stanford, Calif.: Stanford University Press, 1957.
141. Davis, A., and B. J. Havighurst: Social class and color differences in child-rearing. In C. Kluckhohn and H. A. Murray (eds.), *Personality in nature, society, and culture*. New York: Knopf, 1950.
142. Davis, C. M.: Self selection of diet by newly weaned infants. *Amer. J. Dis. Child.*, 1928, 36, 651–679.
143. Davis, R. C.: Electrical skin resistance before, during, and after a period of noise stimulation. *J. exp. Psychol.*, 1932, 15, 108–117.
144. Davis, R. C.: Modification of the galvanic reflex by daily repetition of a stimulus. *J. exp. Psychol.*, 1934, 17, 504–535.
145. Davis, R. C.: The muscular tension reflex and two of its modifying conditions. *Ind. Univ. Publ. Science Series*, 1935, no. 3.
146. Davis, R. C.: Motor effects of strong auditory stimuli. *J. exp. Psychol.*, 1948, 38, 257–275.
147. Davis, R. C.: Motor responses to auditory stimuli above and below threshold. *J. exp. Psychol.*, 1950, 40, 107–120.
148. Davis, R. C., A. M. Buchwald, and R. W. Frankmann: Autonomic and muscular responses, and their relation to simple stimuli. *Psychol. Monogr.*, 1955, 69, no. 20 (Whole no. 405).
149. Deese, J.: Some problems in the theory of vigilance. *Psychol. Rev.*, 1955, 62, 359–368.
150. Deese, J., and E. Ormond: Studies of detectability during continuous visual search. *WADC Tech. Rept.* 1953, no. 53–8.
151. Dember, W. N.: Response by the rat to environmental change. *J. comp. physiol. Psychol.*, 1956, 49, 93–95.
152. Dember, W. N.: *Psychology of perception*. New York: Holt, 1960.
153. Dempsey, E. W.: Homeostasis. In S. S. Stevens (ed.), *Handbook of experimental psychology*. New York: Wiley, 1951, chap. 6.
154. Dennis, W., and R. T. Sollenberger: Negative adaptation in the maze exploration of albino rats. *J. comp. Psychol.*, 1934, 18, 197–206.
155. DeSoto, C. B., E. B. Coleman, and P. L. Putnam: Predictions of sequences of successes and failures. *J. exp. Psychol.*, 1960, 59, 41–46.
156. DeVito, J. L., and O. A. Smith, Jr.: Effect of temperature and food deprivation on the random activity of *Macaca mulatta*. *J. comp. physiol. Psychol.*, 1959, 52, 29–32.
157. Diamond, S.: *Personality and temperament*. New York: Harper, 1957.
158. Diggory, J. C., E. J. Riley, and R. Blumenfeld: Estimated probability of success for a fixed goal. *Amer. J. Psychol.*, 1960, 73, 41–55.
159. Dinsmoor, J. A.: Punishment. I. The avoidance hypothesis. *Psychol. Rev.*, 1954, 61, 34–46.

160. Dinsmoor, J. A., and L. H. Hughes: Training rats to press a bar to turn off shock. *J. comp. physiol. Psychol.*, 1956, 49, 235–238.
161. Dodson, J. D.: Relative values of reward and punishment in habit formation. *Psychobiology*, 1917, 1, 231–276.
162. Dollard, J., L. W. Doob, N. E. Miller, O. H. Mowrer, and R. R. Sears: *Frustration and aggression.* New Haven, Conn.: Yale University Press, 1939.
163. Duffy, E.: The measurement of muscular tension as a technique for the study of emotional tendencies. *Amer. J. Psychol.*, 1932, 44, 146–162.
164. Duffy, E.: The concept of energy mobilization. *Psychol. Rev.*, 1951, 58, 30–40.
165. Duffy, E.: The psychological significance of the concept of "arousal" or "activation." *Psychol. Rev.*, 1957, 64, 265–275.
166. Dukes, W. F.: Psychological studies of values. *Psychol. Bull.*, 1955, 52, 24–50.
167. Dukes, W. F., and W. Bevan, Jr.: Accentuation and response variability in the perception of personally relevant objects. *J. Pers.*, 1952, 20, 457–465.
168. Dykman, R. A., W. G. Reese, C. R. Galbrecht, and P. J. Thomasson: Psychophysiological reactions to novel stimuli: measurement, adaptation and relationship of psychological and physiological variables in the normal human. *Ann. N.Y. Acad. Sci.*, 1959, 79, 43–107.
169. Easterbrook, J. A.: The effect of emotion on cue utilization and the organization of behavior. *Psychol. Rev.*, 1959, 66, 183–201.
170. Edwards, W.: A perspective on automation and decision making. In D. Willner (ed.), *Decisions, values, and groups.* New York: Pergamon Press, 1960.
171. Edwards, W.: Behavioral decision theory. In P. R. Farnsworth and Q. McNemar (eds.), *Annual review of psychology.* Palo Alto, Calif.: Annual Reviews, 1961.
172. Eliot, T. S.: *The elder statesman.* New York: Farrar, Straus and Cudahy, 1959.
173. Elliott, M. H.: The effect of the change of drive on the maze performance. *Univ. Calif. Publ. Psychol.*, 1929, 4, 185–188.
174. Elwell, J. L., and G. C. Grindley: The effect of knowledge of results on learning and performance. I. A co-ordinated movement of the two hands. *Brit. J. Psychol.*, 1938, 29, 39–53.
175. Estes, H. D.: Adaptability of flying personnel: a longitudinal study of the somatotype in military flying. Randolph Field, Tex.: U.S.A.F. School of Aviation Medicine, 1957, 57–139.
176. Estes, W. K.: Discriminative conditioning. I. A discriminative property of conditioned anticipation. *J. exp. Psychol.*, 1943, 32, 150–155.
177. Estes, W. K.: An experimental study of punishment. *Psychol. Monogr.*, 1944, 57, no. 3.
178. Estes, W. K., and B. F. Skinner: Some quantitative properties of anxiety. *J. exp. Psychol.*, 1941, 29, 390–400.
179. Eysenck, H. J., and H. T. Himmelweit: An experimental study of the reactions of neurotics to experiences of success and failure. *J. gen. Psychol.*, 1946, 35, 59–75.
180. Farber, I. E., and K. W. Spence: Complex learning and conditioning as a function of anxiety. *J. exp. Psychol.*, 1953, 45, 120–125.

181. Farner, D. S.: Comparative physiology: photoperiodicity. *Annu. Rev. Physiol.*, 1961, 23, 71–96.
182. Farner, D. S., L. R. Mewaldt, and J. R. King: The diurnal activity patterns of caged migratory white-crowned sparrows in late winter and spring. *J. comp. physiol. Psychol.*, 1954, 47, 148–153.
183. Fehrer, E.: The effects of hunger and familiarity of locale on exploration. *J. comp. physiol. Psychol.*, 1956, 49, 549–552.
184. Fenchel, G. H., J. H. Monderer, and E. L. Hartley: Subjective status and the equilibration hypothesis. *J. abnorm. soc. Psychol.*, 1951, 46, 476–479.
185. Fenichel, O.: Neurotic acting out. *Psychoanal. Rev.*, 1945, 32, 197–206.
186. Fenichel, O.: *The psychoanalytic theory of neurosis.* New York: Norton, 1945.
187. Ferster, C. B., and B. F. Skinner: *Schedules of reinforcement.* New York: Appleton-Century-Crofts, 1957.
188. Festinger, L.: A theory of cognitive dissonance. Evanston, Ill.: Row Peterson, 1957.
189. Festinger, L.: The motivating effect of cognitive dissonance. In G. Lindzey (ed.), *Assessment of human motives.* New York: Holt, 1958.
190. Filer, R. J.: Frustration, satisfaction, and other factors affecting the attractiveness of goal objects. *J. abnorm. soc. Psychol.*, 1952, 47, 203–212.
191. Finch, G., and E. Culler: Higher order conditioning with constant motivation. *Amer. J. Psychol.*, 1934, 46, 596–602.
192. Finger, F. W., L. S. Reid, and M. H. Weasner: The effect of reinforcement upon activity during cyclic food deprivation. *J. comp. physiol. Psychol.*, 1957, 50, 495–498.
193. Finkle, A. L., and J. R. Poppen: Clinical effects of noise and mechanical vibrations of a turbo-jet engine on man. *J. appl. Physiol.*, 1948, 1, 183–204.
194. Fletcher, F. M.: Effects of quantitative variation of food-incentive on the performance of physical work by chimpanzees. *Comp. Psychol. Monogr.*, 1940, 16, no. 82.
195. Flynn, J. P., and E. A. Jerome: Learning in an automatic multiple-choice box with light as an incentive. *J. comp. physiol. Psychol.*, 1952, 45, 336–340.
196. Fouriezos, N. T., M. L. Hutt, and H. Guetzkow: Measurement of self-oriented needs in discussion groups. *J. abnorm. soc. Psychol.*, 1950, 45, 682–690.
197. Fox, A. L.: The relationship between chemical constitution and taste. *Proc. Nat. Acad. Sci.*, 1932, 18, 115–120.
198. Franks, C. M.: Effect of food, drink, and tobacco deprivation on the conditioning of the eyeblink response. *J. exp. Psychol.*, 1957, 53, 117–120.
199. Fredericson, E., N. Gurney, and E. Dubois: The relationship between environmental temperature and behavior in neonatal puppies. *J. comp. physiol. Psychol.*, 1956, 49, 278–280.
200. Freedman, M. B., T. F. Leary, A. G. Ossorio, and H. S. Coffey: The interpersonal dimension of personality. *J. Pers.*, 1951, 20, 143–161.
201. Freeman, G. L.: Changes in tension-pattern and total energy expenditure during adaptation to "distracting" stimuli. *Amer. J. Psychol.*, 1939, 52, 354–360.

202. Freeman, G. L., and C. I. Hovland: Diurnal variations in performance and related physiological processes. *Psychol. Bull.*, 1934, 31, 777–799.

203. French, G. M., and H. F. Harlow: Locomotor reaction decrement in normal and brain-damaged rhesus monkeys. *J. comp. physiol. Psychol.*, 1955, 48, 496–501.

204. Freud, S.: *The problem of anxiety.* New York: Norton, 1936.

205. Freud, S.: *The ego and the id.* London: Hogarth, 1947.

206. Fries, M. E.: Psychosomatic relationships between mother and infant. *Psychosom. Med.*, 1944, 6, 159–162.

207. Fromm, E.: Selfishness and self-love. In C. L. Stacey and M. F. De-Martino (eds.), *Understanding human motivation.* Cleveland: Howard Allen, 1958.

208. Fuller, J. L.: Individual differences in the reactivity of dogs. *J. comp. physiol. Psychol.*, 1948, 41, 339–347.

209. Fuller, J. L.: Genetics and individual differences. In R. H. Waters, D. A. Rethlingshafer, and W. E. Caldwell (eds.), *Principles of comparative psychology.* New York: McGraw-Hill, 1960, Chap. 11.

210. Fuller, J. L., and E. Gillum: A study of factors influencing performance of dogs on a delayed response test. *J. genet. Psychol.*, 1950, 76, 241–251.

211. Fuller, J. L., and W. R. Thompson: *Behavior genetics.* New York: Wiley, 1960.

212. Funkenstein, D. H., S. H. King, and M. E. Drolette: *Mastery of stress.* Cambridge, Mass.: Harvard University Press, 1957.

213. Fuster, J. M.: Effects of stimulation of brain stem on tachistoscopic perception. *Science*, 1958, 127, 150.

214. Gantt, W. H.: Physiological psychology. In *Annu. Rev. Physiol.*, 1948, 10, 453–478.

215. Gates, G. S.: Anger in college women. In W. Dennis (ed.), *Readings in general psychology.* Englewood Cliffs, N.J.: Prentice-Hall, 1949.

216. Geier, F. M., and E. C. Tolman: Goal distance and restless activity. I. The goal gradient of restless activity. *J. comp. Psychol.*, 1943, 35, 197–204.

217. Geldreich, E. W.: Some physiological concomitants of mental work. *Psychol. Monogr.*, 1953, 67 (Whole no. 358).

218. Gesell, A.: The ontogenesis of infant behavior. In L. Carmichael (ed.), *Manual of child psychology* (2d ed.). New York: Wiley, 1954.

219. Gilchrist, J. C., and L. S. Nesberg: Need and perceptual change in need-related objects. *J. exp. Psychol.*, 1952, 44, 369–376.

220. Gill, M.: The present state of psychoanalytic theory. *J. abnorm. soc. Psychol.*, 1959, 58, 1–8.

221. Glanzer, M.: Stimulus satiation: an explanation of spontaneous alternation and related phenomena. *Psychol. Rev.*, 1953, 60, 257–268.

222. Glueck, S., and E. Glueck: *Unraveling juvenile delinquency.* Cambridge, Mass.: Harvard University Press, 1950.

223. Goldstein, K.: *The organism: a holistic approach to biology derived from pathological data in man.* New York: American Book, 1939.

224. Goldstein, K.: *Human nature in the light of psychopathology.* Cambridge, Mass.: Harvard University Press, 1940.

225. Goldstein, K.: Organismic approach to the problem of motivation. *Trans. N.Y. Acad. Sci.*, 1947, 9, 218–230.

226. Goodenough, Florence L.: *Exceptional children.* New York: Appleton-Century-Crofts, 1956.
227. Graham, C. H.: Visual perception. In S. S. Stevens (ed.) *Handbook of experimental psychology.* New York: Wiley, 1951, Chap. 23.
228. Graham, F. K., W. A. Charwat, A. S. Honig, and P. C. Weltz: Aggression as a function of the attack and the attacker. *J. abnorm. soc. Psychol.,* 1951, 46, 512–520.
229. Grant, D. A., H. W. Hake, and J. P. Hornseth: Acquisition and extinction of a verbal conditioned response with differing percentages of reinforcement. *J. exp. Psychol.,* 1951, 42, 1–5.
230. Grindley, G. C.: Experiments on the influence of the amount of reward on learning in young chickens. *Brit. J. Psychol.,* 1929, 20, 173–180.
231. Grinker, R. R., and J. P. Spiegel: *Men under stress.* New York: McGraw-Hill, 1945.
232. Gruen, E. W.: Level of aspiration in relation to personality factors in adolescents. *Child Developm.,* 1945, 16, 181–188.
233. Guilford, J. P.: *Personality.* New York: McGraw-Hill, 1959.
234. Guilford, J. P., P. R. Christensen, N. A. Bond, Jr., and M. A. Sutton: A factor analysis of human interests. *Psychol. Monogr.,* 1954, 68, no. 4, 1–38.
235. Guilford, J. P., and R. B. Guilford: Personality factors, S, E, and M, and their measurement. *J. Psychol.,* 1936, 2, 109–127.
236. Guilford, J. P., and R. B. Guilford: Personality factors D, R, T, and A. *J. abnorm. soc. Psychol.,* 1939, 34, 21–36.
237. Guilford, J. P., and R. B. Guilford: Personality factors, N, and GD. *J. abnorm. soc. Psychol.,* 1939, 34, 239–248.
238. Guilford, J. P., and W. S. Zimmerman: *The Guilford-Zimmerman temperament survey manual.* Beverly Hills, Calif.: Sheridan Supply Co., 1949.
239. Guilford, J. P., and W. S. Zimmerman: Fourteen dimensions of temperament. *Psychol. Monogr.,* 1956, 70, no. 10.
240. Guthrie, E. R.: *The psychology of learning.* New York: Harper, 1935.
241. Hall, C. S., and G. Lindzey: *Theories of personality.* New York: Wiley, 1957.
242. Hall, J. F.: The relationship between external stimulation, food deprivation, and activity. *J. comp. physiol. Psychol.,* 1956, 49, 339–341.
243. Hall, J. F.: *Psychology of motivation.* New York: Lippincott, 1961.
244. Hansen, R., and W. Langer: Über Geschmacksveränderungen in der Schwangerschaft. *Klin. Wschr.,* 1935, 14, 1173–1176.
245. Harker, J. E.: The diurnal rhythm of activity of mayfly nymphs. *J. exp. Biol.* 1953, 30, 525–533.
246. Harlow, H. F.: Learning and satiation of response in intrinsically motivated complex puzzle performance by monkeys. *J. comp. physiol. Psychol.,* 1950, 43, 289–294.
247. Harlow, H. F.: Motivation as a factor in the acquisition of new responses. In *Current theory and research in motivation: a symposium.* Lincoln, Nebr.: University of Nebraska Press, 1953.
248. Harlow, H. F.: The nature of love. *Amer. Psychologist,* 1958, 13, 673–685.
249. Harlow, H. F.: Primary affectional patterns in primates. *Amer. J. of Orthopsychiat.,* 1960, 30, 676–684.

250. Harlow, H. F., N. C. Blazek, and G. E. McClearn: Manipulatory motivation in the infant rhesus monkey. *J. comp. physiol. Psychol.*, 1956, 49, 444–448.
251. Harlow, H. F., M. K. Harlow, and D. R. Meyer: Learning motivated by a manipulation drive. *J. exp. Psychol.*, 1950, 40, 228–234.
252. Harlow, H. F., and R. R. Zimmermann: Affectional responses in the infant monkey. *Science*, 1959, 130, 421–432.
253. Hartridge, H.: The importance of taste and smell in nutrition. *J. Physiol.*, 1945, 103, 34–35.
254. Hausmann, M. F.: The behavior of albino rats in choosing food and stimulants. *J. comp. Psychol.*, 1932, 13, 279–309.
255. Hauty, G. T., and R. B. Payne: Methods of mitigation of work decrement. *Project No.* 21-1601-0004, *Report No.* 4. Randolph Field, Tex.: U.S.A.F. School of Aviation Medicine, 1953.
256. Hayes, J. R.: The maintenance of play in young children. *J. comp. physiol. Psychol.*, 1958, 51, 788–794.
257. Hebb, D. O.: Elementary school methods. *Teach. Mag.* (Montreal), 1930, 12, 23–26.
258. Hebb, D. O.: *Organization of behavior.* New York: Wiley, 1949.
259. Hebb, D. O.: The role of neurological ideas in psychology. In D. Krech and G. S. Klein (eds.), *Theoretical models and personality theory.* Durham, N.C.: Duke University Press, 1952.
260. Hebb, D. O.: The problem of consciousness and introspection. In *Brain mechanisms and consciousness.* Springfield, Ill.: Charles C Thomas, 1954.
261. Hebb, D. O.: Drives and the C.N.S. (conceptual nervous system). *Psychol. Rev.*, 1955, 62, 243–254.
262. Hebb, D. O.: *A textbook of psychology.* Philadelphia: Saunders, 1958.
263. Hebb, D. O.: The American revolution. *Amer. Psychologist*, 1960, 15, 735–745.
264. Hebb, D. O., and W. R. Thompson: The social significance of animal studies. In G. Lindzey (ed.), *Handbook of social psychology*, Vol. I. Reading, Mass.: Addison-Wesley, 1954.
265. Hediger, H.: *Studies of the psychology and behavior of captive animals in zoos and circuses.* Trans. by Geoffrey Sircom. New York: Criterion Books, 1955.
266. Heider, Fritz: *Psychology of interpersonal relations.* New York: Wiley, 1958.
267. Heilbrunn, L. V.: *An outline of general physiology* (3d ed.). Philadelphia: Saunders, 1952.
268. Helmstadter, G. C., and D. S. Ellis: Rate of manipulative learning as a function of goal-setting techniques. *J. exp. Psychol.*, 1952, 43, 125–129.
269. Helson, H.: Psychiatric screening of flying personnel: perception and personality—a critique of recent experimental literature. *Project No.* 21-0202-0007, *Report No.* 1. Randolph Field, Tex.: U.S.A.F. School of Aviation Medicine, 1953.
270. Hendricks, S. B.: The clocks of life. *Atlantic Monthly*, 1957, 200, 111–115.
271. Hernández-Peón, Raúl, H. Scherrer, and M. Jouvet: Modification of electric activity of cochlear nucleus during 'attention' in unanesthetized cats. *Science*, 1956, 123, 331–332.

272. Heron, W. T., and E. Peake: Qualitative food deficiency as a drive in a discrimination problem. *J. comp. physiol. Psychol.*, 1949, 42, 143–147.

273. Heron, W. T., and S. Yugend: Basal metabolism and maze learning in rats. *J. genet. Psychol.*, 1936, 48, 471–474.

274. Hersey, R.: *Zest for work.* New York: Harper, 1955.

275. Heyer, A. W., Jr.: Studies in motivation and retention. IV. The influence of dehydration on acquistion and retention of the maze habit. *Comp. Psychol. Monogr.*, 1951, 20, 273–286.

276. Heyns, R. W., and R. Lippitt: Systematic observational techniques. In G. Lindzey (ed.), *Handbook of social psychology*, Vol. 1. Reading, Mass.: Addison-Wesley, 1954.

277. Hickam, J. B., W. H. Cargill, and A. Golden: Cardiovascular reactions to emotional stimuli: effect on cardiac output, A-V oxygen difference, arterial pressure and peripheral resistance. *J. clin. Invest.*, 1948, 27, 290–298.

278. Highet, G.: Life behind the ivy. *Horizon*, September, 1960.

279. Hilgard, E. R.: *Theories of learning.* New York: Appleton-Century-Crofts, 1948.

280. Hilgard, E. R., L. V. Jones, and S. J. Kaplan: Conditioned discrimination as related to anxiety. *J. exp. Psychol.*, 1951, 42, 94–99.

281. Hill, H. E., H. G. Flanary, C. H. Kornetsky, and A. Wikler: Effects of anxiety and morphine on discrimination of intensities of painful stimuli. *J. clin. Invest.*, 1952, 31, 473–480.

282. Hill, W. F.: Activity as an autonomous drive. *J. comp. physiol. Psychol.*, 1956, 49, 15–19.

283. Hill, W. F.: The effect of long confinement on voluntary wheel-running by rats. *J. comp. physiol. Psychol.*, 1958, 51, 770–773.

284. Hill, W. F.: The effect of varying periods of confinement on activity in tilt cages. *J. comp. physiol. Psychol.*, 1958, 51, 570–574.

285. Hill, W. F.: Learning theory and the acquisition of values. *Psychol. Rev.*, 1960, 67, 317–331.

286. Hillman, B., W. S. Hunter, and G. A. Kimble: The effect of drive level on the maze performance of the white rat. *J. comp. physiol. Psychol.*, 1953, 46, 87–89.

287. Himmelweit, H. T.: A comparative study of the level of aspiration of normal and of neurotic persons. *Brit. J. Psychol.*, 1947, 37, 41–59.

288. Hobbes, T.: *Leviathan,* Part I, 1651. New York: Liberal Arts Press, 1958.

289. Hokanson, J. E.: The effects of frustration and anxiety on overt aggression. *J. abnorm. soc. Psychol.*, 1961, 62, 346–351.

290. Hollingworth, H. L.: *Psychology and ethics.* New York: Ronald, 1949.

291. Holmberg, A. R.: The Siriono. A study of the effect of hunger frustration on the culture of a semi-nomadic Bolivian Indian society. Unpublished doctoral dissertation, Yale University, 1946.

292. Holtzman, W. H., and M. E. Bitterman: Psychiatric screening of flying personnel. VI. Anxiety and reactions to stress. *Project No.* 21-37-002, *Report No.* 6. Randolph Field, Tex.: U.S.A.F. School of Aviation Medicine, 1952.

293. Hoppe, F.: Erfolg und Misserfolg. *Psychol. Forsch.*, 1930, 14, 1–62.

294. Horney, K.: *Self-analysis.* New York: Norton, 1942.

295. Hovland, C. I., and R. R. Sears: Experiments on motor conflict. I. Types of conflict and their mode of resolution. *J. exp. Psychol.*, 1938, 23, 477–493.
296. Howes, D. H., and R. L. Solomon: A note on McGinnies' "Emotionality and perceptual defense." *Psychol. Rev.*, 1950, 57, 229–234.
297. Hubbard, W. R.: Secondary reinforcement of a simple discrimination in human beings. *J. exp. Psychol.*, 1951, 41, 233–241.
298. Hull, C. L.: The rat's speed-of-locomotion gradient in the approach to food. *J. comp. Psychol.*, 1934, 17, 393–422.
299. Hull, C. L.: *Principles of behavior.* New York: Appleton-Century-Crofts, 1943.
300. Hull, C. L.: Stimulus intensity dynamism (V) and stimulus generalization. *Psychol. Rev.*, 1949, 56, 67–76.
301. Hull, C. L.: *A behavior system: an introduction to behavior theory concerning the individual organism.* New Haven, Conn.: Yale University Press, 1952.
302. Humphreys, L. G.: Characteristics of type concepts with special reference to Sheldon's typology. *Psychol. Bull.*, 1957, 54, 218–228.
303. Hutt, P. J.: Rate of bar pressing as a function of quality and quantity of food reward. *J. comp. physiol. Psychol.*, 1954, 47, 235–239.
304. Igel, G. J., and A. D. Calvin: The development of affectional responses in infant dogs. *J. comp. physiol. Psychol.*, 1960, 53, 302–305.
305. Irwin, F. W.: Stated expectations as functions of probability and desirability of outcomes. *J. Pers.*, 1953, 21, 329–335.
306. Irwin, O. C.: The amount and nature of activities of newborn infants under constant external stimulating conditions during the first ten days of life. *Genet. Psychol. Monogr.*, 1930, 8, 1–92.
307. Irwin, O. C.: The distribution of the amount of mobility in young infants between two nursing periods. *J. comp. Psychol.*, 1932, 14, 429–445.
308. James, W. T.: Morphologic form and its relation to behavior. In C. R. Stockard et al., *Genetic and endocrine basis for differences in form and behavior.* Philadelphia: Wistar Institute Press, 1941.
309. James, W. T.: Social organization among dogs of different temperaments, terriers and beagles, reared together. *J. comp. physiol. Psychol.*, 1951, 44, 71–77.
310. James, W. T.: Social facilitation of eating behavior in puppies after satiation. *J. comp. physiol. Psychol.*, 1953, 46, 427–428.
311. Jarrard, L. E.: The role of visual cues in the performance of ergographic work. *J. exp. Psychol.*, 1960, 60, 57–63.
312. Jarvik, M. E.: Probability learning and a negative recency effect in the serial anticipation of alternative symbols. *J. exp. Psychol.*, 1951, 41, 291–297.
313. Jasper, H. H.: Electroencephalography. In W. Penfield and T. C. Erickson (eds.), *Epilepsy and cerebral localization.* Springfield, Ill.: Charles C Thomas, 1941.
314. Jenkin, N.: Affective processes in perception. *Psychol. Bull.*, 1957, 54, 100–127.
315. Jenkins, T. N., L. H. Warner, and C. J. Warden: Standard apparatus for the study of animal motivation. *J. comp. Psychol.*, 1926, 6, 361–382.
316. Jenkins, W. O., and J. C. Stanley, Jr.: Partial reinforcement: a review and critique. *Psychol. Bull.*, 1950, 47, 193–234.

317. Jersild, A. T.: Emotional development. In L. Carmichael (ed.), *Manual of child psychology.* New York: Wiley, 1946.
318. Jersild, A. T.: *Child psychology* (4th ed.). Englewood Cliffs, N.J.: Prentice-Hall, 1954.
319. Jersild, A. T., and F. B. Holmes: Children's fears. *Child Develpm. Monogr.,* 1935, 20, ix–358.
320. Jessor, R., and J. Readio: The influence of the value of an event upon the expectancy of its occurrence. *J. gen. Psychol.,* 1957, 56, 219–228.
321. Johnson, E. E.: The role of motivational strength in latent learning. *J. comp. physiol. Psychol.,* 1952, 45, 526–530.
322. Jones, A.: The efficiency of utilization of visual information and the effects of stress. *J. exp. Psychol.,* 1959, 58, 428–432.
323. Jost, H., and L. W. Sontag: The genetic factor in autonomic nervous system function. *Psychosom. Med.,* 1944, 6, 308–310.
324. Judd, D. B.: Basic correlates of the visual stimulus. In S. S. Stevens (ed.), *Handbook of experimental psychology.* New York: Wiley, 1951.
325. Jurgensen, C. E.: What job applicants look for in a company. *Personnel Psychol.,* 1948, 4, 433–445.
326. Kagan, J., and M. Berkun: The reward value of running activity. *J. comp. physiol. Psychol.,* 1954, 47, 108.
327. Karsten, A.: Psychische Sättigung. *Psychol. Forsch.,* 1928, 10, 142–254.
328. Kausler, D. H., and E. P. Trapp: Achievement motivation and goal-setting behavior on a learning task. *J. exp. Psychol.,* 1958, 55, 575–578.
329. Kessen, W.: Response strength as a function of conditioned stimulus intensity. *Amer. Psychologist,* 1952, 7, 270–271.
330. Keys, A., J. Brozek, A. Henschel, O. Mickelsen, and H. L. Taylor: *The biology of human starvation,* Vols. I and II, Minneapolis, Minn.: University of Minnesota Press, 1950.
331. Kierkegaard, S.: *The concept of dread.* Trans. by Walter Lowrie. Princeton, N.J.: Princeton University Press, 1944. (Originally published in Danish, 1844.)
332. Kimble, G. A.: Shock intensity and avoidance learning. *J. comp. physiol. Psychol.,* 1955, 48, 281–284.
333. Kimble, G. A.: *Hilgard and Marquis' conditioning and learning* (rev. ed.). New York: Appleton-Century-Crofts, 1961.
334. Kinder, E. F.: Development of personality characteristics. *Amer. Psychologist,* 1947, 2, 267. (Abstract)
335. King, M. S., G. A. Kimble, J. Gorman, and R. A. King: Replication report: two failures to reproduce effects of anxiety on eyelid conditioning. *J. exp. Psychol.,* 1961, 62, 532–533.
336. Klein, G. S.: Need and regulation. In *Nebraska symposium on motivation.* Lincoln, Nebr.: University of Nebraska Press, 1954.
337. Kleitman, N.: *Sleep and wakefulness.* Chicago: University of Chicago Press, 1939.
338. Kleitman, N.: Sleep, wakefulness, and consciousness. *Psychol. Bull.,* 1957, 54, 354–359.
339. Kluckhohn, C.: Values and value-orientations in the theory of action. In T. Parsons and E. A. Shils (eds.), *Toward a general theory of action.* Cambridge, Mass.: Harvard University Press, 1951.
340. Koch, H. L.: The influence of some affective factors upon recall. *J. gen. Psychol.,* 1930, 4, 171–190.

341. Koch, S. (ed.): *Psychology: a study of a science*, Vol. III. New York: McGraw-Hill, 1959.

342. Koffka, K.: *Principles of gestalt psychology*. New York: Harcourt, Brace, 1935.

343. Krause, M. S.: The measurement of transitory anxiety. *Psychol. Rev.*, 1961, 68, 178–189.

344. Krech, D., and R. S. Crutchfield: *Elements of psychology*. New York: Knopf, 1958.

345. Kretschmer, E.: *Physique and character*. London: Routledge, 1925.

346. Kroeber, A. L. (ed.): *Anthropology today: an encyclopedic inventory*. Chicago: University of Chicago Press, 1953.

347. Krueger, W. C. F.: The influence of amount limits and time limits upon rate of work. *J. appl. Psychol.*, 1937, 21, 113–118.

348. Kruse, M.: Food-satiation curves for maze-bright and maze-dull rats. *J. comp. Psychol.*, 1941, 31, 13–21.

349. Külpe, O.: Versuche über Abstraktion, Ber. I. *Kongr. exp. Psychol.*, 1904, 54–68.

350. Kvasov, D. G.: [The reflex organization of reception and the proprio-muscular apparatus (of the sense organs)]. In L. G. Voronin et al. (eds.), *Orientirovochny refleksi orientirovochno-issledovatel'skaia deiatel-nost'* [The orienting reflex and exploratory behavior]. Moscow: Acad. Pedag. Sci., 1958.

351. Lacey, J. I.: Individual differences in somatic response patterns. *J. comp. physiol. Psychol.*, 1950, 43, 338–350.

352. Lacey, J. I., Dorothy E. Bateman, and Ruth Van Lehn: Autonomic response specificity: an experimental study. *Psychosom. Med.*, 1953, 15, 8–21.

353. Lacey, J. I., and B. C. Lacey: Verification and extension of the principle of autonomic response-stereotypy. *Amer. J. Psychol.*, 1958, 71, 50–73.

354. Lacey, J. I., and Ruth Van Lehn: Differential emphasis in somatic response to stress: an experimental study. *Psychosom. Med.*, 1952, 14, 71–81.

355. Lansing, R. W., E. Schwartz, and D. B. Lindsley: Reaction time and EEG activation under alerted and nonalerted conditions. *J. exp. Psychol.*, 1959, 58, 1–7.

356. Lazarus, R. S., J. Deese, and Sonia F. Osler: The effects of psychological stress upon performance. *Psychol. Bull.*, 1952, 49, 293–317.

357. Lazarus, R. S., and C. W. Eriksen: The effects of failure stress upon skilled performance. *J. exp. Psychol.*, 1952, 43, 100–105.

358. Lazarus, R. S., and R. A. McCleary: Autonomic discrimination without awareness: a study of subception. *Psychol. Rev.*, 1951, 58, 113–122.

359. Lazarus, R. S., H. Yousem, and D. Arenberg: Hunger and perception. *J. Pers.*, 1953, 21, 312–328.

360. Leary, T.: *Interpersonal diagnosis of personality*. New York: Ronald, 1957.

361. Leeper, R. W.: A motivational theory of emotion to replace 'Emotion as a disorganized response.' *Psychol. Rev.*, 1948, 55, 5–21.

362. Lehmann, A.: *Die Hauptgesetze des menschlichen Gefühlslebens* (2d ed.). Leipzig: O. R. Raisland, 1914.

363. Leuba, C., and C. Lucas: The effects of attitudes on descriptions of pictures. *J. exp. Psychol.*, 1945, 35, 517–524.

364. Levine, R., I. Chein, and G. Murphy: The relation of the intensity of a need to the amount of perceptual distortion: a preliminary report. *J. Psychol.*, 1942, 13, 283–293.

365. Lewin, K.: *A dynamic theory of personality.* New York: McGraw-Hill, 1935.

366. Lewin, K.: *Principles of topological psychology.* New York: McGraw-Hill, 1936.

367. Lewin, K.: Behavior and development as a function of the total situation. In D. Cartwright (ed.), *Field theory in social science.* New York: Harper, 1951.

368. Lewin, K., T. Dembo, L. Festinger, and P. S. Sears: Level of aspiration. In J. McV. Hunt (ed.), *Personality and the behavior disorders,* Vol. I. New York: Ronald, 1944.

369. Lewinsohn, P. M.: Some individual differences in physiological reactivity to stress. *J. comp. physiol. Psychol.*, 1956, 49, 271–277.

370. Lewis, D. J.: Partial reinforcement: a selective review of the literature since 1950. *Psychol. Bull.*, 1960, 57, 1–28.

371. Lindsley, D. B.: A study of performance under speed stress. OSRD, 1945, Publ. Bldg. No. 1838. Washington: U.S. Dept. Commerce, 1946.

372. Lindsley, D. B.: Emotion. In S. S. Stevens (ed.), *Handbook of experimental psychology.* New York: Wiley, 1951, 473–516.

373. Lindsley, D. B.: Psychological phenomena and the electroencephalogram. *EEG clin. Neurophysiol.*, 1952, 4, 443–456.

374. Lindsley, D. B.: Psychophysiology and motivation. In *Nebraska symposium on motivation.* Lincoln, Nebr.: University of Nebraska Press, 1957.

375. Linton, R. (ed.): *Acculturation in seven American Indian tribes.* New York: Appleton-Century-Crofts, 1940.

376. Little, S. W., and L. D. Cohen: Goal setting behavior of asthmatic children and of their mothers for them. *J. Pers.*, 1951, 19, 376–389.

377. Logan, F. A.: *Incentive.* New Haven, Conn.: Yale University Press, 1960.

378. Lorge, I., J. Eisenson, and B. Epstein: Further experiments in the strength of connections where the connection is punished or rewarded or neither punished nor rewarded. *J. exp. Psychol.*, 1934, 17, 412–423.

379. Lorge, I., and E. L. Thorndike: The comparative strengthening of a connection by one or more occurrences of it in cases where the connection was punished and was neither punished nor rewarded. *J. exp. Psychol.*, 1933, 16, 374–382.

380. Lovell, C.: A study of the factor structure of thirteen personality variables. *Educ. Psychol. Meas.*, 1945, 5, 335–350.

381. Lovell, G. D.: Physiological and motor responses to a regularly recurring sound. *Psychol. Bull.*, 1941, 38, 715. (Abstract)

382. Lowe, C. M.: The self-concept: fact or artifact? *Psychol. Bull.*, 1961, 58, 325–336.

383. Lowell, E. L.: The effect of need for achievement on learning and speed of performance. *J. Psychol.*, 1952, 33, 31–40.

384. Lucas, J. D.: The interactive effects of anxiety, failure, and intraserial duplication. *Amer. J. Psychol.*, 1952, 65, 59–66.

385. MacCorquodale, K., and P. E. Meehl: *Edward C. Tolman.* In W. K. Estes et al., *Modern learning theory.* New York: Appleton-Century-Crofts, 1954.

386. MacDuff, M. M.: The effect on retention of varying degrees of motivation during learning in rats. *J. comp. Psychol.*, 1946, 39, 207–240.
387. Mackworth, N. H.: Researches on the measurement of human performance. *Med. Res. Council, Special Report Ser. No.* 268. London: H. M. Stationery Office, 1950.
388. Madsen, K. B.: *Theories of Motivation.* Copenhagen: Munksgaard, 1959.
389. Maher, W. B., and D. D. Wickens: Effect of differenital quantity of reward on acquisition and performance of a maze habit. *J. comp. physiol. Psychol.*, 1954, 47, 44–46.
390. Mahl, G. F.: Effect of chronic fear on the gastric secretion of HCl in dogs. *Psychosom. Med.*, 1949, 11, 30–44.
391. Maier, N. R. F.: *Frustration: the study of behavior without a goal.* New York: McGraw-Hill, 1949.
392. Maier, N. R. F., and N. M. Glaser: *Studies of abnormal behavior in the rat. II. A comparison of some convulsion-producing situations.* Baltimore: Johns Hopkins Press, 1940.
393. Malmo, R. B.: Measurement of drive: an unsolved problem in psychology. In *Nebraska symposium on motivation.* Lincoln, Nebr.: University of Nebraska Press, 1958.
394. Malmo, R. B.: Activation: a neuropsychological dimension. *Psychol. Rev.*, 1959, 66, 367–386.
395. Malmo, R. B., T. J. Boag, and A. A. Smith: Physiological study of personal interaction. *Psychosom. Med.*, 1957, 19, 105–119.
396. Malmo, R. B., H. Wallerstein, and C. Shagass: Headache proneness and mechanisms of motor conflict in psychiatric patients. *J. Pers.*, 1953, 22, 163–187.
397. Mandler, G., J. M. Mandler, I. Kremen, and R. D. Sholiton: The response to threat: relations among verbal and physiological indices. *Psychol. Monogr.*, 1961, 75, no. 9.
398. Manzer, C. W.: The effect of knowledge of output on muscular work. *J. exp. Psychol.*, 1935, 18, 80–90.
399. Marks, R. W.: The effect of probability, desirability and "privilege" on the stated expectations of children. *J. Pers.*, 1951, 19, 332–351.
400. Martin, B.: The assessment of anxiety by physiological behavioral measures. *Psychol. Bull.*, 1961, 58, 234–255.
401. Masling, J.: The influence of situational and interpersonal variables in projective testing. *Psychol. Bull.*, 1960, 57, 65–85.
402. Maslow, A. H.: Conflict, frustration, and the theory of threat. *J. abnorm. soc. Psychol.*, 1943, 38, 81–86.
403. Maslow, A. H.: The expressive component of behavior. In H. Brand (ed.), *The study of personality: a book of readings.* New York: Wiley, 1954, pp. 363–376.
404. Maslow, A. H.: *Motivation and personality.* New York: Harper, 1954.
405. Mason, W. A., H. F. Harlow, and R. R. Rueping: The development of manipulatory responsiveness in the infant rhesus monkey. *J. comp. physiol. Psychol.*, 1959, 52, 555–558.
406. May, R.: *The meaning of anxiety.* New York: Ronald, 1950.
407. May, R.: The existential approach. In S. Arieti (ed.), *American handbook of psychiatry*, Vol. II. New York: Basic Books, 1959, chap. 66.
408. McCleary, R. A.: The nature of the galvanic skin response. *Psychol. Bull.*, 1950, 47, 97–117.

4)9. McClelland, D. C.: Some social consequences of achievement motivation. In *Nebraska symposium on motivation*. Lincoln, Nebr.: University of Nebraska Press, 1955.

410. McClelland, D. C.: Methods of measuring human motivation. In J. W. Atkinson (ed.), *Motives in fantasy, action, and society*. Princeton, N.J.: Van Nostrand, 1958.

411. McClelland, D. C.: *The achieving society*. Princeton, N.J.: Van Nostrand, 1961.

412. McClelland, D. C., and J. W. Atkinson: The projective expression of needs. I. The effects of different intensities of the hunger drive on perception. *J. Psychol.*, 1948, 25, 205–222.

413. McClelland, D. C., J. W. Atkinson, R. A. Clark, and E. L. Lowell: *The achievement motive*. New York: Appleton-Century-Crofts, 1953.

414. McCormick, E. J.: *Human engineering*. New York: McGraw-Hill, 1957.

415. McDougall, W.: *An introduction to social psychology* (rev. ed.). Boston: Bruce Humphries, 1926.

416. McDougall, W.: Pleasure, pain, and conation. *Brit. J. Psychol.*, 1927, 17, 171–180.

417. McFarland, R. A., A. H. Holway, and L. M. Hurvich: *Studies of visual fatigue*. Cambridge, Mass.: Harvard Graduate School of Business Administration, 1942.

418. McGinnies, E.: Emotionality and perceptual defense. *Psychol. Rev.*, 1949, 56, 244–251.

419. Mednick, S. A., and J. L. Freedman: Stimulus generalization. *Psychol. Bull.*, 1960, 57, 169–200.

420. Meltzer, H.: Individual differences in forgetting pleasant and unpleasant experiences. *J. educ. Psychol.*, 1930, 21, 399–409.

421. Meltzer, H.: Students' adjustments in anger. *J. soc. Psychol.*, 1933, 4, 285–309.

422. Meryman, J. J.: Magnitude of startle response as a function of hunger and fear. Unpublished master's thesis, State University of Iowa, 1952.

423. Meyer, D. R.: Food deprivation and discrimination reversal learning by monkeys. *J. exp. Psychol.*, 1951, 41, 10–16.

424. Miles, R. C.: Discrimination in the squirrel monkey as a function of deprivation and problem difficulty. *J. exp. Psychol.*, 1959, 57, 15–19.

425. Miller, D. R.: Responses of psychiatric patients to threat of failure. *J. abnorm. soc. Psychol.*, 1951, 46, 378–387.

426. Miller, D. R., and G. E. Swanson, with the collaboration of W. Allinsmith et al.: *Inner conflict and defense*. New York: Holt, 1960.

427. Miller, N. E.: Studies of fear as an acquirable drive. I. Fear as motivation and fear-reduction as reinforcement in the learning of new responses. *J. exp. Psychol.*, 1948, 38, 89–101.

428. Miller, N. E.: Theory and experiment relating psychoanalytic displacement to stimulus-response generalization. *J. abnorm. soc. Psychol.*, 1948, 43, 155–178.

429. Miller, N. E.: Comments on multiple process conceptions of learning. *Psychol. Rev.*, 1951, 58, 375–381.

430. Miller, N. E.: Learnable drives and rewards. In S. S. Stevens (ed.), *Handbook of experimental psychology*. New York: Wiley, 1951.

431. Mittelmann, B., H. G. Wolff, and M. P. Scharf: Emotions and gastroduodenal function: experimental studies on patients with gastritis, duodenitis and peptic ulcer. *Psychosom. Med.*, 1942, 4, 5–61.

432. Montgomery, K. C.: A test of two explanations of spontaneous alternation. *J. comp. physiol. Psychol.*, 1952, 45, 287–293.
433. Montgomery, K. C.: The effect of the hunger and thirst drives upon exploratory behavior. *J. comp. physiol. Psychol.*, 1953, 46, 315–319.
434. Montgomery, K. C.: Exploratory behavior as a function of "similarity" of stimulus situations. *J. comp. physiol. Psychol.*, 1953, 46, 129–133.
435. Montgomery, K. C., and J. A. Monkman: Relation between fear and exploratory behavior. *J. comp. physiol. Psychol.*, 1955, 48, 132–136.
436. Morey, R. H.: Swimming speed of rats as a function of the presence or absence of sounds. *J. comp. Psychol.*, 1934, 17, 329–354.
437. Morgan, C. T.: *Physiological psychology* (1st ed.). New York: McGraw-Hill, 1943.
438. Morgan, C. T.: Physiological mechanisms of motivation. In *Nebraska symposium on motivation*. Lincoln, Nebr.: University of Nebraska Press, 1957.
439. Morgan, C. T.: Physiological theory of drive. In S. Koch (ed.), *Psychology: a study of a science*, Vol. I. New York: McGraw-Hill, 1959.
440. Morgan, C. T., and E. Stellar: *Physiological psychology*. New York: McGraw-Hill, 1950.
441. Morgan, J. J. B.: The overcoming of distractions and other resistances. *Arch. Psychol., N.Y.*, 1916, no. 35, 1–84.
442. Morrill, C. S.: Teaching machines: a review. *Psychol. Bull.*, 1961, 58, 363–375.
443. Moss, F. A.: Study of animal drives. *J. exp. Psychol.*, 1924, 7, 165–185.
444. Mowrer, O. H.: A stimulus-response analysis of anxiety and its role as a reinforcing agent. *Psychol. Rev.*, 1939, 46, 553–565.
445. Mowrer, O. H.: *Learning theory and personality dynamics*. New York: Ronald, 1950.
446. Mowrer, O. H.: *Learning theory and behavior*. New York: Wiley, 1960.
447. Muenzinger, K. F.: Motivation in learning. I. Electric shock for correct responses in the visual discrimination habit. *J. comp. Psychol.*, 1934, 17, 267–277.
448. Muenzinger, K. F., and F. M. Fletcher: Motivation in learning. VII. The effect of an enforced delay at the point of choice in the visual discrimination habit. *J. comp. Psychol.*, 1937, 23, 383–392.
449. Muenzinger, K. F., and H. Newcomb: Motivation in learning. V. The relative effectiveness of jumping a gap and crossing an electric grid in a visual discrimination habit. *J. comp. Psychol.*, 1936, 21, 95–104.
450. Muenzinger, K. F., and F. C. Waltz: An analysis of the electrical stimulus producing a shock. *J. comp. Psychol.*, 1932, 13, 157–171.
451. Muenzinger, K. F., and A. Wood: Motivation in learning. IV. The function of punishment as determined by its temporal relation to the act choice in the visual discrimination habit. *J. comp. Psychol.*, 1935, 20, 95–106.
452. Mullahy, P.: A philosophy of personality. In H. Brand (ed.), *The study of personality: a book of readings*. New York: Wiley, 1954.
453. Munn, N. L.: *Handbook of psychological research on the rat*. Boston: Houghton Mifflin, 1950.
454. Murdock, G. P.: How culture changes. In J. E. Nordskog (ed.), *Social Change*. New York: McGraw-Hill, 1960.
455. Murphy, G.: *Personality: a biosocial approach to origins and structures*. New York: Harper, 1947.

456. Murphy, G.: Social motivation. In G. Lindzey (ed.), *Handbook of social psychology*, Vol. II. Reading, Mass.: Addison-Wesley, 1954.

457. Murray, H. A.: *Explorations in personality*. New York: Oxford Press, 1938.

458. Murray, H. A.: Toward a classification of interaction. In T. Parsons and E. A. Shils (eds.), *Toward a general theory of action*. Cambridge, Mass.: Harvard University Press, 1951.

459. Murray, H. A.: Drive, time, strategy, measurement, and our way of life. In G. Lindzey (ed.), *Assessment of human motives*. New York: Holt, 1958.

460. Murstein, B. I.: The projection of hostility on the Rorschach and as a result of ego-threat. *J. proj. Tech.*, 1956, 20, 418–428.

461. Murstein, B. I.: Studies in projection: a critique. *J. proj. Tech.*, 1957, 21, 129–136.

462. Murstein, B. I., and R. S. Pryer: The concept of projection: a review. *Psychol. Bull.*, 1959, 56, 353–374.

463. Myers, J. L.: Secondary reinforcement: a review of recent experimentation. *Psychol. Bull.*, 1958, 55, 284–301.

464. Nissen, H. W.: A study of exploratory behavior in the white rat by means of the obstruction method. *J. genet. Psychol.*, 1930, 37, 361–376.

465. Nissen, H. W.: Phylogenetic comparison. In S. S. Stevens (ed.), *Handbook of experimental psychology*. New York: Wiley, 1951.

466. Nissen, H. W.: The nature of the drive as innate determinant of behavioral organization. In *Nebraska Symposium on Motivation*. Lincoln, Nebr.: University of Nebraska Press, 1954.

467. Novikoff, A. B.: The concept of integrative levels and biology. *Science*, 1945, 101, 209–215.

468. Nowlis, V.: On the use of drugs in the analysis of complex human behavior with emphasis on the study of mood. In *Current trends in psychology*. Pittsburgh: University of Pittsburgh Press, 1956.

469. O'Kelly, L. I.: *Introduction to psychopathology*. Englewood Cliffs, N.J.: Prentice-Hall, 1949.

470. O'Kelly, L. I., and A. W. Heyer, Jr.: Studies in motivation and retention. V. The influence of need reduction on retention of a maze habit. *Comp. Psychol. Monogr.*, 1951, 20, 287–301.

471. Olds, J.: Physiological mechanisms of reward. In *Nebraska symposium on motivation*. Lincoln, Nebr.: University of Nebraska Press, 1955.

472. Olds, J., and P. Milner: Positive reinforcement produced by electrical stimulation of septal area and other regions of rat brain. *J. comp. physiol. Psychol.*, 1954, 47, 419–427.

473. Osgood, C. E.: *Method and theory in experimental psychology*. New York: Oxford Press, 1953.

474. Osgood, C. E.: Motivational dynamics of language behavior. In *Nebraska symposium on motivation*. Lincoln, Nebr.: University of Nebraska Press, 1957.

475. OSS Assessment Staff: *Assessment of men*. New York: Holt, 1948.

476. Packard, V. O.: *The hidden persuaders*. New York: McKay, 1957.

477. Parrack, H. O., D. H. Eldredge, and H. F. Koster: Physiological effects of intense sound. *Aero. Med.*, Lab. Rept. no. MC REXD-695-71B. Mem. Rept. Aero. Med. Lab. Wright-Patterson Air Force Base: U.S.A.F. Air Materiel Command, 1948.

478. Parrish, J., and D. Rethlingshafer: A study of the need to achieve in college achievers and non-achievers. *J. gen. Psychol.*, 1954, 50, 209–226.
479. Pascal, G. R.: The effect of relaxation upon recall. *Amer. J. Psychol.*, 1949, 62, 32–47.
480. Passey, G. E.: The influence of intensity of unconditioned stimulus upon acquisition of a conditioned response. *J. exp. Psychol.*, 1948, 38, 420–428.
481. Pavlov, I. P.: *Conditioned reflexes* Trans. by G. V. Anrep. London: Oxford Press, 1927.
482. Peters, R. S.: *The concept of motivation.* New York: Humanities Press, 1958.
483. Pfaffmann, C.: Taste and smell. In S. S. Stevens (ed.), *Handbook of experimental psychology.* New York: Wiley, 1951.
484. Pfaffmann, C.: The pleasures of sensation. *Psychol. Rev.*, 1960, 67, 253–268.
485. Pfaffmann, C., and J. K. Bare: Gustatory nerve discharges in normal and adrenalectomized rats. *J. comp. physiol. Psychol.*, 1950, 43, 320–324.
486. Philpott, S. J. F.: Fluctuation in human output. *Brit. J. Psychol. Monogr. Suppl.*, 1932, 6, no. 17.
487. Piaget, J.: *The origins of intelligence in children.* New York: International Universities Press, 1952.
488. Pintner, R., and J. Lev: Worries of school children. *J. genet. Psychol.*, 1940, 56, 67–76.
489. Plutchik, R.: The effects of high intensity intermittent sound on performance, feeling, and physiology. *Psychol. Bull.*, 1959, 56, 133–151.
490. Postman, L.: The history and present status of the law of effect. *Psychol. Bull.*, 1947, 44, 489–563.
491. Postman, L., J. S. Bruner, and E. McGinnies: Personal values as selective factors in perception. *J. abnorm. soc. Psychol.*, 1948, 43, 142–154.
492. Postman, L., and B. H. Schneider: Personal values, visual recognition, and recall. *Psychol. Rev.*, 1951, 58, 271–284.
493. Prentice, W. C. H.: Some cognitive aspects of motivation. *Amer. Psychologist*, 1961, 16, 503–511.
494. Pressey, S. L.: Development and appraisal of devices providing immediate automatic scoring of objective tests and concomitant self-instruction. *J. Psychol.*, 1950, 29, 417–447.
495. Pronko, N. H., and W. R. Leith: Behavior under stress: a study of its disintegration. *Psychol. Repts.*, 1956, 2, 205–222.
496. Rapaport, D.: The structure of psychoanalytic theory: a systematizing attempt. In S. Koch (ed.), *Psychology: a study of a science*, Vol. III. New York: McGraw-Hill, 1959.
497. Raush, H. L., A. T. Dittmann, and T. J. Taylor: The interpersonal behavior of children in residential treatment. *J. abnorm. soc. Psychol.*, 1959, 58, 9–26.
498. Reed, J. D.: Spontaneous activity of animals. *Psychol. Bull.*, 1947, 44, 393–412.
499. Rethlingshafer, D.: Comparison of normal and feebleminded children with college adults in their tendency-to-continue interrupted activities. *J. comp. physiol. Psychol.*, 1941, 32, 205–216.
500. Rethlingshafer, D.: Relationship of tests of persistence to other measures of continuance of activities. *J. abnorm. soc. Psychol.*, 1942, 37, 71–82.

501. Rethlingshafer, D.: Experimental evidence for functional autonomy of motives. *Psychol. Rev.*, 1943, 50, 397–407.
502. Rethlingshafer, D.: Effect of various concomitant activities upon the maintenance of a set. *J. exp. Psychol.*, 1945, 35, 312–320.
503. Rethlingshafer, D., A. Eschenbach, and J. T. Stone: Combined drives in learning. *J. exp. Psychol.*, 1951, 41, 226–231.
504. Rethlingshafer, D., and M. Hicks: The role of internal cues in learning differential responses to the same external stimulus. Unpublished study, 1961.
505. Reymert, M. L. (ed.): *Feelings and emotions. The Mooseheart symposium.* New York: McGraw-Hill, 1950.
506. Reynolds, B.: The acquisition of a black-white discrimination habit under two levels of reinforcement. *J. exp. Psychol.*, 1949, 39, 760–769.
507. Reynolds, B.: Acquisition of a simple spatial discrimination as a function of the amount of reinforcement. *J. exp. Psychol.*, 1950, 40, 152–160.
508. Richardson, L. F.: Dr. S. J. F. Philpott's wave theory. *Brit. J. Psychol.*, 1952, 43, 169–176.
509. Richter, C. P.: Biological foundation of personality differences. *Amer. J. Orthopsychiat.*, 1932, 2, 345–354.
510. Richter, C. P.: The effect of early gonadectomy on the gross body activity of rats. *Endocrinology*, 1933, 17, 445–450.
511. Richter, C. P.: Salt taste threshold of normal and adrenalectomized rats. *Endocrinology*, 1939, 24, 367–371.
512. Richter, C. P.: Physiological psychology. *Annu. Rev. Physiol.*, 1942, 4, 561–574.
513. Richter, C. P.: Total self regulatory functions in animals and human beings. *Harvey Lect.*, 1942–1943, 38, 63–103.
514. Richter, C. P.: Biology of drives. *J. comp. physiol. Psychol.*, 1947, 40, 129–134.
515. Richter, C. P.: Taste and solubility of toxic compounds in poisoning of rats and man. *J. comp. physiol. Psychol.*, 1950, 43, 358–374.
516. Richter, C. P., and J. F. Eckert: Mineral appetite of parathyroidectomized rats. *Amer. J. med. Sci.*, 1939, 198, 9–16.
517. Richter, C. P., and M. Hines: Increased spontaneous activity produced in monkeys by brain lesions. *Brain*, 1938, 61, 1–16.
518. Roberts, E. B.: Tests to determine objectively the effectiveness of an industrial relations program. *Office Manag. Series, Americ. Manag. Assoc.*, 1938, no. 84, 32–37.
519. Rogers, C. R.: *Client-centered therapy: its current practice, implications, and theory.* Boston: Houghton Mifflin, 1951.
520. Rogers, C. R.: Perceptual reorganization in client-centered therapy. In R. R. Blake and G. V. Ramsey (eds.), *Perception: an approach to personality.* New York: Ronald, 1951.
521. Rogers, O. E., W. B. Webb, and T. J. Gallagher: Effect on extinction of restricting information in verbal conditioning. *J. exp. Psychol.*, 1959, 57, 219–223.
522. Rosenzweig, S.: An outline of frustration theory. In J. McV. Hunt (ed.), *Personality and the behavior disorders*, Vol. I. New York: Ronald, 1944, 379–388.
523. Ross, C. C.. The influence upon achievement of a knowledge of progress. *J. educ. Psychol.*, 1933, 24, 609–619.

524. Ross, S., and P. D. Bricker: The effect of an amount-set on a repetitive motor task. *J. exp. Psychol.*, 1951, 42, 39–43.
525. Rubinstein, I.: Some factors in probability matching. *J. exp. Psychol.*, 1959, 57, 413–416.
526. Rundquist, E. A.: Inheritance of spontaneous activity in rats. *J. comp. Psychol.*, 1933, 16, 415–438.
527. Rundquist, E. A., and C. J. Bellis: Respiratory metabolism of active and inactive rats. *Amer. J. Physiol.*, 1933, 106, 670–675.
528. Runquist, W. N., and L. E. Ross: The relation between physiological measures of emotionality and performance in eyelid conditioning. *J. exp. Psychol.*, 1959, 57, 329–332.
529. Runquist, W. N., and K. W. Spence: Performance in eyelid conditioning related to changes in muscular tension and physiological measures of emotionality. *J. exp. Psychol.*, 1959, 58, 417–422.
530. Saltz, E., and A. J. Hoehn: A test of the Taylor-Spence theory of anxiety. *J. abnorm. soc. Psychol.*, 1957, 54, 114–117.
531. Saltzman, I. J.: Maze learning in the absence of primary reinforcement: a study of secondary reinforcement. *J. comp. physiol. Psychol.*, 1949, 42, 161–173.
532. Sanford, R. N.: The effects of abstinence from food upon imaginal processes: a preliminary experiment. *J. Psychol.*, 1936, 2, 129–136.
533. Sanford, R. N.: The effects of abstinence from food upon imaginal processes: a further experiment. *J. Psychol.*, 1937, 3, 145–159.
534. Sarason, I. G.: Empirical findings and theoretical problems in the use of anxiety scales. *Psychol. Bull.*, 1960, 57, 403–415.
535. Sarason, S. B., K. S. Davidson, F. F. Lighthall, and R. R. Waite: A test anxiety scale for children. *Child Develpm.*, 1958, 29, 105–113.
536. Sarason, S. B., K. S. Davidson, F. F. Lighthall, R. R. Waite, and B. K. Ruebush: *Anxiety in elementary school children.* New York: Wiley, 1960.
537. Sargent, S. S.: Reaction to frustration—a critique and hypothesis. *Psychol. Rev.*, 1948, 55, 108–114.
538. Schachter, J.: Pain, fear and anger in hypertensives and normotensives. *Psychosom. Med.*, 1957, 19, 17–29.
539. Schlosberg, H.: The description of facial expressions in terms of two dimensions. *J. exp. Psychol.*, 1952, 44, 229–237.
540. Schlosberg, H.: Three dimensions of emotion. *Psychol. Rev.*, 1954, 61, 81–88.
541. Schnore, M. M.: Individual patterns of physiological activity as a function of task differences and degree of arousal. *J. exp. Psychol.*, 1959, 58, 117–128.
542. Schroder, H. M., and D. E. Hunt: Failure-avoidance in situational interpretation and problem solving. *Psychol. Monogr.*, 1957, 71, no. 3 (Whole no. 432).
543. Schutz, W. C.: *FIRO: a three-dimensional theory of interpersonal behavior.* New York: Holt, 1958.
544. Scott, J. P.: Comparative social psychology. In R. H. Waters, D. A. Rethlingshafer, and W. E. Caldwell (eds.), *Principles of comparative psychology.* New York: McGraw-Hill, 1960.
545. Sears, P. S.: Level of aspiration in relation to some variables of personality: clinical studies. *J. soc. Psychol.*, 1941, 14, 311–336.

546. Sears, R. R.: Success and failure. In Q. McNemar and M. A. Merrill (eds.), *Studies in personality*. New York: McGraw-Hill, 1942, chap. 13.

547. Sears, R. R.: Survey of objective studies of psychoanalytic concepts. *Soc. Sci. Res. Council Bull.*, 1943, no. 51.

548. Sears, R. R., E. E. Maccoby, and H. Levin: *Patterns of child rearing*. Evanston, Ill.: Row, Peterson, 1957.

549. Seashore, C. E., and G. H. Kent: Periodicity and progressive change in continuous mental work. *Psychol. Rev. Monogr. Suppl.*, 1905, no. 28, 46-101.

550. Selye, H.: *The stress of life*. New York: McGraw-Hill, 1956.

551. Selye, H., and G. Heuser (eds.): *Fifth annual report on stress, 1955–1956*. New York: MD Publications, 1956.

552. Sharp, A. A.: An experimental test of Freud's doctrine of the relation of hedonic tone to memory revival. *J. exp. Psychol.*, 1938, 22, 395–418.

553. Sheffield, F. D., and T. B. Roby: Reward value of a nonnutritive sweet taste. *J. comp. physiol. Psychol.*, 1950, 43, 471–481.

554. Sheffield, F. D., T. B. Roby, and B. A. Campbell: Drive reduction versus consummatory behavior as determinants of reinforcement. *J. comp. physiol. Psychol.*, 1954, 47, 349–354.

555. Sheldon, W. H.: *The varieties of temperament*. New York: Harper, 1942.

556. Sheldon, W. H.: Constitutional factors in personality. In J. McV. Hunt (ed.), *Personality and the behavior disorders*, Vol. I. New York: Ronald, 1944.

557. Shenstone, W.: Economy, 1763. Quotation reported in *Murry's English Dictionary*. Oxford: Clarendon Press, 1919.

558. Sherif, M., and C. W. Sherif: *An outline of social psychology* (rev. ed.). New York: Harper, 1956.

559. Sherman, M.: The differentiation of emotional responses in infants. I. Judgments of emotional responses from motion picture views and from actual observation. *J. comp. Psychol.*, 1927, 7, 265–284.

560. Shirley, M.: Studies in activity. II. Activity rhythms; age and activity; activity after rest. *J. comp. Psychol.*, 1928, 8, 159–186.

561. Sidman, M.: Two temporal parameters of the maintenance of avoidance behavior by the white rat. *J. comp. physiol. Psychol.*, 1953, 46, 253–261.

562. Siegel, P. S., and D. L. Sparks: Irrelevant aversive stimulation as an activator of an appetitional response: a replication. *Psychol. Repts.*, 1961, 9, 700.

563. Skelly, C. G., and G. M. Haslerud: Music and the general activity of apathetic schizophrenics. *J. abnorm. soc. Psychol.*, 1952, 47, 188–192.

564. Smith, A. A.: An electromyographic study of tension in interrupted and completed tasks. *J. exp. Psychol.*, 1953, 46, 32–36.

565. Smith, E. L., and D. A. Laird: The loudness of auditory stimuli which affect stomach contractions in healthy human beings. *J. acoust. Soc. Amer.*, 1930, 2, 94–98.

566. Smode, A. F.: Learning and performance in a tracking task under two levels of achievement information feedback. *J. exp. Psychol.*, 1958, 56, 297–304.

567. Sokolov, E. N.: Higher nervous activity and the problem of perception. Paper read at Fourteenth International Congress of Psychology, Montreal, 1954.

568. Sokolov, E. N.: [Perception and reflex activity] *Voprosy Psikhol.*, 1957, 3(6), 20–39.
569. Sokolov, E. N.: *Vospriiate i uslovny refleks [Perception and the conditioned reflex]*. Moscow: University of Moscow Press, 1958.
570. Solley, C. M., and R. Stagner: Effects of magnitude of temporal barriers, type of goal, and perception of self. *J. exp. Psychol.*, 1956, 51, 62–70.
571. Solomon, R. L.: The influence of work on behavior. *Psychol. Bull.*, 1948, 45, 1–40.
572. Solomon, R. L., and D. H. Howes: Word frequency, personal values, and visual duration thresholds. *Psychol. Rev.*, 1951, 58, 256–270.
573. Solomon, R. L., and L. C. Wynne: Traumatic avoidance learning: acquisition in normal dogs. *Psychol. Monogr.*, 1953, 67, no. 4 (Whole no. 354).
574. Spector, A. J.: Expectations, fulfillment, and morale. *J. abnorm. soc. Psychol.*, 1956, 52, 51–56.
575. Spence, K. W.: *Behavior theory and conditioning*. New Haven, Conn.: Yale University Press, 1956.
576. Spence, K. W.: A theory of emotionally based drive (D) and its relation to performance in simple learning situations. *Amer. Psychologist*, 1958, 13, 131–141.
577. Spence, K. W., and J. A. Taylor: Anxiety and strength of the UCS as determiners of the amount of eyelid conditioning. *J. exp. Psychol.*, 1951, 42, 183–188.
578. Spencer, H.: *First principles* (Preface dated 1862). New York: Appleton, 1888.
579. Spragg, S. D. S.: Morphine addiction in chimpanzees. *Comp. Psychol. Monogr.*, 1940, 15, no. 7.
580. Stagner, R.: Homeostasis: corruptions or misconceptions? A reply. *Psychol. Rev.*, 1954, 61, 205–208.
581. Stagner, R.: *Psychology of personality* (3d ed.). New York: McGraw-Hill, 1961.
582. Steiner, I. D.: Self-perception and goal-setting behavior. *J. Pers.*, 1957, 25, 344–355.
583. Stellar, E.: The physiology of motivation. *Psychol. Rev.*, 1954, 61, 5–22.
584. Stellar, E., and J. H. Hill: The rat's rate of drinking as a function of water deprivation. *J. comp. physiol. Psychol.*, 1952, 45, 96–102.
585. Stennett, R. G.: The relationship of performance level to level of arousal. *J. exp. Psychol.*, 1957, 54, 54–61.
586. Stephens, J. M.: The influence of punishment on learning. *J. exp. Psychol.*, 1934, 17, 536–555.
587. Stolurow, L. M.: Rodent behavior in the presence of barriers. I. Apparatus and methods. *J. comp. Psychol.*, 1948, 41, 219–231.
588. Stouffer, S. A., L. Guttman, E. A. Suchman, P. F. Lazarsfeld, S. A. Star, and J. A. Clausen: *Measurement and prediction*, Vol. IV. Princeton, N.J.: Princeton University Press, 1950.
589. Strong, E. K., Jr.: *Vocational interests 18 years after college*. Minneapolis: University of Minnesota Press, 1955.
590. Sullivan, H. S.: *Conceptions of modern psychiatry*. Washington, D.C.: William Alanson White Psychiatric Foundations, 1947.
591. Sullivan, H. S.: The theory of anxiety and the nature of psychotherapy. In H. Brand (ed.), *The study of personality: a book of readings*. New York: Wiley, 1954.

592. Talmadge, M.: Expressive graphic movements and their relationship to temperament factors. *Psychol. Monogr.*, 1958, 72, no. 16.

593. Taylor, J. A.: The relationship of anxiety to the conditioned eyelid response. *J. exp. Psychol.*, 1951, 41, 81–92.

594. Taylor, J. A.: A personality scale of manifest anxiety. *J. abnorm. soc. Psychol.*, 1953, 48, 285–290.

595. Taylor, J. A.: Drive theory and manifest anxiety. *Psychol. Bull.*, 1956, 53, 303–320.

596. Taylor, J. A., and K. W. Spence: The relationship of anxiety level to performance in serial learning. *J. exp. Psychol.*, 1952, 44, 61–64.

597. Teel, K. S.: Habit strength as a function of motivation during learning. *J. comp. physiol. Psychol.*, 1952, 45, 188–191.

598. Terman, L. M., et. al.: Mental and physical traits of a thousand gifted children. In L. M. Terman (ed.), *Genetic studies of genius*, Vol. I. Stanford, Calif.: Stanford University Press, 1925.

599. Terman, L. M., and M. H. Oden: The gifted child grows up. In L. M. Terman (ed.), *Genetic studies of genius*, Vol. IV. Stanford, Calif.: Stanford University Press, 1947.

600. Terman, L. M., and M. H. Oden: The gifted group at mid-life. In L. M. Terman (ed.), *Genetic studies of genius*, Vol. V. Stanford, Calif.: Stanford University Press, 1959.

601. Thistlethwaite, D.: A critical review of latent learning and related experiments. *Psychol. Bull.*, 1951, 48, 97–129.

602. Thompson, G. G.: Developmental psychology. In P. R. Farnsworth and Q. McNemar (eds.), *Annual review of psychology*. Palo Alto, Calif.: Annual Reviews, 1959.

603. Thorndike, E. L.: *Animal intelligence: experimental studies*. New York: Macmillan, 1911.

604. Thornton, G. R.: A factor analysis of tests designed to measure persistence. *Psychol. Monogr.*, 1939, 51, no. 229.

605. Thune, L. E.: The effect of different types of preliminary activities on subsequent learning of paired-associate material. *J. exp. Psychol.*, 1950, 40, 423–438.

606. Thurstone, L. L.: The dimensions of temperament. *Psychometrika*, 1951, 16, 11–20.

607. Tiffin, J., and E. J. McCormick: *Industrial psychology*. Englewood Cliffs, N.J.: Prentice-Hall, 1958.

608. Tinbergen, N.: Social releasers and the experimental method required for their study. *Wilson Bull.*, 1948, 60, 6–51.

609. Tinbergen, N.: *The study of instinct*. New York: Oxford Press, 1951.

610. Tinklepaugh, O. L.: An experimental study of representative factors in monkeys. *J. comp. Psychol.*, 1928, 8, 197–236.

611. Titchener, E. B.: *Lectures on the elementary psychology of feeling and attention*. New York: Macmillan, 1908.

612. Tolcott, M. A.: Conflict: a study of some interactions between appetite and aversion in the white rat. *Genetic Psychol. Monogr.*, 1948, 38, 83–142.

613. Tolman, E. C.: Purpose and cognition: the determiners of animal learning. *Psychol. Rev.*, 1925, 32, 285–297.

614. Tolman, E. C.: *Purposive behavior in animals and men*. New York: Appleton-Century-Crofts, 1932.

615. Tolman, E. C.: Operational behaviorism and current trends in psychology. In *Proc. 25th anniv. celebr. inaug. grad. stud.* Los Angeles: University of Southern California Press, 1936.

616. Tolman, E. C.: The law of effect. *Psychol. Rev.*, 1938, 45, 200–203.

617. Tolman, E. C.: A drive-conversion diagram. *Psychol. Rev.*, 1943, 50, 503–513.

618. Tolman, E. C.: Cognitive maps in rats and men. *Psychol. Rev.*, 1948, 55, 189–208.

619. Tolman, E. C.: There is more than one kind of learning. *Psychol. Rev.*, 1949, 56, 144–155.

620. Tolman, E. C.: A cognition motivation model. *Psychol. Rev.*, 1952, 59, 389–400.

621. Tolman, E. C., and C. H. Honzik: Introduction and removal of reward, and maze performance in rats. *Univ. Calif. Publ. Psychol.*, 1930, 4, 257–275.

622. Tracy, H. C.: The development of motility and behavior reactions in the toadfish (*Opsanus tau*). *J. comp. Neurol.*, 1926, 40, 253–369.

623. Troland, L. T.: *Fundamentals of human motivation.* Princeton, N.J.: Van Nostrand, 1928.

624. Trowbridge, M. H., and H. Cason: An experimental study of Thorndike's theory of learning. *J. gen. Psychol.*, 1932, 7, 245–260.

625. Tryon, R. C.: Genetic differences in maze learning in rats. *Yearb. Nat. Soc. Stud. Educ.*, 1940, 39, 111–119.

626. Tsai, L. S.: The laws of minimum effort and maximum satisfaction in animal behavior. *Psychol. Abstr.*, 1932, 6, no. 4329.

627. Ugurel-Semin, R.: Moral behavior and moral judgment of children. *J. abnorm. soc. Psychol.*, 1952, 47, 463–474.

628. Ullman, A. D.: The experimental production and analysis of a "compulsive eating symptom" in rats. *J. comp. physiol. Psychol.*, 1951, 44, 575–581.

629. Updegraff, R., M. E. Keister, L. Heiliger, et al.: Studies in preschool education, I. *Univ. Iowa Studies Child Welf.*, 1938, 14, 1–282.

630. Vernon, P. E., and G. W. Allport: A test for personal values. *J. abnorm. soc. Psychol.*, 1931, 26, 231–248.

631. Viteles, M. S.: *Motivation and morale in industry.* New York: Norton, 1953.

632. Wada, T.: Experimental study of hunger in its relation to activity. *Arch. Psychol., N.Y.*, 1922, no. 57.

633. Wald, G., and B. Jackson: Activity and nutritional deprivation. *Proc. Nat. Acad. Sci.*, 1944, 30, 255–263.

634. Walker, E. L., and J. W. Atkinson, with the collaboration of J. Veroff, R. Birney, W. Dember, and R. Moulton. The expression of fear-related motivation in thematic apperception as a function of proximity to an atomic explosion. In J. W. Atkinson (ed.), *Motives in fantasy, action, and society.* Princeton, N.J.: Van Nostrand, 1958, chap. 10.

635. Waterhouse, I. K., and I. L. Child: Frustration and the quality of performance. III. An experimental study. *J. Pers.*, 1952, 21, 298–311.

636. Waters, R. H.: The specificity of knowledge of results and improvement. *Psychol. Bull.*, 1933, 30, 673. (Abstract.)

637. Waters, R. H.: The principle of least effort in learning. *J. gen. Psychol.*, 1937, 16, 3–20.

638. Watson, J. B., and J. J. B. Morgan: Emotional reactions and psychological experimentation. *Amer. J. Psychol.*, 1917, 28, 163–174.

639. Watson, J. B., and R. Rayner: Conditioned emotional reactions. *J. exp. Psychol.*, 1920, 3, 1–14.

640. Watson, J. B., and R. R. Watson: Studies in infant psychology. *Scient. Mo.*, 1921, 13, 493–515.

641. Webb, W. B.: A motivational theory of emotions. *Psychol. Rev.*, 1948, 55, 329–335.

642. Webb, W. B.: The motivational aspect of an irrelevant drive in the behavior of the white rat. *J. exp. Psychol.*, 1949, 39, 1–14.

643. Webb, W. B., and I. J. Goodman: Activating role of an irrelevant drive in absence of the relevant drive. *Psychol. Repts.*, 1958, 4, 235–238.

644. Webb, W. B., and F. Shafer: A survey of anger in college students. Unpublished study, 1960.

645. Webb, W. B., and R. J. Wherry, Jr.: Vigilance in prolonged and repeated sessions. *Percept. mot. Skills*, 1960, 10, 111–114.

646. Weber, M.: *The protestant ethic and the spirit of capitalism.* Trans. by T. Parsons. London: Allen & Unwin, Ltd., 1930.

647. Weinland, J. D.: A five month strength curve. *J. appl. Psychol.*, 1947, 31, 498–501.

648. Welsh, J. H.: Diurnal rhythms. *Quart. Rev. Biol.*, 1938, 13, 123–139.

649. Wenger, M. A.: Studies of autonomic balance in Army Air Forces personnel. *Comp. Psychol. Monogr.*, 1948, 19, no. 4, 1–111.

650. Wenger, M. A., F. N. Jones, and M. H. Jones: *Physiological psychology.* New York: Holt, 1956.

651. Wessman, A. E., D. F. Ricks, and M. Mc. Tyl: Characteristics and concomitants of mood fluctuation in college women. *J. abnorm. soc. Psychol.*, 1960, 60, 117–126.

652. White, B. V., and E. F. Gildea: "Cold pressor test" in tension and anxiety: a cardiochronographic study. *Arch. Neurol. Psychiat.*, 1937, 38, 964–984.

653. White, R. W.: Motivation reconsidered: the concept of competence. *Psychol. Rev.*, 1959, 66, 297–333.

654. Whyte, W. F., M. Dalton, et al.: *Money and motivation: an analysis of incentives in industry.* New York: Harper, 1955.

655. Wittenborn, J. R.: Inferring the strength of drive. In *Nebraska symposium on motivation*, Lincoln, Nebr.: University of Nebraska Press, 1957.

656. Wolf, S., and H. G. Wolff: Evidence on the genesis of peptic ulcers in man. *J. Amer. Med. Assoc.*, 1942, 120, 670–675.

657. Wolfe, J. B.: Effectiveness of token rewards for chimpanzees. *Comp. Psychol. Monogr.*, 1936, 12, no. 60.

658. Wolfe, J. B., and M. D. Kaplon: Effect of amount of reward and consummative activity on learning in chickens. *J. comp. Psychol.*, 1941, 31, 353–361.

659. Woodworth, R. S.: Reinforcement of perception. *Amer. J. Psychol.*, 1947, 60, 119–124.

660. Woodworth, R. S.: *Dynamics of behavior.* New York: Holt, 1958.

661. Woodworth, R. S., and H. Schlosberg: *Experimental psychology* (rev. ed.). New York: Holt, 1954.

662. Yerkes, R. M., and J. D. Dodson: The relation of strength of stimulus to rapidity of habit-formation. *J. comp. Neurol. Psychol.*, 1908, 18, 459–482.
663. Yerkes, R. M., and A. W. Yerkes: *The great apes.* New Haven: Yale University Press, 1929.
664. Young, P. T.: Appetite, palatibility, and feeding habit: a critical review. *Psychol. Bull.*, 1948, 45, 289–320.
665. Young, P. T.: Emotion as disorganized response—a reply to Professor Leeper. *Psychol. Rev.*, 1949, 56, 184–191.
666. Young, P. T.: Food-seeking drive, affective process, and learning. *Psychol. Rev.*, 1949, 56, 98–121.
667. Young, P. T.: The role of hedonic processes in the organization of behavior. *Psychol. Rev.*, 1952, 59, 249–262.
668. Young, P. T.: The role of hedonic processes in motivation. In *Nebraska symposium on motivation.* Lincoln, Nebr.: University of Nebraska Press, 1955.
669. Young, P. T.: *Motivation and emotions.* New York: Wiley, 1961.
670. Young, P. T., and E. H. Shuford, Jr.: Intensity, duration, and repetition of hedonic processes as related to acquisition of motives. *J. comp. physiol. Psychol.*, 1954, 47, 298–305.
671. Zeaman, D.: Response latency as a function of the amount of reinforcement. *J. exp. Psychol.*, 1949, 39, 466–483.
672. Zeller, A. F.: An experimental analogue of repression. I. Historical summary. *Psychol. Bull.*, 1950, 47, 39–51.
673. Zeller, A. F.: An experimental analogue of repression. II. The effect of individual failure and success on memory measured by relearning. *J. exp. Psychol.*, 1950, 40, 411–422.
674. Zilboorg, G.: *The medical man and the witch during the Renaissance.* Baltimore: Johns Hopkins Press, 1935.
675. Zimmer, H., and J. Foy: Depression: definition and determinants. In D. Willner (ed.), *Decisions, values, and groups.* New York: Pergamon Press, 1960.

NAME INDEX

Page references in **boldface** type indicate bibliographic entries

SUBJECT INDEX

48352

BF   Motivation as related to
683   personality.
R4   Rethlingshafer, Dorothy